HEMPSONS
con copy 2

20 JUL 2006

Health and Social Care Handbook

AF743953

002534

Related titles available from Law Society Publishing:

Child Abuse Compensation Claims
Elizabeth-Anne Gumbel, Malcolm Johnson and Richard Scorer

Child Law Handbook
Guide to Good Practice
Liz Goldthorpe with Pat Monro

Elderly Client Handbook (3rd edn)
General Editors: Caroline Bielanska and Martin Terrell. Consultant Editor: Gordon R. Ashton

Family Law Protocol (2nd edn)
The Law Society with Resolution, LSC and DCA

Good Practice in Child Care Cases
A Guide for Solicitors Acting in Public Law Children Act Proceedings Including Cases Involving Adoption
The Law Society in association with ALC, CCJLG and Resolution

Mental Capacity Act 2005
A Guide to the New Law
Nicola Greaney, Fenella Morris and Beverley Taylor

Practical Education Law
Angela Jackman, Deborah Hay and Pat Wilkins

Resolution Family Law Handbook (due November 2006)
General Editor: Andrew Greensmith

All books from Law Society Publishing can be ordered from good bookshops or direct from our distributors, Marston Book Services, by telephone 01235 465656 or email law.society@marston.co.uk. Please confirm the price before ordering.

For further information or a catalogue, please contact our editorial and marketing office by email: publishing@lawsociety.co.uk.

HEALTH AND SOCIAL CARE HANDBOOK

Caroline Bielanska with Fiona Scolding

The Law Society

All rights reserved. No part of this publication may be reproduced in any material form, whether by photocopying, scanning, downloading onto computer or otherwise without the written permission of the Law Society and the author except in accordance with the provisions of the Copyright, Designs and Patents Act 1988. Applications should be addressed in the first instance, in writing, to Law Society Publishing.

Whilst all reasonable care has been taken in the preparation of this publication, neither the publisher nor the author can accept any responsibility for any loss occasioned to any person acting or refraining from action as a result of relying upon its contents.

The views expressed in this publication should be taken as those of the authors only unless it is specifically indicated that the Law Society has given its endorsement. The authors have asserted the right under the Copyright, Designs and Patents Act 1988 to be identified as the authors of this work.

© Caroline Bielanska and Fiona Scolding 2006

ISBN-10: 1–85328–990–6
ISBN-13: 978–1–85328–990–3

Published in 2006 by Law Society Publishing
113 Chancery Lane, London WC2A 1PL

Typeset by J&L Composition, Filey, North Yorkshire
Printed by Antony Rowe Ltd, Chippenham, Wilts

Contents

Preface and acknowledgements

Health and social care law affects millions of people. Although it is a specialism in its own right, it may form part of the advice that needs to be given to clients with wider problems. As a private client solicitor specialising in advising older and vulnerable clients, their families and carers, I found it necessary to advise on numerous health and social care law issues that affect such people. Many lawyers who specialise in health and social care law, which encompasses 'community care law' may also have expertise in mental health, education, childcare, personal injury, asylum or elder law. So perhaps it is not surprising that health and social care law is for many, part of a holistic approach adopted by lawyers in advising their clients.

I consider myself fortunate that just after I qualified, I worked with Eileen Loughridge, then of Bindley Twist Tafft and James in Coventry, who encouraged me to undertake Court of Protection work. The Court of Protection client groups include those who are mentally ill, learning disabled, brain damaged and people who suffer from mentally degenerative conditions, such as dementia. The common thread is that they are all mentally incapacitated, and many also have additional physical disabilities. As a single client group, older people are the largest health and social care service users, as age is a significant factor in disability. Some older clients have no known living relatives as a result of the Second World War, where loved ones were killed, lost or displaced. For some, I have been named as their next of kin. I know that there will be many lawyers reading this who have had similar experiences. In practice, my work consisted of not only managing my clients' finances but also ensuring that their welfare needs were being met. There is at times a very fine line between financial and welfare decisions and as such the provision and funding of care forms an important element of advice.

Before the introduction of the National Health Service and Community Care Act 1990, relations with social services were in the main a positive experience. The level of case law and legislation was relatively small. Funding for residential-based care was provided by the then DHSS which was not involved in any consideration of the service user's needs. Those early days of the 1990 Act were a sharp learning curve for all concerned. It did not take too long before social services were struggling to carry out assessments, running out of financial resources and at times failing to provide. They were acting as collectors of charges, which led to a growth in advice being sought on the funding and recovery of care costs, as well as estate planning to avoid or mitigate potential charges levied. Increasingly issues about whether care was the responsibility of the NHS or social services occurred. All these issues still remain relevant.

Demands on the NHS have continued since its inception but have been compounded by higher expectations, an increase in life expectancy, and improvements and increased availability of treatments and services. The NHS will never have enough money or human resources to meet all needs all of the time as budgetary restrictions have become the norm.

Directions and guidance were often issued without consultation, sometimes as a solution to one particular issue. The status of guidance and directions was often ignored. Getting hold of guidance was also problematic – even for those in social services. Now with the internet and the volume of paper that the Department of Health has produced, it can be overwhelming at times. The feeling 'I know I have read it somewhere but where?' will be all too familiar. Although since 2002, the number of formal circulars issued by the Department of Health has reduced in an effort to adopt a less hands-on approach, this means that sometimes guidance and directions are harder to locate. Information can of course be accessed via the internet, but the Government is constantly introducing new legislation and Codes of Practice, which can be confusing and difficult to decipher if you do not already have a basic understanding of the principles at play.

I wanted to write a book for the busy practitioner who needs a readily accessible guide to legal rights to health and social care. The Law Society was seeking to commission the writing of such a book and so it was fortuitous that our wishes coincided. One of the hardest things in writing a book of this nature is making the decision about what should be left out, particularly when the law and the structures that are in place in health and social services are constantly moving. At the time of writing we have been waiting for the government's White Paper on their planned reforms to the NHS and social care provision. As a handbook, the aim of this book is to provide basic information and where necessary point users to other sources of help. I have listed relevant websites and addresses, with case law mentioned briefly within the text. To aid the location of specific documents, specific URLs can be found in Appendix 4.

The book is divided into five distinct sections. The first covers the overarching principles and responsibilities of health and social care providers. The second and third sections cover all the legal aspects of the provision of social services and health care and explain the law in relation to an individual's rights to access and receive services. The fourth section highlights specific user groups who are affected by community care, so that further additional information is available to advisers. The final section explains how to enforce those rights and how to complain when services are not present or are inadequate. It covers non-litigation-based remedies for failure/inadequate provision through to the use of judicial review, the Ombudsman and even applications to the European Court of Human Rights.

For simplicity, the masculine pronoun is used throughout to include the feminine.

I am grateful to Fiona Scolding of Hardwicke Building for her valuable contribution to the book, in particular for undertaking to write the chapters relating to children, asylum seekers and the judicial remedies.

When my young son, Max asked me what I was writing, he made it very clear he was not impressed with the title, as it did not sound 'any fun'. Much as I would have liked this book to have appealed to him, I don't think The Law Society would have let me get away with having 'Pokemon' in the title. I would have loved for this book to have been fun but given the subject matter I think it is unlikely. If the book cannot be fun then I do hope that it will serve to be useful.

Caroline Bielanska
May 2006

I would like to thank my husband, Jimmy, and my parents for their patience, and my grandmother, Pamela Darkens, for teaching me never to give up.

Fiona Scolding
May 2006

Table of cases

Table of statutes

Table of statutory instruments

Table of international conventions and treaties

List of abbreviations

1977 Act	National Health Service Act 1977
1983 Act	Health and Social Services and Social Security Adjudications Act 1983
1989 Act	Children Act 1989
2002 Act	National Health Service Reform and Health Care Professions Act 2002
2003 Act	Community Care (Delayed Discharges etc.) Act 2003
ADR	alternative dispute resolution
BCHS	Better Care Higher Standards
CDCA 2000	Carers and Disabled Children Act 2000
CDRP	Crime and Disorder Reduction Partnership
CIL	Chief Inspector Letter
CPA	Care Programme Approach
CPR	Civil Procedure Rules 1998, SI 1998/3132
CRAG	*Charging for Residential Accommodation Guide*
CRB	Criminal Records Bureau
CRSA 1995	Carers (Recognition and Services) Act 1995
CSA 2000	Care Standards Act 2000
CSCI	Commission for Social Care Inspection
CSDPA 1970	Chronically Sick and Disabled Persons Act 1970
CSIW	Care Standards Inspectorate for Wales
DASS	director of adult social services
DAT	Drug and Alcohol Action Team
DFG	disabled facilities grant
DGM	District General Manger
DLA	disability living allowance
DPA	deferred payment agreement
DPSCRA 1986	Disabled Persons (Services, Consultation and Representation) Act 1986
DWP	Department for Work and Pensions
EA 1996	Education Act 1996
EEA	European Economic Area
EL	Executive Letter

EPA	enduring power of attorney
EPAA 1985	Enduring Powers of Attorney Act 1985
FACS	*Fair Access to Care Services*, LAC (2002) 13
GMC	General Medical Council
HA 1996	Housing Act 1996
HGCRA 1996	Housing Grants, Construction and Regeneration Act 1996
HSC	Health Service Circular
HSC(CHS)A 2003	Health and Social Care (Community Health and Standards) Act 2003
HSCA 1993	Health Service Commissioners Act 1993
HSG	Health Service Guidelines
HSO	Health Service Ombudsman
IAA 1999	Immigration and Asylum Act 1999
ICCPR	International Covenant on Civil and Political Rights
IMCA	Independent Mental Capacity Advocate
LAC	Local Authority Circular
LDP	Local Delivery Plan
LEA	local education authority
LASSA 1970	Local Authority Social Services Act 1970
LASSL	Local Authority Social Services Letter
LGA 1974	Local Government Act 1974
LGA 2000	Local Government Act 2000
LGHA 1989	Local Government and Housing Act 1989
LGO	Local Government Ombudsman
LHB	Local Health Board
LPA	lasting power of attorney
MCA 2005	Mental Capacity Act 2005
MHA 1983	Mental Health Act 1983
NAARR 1992	National Assistance (Assessment of Resources) Regulations 1992, SI 1992/2977
NAFWC	National Assembly for Wales Circular
NASS	National Asylum Support Service
NHS Complaints Regulations 2004	National Health Service (Complaints) Regulations 2004, SI 2004/1768
NHS	National Health Service
NIAA 2002	National Immigration and Asylum Act 2002
NICE	National Institute for Health and Clinical Excellence
NSF	National Service Framework
NTA	National Treatment Agency
Ofsted	Office for Standards in Education
PCT	Primary Care Trust
PGO	Public Guardianship Office
POVA	Protection of Vulnerable Adults

PSCI	person subject to immigration control
RMO	responsible medical officer
RNC	registered nursing care
RNCC	Registered Nursing Care Contribution
SAP	Single Assessment Process
SEN	special educational needs
SHA	Strategic Health Authority
SSI	Social Services Inspectorate
SSIW	Social Services Inspectorate for Wales
UFSAMC	*Creating a Unified and Fair System for Assessing and Managing Care*
UN	United Nations
WHC	Welsh Health Circular
WOC	Welsh Office Circular

PART I

The overarching principles and responsibilities of health and social care providers

CHAPTER 1

Health care providers

1.1 WHAT IS THE NHS?

The National Health Service (NHS) was established on 5 July 1948 with the introduction of the National Health Service Act 1946, to provide health care for all citizens in the UK, based on need and not the ability to pay. Health services are free of charge unless charges are expressly provided for by statute. (See **Chapter 10** for further discussion of health care charges.)

Since 1948 there have been significant changes to both the organisational structure of the NHS and the way that services are provided, such as:

- The National Health Service Act 1946 was superseded by the National Health Service Act 1977 (as amended) (the 1977 Act).
- The National Health Service and Community Care Act 1990 provided for the establishment of NHS Trusts (s.5(1), Sched.2) and allowed the NHS to be both purchaser and provider of health care.
- The Health Act 1999 created Primary Care Trusts (PCTs) in England and Wales (s.2) and allows for the pooling of resources between health and social care bodies (s.31).

More recently, in July 2000 the Labour Government published *The NHS Plan: A Plan for Investment, a Plan for Reform* which was followed in 2001 by *Shifting the Balance of Power within the NHS: Securing Delivery* and in April 2002 by *Delivering the NHS Plan: Next Steps on Investment, Next Steps on Reform*. The National Assembly for Wales published in February 2001 *Improving Health in Wales – A Plan for the NHS with its Partners*. These strategy documents have resulted in the following legislation.

- The Health and Social Care Act 2001 provided for the establishment of Care Trusts and Independent Advocacy Services for NHS complaints.
- The National Health Service Reform and Health Care Professions Act 2002 created Strategic Health Authorities (SHAs) as well as creating Patient's Forums in England, to supersede the role of the Community Health Councils.

- PCTs are now Local Health Boards (LHBs) in Wales by virtue of the National Health Service Reform and Health Care Professions Act 2002, s.6.
- Foundation Trust Hospitals and new regulatory bodies were created by the Health and Social Care (Community Health and Standards) Act 2003.

The NHS is funded out of central taxation and managed by the Department of Health in England and the NHS Wales Department in Wales, which set policy on health issues. It is the responsibility of the Departments to provide health services to the general public through the NHS. Technological and medical advances, and improvements in standards of living, have created an overall healthier nation where people are living longer, but health care demands have as a result also increased. This has had an impact on resources, both human and financial, and has led to the development of prioritising practices to attempt to meet the demands of those with the greatest needs.

1.2 HOW THE NHS WORKS IN ENGLAND

1.2.1 Responsibility of the Secretary of State

The Secretary of State retains overall responsibility for the NHS in England. In addition to setting the strategic direction he has a number of other specific functions and may:

- provide any services which he considers appropriate for the purpose of discharging any of his statutory duties (1977 Act, s.2(a));
- do any other thing calculated to facilitate, or conducive or incidental to, the discharge of such duties (1977 Act, s.2(b)).

1.2.2 Strategic Health Authorities

Since April 2002 regional and district health authorities merged and there are now 28 Strategic Health Authorities (SHAs). They are responsible for developing and implementing the health policy at local level for their area. They manage the performance of the PCT in their area and are a key link between the Department of Health and the NHS to ensure national priorities are integrated into local plans. See the 1977 Act, s.8 as amended by the National Health Service Reform and Health Care Professions Act 2002 and the National Health Service (Functions of Strategic Health Authorities and Primary Care Trusts and Administration Arrangements) (England) Regulations 2002, SI 2002/2375 (as amended). In July 2005, in *Commissioning a Patient-led NHS* the Government announced plans to streamline SHAs by reducing the number of SHAs to nine.

1.2.3 Special Health Authorities

These have particular functions, such as the National Blood Authority and provide services for the whole population in England and Wales. They are set up under the 1977 Act, s.11.

National Institute for Health and Clinical Excellence

Formerly the National Institute for Clinical Excellence, from 1 April 2005, NICE has taken over the work of the Health Development Agency. Its role is to provide patients, health professionals and the public with authoritative and reliable guidance on current best practice and so use NHS resources effectively. The guidance covers both individual health technologies (including medicines, medical devices, diagnostic techniques, and procedures) and the clinical management of specific conditions. The NHS is expected to make drugs available throughout England and Wales where NICE advises that they are clinically and cost effective (National Institute for Clinical Excellence (Establishment and Constitution) Order 1999, SI 1999/220 (as amended) and the National Institute for Clinical Excellence Regulations 1999, SI 1999/260 (as amended)).

NHS Direct

The NHS Direct Special Health Authority's main function is to provide free 24-hour telephone assistance (NHS Direct (Establishment and Constitution) Order 2004, SI 2004/569 and the NHS Direct Regulations 2004, SI 2004/570). Some GPs use this as their initial out-of-hours service. The Authority's responsibilities also cover managing a website (**www.nhsdirect.nhs.uk**) and producing self-help guides. NHS Direct Wales is not part of its English counterpart and responsibility is with the Local Health Boards and NHS Trusts.

1.2.4 NHS Trusts

Hospital trusts, also known as 'acute trusts', usually offer a range of services to meet general health needs. Some trusts also act as regional or national centres of expertise for more specialised care, while some are attached to universities and help to train health professionals. Trusts can also provide services in the community such as through health centres, clinics or in people's homes. Other than in an emergency, hospital treatment is arranged by a referral through a GP. Appointments and treatment are free. Their funding is obtained in the main by contracts from PCTs, which receive their funding direct from central government. However, the funding is to alter over time as the Government is in the process of rolling out a programme of payment by results, a system whereby the money follows the patient around. At present elective care is paid for in this way, with the aim that by April 2006 it will extend to A&E and emergency care.

1.2.5 Mental Health Trusts

Mental health services can be provided through the patient's GP, other primary care services and through more specialist care. This can include various counselling and psychological therapies. Specialist care however, can be provided by specialist mental health services within an NHS Hospital Trust.

1.2.6 Foundation Hospital Trusts

The Health and Social Care (Community Health and Standards) Act 2003 created the power to establish Foundation Hospital Trusts, which are public benefit corporations, whose members are made up of local people, patients, carers and staff. The members can vote, and stand as governors of the trust. NHS Foundation Trusts are part of the NHS but they have greater financial and management freedoms including freedom to retain surpluses and to invest in delivery of new services, to manage and reward their staff flexibly and to access a wider range of options for capital funding. An independent regulator, known as 'Monitor', authorises, monitors and regulates the trusts (see **www.monitor-nhsft.gov.uk**).

1.2.7 Primary Care Trusts

PCTs are responsible for the planning and provision of local hospital and family practitioner services. The 303 PCTs in England control 80 per cent of the NHS budget to plan and commission health services for their local communities (National Health Service (Functions of Strategic Health Authorities and Primary Care Trusts and Administration Arrangements) (England) Regulations 2002, SI 2002/2375 (as amended)). Guidance has been issued in HSC 1999/167 and HSC 1999/ 246 on the establishment and operation of PCTs. The July 2005 document *Commissioning a Patient-led NHS* sets out plans to reduce the number of PCTs to between 70 and 130.

PCTs are responsible for:

- purchasing hospital and community health services on behalf of local people;
- ensuring that there are enough GPs to provide services as well as securing the provision of other health services including hospitals, dentists, mental health care, walk-in centres, NHS Direct, population screening, patient transport (A&E) and pharmaceutical and optical services;

- integrating health and social care so that the two systems work together for patients.

1.2.8 Care Trusts

The Health Act 1999 created flexibility for the NHS and social care to work together to provide better integrated services. This is particularly important with regard to certain user groups such as the elderly infirm, but it is made difficult by the fact that health and local authority boundaries do not coincide.

A Care Trust is an NHS organisation to which local authorities can delegate health-related functions, in order to provide integrated health and social care to their local communities (Health and Social Care Act 2001, s.45 and the Care Trusts (Applications and Consultation) Regulations 2001, SI 2001/3788). They are established on a voluntary basis and in partnership where there is a joint agreement at a local level that this will be the best way to deliver better health and social care services. There is only a small number of such trusts in existence and these are often linked to the provision of mental health services.

1.3 HOW THE NHS WORKS IN WALES

The Minister for Health and Social Services has overall responsibility for the NHS in Wales. The NHS Wales Department is responsible for implementing and developing the health policies of the Welsh Assembly and providing advice to the Minister about required resources.

It is up to the Welsh Assembly how it sets Welsh policy and allocates NHS funds. The three regional offices of the National Assembly for Wales, based in Mid, North, South and East Wales work with LHBs, local authorities and NHS Trusts in their area to monitor and ensure that Assembly initiatives are carried out.

The running of NHS Trust hospitals is as in England.

1.3.1 Local Health Boards

LHBs, similar to the English PCTs, hold three-quarters of the budget for the NHS in Wales, so they can plan and pay for health services for people living in their area (Local Health Boards (Establishment) (Wales) Order 2003, SI 2003/148 (W.18) (as amended); Local Health Boards (Constitution, Membership and Procedures) (Wales) Regulations 2003, SI 2003/149 (W.19)).

Guidance has been issued by the Welsh Assembly on the establishment of LHBs and is available from the Welsh Assembly's website (**www.wales.gov.uk**).

Each of the 22 LHBs has a decision-making board, made up of local doctors, a nurse, other health professionals, members of the local council and voluntary organisations, and others to represent patients. They also have an executive team to put the decisions into action and provide services for the public. They plan and pay for most hospital and family health services with the exception of certain specialist services. These are the responsibility of the Health Commission Wales (Specialist Services).

The LHBs cover exactly the same areas as the 22 local authorities in Wales to allow much closer working between the NHS and the local councils with the aim to tackle long-term problems with health.

1.3.2 The Health Commission Wales (Specialist Services)

This is an executive agency of the Assembly, which has responsibility for the planning and commissioning of specialist health services such as treatment for rare forms of cancer, cardiac services, plastic surgery, specialised services for children and people with complex physical disabilities; neurosciences; mental health services; NHS Direct; national population screening programmes; emergency ambulance services; blood transfusion and tissue typing; and regional pharmaceutical services.

1.4 REGULATION OF NHS BODIES

1.4.1 Commission for Healthcare Audit and Inspection

The Commission for Healthcare Audit and Inspection, known as 'the Healthcare Commission' was established by the Health and Social Care (Community Health and Standards) Act 2003, s.41. Its general powers and duties are contained in Sched.6. Sections 45–47 impose a duty of quality on all NHS bodies that provide or commission health care, and provides for the standards which are to be taken into account by NHS bodies in discharging the duty of quality and by the Healthcare Commission in reviewing health care provision. The Healthcare Commission's functions are contained in ss.48–69, and include conducting general reviews of health care across NHS bodies in England and producing a report to Parliament each year. Reviews and investigations of health care provided by or for particular NHS bodies in Wales are the responsibility of the Assembly under ss.70–75.

The Healthcare Commission is also responsible for the independent review process of NHS complaints about the NHS in England. In Wales the Independent Review Secretariat manages the independent review stage. (For information on complaints see **Chapter 18.**) For more information on the role of the Healthcare Commission in inspecting and regulating services see **Chapter 17**.

1.4.2 Commission for Health Improvement in Wales

Established by the Health Act 1999, s.19, the Commission for Health Improvement in Wales provides advice, reviews and investigates the management, provision and quality of health care by LHBs and NHS Trusts to the Welsh Assembly and those NHS bodies. Its functions are set out in the 1999 Act, s.20 and the Commission for Health Improvement (Functions) (Wales) Regulations 2003, SI 2003/993 (W.142).

1.5 PROVISION OF PLANS BY THE NHS

1.5.1 Health Improvement and Modernisation Plans

Section 28(1) of the Health Act 1999 creates a duty on every SHA, PCT and LHB to prepare a strategic plan (as the Secretary of State directs) which sets out a strategy for improving the health of the people for whom they are responsible, and the provision of health care to such people. There is a duty to keep the plans under review (s.28(2)). Monitoring and implementation of the plans are the responsibility of the SHA, which has power to ensure that major decisions taken by the PCT and NHS Trusts are in line with the plan. Section 11 of the Health and Social Care Act 2001 places a duty on NHS bodies to consult and involve the public in the planning, development and implementation of health services. This is underpinned by the joint duty of NHS bodies and local authorities to cooperate (1977 Act, s.22 (as amended)), in order to secure and advance the health and welfare of the people of England and Wales. For more on cooperation and collaborating with social services see **para.2.6**.

Local Delivery Plans

Under the Planning and Priorities Framework guidance, which was issued by the Department of Health on 2 October 2002, PCTs no longer need to prepare Health Improvement and Modernisation Plans. Instead they are to prepare Local Delivery Plans (LDPs), which should focus on health and social care priorities. The LDPs will be collated by the SHA to be prepared into a report to ensure that it is consistent with the guidance. For a copy of the 2002 guidance see *Improvement, Expansion and Reform – The Next 3 Years: Priorities and Planning Framework 2003–2006* which is available from the Department of Health's website (**www.dh.gov.uk**).

1.5.2 Joint Investment Plans

The Department of Health requires health and local authorities to produce Joint Investment Plans for older people, adult mental health services, learning disabilities and welfare to work for disabled people, and carers (HSC 1999/244, LAC (99) 39). Health and local authorities, together with partner agencies, are required to assess the service needs of local people and compare this with existing services. The aim of the Joint Investment Plan is to deliver better services and improve outcomes for service users. Guidance has been issued and can be accessed from the Department of Health's website (**www.dh.gov.uk**).

1.5.3 Planning and the provision of plans in Wales

Section 24 of the National Health Service Reform and Health Care Professions Act 2002 establishes a duty on each LHB and local authority in Wales to formulate and implement a strategy for the health and well-being of the population in the area, and to have regard to the strategy in exercising their functions. It builds on the strategy document *Improving Health in Wales – A Plan for the NHS with its Partners*.

The Health, Social Care and Well-being Strategies (Wales) Regulations 2003, SI 2003/154 (W.24) sets out how these strategies should be prepared, consulted upon, what they must address, commissioning arrangements, and how they should be adopted, reviewed and published.

1.6 DUTY TO PROVIDE NHS SERVICES

1.6.1 Duty to provide hospital and community health services

The Secretary of State in England and the National Assembly for Wales owe a general duty to the population of England and Wales to continue to promote a comprehensive health service which is designed to secure improvement in the physical and mental health of the population and to prevent, diagnose and treat illness (1977 Act, s.1(1)). Services that can be provided are those that the Secretary of State thinks are appropriate to discharge any duty he may have under the 1977 Act (s.2). A general power exists to provide the following services, to such extent as the Secretary of State considers necessary to meet all reasonable requirements (1977 Act, s.3):

- hospital and other accommodation;
- medical, dental, nursing and ambulance services;
- facilities for the care of expectant and nursing mothers and young children;
- facilities for the prevention of illness, care of people who are ill and after-care services; and
- providing other services required for the diagnosis or treatment of illness.

Not all health services have to be met, provided the Secretary of State pays due regard to the general duty under s.1(1). The duty is to 'continue to promote a comprehensive health care service' and as such it is not an absolute duty to provide, as a comprehensive health care system will never be achieved due to the limits of human and financial resources (*R* v. *North and East Devon Health Authority ex p Coughlan* [2001] QB 213; [2000] 3 All ER 850, paras.22–24).

Delegation of provision to local NHS bodies

The 1977 Act contains powers for delegation of the Secretary of State's functions under ss.16, 16B, 17, 17A(4), 18, 51(2) and 126. The National Health Service (Functions of Strategic Health Authorities and Primary Care Trusts and Administration Arrangements) (England) Regulations 2002, SI 2002/2375 (as amended) have delegated the Secretary of State's functions to SHAs and PCTs.

Similar regulations are in force in Wales which delegate the function to LHBs (Local Health Board (Functions) (Wales) Regulations 2003, SI 2003/150 (W.20)).

Services provision

The 1977 Act does not contain detail of the specialist services that can be provided, but in practice it includes community health services such as district nurses, midwives and health visitors. The word 'facilities' is widely interpreted and includes not only the accommodation, plant and other means by which health services are provided, but also the personnel involved in providing the services. A local NHS body has the power to fund a project providing a service of advice and assistance in relation to access to state benefits for those with mental health problems (*R (on the application of Keating)* v. *Cardiff Local Health Board* [2005] 3 All ER 1000).

NHS walk-in centres were established under the National Health Service (Primary Care) Act 1997, amending the 1977 Act, which provides for non-appointment access to medical and dental services, including health information, advice and treatment for a range of minor illnesses and injuries. The services are commissioned by the PCT (HSC 1999/116 *NHS Primary Care Walk-in Centres Selection of Pilot Sites for 1999/2000*). The 1977 Act also creates a duty to provide medical and dental inspection and treatment of pupils at local authority schools (s.5(1)(a) and Sched.1) and family planning services (s.5(1)(b)).

Services can be secured from private hospitals, nursing homes or other private facilities (1977 Act, s.23) or from outside England and Wales (1977 Act, s.3(1A)). This will generally be used where there is a long waiting list and there is undue delay in receiving the necessary treatment, and the service cannot be secured elsewhere (*R (on the application of Watts)* v. *Bedford Primary Care Trust* [2004] EWCA Civ 166). The general policy is to secure such treatment within the European Economic Area. Guidance has been issued and is available from the Department of Health's website (**www.dh.gov.uk**). The case of *Watts* has been taken to the European Court of Justice and a final ruling is expected in Spring 2006. However, the court's Advocate General, who provides guidance to the judges, has said that the NHS has no proper procedures to assess applications for treatment abroad, which restricts the possibilities for patients to seek treatments outside the system, and therefore is a restriction of their freedom to receive services. He also said NHS waiting targets were not flexible enough to judge patient need.

Third party provision

Section 23 of the 1977 Act provides for arrangements to be made with any person or body (including a voluntary organisation) for that person or body to provide, or assist in providing, any service under the Act. As such agencies can provide services for the NHS body, in exercise of its functions. A voluntary organisation is defined as 'a body the activities of which are carried on otherwise than for profit, but does not include any public or local authority' (s.128(1)). In addition, a wide power exists in para.12 of Sched.5A to the 1977 Act, which allows a PCT to do what appears to it to be necessary or expedient for the purpose of or in connection with the exercise of its functions, which includes amongst other things power to enter into contracts (*Gunter* v. *South Western Staffordshire Primary Care Trust* [2005] EWHC 1894 (Admin)).

Limits on NHS resources

Individuals are not specifically owed the duty under s.3 and as such the Secretary of State and the National Assembly for Wales can take into account available resources and the demands on those resources when deciding NHS policy. This general duty is often perceived to operate as a power to provide, as services can be rationed or not provided at all. However, the level of service provision should be justifiable within local priorities and resources (*R* v. *Secretary of State for Social Services ex p Hincks* (1980) 1 BMLR 93). See also *R* v. *Cambridge District Health Authority ex p B (No. 1)* [1995] 2 All ER 129, CA; *R* v. *Central Birmingham Health Authority ex p Walker* (1987) 3 BMLR 32, CA.

That is not to say the courts will never intervene in the resource issue. In *North West Lancashire Health Authority* v. *A* [2000] 1 WLR 977, the Court of Appeal held that the health authority's policy to refuse surgery to transsexuals suffering from general identity dysphoria was unlawful, because having accepted transsexualism as an illness, the policy and the stated exceptions to it failed to reflect that medical judgment. The NHS body should not fetter their discretion by operating a blanket policy, which does not allow for flexibility. It may have to account for such policy through the judicial review process, which will also ensure that no human right has been infringed.

1.6.2 Duty to provide family health services

Part II of the 1977 Act governs the arrangements for the provision of services such as GPs, dentists, opticians and chemists. PCT/LHBs are under a duty to contract with GPs, who are independent professionals, to provide general medical services (s.28Q). See **Chapter 9** for more details.

1.6.3 NHS directions and guidance

Section 17 of the 1977 Act empowers the Secretary of State to issue directions to NHS bodies but there is no power for him to issue guidance in the same way as he can to social services under the Local Authority Social Services Act 1970 (LASSA 1970), s.7A. Care Trusts, however, are subject to guidance issued under LASSA 1970, s.7 by virtue of the Health and Social Care Act 2001, s.45(10). The issuing of guidance by the Secretary of State is authorised by the general provisions of the 1977 Act, s.2(b), although these provisions are silent as to the status of such guidance.

In England, important guidance is usually issued within a Health Service Circular (HSC) (prior to 1998, guidance was issued within Health Service Guidelines (HSG)). The same guidance may be issued to local authorities at the same time under its equivalent Local Authority Circular (LAC). There is strong argument that where this occurs and is issued to the local authority under LASSA 1970, s.7 then the NHS must follow it in the same way as local authorities (*R* v. *Islington LBC ex p Rixon* (1997–98) 1 CCLR 119).

Guidance can also be contained within an Executive Letter (EL). It is possible for a direction to be contained within such a letter, provided the wording is sufficiently mandatory to be a direction. Strong guidance, although not obligatory, should be followed unless there are clear reasons for not doing so. Such reasons can of course be subject to judicial review (*R* v. *North Derbyshire Health Authority ex p Fisher* (1997–98) 1 CCLR 150).

English guidance can be obtained from the Department of Health (see Appendix 3). In Wales, important guidance is issued within Welsh Health Circulars (WHC). Less important guidance is issued as District General Manager (DGM) guidance. Copies of guidance can be obtained from the Welsh Assembly (see Appendix 3).

1.7 RIGHTS TO INFORMATION

1.7.1 Code of Practice on Openness in the NHS

The Code of Practice, issued in England (August 2003) and Wales (1999), sets out the basic principles underlying public access to information about the NHS. NHS bodies must publish or otherwise make available the following information:

- information about what services are provided, the targets and standards set and results achieved, and the costs and effectiveness of the service;
- details about important proposals on health policies or proposed changes in the way services are delivered, including the reasons for those proposals;
- details about important decisions on health policies and decisions on changes to the delivery of services;
- information about the way in which health services are managed and provided and who is responsible;
- information about how the NHS communicates with the public, such as details of public meetings, consultation procedures, suggestion and complaints systems and contact details;
- information about how people can have access to their own personal health records.

The NHS body does not have to give access to:

- personal information about third parties;
- information which is manifestly unreasonable, far too general, or would require unreasonable resources to answer;
- information about internal discussion and advice, where disclosure would harm frank internal debate, except where this disclosure would be outweighed by the public interest;
- management information, where disclosure would harm the proper and effective operation of the NHS organisation;
- information about legal matters and proceedings, where disclosure would prejudice the administration of justice and the law;
- information which could prejudice negotiations or the effective conduct of personnel management or commercial or contractual activities;
- information given in confidence;
- information which will soon be published or where disclosure would be premature in relation to a planned announcement or publication;
- information relating to incomplete analysis, research or statistics where disclosure could be misleading or prevent the holder from publishing it first.

1.7.2 Freedom of Information Act 2000

The Freedom of Information Act 2000, fully in force from January 2005, creates a general right of access to information held by a public authority, such as local government, NHS bodies, and other public bodies and offices. The provisions in the Act are regulated by the Information Commissioner (who is the same person who acts as Commissioner under the Data Protection Act) to whom the public have direct access. The Act permits people to apply for access to documents, or copies of documents, as well as to the information itself. The information sought however, is of public interest, such as minutes of committee meeting or accounts, rather than of a personal interest, such as under the Data Protection Act 1998.

The Freedom of Information Act 2000:

- provides a right of access to recorded information held by public authorities and specifies the conditions which need to be fulfilled before an authority is obliged to comply with a request;
- creates exemptions from the duty to disclose information;
- establishes the arrangements for enforcement and appeal;
- allows public authorities to charge fees in accordance with regulations made by the Secretary of State;
- provides for time limits for complying with a request;
- requires public authorities to provide advice and assistance to applicants;
- requires public authorities to state the basis for refusal of a request;
- requires public authorities to adopt and maintain a publication scheme and to publish information in accordance with it.

Information on the Data Protection Act 1998 and the Freedom of Information Act 2000 is available from the Information Commissioner (see Appendix 3).

Paragraph 15.9.6 sets out how to obtain personal data.

CHAPTER 2

Social care providers

2.1 WHAT ARE SOCIAL SERVICES?

Social services were established by LASSA 1970, which provides for the management and administration of social services. Social services functions are listed in the first Schedule to the Act. The list is extensive and includes such functions under the National Assistance Act 1948, the Children Act 1989 (the 1989 Act), the National Health Service and Community Care Act 1990 and the Carers and Disabled Children Act 2000 (CDCA 2000). The work of social services has been extended by the Local Government Act 2000 (LGA 2000), Part I which empowers local authorities to undertake activities which they consider will promote the economic, social or environmental well-being of their area (s.2).

Mandatory guidance has been issued as *Power to Promote or Improve Economic, Social or Environmental Well-being* (March 2001) and is available from the Department for Communities and Local Government on its website (**www.odpm.gov.uk**) (LGA 2000, s.3(5)). Although this wide discretionary power can be used as a 'safety net' to make service provision that would not otherwise be possible, it cannot be used to do anything that is specifically prohibited or limited in other statutory provisions (LGA 2000, s.3). The Local Government Act 2003 extends local authorities' financial powers and importantly includes powers to charge for the provision of discretionary services (s.93).

2.2 HOW DO SOCIAL SERVICES WORK?

Local authorities are known by different names depending on their role and location.

District councils take on different responsibilities within the same area as county councils, but metropolitan districts, unitary authorities and London boroughs take on the same responsibilities as county and district councils together. Not all councils have social services responsibilities. The executive of the local authority can take one of three broad forms: an elected mayor with a cabinet; an elected leader with a cabinet; or an elected mayor with a council manager.

The elected leader or mayor will appoint an executive from the elected councillors to make decisions about policies and budgets. These are put to the full council for approval.

The various departments of the local authority, such as social services, employ officers of the council to put policy into practice. The director of social services is appointed by the local authority to carry out social services functions (LASSA 1970, s.6(1)) and adequate staff should be appointed to assist him in carrying out his functions (LASSA 1970, s.6(6)).

The Green Paper on adult social care *Independence, Well-being and Choice: Our Vision for the Future of Social Care for Adults in England* was published in March 2005, and proposed the introduction of the post of director of adult social services (DASS), alongside the director of children's services. The DASS has seven key roles: to provide accountability for spending and delivering quality services; to provide professional leadership for the social care workforce and the rights of adults with social care needs in the wider community; to lead the implementation of standards to drive up quality of care; to manage a process of change to implement person-centred planning; to promote local access and ownership to deliver a whole system approach to social care; to develop an integrated approach in conjunction with the director of children's services; and to promote social inclusion and well-being.

The Green Paper envisages that the DASS and the local authority will carry out regular strategic needs assessments to enable them to plan ahead to ensure that adequate services are available in the future. The strategic assessment should be linked with the wider housing needs in the area, with greater emphasis on supporting people to live in their own homes.

2.3 REGULATION OF SOCIAL SERVICES

The Commission for Social Care Inspection (CSCI) took over the work of the Social Services Inspectorate from 1 April 2004. Its role includes inspection, assessment and evaluation of all social care provision against national standards. Star ratings are published annually and a report is submitted to Parliament. Inspection Reports are published on the CSCI website (**www.csci.org.uk**). It was planned that from October 2005, the CSCI would take over the independent complaints stage of adult social services complaints. However, this has been subject to repeated delay. **Chapter 18** has more detail on the complaints process.

The National Assembly for Wales has responsibility for the delivery of social care services in Wales. Social care registrations, inspection, and enforcement is undertaken by the Care Standards Inspectorate for Wales

(CSIW) and the Social Services Inspectorate for Wales (SSIW), whilst the Audit Commission in Wales carries out value for money studies.

2.4 PLANNING AND THE PROVISION OF SERVICES BY SOCIAL SERVICES

2.4.1 Register of disabled persons

Section 29(4)(g) of the National Assistance Act 1948 creates a duty on local authorities to keep a register of disabled persons in their area. (See LAC (93) 10, Appendix 4, which sets out the registration practice and related statistical requirements.)

The register is used for planning purposes, but has limitations as it does not contain details of all people in the local authority area who are disabled, as being on the register is optional and is not a condition of receiving assistance. However, being on the register may be necessary to receive certain benefits, such as the blind person's personal allowance for income tax. The local authority must submit annual statistical returns to the Department of Health based on the information contained in the register.

The 1989 Act, Sched.2, Part I, para.2 sets out the equivalent registration duty in respect of children.

2.4.2 Planning for services

Section 1(1) of the Chronically Sick and Disabled Persons Act 1970 (CSDPA 1970) requires local authorities to inform themselves of the number of disabled people in their area, although this does not extend to 100 per cent identification (DHSS Circular 12/70).

Under the National Health Service and Community Care Act 1990, local authorities were under a duty to produce annual community care plans but in England there are now a range of plans and planning mechanisms, such as: Community Care Charters, Local Strategic Partnerships, Local Health Partnership and Modernisation Boards Plans, Health and Modernisation Plans, Joint Investment Plans, National Service Frameworks, Local Action Plans, Better Care, Higher Standards Charters, Local Community Strategy Initiatives, Carers Strategies and Best Value Plans. So to rationalise and streamline planning, the requirement to prepare community care plans was removed by the Community Care Plans (Disapplication) (England) Order 2003, SI 2003/1716.

Policy guidance and related good practice on the development of joint local 'Better Care Higher Standards' charters (BCHS) for people aged over 18 who need long-term care and their carers was published in LAC (2001) 6, HSC 2001/006, and is underpinned by the duty on social services, health and housing authorities to work together to prepare community strategies (LGA

2000, s.4). The local authorities must consult and seek the participation of such persons as they consider appropriate in preparing or modifying their community strategies (LGA 2000, s.4(3)(a)). The BCHS guidance can be found on the Department of Health's website (**www.dh.gov.uk**).

The BCHS charters should set out the standards and goals for improvement in the following areas:

- information to help users and carers to find out about services;
- understanding and responding to the needs of users and carers;
- finding a suitable place to live;
- helping people to stay independent;
- getting the right health care;
- helping carers to care.

It includes being told how long the user should wait for an assessment, how long the process will take, the right to be given a copy of the decision in writing and how to challenge the decision if the user is not satisfied.

The BCHS Charters and Joint Investment Plans (see **para.1.5.2**) are currently the main vehicles for strategic planning.

The requirement for community care plans still exists in Wales, although it has been updated by the wider functions of the LGA 2000. Community care plans must be integrated with health, social care and well-being strategies under the Health, Social Care and Well-being Strategies (Wales) Regulations 2003, SI 2003/154 (W.24). Guidance has been issued by the Welsh Assembly in NAFWC 36/00 and *Social Services Guidance on Planning* (Nov 2000) (available from the Welsh Assembly's website **www.wales.gov.uk**).

It is also envisaged that the Welsh Unified Assessment and Care Management systems should influence and affect the development of local social and health plans (paras.1.12–1.16 of *Creating a Unified and Fair System for Assessing and Managing Care* (UFSAMC) (NAFWC 09/02, WHC (2002) 32) (available from **www.wales.gov.uk**).

2.4.3 Access to information

The Code of Practice on Access to Government Information has now been completely superseded by the Freedom of Information Act 2000, which gives every individual a right to access information from a public authority and (see **para.1.7.2**). The service user's and carer's right to obtain personal data under the Data Protection Act 1998 is discussed at **para.15.9.6**.

2.5 WHAT DUTIES AND POWERS DO THEY HAVE?

The local authority will either have a statutory duty, in which case it must carry out the particular function, or a statutory power, where it has discretion. In any event discretion must be shown to have been exercised in each case, as failure to do so may be subject to judicial review on the basis that the local authority has fettered its discretion. Service provision is generally dependent on whether:

- the individual is a disabled person;
- the relevant statute contains a power or duty to provide;
- the duty is a target duty or specific to the individual.

For some service provision, such as in the case of residential accommodation, the duty can apply to a wider section of people.

2.5.1 Provision of residential accommodation

Residential accommodation is further considered in **Chapters 13** and **14**.

National Assistance Act 1948

Local authorities are under a duty by virtue of the National Assistance Act 1948, s.21(1)(a) 'to provide residential accommodation for persons aged eighteen or over who, by reason of age, illness, disability or any other circumstances are in need of care and attention which is not otherwise available to them'. The duty applies to people who are ordinarily resident in the local authority area (s.24(1)) (see **para.2.5.4** below). Directions have been issued in England (LAC (93) 10, Appendix 1) and in Wales (WOC 35/93), which are virtually identical. The local authority has a discretionary power to make provision for those of no settled residence or who are ordinarily resident in another local authority area but are in urgent need of residential accommodation (s.24(3)). In all other cases provision is to be made where the person is ordinarily resident in the area and in urgent need (LAC (93) 10, Appendix 1, para.2(1)(b) (*R (on the application of Wahid)* v. *Tower Hamlets LBC* [2002] EWCA Civ 287).

There are no limits to the potential conditions that may arise for entitlement to provision under s.21; however the directions specifically create a duty to provide for people who are or have been suffering from a mental disorder and to prevent mental disorder, even where they are not ordinarily resident in the local authority area (LAC (93) 10, Appendix 1, paras.2(3), 4(c) and 4(4)(1)).

There is a power, within the directions, to provide for those who are alcohol or drug dependent (para.4(6)) and a separate power to provide hostel accommodation for disabled people engaged in workshops provided by the authority (s.29(4)(c) and LAC (93) 10, Appendix 2, para.2(4)). Such accommodation is subject to charging under the National Assistance Act 1948, s.22 (s.29(4A)).

Power exists under s.21(1)(aa) for expectant and nursing mothers who are in need of care and attention, which is not otherwise available to them, irrespective of age (LAC (93) 10, Appendix 1, para.3).

The provision does not extend to able-bodied asylum-seekers by virtue of s.21(1A), which was inserted by the Immigration and Asylum Act 1999, s.116. Those who are solely destitute or suffer or may suffer the physical effects of being destitute must apply for accommodation from the National Asylum Support Service (NASS). Useful information is available from its website (**www.asylumsupport.info/nass.htm**). **Chapter 14** sets out what provision may be available to asylum-seekers.

Mental Health Act 1983, s.117

Provision can also be made for residential accommodation under the Mental Health Act 1983 (MHA 1983), s.117 and must not be charged for (see **para.12.3.4**).

Local Government Act 2000

The local authority has a wide general power under LGA 2000, s.2 to do anything which it considers is likely to promote or improve the social well-being of its area, which may be for the benefit of all persons or an individual person, either resident or present in its area. The power includes provision for a local authority to provide accommodation to any person (s.2(4)(f) and *R (on the application of J) (Ghanian Citizen)* v. *Enfield LBC* (2002) 5 CCLR 434).

There is a wide general power to charge for services provided under LGA 2000 but it is limited by the restrictions that the recipient must agree to the provision of the service; taking one financial year with another, income does not exceed costs; and it cannot be used to charge for services that the authority is under a duty to provide (Local Government Act 2003, s.93). Guidance was issued by the Office of the Deputy Prime Minister (now the Department for Communities and Local Government), entitled *General Power for Best Value Authorities to charge for Discretionary Services – Guidance on the Power in the Local Government Act 2003* (November 2003) (available from **www.odpm.gov.uk**) and by the National Assembly for Wales in November 2004 (available from **www.wales.gov.uk**).

Children Act 1989, s.17

Local authorities owe a duty to children in need which requires them to safeguard and promote the welfare of such children in their area, including the provision of residential accommodation as well as a range of other services (1989 Act, s.17). **Chapter 11** contains more detail on provision for children and young adults.

2.5.2 Provision of non-residential services

A wide range of services can be provided in the home as domiciliary services or community-based services, including help in the home, disability equipment, home adaptations, transport, day care and recreational facilities. Service provision is dependent on which client group the individual falls within, as different services are available under different statutory provisions.

National Assistance Act 1948, s.29(1)

The local authority has a duty to make arrangements in relation to people who are ordinarily resident in the local authority area; for promoting the welfare of people aged 18 or over who are blind, deaf or dumb or who suffer from mental disorder of any description; and other persons aged 18 and over who are substantially and permanently handicapped by illness, injury or congenital deformity or such other disabilities as may be prescribed by the Secretary of State. The duty however is a target duty as opposed to a specific duty to an individual (*R* v. *Islington LBC ex p Rixon* (1997–98) 1 CCLR 119). Services can be provided at the discretion of the local authority for people who are outside its area (*R* v. *Berkshire CC ex p P* (1997–98) CCLR 141). To create a level of clarity as to the health and social divide, no service can be provided under s.29 if services are required to be provided under the 1977 Act (s.29(6)(b)).

Most people who fall within the s.29(1) definition are entitled to services by virtue of CSDPA 1970, s.2; however, frail older people are not covered and provision may be available under the Health Services and Public Health Act 1968, s.45. Those who are partially sighted and/or hard of hearing are covered by s.29(1), following previous guidance issued in LAC 13/74, para.11(i) (LAC (93) 10, Appendix 4, Annex 2, para.2).

LAC (93) 10, Appendix 2, para.2(2) sets out which services the local authority has a duty to provide:

- social work support and advice (welfare benefits advice and counselling fall within this aspect);
- facilities for social rehabilitation and adjustment to disability (medical rehabilitation is excluded);
- facilities for occupational, social, cultural and recreational activities, and where appropriate making payments to people for work undertaken by them.

The following are services which the local authority has a power to provide under LAC (93) 10, Appendix 2, para.2(3):

- holiday homes;
- free or subsidised travel for those who do not qualify for travel concessions where such concessions are available;

- assistance in finding suitable accommodation;
- contributions towards the cost of employing a warden on welfare functions in warden-assisted living schemes or providing warden services in private housing.

Chronically Sick and Disabled Persons Act 1970, s.2

The local authority is under an absolute duty to provide services, having functions under the National Assistance Act 1948, s.29, if it is satisfied following an assessment that it is necessary to make provision in order to meet the needs of a disabled person who is ordinarily resident in the local authority area (*R* v. *Gloucestershire CC ex p Barry* (1997–98) 1 CCLR 7). See **para.2.5.4** below on the term, 'ordinarily resident'. Services can be provided to a disabled adult or child (CSDPA 1970, s.28A and 1989 Act, s.17(11)). Although service provision under CSDPA 1970 is not listed as a community care service under the National Health Service and Community Care Act 1990, s.46, the courts have held that provision for adults is made under the National Assistance Act 1948, s.29 and as such a charge can be made (*R* v. *Powys CC ex p Hambridge (No.1)* [1998] 1 FLR 643).

Provision includes the following:

- practical assistance within the home;
- provision of or assistance in obtaining a radio or television, and help in using the local library or similar recreational facilities;
- provision of lectures, games, outings or other recreational facilities outside the home or assistance in taking advantage of educational facilities available;
- help with travelling to any of these or similar activities;
- adaptations, such as a ramp or lift or provision of disability aids and equipment needed in the home for the greater safety, comfort or convenience of the disabled person;
- facilitating the taking of holidays;
- meals in the home or elsewhere such as at a local centre;
- a telephone and any special equipment needed to use it.

National Health Service Act 1977, s.21 and Sched.8, para.2(1)

Local authorities have a discretionary power to make arrangements to prevent illness or mental disorder, to care for those suffering from illness and assist in their after-care, which is aimed at those who do not qualify for services under CSDPA 1970, s.2 or the National Assistance Act 1948, s.29, irrespective of whether the person is ordinarily resident in the local authority area.

Provision includes under LAC (93) 10, Appendix 3, para.3(3):

- advice and support;
- making payments to ill people for work undertaken by them at centres;
- meals on wheels;
- night sitting service;
- recuperation holidays;
- facilities for social and recreational activities;
- services for alcoholic or drug dependent persons.

A duty is owned to those who suffer a mental disorder, for the purposes of their after-care or for the prevention of a mental disorder, to provide centres, such as training and day centres or other domiciliary facilities, for training or occupation, including paying the service user for work undertaken at the centres or other facilities. In addition, social work support, domiciliary and care services, as well as services to help in the identification, diagnosis, assessment and social treatment of the mental disorder (LAC (93) 10, Appendix 3, para.3(2)).

National Health Service Act 1977, Sched.8, para.3(1)

Local authorities have a duty to provide, on a scale that is adequate for the needs of their area, home help for households where there is a person suffering from an illness, an expectant or a nursing mother, an aged person, a person handicapped as a result of illness or congenital deformity, irrespective of whether that person is ordinarily resident in the local authority area. There is a discretion to provide laundry services where a home help is provided.

Health Services and Public Health Act 1968, s.45

The local authority has a power to make arrangements for promoting the welfare of older people. DHSS 19/71, para.4 directs that the local authority may provide:

- meals and recreation in the home and elsewhere;
- information about available services;
- transport to and from any services provided by the authority or any other similar service;
- assistance in finding boarding accommodation;
- support from visitors, advisory services and social workers;
- practical assistance in the home, including adaptations in order to secure greater safety, comfort or convenience;
- home helps, laundry services and aids to independent living;

- a contribution towards the cost of employing a warden on welfare functions in warden-assisted housing schemes or providing warden services in private housing.

Health and Social Services and Social Security Adjudications Act 1983, Sched.9, Part II

District councils, Welsh county councils or county borough councils have discretionary power to provide meals and recreation for elderly people in their homes or elsewhere, such as at a day centre. Such councils do not have social services responsibilities and can work with councils with social services responsibilities for provision.

Mental Health Act 1983, s.117(2)

Section 117 of MHA 1983 imposes a duty on local and health authorities to provide after-care services, which include non-residential care services, to those who leave hospital after ceasing to be detained under ss.3, 37, 47 and 48. No charge can be made for these services. See **Chapter 12** for more detail.

Children Act 1989, s.17

Local authorities owe a duty to children in need and are required to safeguard and promote the welfare of such children in their area, which includes the provision of a range of services. **Chapter 11** contains more detail on provision for children and young adults.

Local Government Act 2000

Local authorities have wide power to provide services for individuals in their area. See **para.2.5.1** above.

2.5.3 The status of directions and guidance

Government directions and guidance may underpin statutes and regulations. The status of such directions and guidance can at times be unclear. Section 7(1) of LASSA 1970 provides that 'local authorities shall, in exercise of their social services functions, including the exercise of any discretion, conferred by any relevant enactment, act under the general guidance of the Secretary of State'. In addition, s.7A(1) and (2) states:

> . . . every local authority shall exercise their social services functions in accordance with such directions as may be given to them under this section by the Secretary of State.

(2) Directions under this section –

(a) shall be given in writing; and
(b) may be given to a particular authority, or to authorities of a particular class, or to authorities generally.

As such, directions are mandatory and attract a statutory duty of compliance (*R* v. *North Derbyshire Health Authority ex p Fisher* (1997–98) 1 CCLR 150).

There are two types of social services guidance:

(a) policy guidance, issued under s.7(1), which is mandatory and should be followed unless there are good reasons not to (*R v. Islington LBC ex p Rixon* (1997–98) 1 CCLR 119); and
(b) practice guidance, which essentially sets out best practice of how the local authority should implement a policy.

Guidance may be contained within: a Local Authority Circular (LAC); a Local Authority Social Services Letter (LASSL); a Chief Inspector Letter (CIL); or may have been issued prior to its abolition, by the Social Services Inspectorate (SSI). In Wales, prior to 1999 guidance was issued as a Welsh Office Circular (WOC) rather than an LAC. Since 1999, guidance is issued as a National Assembly for Wales Circular (NAFWC).

The Government issued general policy guidance at the time of the passing of the National Health Service and Community Care Act 1990, entitled *Caring for People: Community Care in the Next Decade and Beyond* (1990). Subsequent policy guidance has been issued in respect of many aspects of community care law which were originally contained in the 1990 guidance. It is generally accepted that the 1990 policy guidance should be referred to when there are gaps or uncertainty in the more recent policy guidance.

English guidance can be obtained from the Department of Health and its website (see Appendix 3). Copies of Welsh guidance can be obtained from the Welsh Assembly and its website (see Appendix 3).

2.5.4 Ordinarily resident

The term defined

Much of the provision of community care services is determined by whether or not the individual is ordinarily resident in the local authority area. To assist local authorities in determining whether they have a responsibility to a particular individual guidance has been published in LAC (93) 7 in England (available from **www.dh.gov.uk**) and WOC 41/93 in Wales (available from **www.wales.gov.uk**).

There is no set definition of 'ordinarily resident' and it is ultimately a judicial question to be resolved, unless it relates to residential accommodation, in which case determination rests with the Secretary of State.

The concept of ordinarily resident or ordinary residence involves questions of fact and degree, and factors such as time, intention and continuity, each of which may be given different weight according to the context, and which have to be taken into account. Of this definition, Lord Scarman said in *R* v. *Barnet LBC ex p Shah (Nilish)* [1983] 1 All ER 226 at 239:

> unless . . . it can be shown that the statutory framework or the legal context in which the words are used requires a different meaning I unhesitatingly subscribe to the view that 'ordinarily resident' refers to a man's abode in a particular place or country which he has adopted voluntarily and for settled purposes as part of the regular order of his life for the time being, whether of short or long duration.

The term 'ordinary residence' in *Levene* v. *IRC* [1928] AC 217 was said by Viscount Care to be in a place with some degree of continuity apart from accidental or temporary absences. For other relevant cases see *R* v. *Waltham Forest LBC ex p Vale* (1985) *The Times*, 25 February (where the applicant's parents' home was found to be her base and as such determined her ordinary residence), and *R* v. *Redbridge LBC ex p East Sussex CC* (1993) *The Times*, 3 January.

Ordinary residence and the Community Care (Delayed Discharges etc.) Act 2003

Delays should not occur where there is uncertainty about which local authority is responsible for commissioning care. It is for the local authority where the potential service user is living at that time to provide the care to meet the assessed needs. This is particularly relevant under the Community Care (Delayed Discharges etc.) Act 2003, when the local authority where the person is situated may be responsible for assessing and putting into placc service provision, even if the person is not ordinarily resident in its area (s.10 and the Community Care (Delayed Discharges etc.) Act 2003 (Commencement No.1) (England) Order 2003, SI 2003/2280).

Disputes as to ordinary residence

Disputes in respect of provision under the National Assistance Act 1948 should be resolved by negotiation between local authorities but failing any resolution they can seek a determination of which authority the person is deemed to be ordinarily resident within from the Secretary of State (LAC (93) 7, paras.23–29; National Assistance Act 1948, s.32(3)). This is unlike disputes regarding provision under CSDPA 1970, the 1989 Act and MHA 1983, where the court is the arbitrator (*R* v. *Kent CC ex p S and Pierre* (2000) 3 CCLR 38).

Ordinary residence and Mental Health Act 1983, s.117

The Court of Appeal in the case of *R* v. *Mental Health Review Tribunal ex p Hall* [2000] 1 WLR 1323, confirmed that the health and social services authorities where the patient was resident at the time of admission to hospital have legal responsibility for providing after-care under s.117. The respondent had been detained indefinitely under MHA 1983 in 1991. In May 1996 he applied to the tribunal to be discharged. The tribunal found that the respondent was suffering from a mental illness for which treatment was not required but that he might relapse and so should be liable for recall. One of the conditions set by the tribunal was that the patient should not return to where he lived before admission to hospital. Detention under MHA 1983 does not alter a patient's ordinary residence. If a patient with ordinary residence in one area is sent to another area on discharge, it is the responsibility of the health and social services authorities in the area where the patient was resident before admission to make the necessary arrangements under s.117. Where the patient has no current residence when admitted to hospital, the authorities for the area where the patient must reside as part of his conditional discharge have responsibility for providing after-care under s.117.

Moving between local authority areas

Where a user moves residence from one local authority area to another, the responsibility for providing services is transferred across, except where the move is the result of the person being placed in residential accommodation arranged by the local authority (National Assistance Act 1948, s.24(5)). If any change in services is contemplated, the individual should be reassessed in accordance with the new authority's policies and priorities, always ensuring that the individual's needs are properly taken into account.

For people moving independently to a new local authority area, such as self-funders, they will need to be assessed by the new local authority for service provision, although the local authority may want to be satisfied that it has a responsibility for them and so clarify whether the person is now ordinarily resident in its area (LAC (93) 7, paras.10 and 15). For those of no settled residence the local authority should take responsibility (LAC (93) 7, para.16).

In the *Fair Access to Care Services* (FACS) policy guidance (LAC (2002) 13) para.56, and para.5.43 of UFSAMC, where the service user moves from one area to another, 'the receiving council' should, pending an assessment, take into account the services that were previously received and the effect of the substantial changes on the service user when taking an interim decision about what services to provide. The 'receiving council' should have regard to these factors, as well as the outcomes that were previously pursued, when carrying out the assessment and taking long-term decisions about what services will be provided. When 'receiving councils' intend to pursue significantly different outcomes, or provide significantly different services, they should produce clear and written explanations for the service user.

2.6 THE OVERLAP BETWEEN HEALTH CARE AND SOCIAL SERVICES

It can be unclear at times whether a particular service is the responsibility of the NHS or social services, with the additional problem that NHS provision is free at the point of delivery, whereas provision by social services is means tested. This has led to the Government issuing guidance in respect of continuing NHS health care, intermediate care and community equipment services, in an attempt to clarify the position and has led to increase legislation to improve the joint working of health and social care bodies, so effectively there should be no gaps in the system (see **Chapter 8** for more detail on NHS continuing health care). Despite this, service users are frequently pushed between both organisations, with arguments as to which body is responsible, in which case a complaint can be made against each organisation for failure to cooperate at the very least.

2.6.1 The duty to cooperate and collaborate

Section 22 of the 1977 Act (as amended by the Health Act 1999, s.27) imposes on NHS bodies and local authorities a wide duty to cooperate with each other, in order to secure and advance the health and welfare of the people of England and Wales. The duty to cooperate specifically arises within the assessment process, where the individual appears to have a health or housing need, as the local authority must notify the appropriate body and invite it to assist in the assessment, and can take into account any service that would be provided by that body (National Health Service and Community Care Act 1990, s.47(3)). (See **para.3.1.3**.) There is however no duty on the health or housing body to cooperate with social services, unlike the similar provision in respect of children (1989 Act, s.27). Health authority staff should be made available to enable the local authority to discharge its functions, and vice versa, so far as is reasonably necessary and practical (1977 Act, ss.26 and 27).

The local authority should collaborate with the NHS body when it is exercising its duty to consult under the Health and Social Care Act 2001, s.11 in respect of health care planning and development, as well as discharge under the Community Care (Delayed Discharges etc.) Act 2003 (see **para.7.3**).

The NHS and local authority also have a joint duty to arrange after-care services for certain people who were previously detained under MHA 1983 (s.117(2)) (see **Chapter 12**). This joint responsibility has lead to the setting up of a number of 'Care Trusts', where local authorities can delegate their health responsibilities to the NHS body (see **para.1.2.8**).

Section 113 of the Local Government Act 1972 creates a power for the local authority to enter into agreements with a health authority, special authority or NHS Trust to delegate its functions to an NHS officer or for local authority staff to work within the NHS.

2.6.2 Financial arrangements between the NHS and social services

The Health Act 1999 amended the reciprocal powers (1977 Act, ss.28A and 28BB) of NHS bodies and social services to make payments to the other body in respect of local authority functions that are health related and 'prescribed functions', which are defined by the National Health Service (Payments by Local Authorities to NHS Bodies) (Prescribed Functions) Regulations 2000, SI 2000/618 and the National Health Service (Payments by Local Authorities to Health Authorities) (Prescribed Functions) (Wales) Regulations 2001, SI 2001/1543 (W.108). In particular it allows for payments to be made in respect of the provision of after-care services under MHA 1983 (s.117).

Strategic Health Authorities, Primary Care Trusts and Local Health Boards, and social services have power under the Health Act 1999, s.31 to arrange:

- pooled funds – each contributes agreed funds to a single pot, to be spent on agreed projects for designated services;
- lead commissioning – agree to delegate commissioning of a service to one lead organisation;
- integrated provision – their staff, resources and management structures work together to integrate the provision of a service from managerial level to the front line.

See the NHS Bodies and Local Authorities Partnership Arrangements Regulations 2000, SI 2000/617 (as amended) and the National Health Service Bodies and Local Authorities Partnership Arrangements (Wales) Regulations 2000, SI 2000/2993 (W.193). Guidance has been issued in HSC 2000/10, LAC (2000) 9 for England and *Increased Flexibilities Partnership Framework: A User Guide* was published in May 2002 by the Welsh Assembly.

2.7 COOPERATION AND COLLABORATION REGARDING EDUCATION

There is a clear overlap between the role of social services and NHS bodies in their provision of services for disabled children and young adults and the local education authority (LEA). The Government in its 10-year strategy for children called *Every Child Matters* has been concerned to ensure that authorities work together in a collaborative fashion (see further **www.everychildmatters.gov.uk**).

Often, service users of social care will also require assistance in navigating the education legislation in respect of children with special educational needs. Children's social services needs have, since May 2004, been looked after by the Department for Education and Skills.

2.7.1 Children Act 1989

Section 27 of the 1989 Act provides that where it appears to a local authority that an LEA could assist in providing services for a child in need, then it may ask the LEA to help by the taking of a specified action. Section 27(2) provides that the LEA has to comply with the request providing that:

- it is compatible with its own statutory or other duties and obligations; and
- does not unduly prejudice the discharge of any of its functions.

Effectively therefore, this provision only provides a duty for the LEA to act in limited circumstances.

Under the 1989 Act, s.47 the LEA must cooperate with social services departments if the child is suffering from significant harm with the same caveats as are set out in s.27 of the same Act.

2.7.2 Framework for Assessment of Children in Need and Their Families

All social services departments must have regard to the *Framework for Assessment of Children in Need and their Families* (DOH, 2000), which provides extensive guidance to support the principle that in order to secure optimal outcomes, authorities must cooperate and work in a coordinated way. Education professionals will be in most cases expected to contribute to assessments and care planning which takes place in accordance with this framework. A copy of the framework can be obtained from the Department of Health website (**www.dh.gov.uk**).

2.7.3 Education Act 1996

Section 322 of the Education Act 1996 provides that health authorities and social services, subject to the reasonableness of the request in the light of the resources available to them, must comply with a request for help from an LEA in connection with a child with special educational needs, unless they consider that the help is not necessary for the exercise of the functions of the LEA.

Again this provision is therefore only mandatory in limited circumstances and does not provide a mandatory obligation for social services to provide assistance (for example, by paying for a portion of the fees of residential schooling) in all cases.

The social services department usually designates an officer or officers who deals with special education cases and who provides the advice which is requested by the LEA to be contributed as part of a child's statutory assessment of special educational needs under the Education Act 1996, s.323.

2.7.4 Children Act 2004

The Children Act 2004 adds to these duties by creating the post of 'director of children's services' and the department of children's services. Section 18 of the Children Act 2004 provides that each local authority must have a 'director of children's services' in order to direct all functions of the authority in respect of education, social services functions as they relate to children, and functions of the authority in relation to pooled funding under the Health Act 1999, s.31 (see **para.2.6.2** above). This provides for one system of management and responsibility for most local authority functions which relate to children.

It is mandatory for each children's services authority in England to promote cooperation between itself and the district council, police authority and relevant youth justice agencies and the Strategic Health Authority and the Learning and Skills Council (which governs education for adults and young adults over 16 who enter the further or higher education sector) (Children Act 2004, s.10). Such arrangements must be made to improve the well-being of children in the authority's area relating to the following:

- physical and mental health and emotional well-being;
- protection from harm and neglect;
- education, training and recreation;
- the contribution made by them to society;
- social and economic well-being.

The authority is told that it must have regard to the importance of parents and other persons caring for children when improving the well-being of children (Children Act 2004, s.10(3)).

In furtherance of this duty, the children's services authority can provide staff, goods, services, accommodation or other resources, and establish and maintain a pooled fund which is made out of contributions by the authority and relevant partners (Children Act 2004, s.10(6) and (7)). Such services can be provided to persons aged 18 and 19, those who are care leavers (1989 Act, ss.23C–24D) and those between the ages of 19 and 25 who have a learning difficulty as defined by the Learning and Skills Act 2000, s.13 and are receiving services under that Act (principally young adults with learning disabilities receiving education and training in further education or specialist residential colleges) (Children Act 2004, s.10(9)).

Section 11 of the Children Act 2004 provides that a children's services authority in England, a district council, Strategic Health Authority, Special Health Authority, Primary Care Trust, NHS Trust, NHS Foundation Trust, bodies representing youth justice and the Learning and Skills providers must make arrangements for ensuring that:

- their functions are discharged having regard to the need to safeguard and promote the welfare of children; and
- any services provided by another person pursuant to arrangements made by the person or body in the discharge of their functions are provided having regard to that need and having regard to the Secretary of State's guidance.

These provisions came into force in March and April 2005 (Children Act 2004 (Commencement No.1) Order 2005, SI 2005/394). Multiple guidance is available on the role of children's trusts and their impact and remit (see **www.everychildmatters.gov.uk**). The Department of Health and the Department for Education and Skills have also published a National Service Framework for children, which sets out a number of standards that should be reached in respect of all children, with several of those standards involving improvement of planning and care for disabled children and young adults (see policy and guidance on children's services on the Department of Health's website: **www.dh.gov.uk**).

There is also a duty upon the local authority to prepare a children's plan, and for that plan to set out the arrangements made for children's services (which will include both education and social care provision). The Children and Young People's Plan (England) Regulations 2005, SI 2005/2149 sets out the obligations and nature of the plan and in particular provides that the authority must indicate what proportion of its budget will be spent on improving children's welfare and well-being. Every authority must publish the first plan by 1 April 2006.

The duty to cooperate for Welsh authorities is broadly similar to that set out in England. The cooperation and well-being duties of the Children Act 2004 for Welsh authorities are set out at ss.25–34 of the Act, and these provisions also came into force in March and April 2005.

2.8 COOPERATION AND COLLABORATION REGARDING HOUSING

Many individuals who present themselves to social services will have related difficulties in respect of housing, or may indeed be presenting themselves to social services because they are homeless. The duties to provide housing are governed by the Housing Act 1996 and are dealt with in **Chapter 14**. The legislation for England and Wales is identical. LAC (92) 12, DOE Circular 10/92 provides explicit guidance to ensure cooperation in order to maintain an effective package of care and a seamless service with joint discussion, understanding and agreement between housing authorities and social services.

2.8.1 National Health Service and Community Care Act 1990

Section 47(3) of the National Health Service and Community Care Act 1990 provides that, where there may be a requirement for housing or some kind of housing function (for a definition of which, see the Housing Act 1985, s.228), which is disclosed during a community care assessment, then social services must notify the housing authority, telling it what assistance the housing authority may provide in order to assist in making the community care assessment (s.47(3)(b)). This applies only to those authorities which are not unitary. Unfortunately, this provision is somewhat toothless as the housing authority is under no statutory duty to respond or cooperate. However, social services may remain responsible for provision (*R* v. *Islington LBC, ex p Batantu* (2001) 4 CCLR 445).

2.8.2 Housing Act 1996

If social services have notified the housing authority of an individual who has a housing need, separate duties may arise under the Housing Act 1996. If an individual makes an application (which need not be in any particular form) and he is either homeless or threatened with homelessness, the housing authority will owe him a duty to make enquiries, notify him of the decision, and accommodate him pending the outcome of such enquiries (Housing Act 1996, s.184).

A housing authority may request social services to exercise any of their functions in relation to a case which is being dealt with under the homelessness provisions of the Housing Act 1996. Social services must cooperate in rendering such assistance to discharge these functions 'as is reasonable in the circumstances' (Housing Act 1996, s.213).

2.8.3 Children Act 1989

For those under 18 years of age, the duty to cooperate under the 1989 Act, s.27 provides that social services can ask the housing authority to assist them, in which case the request must be complied with if it is compatible with the housing authority's own statutory or other duties and obligations and does not unduly prejudice the discharge of its own functions. In *R* v. *Northavon DC ex p Smith* [1994] 2 AC 402, the housing authority refused a request from social services for assistance in housing a family with children whom

Northavon had previously found to be intentionally homeless. In the Court of Appeal this challenge was upheld. This decision is somewhat in doubt following *R (on the application of A)* v. *Lambeth LBC* [2003] UKHL 57, where it was found that no specifically enforceable duty is owed to house homeless children and their families together pursuant to 1989 Act, s.17.

2.8.4 Homelessness Act 2002

As a result of the *Lambeth* decision, the Homelessness Act 2002 imposes a specific referral and cooperation duty on the housing authority to inform social services (Housing Act 1996, s.213A). This duty arises where the housing authority has reason to believe that a homeless applicant with children may be:

- ineligible for assistance; i.e. mainly asylum seekers (under the Asylum and Immigration Act 1996 and the Immigration and Asylum Act 1999) or those who lack the capacity to accept or reject an offer of accommodation (*R* v. *Tower Hamlets LBC ex p Begum* [1993] AC 509);
- homeless intentionally; or
- threatened with homelessness intentionally.

Once social services is made aware that an applicant is ineligible for assistance by the housing authority, it may request that the housing authority provides it with advice and assistance as part and parcel of its duties under the 1989 Act.

2.8.5 National Assistance Act 1948 and Local Government Act 2000

In any event, social services have a residual duty to provide housing under the National Assistance Act 1948, s.21 or even LGA 2000, s.2 (see **para.2.5.1** above).

PART II

Responsibility for the provision of social care

CHAPTER 3

Assessment by social services

Provision of services is subject to the individual coming to the attention of the local authority, being assessed and social services then concluding that the individual qualifies to have their needs met by them. The assessment of children and young adults, mentally ill individuals and carers is dealt with in **Chapters 11**, **12** and **15** respectively. Provision of services is covered in **Chapter 4**. This chapter deals with the assessment of adults, including those over 65 through the Single Assessment Process (SAP) and those who are learning disabled. **Chapter 13** expands on issues that affect the vulnerable adult, such as those who misuse drugs and alcohol.

3.1 ELIGIBILITY FOR ASSESSMENT

The duty to assess the individual arises where the person is disabled or may, in the local authority's view, be in need of community care services.

3.1.1 Assessment under the Disabled Persons (Services, Consultation and Representation) Act 1986

Under the Disabled Persons (Services, Consultation and Representation) Act 1986, s.4 there is a duty to assess the need for services under the Chronically Sick and Disabled Persons Act 1970 (CSDPA 1970), s.2(1) when requested by a disabled person, or any person who provides care for him (but who is not employed to care). As such, the assessment will only occur when there has been a request. 'A disabled person' is defined under the National Assistance Act 1948, s.29 as persons aged 18 and over who are blind, deaf or dumb or suffer a mental disorder of any description and other persons who are substantially and permanently handicapped by illness, injury, congenital deformity and other disabilities as may be prescribed.

Where assessments are conducted under the 1986 Act, s.4, the duty extends to providing a written statement, which sets out the needs of the disabled person which the local authority should provide, and the authority's proposals as to how it will meet those needs.

Section 2(1) of CSDPA 1970 places a duty on the local authority to make arrangements for the provision of welfare services for disabled people who are ordinarily resident in their area, where the authority is satisfied that it is necessary in order to meet the needs of that person. The concept of 'ordinarily resident' is considered at **para.2.5.4** and at **para.3.6** below.

3.1.2 Assessment under the National Health Service and Community Care Act 1990

As the key to provision under the Disabled Persons (Services, Consultation and Representation) Act 1986, s.4 is a request for an assessment, it was possible for disabled people to fail to obtain services if they were unaware that they had to make such a request before they obtained services. As a consequence, the National Health Service and Community Care Act 1990, s.47(1) creates a freestanding duty to assess without the need to make a request for an assessment, which provides:

> . . . where it appears to a local authority that any person for whom they may provide or arrange for the provision of community care services may be in need of any such services, the authority –
>
> (a) shall carry out an assessment of his needs for those services; and
> (b) having regard to the results of that assessment shall then decide whether his needs call for the provision by them of any such services.

As such the section creates a duty to assess (although not a duty to provide), once there is the possibility that the individual may need community care services, irrespective of whether that person is ordinarily resident in the local authority area, or whether the local authority has the legal power to provide or arrange services (*R* v. *Berkshire CC ex p P* (1997–98) 1 CCLR 141).

Definition of community care services

Community care services are defined in the National Health Service and Community Care Act 1990, s.46 by reference to services arranged or provided under the following statutory provisions:

(a) National Assistance Act 1948, Part III;
(b) Health Services and Public Health Act 1968, s.45;
(c) 1977 Act, s.21 and Sched.8; and
(d) MHA 1983, s.117.

Section 2 of the CSDPA 1970 is omitted from the above list, although the courts are of the view that s.2 is an extension of the National Assistance Act 1948, s.29 so that services identified under s.2 are actually provided under s.29

(*R* v. *Powys CC ex p Hambridge (No.1)* [1998] 1 FLR 643). These statutory provisions are covered in more detail at **para.2.5**.

Coming to the attention of the local authority

Although there is no longer a need to request an assessment, the fact that a person may need community care services will have to be brought to the attention of the local authority, before it will assess that person's needs. In the main this will come about through direct contact from the potential service user or someone acting on his behalf. As the duty applies to the local authority rather than an individual department, there is a practical requirement that all departments work together and refer cases that are brought to their attention to social services for assessment (*R (on the application of P)* v. *Newham LBC* (2001) 4 CCLR 48). The threshold for appearing to need community care services is a low one (*R* v. *Bristol City Council ex p Penfold* (1997–98) 1 CCLR 315), although inevitably due to demand for assessments, social services operate a screening process to ascertain whether the individual seeking help may be someone whom they have a duty to assess (see **para.3.4.2** below).

The link between the assessment and the Chronically Sick and Disabled Persons Act 1970, s.2

If during the needs assessment under the National Health Service and Community Care Act 1990, s.47(1)(a) it appears to the local authority that the person is a disabled person, the authority must conduct the assessment under the Disabled Persons (Services, Consultation and Representation) Act 1986, s.4 and inform the person that they are doing this and of the rights under that Act (s.47(2)). In effect, the National Health Service and Community Care Act 1990, s.47 and CSDPA 1970, s.2 are intrinsically linked (*R* v. *Kirklees MBC ex p Daykin* (1997–98) 1 CCLR 512).

3.1.3 Health or housing needs

If it appears to the local authority that the person being assessed has health or housing needs the local authority must notify the appropriate PCT, LHB, NHS Trust or health or housing authority, and invite them to assist in the assessment, to such extent as is reasonable in the circumstances (National Health Service and Community Care Act 1990, s.47(3)). There is no duty on the approached authority to cooperate with the assessment and if the health authority refuses to assist, in practice the social services department will have to make its own assessment as best it can. Increasingly with the Department of Health's requirement to have joint eligibility criteria for continuing care needs to prevent gaps in the health and social care system and with more partnership arrangements under the Health Act 1999, there is greater cooperation in the assessment process (see **para.3.3.2** below). Cooperation is covered more fully at **paras.2.6.1** and **2.8**.

3.1.4 Emergency provision

In an emergency, it is possible under the National Health Service and Community Care Act 1990, s.47(5) for the local authority to provide community care services, even if an assessment has not been carried out. Provision will be made subject to a full assessment being conducted at a later date, and depending on the outcome, the service may continue, be reduced, altered or withdrawn (see **para.3.5.6** below).

3.2 DEFINITION OF AN ASSESSMENT

The Secretary of State may give directions about how an assessment is to be carried out but it should be carried out in a manner and take such form as the local authority considers appropriate (National Health Service and Community Care Act 1990, s.47(4) and the Carers (Recognition and Services) Act 1995, s.1). Section 3 of the Disabled Persons (Services, Consultation and Representation) Act 1986 sets out how assessments should be carried out, although it has not been brought into force.

The Community Care Assessment Directions 2004, made under the National Health Service and Community Care Act 1990, s.47(4), apply to every local authority in England and are covered in LAC (2004) 24. The brief Directions provide that in assessing needs under s.47(1) a local authority must:

(a) consult the person being assessed and, where appropriate, any carer;
(b) take all reasonable steps to reach agreement with the person and, where appropriate, any carer, on the community care services that they are considering providing to him; and
(c) give details of liable charges for those services to the assessed person and, where appropriate, any carer.

However an assessment is conducted, enough information should be obtained to ascertain what are the presenting needs.

3.3 ASSESSMENT CRITERIA

3.3.1 Framework for eligibility

Policy and practice guidance

The need for guidance on the setting of eligibility criteria was highlighted in the 1998 White Paper *Modernising Social Services* (Cm 4169, DH TSO) as different local authorities used different criteria and reviews of eligibility were patchy, which led to national variations and, at times, unfairness. In addition, some local authorities used different or stricter criteria for certain groups of adults who requested help.

Following the White Paper, mandatory policy guidance has been issued in England as *Fair Access to Care Services* (FACS) in LAC (2002) 13, and in Wales in *Creating a Unified and Fair System for Assessing and Managing Care* (UFSAMC) (NAFWC 09/02, WHC (2002) 32). They are virtually identical and are available on the Department of Health and the Welsh Assembly websites (**www.dh.gov.uk** and **www.wales.gov.uk**).

Practice guidance has also been published in England as a series of questions and answers, with accompanying case studies (March 2003). The guidance builds on the original practice guidance *Care Management and Assessment: Practitioners' Guide* (the 1991 practice guidance) and this can be referred to if the FACS guidance is inadequate (Q8.1 practice guidance).

The overall objective

The aim of the guidance is to provide local authorities with a framework for determining eligibility for adult care services and covers how assessments and reviews should be carried out. Each local authority should make similar decisions, which should ensure fairer decisions in their area. However, the guidance does not go as far as to say that every local authority should make identical decisions about eligibility or what services should be provided.

The individual's presenting needs should be assessed, and his eligible needs should be prioritised, according to the risks to his independence were help not provided. Both a short-term and a longer-term view should be adopted, with particular consideration of preventing problems escalating. However, focus will be on those who have the greatest immediate or longer-term needs. 'Presenting needs' are defined in the guidance as 'the issues and problems that are identified when adults contact or are referred to social services for assistance'. 'Eligible needs' are defined as 'those needs that are assessed as falling within the eligibility criteria, which the local authority has a duty to meet'. The framework document makes no reference to age, gender, ethnic group, religion, disabilities, impairments or similar difficulties, personal relationships, location, living and caring arrangements, and similar factors (FACS, para.15; UFSAMC, para.5.16).

The bands of eligibility

The framework for eligibility is graded into four bands, based on the seriousness of the risk to independence if problems and issues are not addressed. UFSAMC, para.5.16 uses slightly different wording to para.16 of FACS, which sets the following framework.

CRITICAL – WHEN

- life is, or will be, threatened; and/or
- significant health problems have developed or will develop; and/or
- there is, or will be, little or no choice and control over vital aspects of the immediate environment; and/or
- serious abuse or neglect has occurred or will occur; and/or
- there is, or will be, an inability to carry out vital personal care or domestic routines; and/or
- vital involvement in work, education or learning cannot or will not be sustained; and/or
- vital social support systems and relationships cannot or will not be sustained; and/or
- vital family and other social roles and responsibilities cannot or will not be undertaken.

SUBSTANTIAL – WHEN

- there is, or will be, only partial choice and control over the immediate environment; and/or
- abuse or neglect has occurred or will occur; and/or
- there is, or will be, an inability to carry out the majority of personal care or domestic routines; and/or
- involvement in many aspects of work, education or learning cannot or will not be sustained; and/or
- the majority of social support systems and relationships cannot or will not be sustained; and/or
- the majority of family and other social roles and responsibilities cannot or will not be undertaken.

MODERATE – WHEN

- there is, or will be, an inability to carry out several personal care or domestic routines; and/or

- involvement in several aspects of work, education or learning cannot or will not be sustained; and/or
- several social support systems and relationships cannot or will not be sustained; and/or
- several family and other social roles and responsibilities cannot or will not be undertaken.

LOW – WHEN

- there is, or will be, an inability to carry out one or two personal care or domestic routines; and/or
- involvement in one or two aspects of work, education or learning cannot or will not be sustained; and/or
- one or two social support systems and relationships cannot or will not be sustained; and/or
- one or two family and other social roles and responsibilities cannot or will not be undertaken.

Local authorities cannot vary the wording of the bands, although they can add extra bullet points (Q3.1 FACS practice guidance).

3.3.2 Joint health and social eligibility criteria

To ensure that potential service users have the totality of their care needs addressed, where eligible, joint eligibility criteria for continuing health and social care should be agreed locally between health and social services, which cover the full range of health and social care services, without any gaps in service, regardless of age (LAC (2001) 18, HSC 2001/15, FACS, para.7, UFSAMC, para.5.46, WHC (2004) 54, NAFWC 41/2004).

3.3.3 Resources and eligibility criteria

Local authority resources

Local authorities are allowed to take into account their available resources when setting their eligibility criteria (*R* v. *Gloucestershire CC ex p Barry* [1997] AC 584). In *R* v. *East Sussex CC ex p Tandy* [1997] 3 WLR 884 and *R* v. *Birmingham City Council ex p Mohammed* [1999] 1 WLR 33, resources were not relevant in considering suitable education and disabled facilities grants respectively and so the *Barry* case is limited to provision under CSDPA 1970, s.2. Guidance to local authorities on the *Barry* judgment was issued under LASSL (97) 13 and WOC 59/97.

In addition to available resources, local authorities must take into account local expectations, local costs and any agreements with the NHS when setting eligibility criteria. They are not obliged to cover all bands: for example, they may only have sufficient resources to meet the critical and substantial bands. However, the criteria must be flexible enough to allow for exceptional cases, as failure to do so may be a breach of human rights, for example to deny a person provision when his life was at risk.

Service user's resources

An individual's financial circumstances should have no bearing on whether or not the local authority carries out an assessment of need. It should also not affect the level or detail of the assessment process (FACS policy guidance, para.70, LAC (98) 19, WOC 27/98). This point was also made by Hardy J in the Scottish case of *Macgregor* v. *South Lanarkshire Council* (2001) 4 CCLR 188; only the relevant issues of the individual are to be taken into account in the assessment. Resources are relevant in determining what provision to make after the person has been assessed, as the individual may have sufficient funds to pay for the cost of their own care. Even if the resource in question is notional capital, it is wrong for a local authority to take such capital into account when assessing a person's need for the provision of residential nursing care (*Robertson* v. *Fife Council* (2002) 68 BMLR 229) See **para.4.13** on the relevance of the service user's resources in the provision of services.

3.3.4 Review of eligibility criteria

Local authorities should review their criteria at least annually, although if there are any major changes, financial or otherwise, criteria may be reviewed more frequently (FACS, para.19; UFSAMC, para.5.22). In the event that criteria are more restrictive, service users need to be fully reassessed against the revised criteria and it must be concluded that they no longer need the service, the need is being met in another way or that they no longer meet the criteria before the service is withdrawn. However, services should not be withdrawn if this will leave the service user at serious risk (*R* v. *Gloucestershire CC ex p Barry* [1997] AC 584 and *R* v. *Birmingham City Council ex p Killigrew* (2000) 3 CCLR 109).

3.4 THE NATURE OF AN ASSESSMENT

The initial assessment process is a fact-finding mission by the assessor to identify and evaluate the individual's presenting needs and whether they have a need for community care services. The assessment should be rounded and person-centred, in which the individual should be an active participant. Any carer should also be consulted and advised of the right to a carer's assessment (see further **Chapter 15**).

FACS, para.36 and UFSMAC at para.2.4 provide that the assessment should be carried out in such a way, and be sufficiently transparent, for individuals to:

- gain a better understanding of their situation;
- identify the options that are available for managing their own lives;
- identify the outcomes required from any help that is provided;
- understand the basis on which decisions are reached.

The scale and depth of the assessment should be proportionate to the individual's presenting needs and circumstances but it should be simple and timely. Details of the assessment types are set out in **para.3.4.4** below.

3.4.1 Areas to be assessed

The areas (or domains) that may be assessed are contained in annexes F and I of SAP and para.4.24 of UFSAMC. Annexes F and I are set out in the table below. The Welsh guidance contains more detail and has a number of additional domains. Not all the domains have to be assessed, as it will depend on the potential service user's presenting needs. The FACS guidance does not specify what areas are to be assessed but should include recreational and leisure needs (*R* v. *Haringey LBC ex p Norton* (1997–98) 1 CCLR 168) and psychological needs (*R* v. *Avon CC ex p M* [1994] 2 FLR 1006). In any event much depends on the quality of any assessment tool and scales used and the skill of the assessor in gaining, evaluating and recording the relevant information. Failure to consider all relevant factors could result in any subsequent care plan being quashed by the court (*R* v. *Birmingham City Council ex p Killigrew* (2000) 3 CCLR 109).

There are a number of accredited assessment tools, scales (a means of identifying the presence and/or severity of a particular problem), questions and checklists used to assist with the assessment of the older person but there is no compulsion on local authorities to use them. They can be used for any type of assessment (see further **www.dh.gov.uk**).

Annex F from the Single Assessment Process guidance

User's perspective

- Recent life events – including strengths and coping mechanisms.
- Advocacy needs.

Carer's perspective and need for carer assessment

- Physical difficulties in caring.
- Psychological difficulties and pressures arising from caring role, including shock, grief, felt inadequacy.

- Life constraints arising from caring role e.g. clashes with employment, child care responsibilities, leisure activity.
- Carer's strengths, expectations, motivation and perceptions of her/his needs and user's needs.

Clinical background

- Recent hospitalisation.
- Breathing difficulties.

Activities of daily living

- Washing.
- Bathing.
- Grooming, including hair care and shaving.
- Dressing.
- Accessing and using toilet.
- Transfer in/out of chair.
- Transfer from bed.
- Eating and drinking.
- Ability to make choices and have control over environment.
- Suitable equipment.

Senses

- Smell.
- Taste.

Mental health

- Substance misuse (including tranquilisers or alcohol).

Relationships

- Ability to care for others where necessary e.g. partner.

Safety

- Manual handling assessment (risk assessment).

Instrumental activities of daily living

- Meal and snack preparation.
- Make hot drink.
- Heavy housework (cleaning).
- Keeping warm.
- Shopping.
- Care of the home.
- Managing affairs (financial paperwork).

Immediate environment and resources

- Work, education, learning and participating in community activities.
- Transport needs.

Additional domains extracted from Annex I of UFSAMC

User's perspective

- Needs and issues in the user's own words.
- User's expectations, strengths, abilities and motivation.

Clinical background

- History of medical conditions and diagnoses.
- History of falls.
- Medication use and ability to self-medicate.

Disease prevention

- History of blood pressure monitoring.
- Nutrition, diet and fluids.
- Vaccination history.
- Drinking and smoking history.
- Exercise pattern.
- History of cervical and breast screening.

Personal care and physical well-being

- Personal hygiene, including washing, bathing, toileting and grooming.
- Dressing.
- Pain.
- Oral health.
- Foot care.
- Tissue viability.
- Mobility.
- Continence and other aspects of elimination.
- Sleeping patterns.

Senses

- Sight.
- Hearing.
- Communication.

Mental health

- Cognition and dementia, including orientation and memory.
- Mental health including depression, reactions to loss, and emotional difficulties.

Relationships

- Social contacts, relationships, and involvement in leisure, hobbies, work and learning.
- Carer support and strength of caring arrangements, including the carer's perspective.

Safety

- Abuse and neglect.
- Other aspects of personal safety.
- Public safety.

Immediate environment and resources

- Care of the home and managing daily tasks such as food preparation, cleaning and shopping.
- Housing – location, access, amenities and heating.
- Level and management of finances.
- Access to local facilities and services.

Additional sub-domains for people likely receive intensive or prolonged support

(User's perspective)

- Personal fulfilment.
- Spiritual fulfilment.

(Personal care and physical well-being)

- Eating, drinking and swallowing.
- Breathing difficulties.

(Relationships)

- Personal relationships.
- Lifestyle choices.

Note: the terms in brackets are current domains into which the additional sub-domains fit.

3.4.2 The screening process

Most local authorities operate a screening procedure. Although only a pre-assessment stage, screening can determine what happens to people and enables local authorities to determine their response to demands made on them. FACS at para.30 and UFSAMC at para.2.23 make it clear that local authorities should avoid screening individuals out of the assessment process before sufficient information is known about them, as the threshold for needing community care services is a low one (*R* v. *Bristol City Council ex p Penfold* (1997–98) 1 CCLR 315). The UFSAMC guidance, unlike its English counterpart, makes it clear that the initial inquiry should develop protocols to distinguish between those callers that need simple information; straightforward service requests; and enquiries leading to a contact assessment (4.7–4.11). The FACS practice guidance at Q8.2 makes it clear that local authorities must not operate a policy of declaring they will not help certain groups of individuals, such as those with higher functioning autism/Asperger's Syndrome or turning people away before their needs can be identified.

The *Penfold* case confirmed that the practice of sifting out assessments where there was no hope of meeting any need was unlawful and that the local authority was not allowed to consider its own resources in deciding not to conduct a s.47 assessment. A common practice has been for individuals seeking help to be asked about their own resources before needs are identified and being told that those with assets will not receive help. Such action is unlawful and should be challenged as the individual's own resources are not relevant in considering whether to assess (FACS policy guidance, para.70; UFSAMC, para.2.33; LAC (98) 19, para.8; WOC 27/98). The relevance of the local authority's resources and the individual's resources are considered further in **paras.4.4**, **4.7** and **4.13** in relation to the provision of services.

3.4.3 The Single Assessment Process for older people

Older people can expect as part of the Government's National Service Framework aimed at improving standards, to have a single assessment of their health and social care needs (LAC (2002) 1, HSC 2001/1, NSF for Older People (March 2001)) (see further **www.dh.gov.uk**).

The purpose of the SAP is to ensure that older people receive appropriate, effective and timely responses to their health and social care needs, and that professional resources are used effectively. As with an assessment under FACS and UFSAMC, the process should ensure that the scale and depth of the assessment is kept in proportion to the older person's needs; agencies do not duplicate each assessment; and professionals contribute to assessments in the most effective way. SAP and UFSAMC state that the key attributes to the approach to assessment should be that it must be person-centred, standardised and outcome-centred.

3.4.4 Types of assessments

The SAP and UFSAMC set out a description of types of assessment that can occur, although they should not be prescriptive and therefore allow for flexibility. For example, an overview assessment would not be appropriate for a person who simply seeks a grab rail, whereas a person with a considerable number of care needs requiring intensive support would need a comprehensive assessment. In many cases, combinations of these assessment types may be used and will be dependent on the judgement of the assessor. Whatever the type of assessment conducted, sufficient data should be collected concerning the presenting needs of the individual. Most local authorities adopt a standardised assessment form for consistency but there is no universally adopted format.

Contact assessment

This refers to the initial contact of the person and the department agencies, where basic information is obtained and the nature of the problem established, with wider issues which might be explored.

The initial contact should look beyond the presenting problems and should establish seven key issues:

1. The nature of the presenting need.
2. The significance of the need for the older person.
3. The length of time the need has been experienced.
4. Potential solutions identified by the older person.
5. Other needs experienced by the older person.
6. Recent life events or changes relevant to the problem(s).
7. Perceptions of the family and carers.

Where the individual has indicated that there are no other problems or issues and the request is straightforward, then there is no need for a wider assessment.

Overview assessment

This will be carried out if a more rounded assessment needs to be undertaken, which may be apparent immediately. The overview assessment can occur after the contact assessment or may be relevant during an in-depth assessment of a specific problem. All or some of the domains as contained in the SAP will usually be explored. The detail will depend on the judgement of the assessor and the assessor's ability to recognise the signposts that other issues need to be explored, and whether any assessment tools are used to guide the process.

In-depth/specialist assessment

This offers a way of exploring specific problems in detail. For example, professionals should be able to confirm the presence, extent, cause and likely development of a health condition. Qualified and experienced professionals will be involved in this assessment, such as occupational therapists, registered nurses, and physiotherapists.

Comprehensive old age assessment/comprehensive assessment or comprehensive geriatric assessment

These should be completed for people where the level of support and treatment likely to be offered is intensive or complex, including permanent admission to a care home, intermediate care services or intensive home care packages, although this type of assessment can arise at other times. The assessment will involve an in-depth assessment of all or most of the domains of the SAP.

3.4.5 Care Programme Approach

The Care Programme Approach (CPA) applies to patients who are receiving treatment and care from the specialist psychiatric services, irrespective of whether or not they have be detained under MHA 1983. Assessment under the CPA is dealt with at **para.12.3.2**.

3.5 THE ASSESSMENT PROCEDURE

3.5.1 Publishing information about services

Section 1(2)(b) of CSDPA 1970 requires social services to ensure that a disabled person who uses any welfare services is informed of any other service considered by social services to be relevant to his needs. Section 9 of the Disabled Persons (Services, Consultation and Representation) Act 1986 extends this provision to require the local authority to provide information about other services provided by the same authority and about other relevant services provided by other organisations, of which the local authority is aware. In addition, under the Department of Health's 'Better Care, Higher Standards' Charter local authorities must publish information as to how a person can get an assessment and what services are available (LAC (2001) 6, HSC 2001/6). Paragraph 2.17 and Annex 10 of UFSAMC require agencies to work together to publish and disseminate information about services and eligibility.

3.5.2 When and where assessments are made

The location of the assessment may have an impact on the outcome, as individuals may be more comfortable being assessed in their own homes, particularly if domiciliary care services are sought. An assessment may occur over the telephone or the internet where the service user or someone on their behalf recognises the service needed, such as a minor aid or appliance, but such assessments are not appropriate for complex needs. If the person is planning to move into a care home, then the individual should have an opportunity to spend some time in the chosen home before making the decision to move (paras.3.12–3.15 of the 1991 Practice Guidance). However in practice, this is rare (Office of Fair Trading's report *Care Homes for Older People in the UK – A Market Study* (May 2005)).

Assessments can occur at any time, but in particular they should occur as part of the discharge from hospital planning stage (see **Chapter 7**); where the individual needs registered nursing care by a registered nurse in a care home; where the person is to move permanently into a care home or receive an intensive package of care; where the person is moving from youth to adulthood; and where the person has made a request to be assessed. It may be unwise to move into a care home without an assessment having been carried out if there is a chance that the individual might need local authority assistance at a later date, as the local authority may not be prepared to fund the care in the preferred home.

Where an individual needs nursing home care and so qualifies for the cost of care by a registered nurse to be funded by the NHS, there must be a joint assessment by health and social services, irrespective of whether social services are to make any assistance (HSC 2003/006, LAC (2003) 7, para.8). The NHS also owes a duty to assess for continuing health care needs, which is explored further at **para.8.9**.

3.5.3 Who assesses?

Trained non-professional staff, whose role it is to collect and verify basic personal information, often conduct contact assessments. Otherwise, a professional assessor conducts assessments, although trained and experienced non-professional staff may assess for presenting problems. A single professional will usually conduct overview assessments. In-depth assessments by their nature will involve a multidisciplinary team which will assess on the separate specialist problems. **Paragraph 2.5.4** covers the assessment of service users moving between local authority areas. In Wales, the Care Coordinator is given the role of coordinating the plan (para.2.39 and Chapter 6 of UFSAMC).

There is no general power for social services to delegate assessment to other bodies, unless a formal partnership arrangement exists with an NHS body (Health Act 1999, s.31). There may also be partnership agreements entered into under the Local Government Act 1972, s.113 where the local authority can delegate local authority agreed functions to an NHS officer who may assess the individual. In practice some aspects of the assessment will be delegated, such as to occupational therapists employed by PCTs for assessment of equipment and adaptation needs and probation officers for some clients who misuse alcohol and/or drugs (LAC (93) 2 at paras.14, 25 and 27). Whoever the assessor may be, he should possess the required skills to assess the presenting needs of the individual.

3.5.4 Assessing presenting needs

The individual should be given help to prepare for the assessment process and it may be that translators, advocates or supporters are involved before and during the assessment. Advocacy services may be provided, particularly where the potential service user has difficulty expressing himself and may not otherwise be able to be an active participant, such as a person with severe learning disabilities or dementia. The assessed person's preferences should be included in the assessment process (*R (on the application of A) v East Sussex CC (No.2)* (2003) 6 CCLR 194 (see also **para.4.11**).

Presenting needs should be fully described and explored. Consideration should be given to the intensity of needs, as well as external and environmental factors that may exacerbate the problems and how the various needs interact with each other. The individual and the assessor should consider and evaluate the risks to independence that result from the needs in both the immediate and longer term and the likely outcome if help were not to be provided. The evaluation of risks should focus on the following aspects that are central to an individual's independence:

- autonomy and freedom to make choices;
- health and safety including freedom from harm, abuse and neglect, and taking wider issues of housing and community safety into account;
- the ability to manage personal and other daily routines;
- involvement in family and wider community life, including leisure, hobbies, unpaid and paid work, learning and volunteering. Individuals and professionals should consider risks faced not only by individuals but also by those close to them, such as carers. They should consider which risks cause serious concern, and which risks may be acceptable or viewed as a natural and healthy part of independent living (FACS, para.40; SAP, p.16; UFSAMC, para.2.36).

3.5.5 Evaluating assessment information and deciding what help to provide

A common sense approach

Determining eligibility is by its nature imprecise and depends on the assessor adopting a common sense approach to the presenting needs. There is a huge subjective element, which is dependent on the assessor understanding and recognising the nature of the disability and problems encountered. In *R (on the application of Heffernan)* v. *Sheffield City Council* [2004] EWHC 1377 (Admin), the applicant, who was severely disabled due to Still's Disease and was blind, sought judicial review of his care plan. The court held that the local authority had wrongly relegated his significant health care problems to 'substantial' and wrongly asserted that the references to health problems in the other bands were words that had been specified by the Department of Health and could not be changed. The existence of significant health problems would not of itself result in any particular care need; however, the relevant care needs arose from the health problems. The applicant's needs had been caused by a significant health problem, and so should be provided for. The court made clear that it is not appropriate to consider the various individual criteria, as explained in the FACS guidance (Q3.12), when there were significant health problems (para.19).

The policy intention is that the local authority will identify each need that gives rise to an eligible risk, which if addressed will ameliorate, contain or reduce the risk. This has the effect that not all eligible risks will have to be met, only those that improve, contain or reduce the risk. Eligibility is determined by comparing the risks to the individual's autonomy, health and safety, ability to manage daily routines and involvement in family and wider community life with the eligibility criteria (FACS policy guidance, para.42; UFSAMC, para.2.41).

Taking a preventative approach

The local authority must prioritise the eligible needs according to the risks to the individual's independence in both the short term and longer term, if help were not provided, and so it must take a longer-term preventative view of the individual's needs and circumstances. Adopting such an approach is an aspect of assessments to which local authorities may, due to lack of resources, attach little weight, as illustrated in the case of *R (on the application of Wahid)* v. *Tower Hamlets LBC* [2002] EWCA Civ 287. Mr Wahid was a long-term schizophrenia sufferer whose condition had in the past necessitated in-patient treatment but was manageable with community support. He was on the local authority's housing waiting list. An assessment of Mr Wahid's community care needs concluded that his mental stability could only be safely maintained by his transfer into a more congenial and relaxed living environment. However, whilst he did need better accommodation, he did not need care and attention under the National Assistance Act 1948, s.21 to justify immediate rehousing. The Court of Appeal held that Mr Wahid was assessed as receiving suitable care and attention and his need for suitable accommodation was not urgent. The Government has, within the Green Paper *Independence, Well-being and Choice: Our Vision for the Future of Social Care for Adults in England* (Cm 6499) March 2005, recognised the need to take a preventative approach as it may prevent increased support and cost at a later date.

Through identifying the risks that fall within the eligibility criteria, eligible needs should be identified, which should then be met by the local authority (*R* v. *Gloucestershire CC ex p Barry* [1997] AC 584; FACS, para.52). It may be that the local authority meets a low level need on the basis that it might otherwise worsen considerably without timely help. Services can also be provided to meet some presenting needs as a consequence of, or to facilitate the meeting of, eligible needs.

3.5.6 Reviews and reassessments

To ensure that the services provided have achieved the proposed outcomes set out in the care plan and that the person still qualifies for support, there should generally be an initial review after three months and thereafter the person should be reassessed annually, unless the situation justifies more frequent reviews (FACS policy guidance, para.58; UFSAMC, para.2.54). The service user, service provider and other appropriate individuals or agencies, can request a review. **Paragraph 4.8.6** contains more details on reviews of the care plan.

The personnel who undertook the original assessment will usually be the same personnel who undertake any review and reassessment. Where the local authority provides the service, then the service provider can undertake the review, but FACS practice guidance at Q10.5 takes a cautionary approach to this, as it will not make sense if the assessor is not skilled in assessments, does not carry care management responsibilities, and lacks the authority to make a decision about eligibility. It is best if reviews are carried out by competent professionals who are independent of the services they are receiving, although service providers can give great insight into the needs and issues which affect the service user.

The review should consist of a meeting and involve the service user, any carer and the service user's representative, where appropriate, agencies that have purchased the service, key providers of the service and the local authority professional who is responsible for the review (FACS policy guidance, para.62; UFSAMC, para.2.56). The review may lead to confirmation of the current level of service, an amendment to the care plan or lead to closure, such as where the service user no longer needs the service, it can be met in another way, or the service user no longer qualifies for the service. Reasons should be provided, failing which the resulting care plan may be quashed (*R* v. *Birmingham City Council ex p Killigrew* (2000) 3 CCLR 109).

3.6 WHICH LOCAL AUTHORITY ASSESSES?

Problems can arise where it is unclear which local authority is responsible for assessing the person's need for community care services. Guidance has been issued in LAC (93) 7 (Ordinary Residence) and in Wales under WOC 41/93 *Ordinary Residence – Personal Social Services*. Local authorities will be under a duty to assess for community care services where the person is ordinarily resident in their area. There is no set definition of ordinarily resident and in the end it is for the courts to determine. This will involve questions of fact and degree and factors such as time, intention and continuity, each of which may be given different weight according to the context, and which have to be taken into account (*R* v. *Barnet LBC ex p Shah (Nilish)* [1983] 1 All ER 226). The duty to assess arises even if the applicant is not ordinarily resident in the local authority area (*R* v. *Berkshire CC ex p P* (1997–98) 1 CCLR 141). See **para.2.5.4** on 'ordinarily resident'.

3.7 TIMESCALE FOR ASSESSMENT

Local authorities must carry out an assessment within a reasonable period of time, which will depend on the circumstances of the case. In the FACS practice guidance at Q8.7, the assessment process for older people should have commenced within 48 hours of a request and be completed within a month. Local authorities should publish timescales as part of their 'Better Care Higher, Standards' Charter and in Wales in accordance with para.2.17 and Annex 10 of UFSAMC. Such timescales should be realistic. The Ombudsman in a complaint against Ealing LBC (97/A/4069) found maladministration where the published Charter stated an unrealistic time to be assessed by an occupational therapist.

For patients being discharged from hospital under the Community Care (Delayed Discharges etc.) Act 2003, an assessment should be conducted within prescribed period of time (see **para.7.3**).

In the event of an unreasonable delay, the person seeking an assessment should consider making a complaint as the matter will then need to be dealt with within the set timescales under the social services complaints process (see **Chapter 18**).

3.8 RECORD OF ASSESSMENT

Social services are under no statutory duty to record assessments in writing. However, as most now have standardised assessment forms, tools and scales, they are likely to keep a record of more complex cases although simple decisions may still be unrecorded. In the event that there is a disputed care plan but no assessment recorded, it could be argued that there has been no lawful assessment (*R* v. *Berkshire CC ex p P* (1997–98) 1 CCLR 141).

Paragraph 42 of FACS states that as part of the assessment, information about an individual's presenting needs and related circumstances should be recorded. Once eligible needs and associated risks to independence have been identified they should be recorded and agreed with the individual or their representative (FACS, para.46). The FACS guidance at para.49, page 18 of SAP and UFSAMC guidance at para.2.49 are clear that service users should receive a copy of their care plan but they are silent on the provision of the assessment record, although the 1991 Practice Guidance indicates that service users, their representatives and the service providers should be given a copy of the assessment. If a request for the assessment is denied, a formal application for the record under the Data Protection Act 1998 should be made (see **para.15.9.6**).

CHAPTER 4

Service provision

4.1 ASSESSMENT AND SERVICES

4.1.1 Decisions following assessment

Service provision, other than in an emergency, is subject to an assessment of need. Once the local authority has assessed the individual for community care services, it must decide whether those needs call for it to arrange services (National Health Service and Community Care Act 1990, s.47(1)(b)). This will largely depend on whether the local authority is under a duty to provide the service and whether the individual meets the eligibility criteria. **Paragraph 2.4** covers these duties and powers and **Chapter 3** deals with the assessment process and eligibility in detail. Where the local authority has decided that it should provide a particular service then it must do so, one way or another (*R* v. *Sefton BC ex p Help the Aged* [1997] 4 All ER 532 at 543 b–e). As such, it has discretion as to how to meet the eligible need but no discretion as to whether to meet the need. The duty continues until the need has been fulfilled (*R* v. *Wigan MBC ex p Tammadge* (1997–98) 1 CCLR 581; *R* v. *Islington LBC ex p Batantu* (2001) 4 CCLR 445).

Services that may be provided are varied but common services include care home provision, meals on wheels, the provision of personal care and home help services, equipment and aids, home adaptations, day centres, holidays and leisure activities. According to the 'Better Care, Higher Standards' Charters, in England the local authority should publish the type of services that may be provided, although actual service provision will be tailored to the individual service user (HSC 2001/006, LAC (2001) 6, para.2). Similar information should be provided in Wales as part of the authority's public information strategy (Annex 10 and para.2.17 of UFSAMC (available from **www.wales.gov.uk**)).

4.1.2 Emergency situations

Despite the general prerequisite to have been assessed, services can be provided in exceptional circumstances without an assessment having been carried out, such as in an emergency (National Health Service and Community Care Act 1990, s.47(5)). Service users should be informed by the local authority that the provision made may be subject to change, as a full assessment will eventually be conducted (FACS policy guidance, para.69 and UFSAMC policy guidance, para 5.36).

4.2 UNMET NEEDS

4.2.1 Reasons to record unmet needs

Not all needs following an assessment will be met by social services, as provision is dependent on the need being an eligible need. Unmet needs, that is the difference between the 'presenting need' (the needs described by adults seeking social care support and others on their behalf) and the 'eligible needs' (those needs that are assessed as falling within the local authority's eligibility criteria) should be monitored and recorded so the results can be used to inform service delivery, planning and commissioning (FACS practice guidance, Q11.1, and UFSAMC, paras.2.45 and 8.8). There is a benefit in assessing an individual, even if there is no chance of provision, as it allows a clearer way of identifying and recording unmet need (*R* v. *Bristol City Council ex p Penfold* (1997–98) 1 CCLR 315).

4.2.2 Information given on unmet need

The FACS practice guidance requires a note of eligible needs and associated risks to be recorded in the service user's care plan, although a record of any unmet need only has to be placed on the individual's file, and not in the care plan. However, it can be obtained from the file to clarify any presenting needs that are unmet (Q11.2). The Welsh guidance is clearer as it states that the record of unmet need should be included in the care plan with reasons given (paras.2.45 and 6.22).

Following the assessment, where the local authority does not offer any help, a written record with reasons for the decision should be made, which should also be available to the individual. Useful information and advice about other sources of support to address any outstanding issues and problems should be given, including facilitating access to relevant services (FACS policy guidance, para.68). Should the situation change, individuals can reapply to be assessed at any time, although they may prefer to challenge the decision through the complaints procedure.

4.3 TIMESCALE FOR PROVISION

Local authorities should ensure that services are promptly put into place once eligibility has been determined to meet the eligible needs (FACS policy guidance, para.23; UFSAMC guidance, para.5.35). Where waiting is unavoidable, they should ensure alternative services are in place to meet the assessed needs (FACS policy guidance, para.53; UFSAMC policy guidance, para.5.35).

'Better Care, Higher Standards' Charters state that where the local authority has agreed to supply disability equipment, items that cost less than £1,000 should be provided within three weeks. The Secretary of State for Health said in his statement on older people's services on 23 July 2002 that by December 2004, all equipment should be provided within one week, and all other services should be provided within a month after the completion of the assessment. These targets have been repeated in the FACS practice guidance at Q9.3. In any event, any failure to provide the service within a reasonable period of time is open to challenge. What is a reasonable period of time will depend on the facts and circumstances of each case. In a complaint against Harrow LBC (02/B/03622) (2004), the Ombudsman recommended that the provision of the appropriate care package should be made within three months of the assessment in respect of day care services.

Delays frequently occur with adaptations to the home, when the case is referred to the housing department to process. The responsibility for provision remains with the social services department which continues to owe a duty to meet the individual's needs and it cannot refuse to provide the service due to resource shortages (*R* v. *Wigan MBC ex p Tammadge* (1997–98) 1 CCLR 581; *R* v. *Islington LBC ex p Batantu* (2001) 4 CCLR 445).

4.4 BUDGET RESTRICTIONS

Once the local authority has determined eligibility for a particular service it must provide that service and cannot use lack of resources as an excuse for not doing so (FACS policy guidance, para.52, LASSL (97) 13, WOC 59/97, and *R* v. *Gloucestershire CC ex p Barry* [1997] AC 584). However, the local authority is able to decide how best to meet the need within its budget (*R* v. *Kirklees MBC ex p Daykin* (1997–98) 1 CCLR 512). Budgetary considerations should not be prioritised over the legal requirement to meet the assessed need, which would amount to maladministration (Bolton MBC (02/C/17068) (2004)) and be unlawful (*R* v. *Wigan MBC ex p Tammadge* (1997–98) 1 CCLR 581).

The local authority should be flexible when applying specific budgets to particular services, and may move from one budget to another to achieve service provision (FACS policy guidance, para.23). It is acceptable for budgetary purposes to operate a ceiling on what the local authority will pay for a package of care; however, this should only ever be used as a guide and not be inflexible (FACS practice guidance, Q6.4, and UFSAMC, para.5.37). The Ombudsman found maladministration against Liverpool CC (96/C/4315), where it operated a fixed ceiling on care packages available to elderly people, but not for people with learning disabilities or mental health problems. Such a policy discriminated against elderly people and fettered the local authority's discretion. It may be that more needs to be spent on certain service users, because the cost of providing services to them are higher, such as for people with profound learning disabilities or for older people. The local authority should spend above the cost ceiling where it will make a significant difference to the service user. Persistently sticking to cost ceilings fetters the local authority's discretion and is amenable to judicial review or a complaint to the Ombudsman.

4.5 ALTERNATIVE CARE PACKAGES

4.5.1 Choosing the cheaper option

Where the local authority can meet the assessed need by an alternative care package, it is at liberty to select the cheaper option (*R* v. *Gloucestershire CC ex p Barry* [1996] 4 All ER 421, CA at 439d). In effect the local authority may decide to provide residential home care rather than 24-hour care in the home, provided that it is suitable to meet the assessed need (*R* v. *Lancashire CC ex p Ingham and Whalley* (unreported) 5 July 1995; *Khana* v. *Southwark LBC* [2002] BLGR 15) or one type of residential accommodation over another (*R* v. *Kensington and Chelsea RLBC ex p Kujtim* [1999] 4 All ER 161). A fundamental aim of the care plan should be to preserve independence of people in the community and in their own home for as long as possible, with an acceptable degree of risk or if it would provide them with a better quality of life (*Caring for People: Community Care in the Next Decade and Beyond* (the 1990 policy guidance), para.3.25) and so it would improper to place a person in a care home unnecessarily. If this were to occur then the local authority may be subject to a challenge on the basis that such decision infringed the individual's right to a private and family life under Art.8 of the European Convention on Human Rights. Where cost is the reason put forward for the alternative option, evidence would need to be produced as to the cost of the various options (*Khana* (above)). Whatever the option chosen it must meet the assessed needs and not purely be determined by cost.

In the Green Paper *Independence, Well-being and Choice: Our Vision for the Future of Social Care for Adults in England* (Cm 6499) March 2005, the Government consulted on the right to request not to live in a care home setting, taking into account the individual's circumstances and consideration of the financial, organisational and legal implications of the status quo and the alternative options. Service providers would be under an obligation to provide explicit reasons behind the decision to recommend residential care including the cost considerations.

4.5.2 The need for real alternatives

There must however be a real option, as was highlighted in the case of *R* v. *Avon CC ex p M* (1999) 2 CCLR 185, which concerned a young man with Down's Syndrome, who had an entrenched preference to go to a particular care home. The local authority wished to place him in a cheaper home. The court agreed with the evidence that the entrenched preference amounted to a psychological need. There was only one way to meet this need and that was in the preferred home. Similar conclusions were drawn in *R* v. *Sutton LBC ex p Tucker* (1997–98) 1 CCLR 251. In *R* v. *Bromley LBC ex p A* (LTL 18/8/2004), the High Court held that the local authority's decision to refuse to place a profoundly autistic young adult in a particular care home had been flawed, as the home had been ruled out as too expensive before alternative placements had been adequately investigated in terms of meeting needs and costs.

4.6 WITHDRAWAL OF SERVICES

Owing to the financial limits of most local authorities, eligibility criteria have increasingly become more restrictive, despite the introduction of the national framework for eligibility, contained in the FACS and UFSAMC policy guidance. The House of Lords held in *R* v. *Gloucestershire CC ex p Barry* [1997] AC 584 that services may be withdrawn, following a full reassessment of the individual where it is shown that:

(a) the need for the service no longer exists;
(b) the need can be met another way; or
(c) the service user no longer meets the revised eligibility criteria for that service.

Withdrawal of services should only occur if the local authority is satisfied that the person will not be placed at serious risk as a result of the withdrawal or it may not be practical (FACS policy guidance, para.66). Local authorities are also reminded in the policy guidance to check any commitments they gave to service users at the outset of the provision about the longevity of service receipt, for example if service users were promised that the care home would be their home for their life, as the authority may be under an obligation to continue to provide that service (see **para.13.3**). The decision to withdraw the service with reasons should be recorded in writing and made available to the service user. Challenges to the withdrawal are made in the first instance through the social services complaints process.

Problems can arise where local authority boundaries change, as was highlighted in *R (on the application of J)* v. *Southend BC* (2005) 102(33) LSG 25, where the claimants had attended day centres in Southend BC's catchments area for over 18 years, whilst being under the statutory care of Essex CC. As a result of Southend becoming a unitary authority it continued to provide day centre services, although it was not responsible for assessment or service provision. When Southend decided to close the centres, Southend owned no duty to assess the service users, as it remained Essex's responsibility. Any assumption that the exclusion of the claimants from the day centre was likely to affect their private lives and so evoke Art.8 of the European Convention on Human Rights was limited in the circumstances, taking into account proportionality and balancing the effects of the changes upon all concerned, and so there was no breach.

4.7 WAITING LISTS AND LACK OF PERSONNEL

4.7.1 The use of waiting lists

Whilst waiting times for care services have been reduced in England by the introduction of the Community Care (Delayed Discharges etc.) Act 2003, waiting lists still exist because of a lack of some service provision and as a way to manage budgets, in particular for certain types of care homes, such as for profoundly disabled young adults, and for major adaptations to the home. The problem of bed blocking in hospitals to manage resources was highlighted in the Scottish case of *Macgregor* v. *South Lanarkshire Council* (2001) 4 CCLR 188, where Mr Macgregor was assessed as needing a nursing home place and was waiting in hospital. It was estimated that it would be between seven to eight months before a bed became available. At 90 years of age there was a high chance that Mr Macgregor might never move out of hospital, while 199 other people were waiting for an available bed, of whom 106 were in hospital. The court held that the council's failure to do anything other than place Mr Macgregor on a waiting list was an abdication of its responsibility and was unlawful. The court was critical of the lack of any system of prioritisation and held unlawful the council's failure to put into place interim measures to meet Mr Macgregor's needs.

Interim arrangements

Local authorities are expected to commission adequate services, although inevitably delays will occur at times, for example, if the individual has a preference to move to a particular care home where there are no vacancies. Guidance issued under LAC (2004) 20 on the National Assistance Act 1948 (Choice of Accommodation) Directions 1992 sets out local authorities' responsibility to have contingency plans in place for situations where a place at the preferred home is not available, particularly in the light of their obligation to effect a quick discharge from hospital under the Community Care (Delayed Discharges etc.) Act 2003.

Adequate interim arrangements must be commissioned to meet the eligible needs and sustain or improve the individual's level of independence, which could be an enhanced care package at home (para.2.5.9). The local authority should estimate the duration of the interim arrangements, the details of which should be agreed between all parties. If no agreement is reached, the local authority must ensure that the individual, his family and any carer understand the effect of this. If the individual unreasonably refuses to agree to the interim arrangements, the local authority could be discharged from responsibility (*R* v. *Kensington and Chelsea RLBC ex p Kujtim* [1999] 4 All ER 161).

The individual should be placed on a waiting list for the preferred home with the aim that a move will occur as soon as a bed becomes available. The operation of the waiting list should be set out clearly and the individual kept informed of any progress (para.2.5.10). Where the interim arrangement exceeds a reasonable period, for example 12 weeks, the individual should be reassessed to ensure that the arrangements still meet the eligible needs and that the preferred home is still suitable to meet those needs. Some individuals may decide to remain in the interim accommodation and thus no longer wish to wait for the preferred home, and as such will be removed from the waiting list. In practice, a change of mind often occurs, as the individual may not want the uncertainty to continue and may wish to be settled.

Failure to make interim arrangements may amount to an infringement of the individual's human rights under Art.8 of the European Convention on Human Rights. In *R (on the application of Bernard)* v. *Enfield LBC* [2003] HRLR 4, the court awarded £10,000 to a severely disabled woman and her husband-carer, who had been left in unsuitable accommodation for 20 months which breached their rights under Art.8.

4.7.2 Funding panels

It is not uncommon for the local authority to refer the proposed care package to a panel to agree the level of care and resulting level of funding. In effect, the panel can budget and restrict costs. If the panel denies the service user the service that he has been assessed as needing, it will be unlawful (*R* v. *Wigan MBC ex p Tammadge* (1997–98) 1 CCLR 581). However, if the role of the panel is to review complex care packages and the panel members consist of experts whose role is to determine the type of accommodation that is required, then it is not objectionable (*R (on the application of Rodriguez-Bannister)* v. *Somerset Partnership NHS and Social Care Trust* [2003] EWHC 2184 (Admin)). The panel should provide reasons for their recommendations, record the minutes of meetings and allow close relatives an opportunity to be heard before the panel (*R (on the application of Goldsmith)* v. *Wandsworth LBC* [2004] EWCA Civ 1170).

The main route for challenging panel decisions has been through the Ombudsman and a number of complaints about funding panels have been upheld. The Ombudsman found maladministration against Essex CC (00/B/00599) (2001), when a panel decided that the need for residential care was not of sufficient priority to justify immediate funding and so placed the service user on a waiting list. There was no reason for the local authority to use the waiting list, when the service was available. For another example of an upheld complaint, see complaint against East Sussex CC (00/B/18600) (2003).

4.7.3 Physical resource problems

Problems can emerge where there is a shortage of people to deliver the care or shortages of service facilities. Provided the local authority has a settled and determined resolve to search for a solution, the courts are unlikely to treat the local authority as acting unreasonably in failing to provide. In *R* v. *Lambeth LBC ex p A1 and A2* (1997–98) 1 CCLR 336, the Court of Appeal held that the local authority had not acted unreasonably in failing to provide suitable housing for the family with a severely disabled child. The local authority was aware of the serious and urgent need for rehousing but did not have any suitable properties available. It had attempted to provide facilities in the home to alleviate the problems but little could be achieved in the circumstances. However, it may be unlawful for the local authority to fail to make provision, where no service is available and no effort is made to find a way to meet the assessed need (*R* v. *Islington LBC ex p Rixon* (1997–98) 1 CCLR 119).

The Ombudsman found maladministration against Essex CC (99/B/00799) (2001), when the local authority refused to pay travel costs to agency staff to provide home care to a severely disabled man and his main carer. The local authority could not find any agency to provide the service, unless travel costs were paid. The local authority fettered its discretion by refusing to make such payments.

4.8 THE CARE PLAN

4.8.1 The purpose of a care plan

A central feature in establishing good service provision is understanding what will be provided, when, and by which service provider, and the objectives in providing that service. It is envisaged from paras.3.24–3.26 of *Caring for People: Community Care in the Next Decade and Beyond* (the 1990 policy guidance), that following the decision to provide services, the local authority will establish a care plan, a copy of which should be shared with the service user. The agreed care plan should as far as possible preserve or restore normal living in the following order of preference:

- support for the user in his own home including day and domiciliary care, respite care, the provision of disability equipment and adaptations to accommodation as necessary;
- a move to more suitable accommodation, which might be sheltered or very sheltered housing, together with the provision of social services support;
- a move to another private household, such as a move to live with relatives or friends or as part of an adult fostering scheme;
- residential care;
- nursing home care;
- long-stay hospital care.

At the care planning stage, services should be matched to eligible needs through the use of 'statements of purpose', which all service providers are expected to prepare. These statements set out the objectives and philosophy of care underpinning the service, the nature of services, facilities, physical and geographical access, and likely charges. They should also describe the types and circumstances, and the people for whom the service is designed. For registered services, such as domiciliary care services and care homes, statements of purpose must been provided to the CSCI or the CSIW.

The Single Assessment Process (SAP) policy guidance (LAC (2002) 1, HSC (2002) 1, available from **www.dh.gov.uk**) describes the care planning process in that it should:

- involve users and professionals discussing the support and treatment that can best meet identified/eligible needs and achieve agreed goals;
- be responsive to, but not prejudiced against the age, living circumstances, geographic location, disabilities, gender, culture, faith, personal relationships and lifestyle choices of service users;
- build on the strengths and abilities of individuals and the part they can play in addressing their needs;
- address external or environmental factors that have caused the needs to arise, or will hamper the resolution of needs if not addressed;
- involve all agencies providing or commissioning services that are part of the individual's package of care.

4.8.2 The status of the care plan

The importance of the care plan was highlighted in *R* v. *Islington LBC ex p Rixon* (1997–98) 1 CCLR 119, where Sedley J confirmed its status as being 'the means by which the local authority assembles the relevant information and applies it to the statutory ends and hence affords good evidence to any inquirer of the due discharge of its statutory duties'. The standardisation of the format of a care plan increasingly occurs, as failure to address core factors may mean that no care plan exists, as was held in *R* v. *Sutton LBC ex p Tucker* (1997–98) 1 CCLR 251, where a lady with learning disabilities was placed in an NHS facility pending an assessment, where she remained for nearly three years. There was a disagreement as to provision between the lady's mother and the local authority. The court held there was a breach of the 1990 policy guidance, in that there was no care plan, as well as a failure to make a decision about provision under s.47(1)(b).

4.8.3 The contents of the care plan

There is no consistent or exhaustive list of the factors that should be contained in a care plan, although *Care Management and Assessment: Practitioners' Guide* at para.4.37 (the 1991 practice guidance) provides some detail:

- the overall objectives;
- the specific objectives for all parties involved;
- the criteria for measuring those objectives;
- the service to be provided and by which agency or personnel;
- other considered options;
- any points of difference;
- any unmet need, with reasons, which should be separately notified to the service user planning system;
- the named person responsible for implementing, monitoring and reviewing the care plan;
- the date of the first review.

The Fair Access to Care Services guidance

The FACS policy guidance at para.47 states that the care plan should contain at a minimum the following:

- a note of the eligible needs and associated risks;
- the preferred outcomes of service provision;
- contingency plans to manage emergency changes;
- details of services to be provided, and any changes the individual is assessed to pay, or if direct payments have been agreed;
- contributions which carers and others are willing and able to make;
- a review date.

The Welsh guidance

The UFSAMC policy guidance at para.2.44, expands on the FACS guidance and confirms that the personal plans of care should also include:

- the eligibility decision and the basis for that decision;
- a clear statement of the objectives for providing help and care;
- contact details of the service provider;
- record of unmet needs with reasons;
- coordination, monitoring the plan with contact details.

The Single Assessment Process

Under the SAP (Annex E, LAC (2002) 1, HSC 2002/001) the details of the care plan are more extensive, as older people are singularly the largest user group of support services. Paragraph 6.22 of UFSAMC contains similar provisions, save that estimates of timescales for provision should be included and details of any manual handling assessment.

The care plan should include the following.

- a summary of assessed needs indicating the intensity, instability, predictability and complexity of problems, the associated risks to independence, and the potential for rehabilitation;
- a note on whether or not the service user has agreed the care plan, and where this was not possible, the reason why;
- the objectives of providing help and anticipated outcomes for users;
- a summary of how services will impact on assessed need and associated risks. Details on managing risk as appropriate. Where it has been agreed that users will accept a certain degree of risk, this must be written in the care plan;
- details of what carers are willing to do, and related needs and support;
- a description of the level and frequency of the help that is to be provided, stating which agency is providing what service;
- a nursing plan, where appropriate;
- the level of Registered Nursing Care Contribution for nursing home admissions;
- the name of the person coordinating the care plan and that person's contact number;
- a contact number or office in case of emergencies and the contingency plan if things go wrong;
- monitoring arrangements and a date for review.

4.8.4 Provision of copy of the care plan

The service user should be given a copy of the care plan, which should be explained and agreed. They should be made aware of review arrangements and advised, where appropriate, that the service may be withdrawn or altered as a consequence of the review (FACS policy guidance, para.49). Failure to provide a copy of the care plan has been criticised by the Ombudsman and may form part of a bigger picture of a failure to keep accurate records (complaint against Cumbria CC (03/C/03660) (2005)).

4.8.5 Disagreement with the care plan

If the care plan cannot be agreed, then the points of difference should be recorded. Within the 1990 policy guidance, local authorities are reminded that if they fail to meet a particular care service, it may bring about an increasing burden on the authority (para.3.25). This has been reflected in both the FACS and UFSAMC policy guidance, where local authorities are to adopt a preventative approach when assessing eligible needs (paras.21 and 5.20 and 5.27). As such they may meet a low level need (which may not be an eligible need) that would considerably worsen for the lack of timely help (FACS practice guidance Q3.9). The process for disputing the care plan is through the complaints procedure rather than through the courts (*R* v. *Barking and Dagenham LBC ex p L* (2001) 4 CCLR 196). However, it may be appropriate to progress the matter through the court, where a material consideration has been ignored in the assessment, or if reasons have not been provided to explain a reduction in service, as the courts have quashed the resulting care plan in such situations (*R* v. *Birmingham City Council ex p Killigrew* (2000) 3 CCLR 109).

4.8.6 Review of the care plan

Where adjustments to the care plan are minor, it is not necessary for a review and reassessment of the individual's needs. However, most care plans will need to be reviewed over time, particularly when significant changes are contemplated, such as a withdrawal or reduction in care. With one-off items of equipment there should be an initial review of their suitability but thereafter there is no need to conduct a review. Major items of equipment should be reviewed annually to ensure they are still suitable and safe to use. Periodic services, such as short-term breaks should be reviewed shortly after the first service period and thereafter annually (FACS policy guidance, para.63; SAP, p.19; UFSAMC, para.2.55).

For older people, SAP and the UFSAMC policy guidance remind local authorities that there should not be assumptions about the individual's needs and either the overview assessment should be conducted or the same domains that were covered in the previous assessment should be explored again. Following a review and reassessment (see **para.3.5.6**), the care plan should be updated. Where the service user is no longer eligible for services, this should be recorded in the care plan with reasons, and shared with the service user.

4.9 DIRECT PAYMENTS FOR SERVICES

The Community Care, Services for Carers and Children's Services (Direct Payments) (England) Regulations 2003, SI 2003/762 and the Community Care, Services for Carers and Children's Services (Direct Payments) (Wales) Regulations 2004, SI 2004/1748 (W.185) were made under the Health and Social Care Act 2001, s.57, making it a duty for local authorities to make direct payments to certain prescribed people who are assessed as needing community care services, children's services or carers' services, whether short term or long term. This includes adults, parent carers or 16- and 17-year-old carers. Payments for carers and children's services are also covered in **para.15.8**.

Local authorities have to specifically consider direct payments in the written care plan as part of the mandatory FACS guidance (LAC (2002) 13). Guidance has been published by the Department of Health as *Direct Payments Guidance: Community Care, Services for Carers and Children's Services (Direct Payments) Guidance England 2003* (September 2003) (the Direct Payments Guidance), with a user guide *A Guide to Receiving Direct Payments from your Local Council: A Route to Independent Living* (September 2004 edition). An equivalent publication, *Direct Payments Guidance*, was issued by the Welsh Assembly in September 2004, and this should be read alongside *Creating a Unified and Fair System for Assessing and Managing Care* (NAFWC 09/02, WHC (2002) 32).

For more information on direct payments see the Department of Health's website (**www.dh.gov.uk**) and in Wales, the Welsh Assembly's website (**www.wales.gov.uk**).

4.9.1 What are direct payments?

Direct payments are an alternative to direct local authority provision. The day-to-day control of the money and care package passes from social services to the service user, who contracts directly with the provider, creating greater flexibility in choice and control in arranging services. It also gives the recipient an opportunity to be independent, socially included and may raise self-esteem. However, for some it can add another headache to their problems, such as negotiating contracts, levels of service and contingency plans in case arrangements break down. Numerous local support networks are established to resolve and assist in these issues. Details of available networks and support can be obtained through local social services departments as part of their 'Better Care, Higher Standards' Charter.

The term 'direct payment' is derived from the legislation; however, it is often confused with direct payments made by the Department for Work and Pensions to claimants of benefits and allowances. The Government in the Green Paper on the future of social care *Independence, Well-being and Choice* (Cm 6499) March 2005 proposed a change to the term as it may hinder the uptake. Suggested name changes include direct service payments, individual service payments, individualised funding and personal budget.

4.9.2 Who can have a direct payment?

The disabled person must be able to consent and be capable of managing a direct payment either on his own or with assistance (SI 2003/762, reg.2(1)(a)). The responsible local authority must be satisfied that the direct payment can be used to secure services to meet the eligible needs. Direct payments cannot be made for services provided by close relatives or a cohabitee living in the same household, unless the local authority is satisfied that it is necessary to meet the eligible needs and in the case of a child is necessary for promoting the welfare of the disabled child (SI 2003/762, reg.6(1) and (2)).

Anyone undergoing treatment for a mental condition or for drug or alcohol dependency as a result of a court order cannot receive a direct payment, nor can those subject to certain orders arising under MHA 1983 and the Criminal Justice Act 1991.

Direct payments to 16- and 17-year-olds

Young persons aged 16 or 17 may have a direct payment to manage part or all of their care package. The local authority will balance the wishes of the young persons with those of the person with parental responsibility and the requirement to promote and safeguard the welfare of the young person. The young person's wishes will take precedence over the person with parental responsibility, provided the individual is capable of managing the direct payment, either alone or with assistance (para.38 of the guidance).

Transition to adulthood for the disabled child

As the disabled child reaches adulthood, the availability of direct payments for children's services to the person with parental responsibility will end and the disabled child will need to be reassessed as an adult to receive direct payments for community care services, provided that the young adult consents and can manage a direct payment. The person who previously had parental responsibility may be entitled to receive a direct payment for carer's services.

4.9.3 Help with managing the direct payment

A direct payment may be made to the individual, a nominee, an attorney acting under a power of attorney or a user-controlled trust for the recipient, provided that he is able to consent to the making of the payment and has control over how services are delivered. This will depend largely on the degree of management required. Family or friends, advocacy or support groups or local groups for independent living may provide assistance. The Green Paper proposed extending the scope of direct payments to adults without mental capacity and those who cannot manage such payments even with assistance. This will require legislative change.

The regulations provide that if the recipient ceases to be capable of managing the payments, the payments can continue if the incapability is temporary and the service provider agrees to accept payment from another person who has agreed to manage the payments (SI 2003/762, reg.10(3)).

Enduring power of attorney

In the case of a registered enduring power of attorney (where the donor of the power has lost mental capacity to manage his finances) the attorney will be able to continue to receive direct payments, provided the power allows for this and the recipient previously consented and had capacity to receive direct payments. An attorney acting under an enduring power cannot use the power to give consent for direct payments or a change in direct payments for alternative or additional services (paras.58–59 of the guidance).

User-controlled trusts

User-controlled trusts are also known as 'independent living trusts'. The trustees manage any money paid via direct payments, but the trust can also include money from other sources, such as housing benefit, family money or from the Independent Living Fund. The trustees make sure the money is being used both as required by the individual and in line with the trust deed, and can be used for example, to employ and pay staff or arrange services from a care agency. See **para.4.13** below on trusts where the user has not the requisite capacity to manage direct payments.

4.9.4 How much direct payment is paid?

It is up to local authorities to decide how frequently payments are made. The sum payable is the amount that the local authority determines (subject to a financial assessment of the individual), which is reasonable for the cost of the type of service needed. In estimating the cost, local authorities should include associated costs that are necessarily incurred in securing provision, without which the service could not be provided, or could not lawfully be provided, such as recruitment costs, national insurance contributions, statutory holiday pay, sick pay, maternity pay, employers' liability insurance, public liability insurance and VAT. Individuals can adjust the amount they use from week to week and save any spare money to use as and when extra needs arise. So long as overall the payments are being used to secure the services they are for and the care plan objectives are met, the actual pattern of service does not need to be predetermined.

If the recipient is unhappy with the amount of the direct payment or the assessed charge, then this should be resolved initially through discussion, failing which it should be pursued through the complaints procedure.

4.9.5 Residential respite care

Direct payments can fund up to 28 days' respite care at any one time, but no more than 120 days in any 12-month period. Where two successive periods of residential care are less than four weeks apart, they are added together to make a cumulative total, which cannot be more than four weeks. If the two periods are more than four weeks apart then they are not added together. Direct payments cannot be used to fund additional respite care, but it is possible for the local authority, where it feels it is necessary, to arrange and fund additional care.

4.9.6 Repayment and termination

The individual is accountable to the local authority for the way in which the money is spent and so conditions can be attached but not so as to frustrate its purpose. If the local authority is satisfied that the direct payment has not been used for securing the assessed services, it can demand that the recipient repay the sum.

If a person becomes permanently incapable of managing a direct payment, whether alone or with help, the local authority is required by the regulations to terminate the making of direct payments, and provide or arrange for the provision of services instead.

4.9.7 Help in running the care package

Support with the care package may be provided in the following ways:

- a list of local provider agencies;
- support and advice in setting up and maintaining a direct payments scheme, including financial management;
- help for people to draft advertisements, job descriptions and contracts;

- help in explaining the safeguards needed in the employment of people to work with children or adults. A person who is considering using a direct payment to employ an individual to care for a child or vulnerable adult may ask the local authority to carry out a Criminal Records Bureau (CRB) check of that person under the Protection of Children Act 1999 or ask to check the Protection of Vulnerable Adults (POVA) list. When a person requests a CRB check the local authority has a duty to comply and the fee due is paid by the person being checked. See *Protection of Vulnerable Adults (POVA) Scheme in England and Wales for Care Homes and Domiciliary Care Agencies: A Practical Guide* issued by the Department of Health in July 2004 (available from **www.dh.gov.uk**);
- rooms for interviews and assistance with interviewing;
- an address for responses to advertisements;
- support and advice about the legal responsibilities of being an employer;
- support and advice about being a good manager of staff;
- information about income tax and national insurance;
- a payroll service;
- advice on health and safety issues, including moving and handling;
- regular training, such as financial management;
- some emergency cover support;
- signposting to other services such as welfare benefits advocacy;
- advice about user-controlled trusts.

4.10 THIRD PARTY SERVICES

Local authorities can contract with voluntary organisations to provide services rather than act as direct providers. Section 30 of the National Assistance Act 1948 provides that:

> A local authority may, in accordance with arrangements made under section 29 of this Act, employ as their agent for the purposes of that section any voluntary organisation or any person carrying on, professionally or by way of trade or business, activities which consist of or include the provision of services for any of the persons to whom the section 29 above applies, being an organisation or person appearing to the authority to be capable of providing the service to which the arrangements apply.

A voluntary organisation is a body the activities of which are carried on otherwise than for profit, but does not include any public or local authority (s.64). Some local authorities have established third party schemes, where they make a payment to a third party, such as a trust fund, which then would purchase the care for the disabled person. These types of trusts are particularly useful where the service user does not have the mental capacity to manage or oversee direct payments. In *R (on the application of A)* v. *East*

Sussex CC (No.2) (2003) 6 CCLR 194, the court held that it was lawful for the local authority to transfer funds to a user independent trust, a company limited by guarantee for two severely disabled sisters. Its purpose was to provide and arrange services for the sisters. The trust was regarded as a voluntary organisation as it was not run for profit and so the local authority could employ the trust as an agent on its behalf to deliver service (National Assistance Act 1948, s.30(1)). Payments could be made to the trust within the scope of provision under the 1948 Act, s.29(1). The trust paid close relatives to care for the sisters, which was held to be legitimate, because under the contract with the local authority the trust was empowered to decide how best to meet the needs. In any event, the scheme was held to have been lawful by virtue of the wide powers contained in the Local Government Act 1972, s.111 and LGA 2000, s.2.

4.11 CHOOSING AND CHANGING SERVICE PROVIDERS

4.11.1 Service user's preference

The 1990 policy guidance, at para.3.25, provides that the local authority should aim to secure the most cost-effective package of services that meet the user's care needs, taking into account the service user's own preferences. In *R* v. *North Yorkshire CC ex p Hargreaves* (1994) *The Times*, 9 November), the local authority made a decision about respite care without taking into account the disabled person's wishes, which was in breach of the policy guidance, and so the decision was held to be unlawful and was quashed. For those who are unable to express a preference, the local authority should use every means possible to ascertain any preference before deciding on the care provision (*R (on the application of A)* v. *East Sussex CC (No.2)* (2003) 6 CCLR 194). LAC (93) 7 at para.12 advises that an adult with learning disabilities should be regarded as capable of forming his own intention of where he wishes to live, unless that person has severe learning difficulties. Specialised advocacy services may be able to provide some assistance and if the service user or his carer would benefit from such help, the local authority should provide details of such support (1991 practice guidance, paras.3.25–3.27). In practice, choice may be limited by the availability of the desired service.

Care should be taken in the assessment to ensure that the preference does not amount to a psychological need, in which case if such need is sufficient to meet the eligibility criteria, it will have to be met (*R* v. *Avon CC ex p M* (1999) 2 CCLR 185).

4.11.2 Specific directions and guidance

Specific directions and guidance on choice have been issued in respect of residential accommodation, where the accommodation is being provided under the National Assistance Act 1948, s.21 (National Assistance Act (Choice of Accommodation) Directions 1992 (LAC (2004) 20); in Wales under WOC 12/93). **Paragraph 5.2.10** contains more detail about choice of accommodation.

There are no equivalent directions or guidance on choice in respect of non-residential care services.

4.11.3 Changes to the service

In the event that local authorities plan to change the way the service is to be provided, they should send written notice of the plan to the service user and any carer. In a complaint against Harrow LBC (02/B/03622) (2004), the Ombudsman found maladministration where the day care service was altered without notice. Changes to the service can also occur where the care arrangements break down. Even where the breakdown is outside the local authority's control, responsibility remains with the authority to find alternative provision. Failing to do so will amount to maladministration (complaint against North Yorkshire (01/C/03521) (2002)). The local authority should deal with such situations robustly, although at times failures will occur (complaint against Wirral MBC (03/C/00120) (2004)). Fundamental questions should be asked about the reasons for the failure and efforts should be made to find solutions, working with the individual, his family and any carers.

4.12 RIGHT TO REFUSE SERVICES

No one can have care services delivered against their wishes, as doing so may bring about claims such as trespass to the person or home, or unlawful detention where care is provided in a care home setting. However disputes can arise about the way the eligible need is to be met. The local authority may eventually contend that if the proposed service is rejected, then it will treat its duty as being discharged. In *R* v. *Kensington and Chelsea RLBC ex p Kujtim* [1999] 4 All ER 161, the Court of Appeal held that the local authority can be discharged from its duty to provide residential accommodation under the National Assistance Act 1948, s.21, if the resident acted unreasonably in refusing accommodation or persistently and unequivocally refuses to observe reasonable conditions of residence. There is no reason why this could not be extended to any service provision by the local authority. What amounts to 'unreasonable' will depend on the facts. However, refusing services because a preferred alternative package is not being offered would not be considered reasonable (*Khana* v. *Southwark LBC* [2002] BLGR 15).

A refusal to receive services should not always be taken at face value. The Ombudsman found maladministration against Sheffield CC (02/C/08690) (2004), which failed to consider whether given the individual's degree of learning difficulty and autistic spectrum disorder, his decision to reject services was an informed decision. In *R* v. *Newham LBC ex p Patrick* (2001) 4 CCLR 48, the court held that where a local authority is dealing with a client with mental health difficulties who has refused accommodation, the local authority's duty was not to treat its duties as discharged, but it should ensure that the applicant was legally represented so that the applicant knew what was offered in terms of location and services, and understood the legal consequences of refusing such an offer.

If at a later date further contact is made with social services regarding the individual, the local authority can reopen the care planning process, if it is satisfied that the individual's needs remain the same, such as to justify the provision of services and there is no longer a reason to think that the individual will persist in refusing such services unreasonably.

4.13 RELEVANCE OF THE INDIVIDUAL'S OWN RESOURCES IN PROVISION

4.13.1 Residential accommodation

Capital under the prescribed capital limit

The local authority will be under a duty to provide residential accommodation when it concludes after an assessment that the individual (aged 18 or over) is by reason of age, illness, disability or any other circumstances in need of care and attention, which is not otherwise available to that person (National Assistance Act 1948, s.21(1)(a)). In *R* v. *Sefton MBC ex p Help the Aged* [1997] 4 All ER 532, the local authority adopted a policy that it would not accept responsibility for people who were already in a care home unless their capital fell to below £1,500, which was below the prescribed limit for local authority financial assistance. The Court of Appeal held that this was unlawful and that care and attention should not be considered as otherwise available when the person is unable to pay for care according to the National Assistance (Assessment of Resources) Regulations 1992, SI 1992/2977 (as amended). Legislation has been brought in to clarify the position, so that in determining whether care and attention is otherwise available to a person, a local authority must disregard so much of the person's resources as does not exceed the capital limit for the purposes of charging under the National Assistance Act 1948, s.22 (s.21(2A) as inserted by the Health and Social Care Act 2001, s.53).

Capital in excess of the prescribed capital limit

Having capital in excess of the upper limit does not in itself constitute adequate access to alternative care and attention. The local authority must satisfy itself that the individual is able to make his own arrangements, or has others who are willing and able to make appropriate care arrangements for him. Where the person has a suitable advocate or representative, such as a close relative, local authorities only have to provide guidance and advice on the availability and appropriate level of services to meet the individual's needs. If there is no identifiable advocate or representative to act on the person's behalf, the local authority will be responsible for making the arrangements and contracting for the person's care (LAC (1998) 19, para.10). This is further clarified in para.72 of the FACS policy guidance, which provides that if an individual is to move into a care home and has both the mental capacity and the financial resources to pay for care, the local authority's responsibility is in practice limited to providing information and advice to assist the person in locating a suitable care home (when requested). However, this will not be the case where the individual is eligible for assistance because he qualifies for the first 12-week property disregard following permanent admission to a care home.

Self-funders becoming supported residents

As soon as capital falls below the upper prescribed threshold, the person should be eligible for local authority financial support. As soon as reasonably practical, the local authority should undertake an assessment of needs and if necessary take over arrangements so that the resident is not forced to use up his remaining capital. The local authority should be proactive in informing the resident of the right to assistance, whether or not the resident has been through the assessment process, when his capital falls below the prescribed limit (para.13). LAC (2001) 25 para.24 advises local authorities that they could be liable to reimburse the resident for any payment made for the accommodation which should have been met by the local authority pursuant to its statutory duties.

4.13.2 Home care services

In respect of home care, the FACS practice guidance at Q8.5 confirms that the local authority should arrange those services irrespective of the resources or capacity of the service user, if that is what the service user wishes. Where individuals have sufficient resources, they will be subject to a means test, the details of which are covered more fully in **Chapter 5**.

The local authority is entitled to have regard to the resources of a third party, such as a parent, in determining whether it is necessary to provide assistance to a disabled child under CSDPA 1970, s.2 (*R (on the application of Spink)* v. *Wandsworth LBC* [2005] EWHC Civ 302). The decision under s.2 requires the individual to have needs within the scope of the list in s.2(1)(a)–(h) and it must be necessary for the local authority to make arrangements to meet those needs. The question of necessity is a matter for the authority, where it is entitled to consider the possibility that a third party could meet the need. Such resources can be taken into account during the decision-making process, unless it can be demonstrated that having regard to the parents' means it is not reasonable to expect the parents to provide the service.

4.13.3 Notional capital as a resource

The House of Lords in *Robertson* v. *Fife Council* (2002) 68 BMLR 229 held that it is wrong for a local authority to take into account capital, including notional capital, when assessing a person's need for the provision of nursing care. The guiding principle is that the provision of community care services to a person in need is not related to the ability of that person to meet the costs. The assessment of needs and the subsequent decision as to whether they call for the provision of community services comes first. The assessment of means follows afterwards. Notional capital can be taken into account at the charging stage and not beforehand. **Paragraph 5.2.7** provides more detail on the treatment of notional capital.

CHAPTER 5

Charging for social services care

The ability of the local authority to charge for services it provides is governed by statute. There is a clear distinction between charging for residential accommodation and non-residential care services. The relevance of the individual's resources in the provision of services is dealt with separately in **para.4.13**.

5.1 FREE SERVICES

Certain services cannot be charged for namely:

- social services support, advice, assessments and the administration associated with arranging and facilitating services;
- services provided as after-care services under MHA 1983, s.117 (see **Chapter 12**);
- intermediate care services, which consist of a time limited structured programme of care provided to assist a person to maintain or regain the ability to live in his home and must be provided free of charge for any period up to six weeks (Community Care (Delayed Discharges etc.) Act (Qualifying Services) (England) Regulations 2003, SI 2003/1196, regs.2(b) and 4(2)). Department of Health Guidance *Intermediate Care* has been published in HSC 2001/01, LAC (2001) 1 as well as LAC (2003) 14 *Changes to Local Authorities Charging Regime for Community Equipment and Intermediate Care Services*. Guidance has been issued in Wales as *Community Care: Six Weeks Support At Home For Vulnerable People* (NAFWC 05/02, WHC (2002) 128, NAFWC 43/2002). For more information on these services see **para.8.4.1**;
- community equipment (aids and minor adaptations) services, which means a service which consists of the provision of an aid, or a minor adaptation to property (£1,000 or less), for the purposes of assisting with nursing at home or aiding daily living. See SI 2003/1196, regs.2(a) and 4(1). No guidance has been published in Wales. For more information on these services see **para.6.1**.

5.2 CHARGES FOR ACCOMMODATION

5.2.1 The statutory basis for charging

Under the National Assistance Act 1948, s.22(1) (as amended) local authorities must charge for providing accommodation that has been arranged under Part III of the Act, but have a discretion to charge a reasonable amount for stays under eight weeks (s.22(5A)).

There can be no charge if the accommodation has been arranged and provided as part of after-care under MHA 1983, s.117 (*R* v. *Manchester City Council ex p Stennett* [2002] 4 All ER 124). In addition, where the accommodation or service has been arranged to meet continuing NHS health care needs there should not be a charge (see **Chapter 8** for further details). Residents under 18 years of age are accommodated under the Children Act 1989 (see **Chapter 11**).

Section 22(2) of the National Assistance Act 1948 requires the local authority to charge a 'standard rate', which is meant to reflect the true cost of providing the accommodation. For independent homes, the rate is the gross cost, being the 'contract rate' to the local authority of providing or purchasing the accommodation under contract.

5.2.2 The means test

If the resident is unable to pay the full rate the resident is means tested to ascertain what contribution (if any) should be made towards the accommodation cost (National Assistance Act 1948, s.22(3)). If the resident is unwilling to be financially assessed then he will be charged the full rate. The local authority will have a contract with the independent home and will recover the assessed contribution from the resident, or the resident may choose to pay the assessed charge directly to the care home (National Assistance Act 1948, s.26(3A)). The local authority will pay any shortfall to the care home.

For the purposes of charging under s.22(3), the National Assistance (Assessment of Resources) Regulations 1992, SI 1992/2977 (NAARR 1992) are used to assess a resident's ability to pay for residential accommodation. The regulations are regularly updated. Guidance is issued by the Department of Health on the interpretation of NAARR 1992 in the *Charging for Residential Accommodation Guide* (also known as CRAG). The most recent publication is LAC (2006) 12 and can be obtained from the Department of Health's website (**www.dh.gov.uk**) or by post from the Publications Department, the Department of Health, PO Box 777, London SE1 6XH. In Wales CRAG is issued on the Welsh Assembly's website (**www.wales.gov.uk**) or available by post from the Publications Department, National Assembly for Wales, Cathays Park Cardiff, CF10 3NQ.

The circular is issued under LASSA 1970, s.7(1) which is mandatory guidance and should be followed unless there is very good reason why it should not be followed (*R* v. *Islington LBC ex p Rixon* (1997–98) 1 CCLR 119).

Para 1.015 of CRAG requires that the local authority give a clear written explanation of how the assessment of ability to pay has been carried out. It should explain the usual weekly assessed charge and give reasons why the charge may fluctuate, for example where a new resident's income from state benefits and allowances is altered as a result of being in a care home.

5.2.3 The resident's income

All income is required to be paid towards the full rate for the accommodation with the exception of the personal expenses allowance and any disregarded income. Income includes earned income, pensions and most social security benefits, annuity income (except home income plans), trust income, income from investment bonds and tariff income from capital (see **para.5.2.5** below). For full details of the source of income which is taken into account see NAARR 1992, Part II and sections 8 and 9 of CRAG.

Notional income

Regulation 17 of NAARR 1992 provides that a resident may be treated as having 'notional' income that he does not actually receive, such as:

- income paid to the local authority as a third party top up;
- income paid to a third party for an item taken into account when the standard rate for the accommodation was fixed;
- income available if applied for;
- income due but not received;
- income of which he has deliberately deprived himself to reduce or avoid charge.

Social services should only consider that a resident has deliberately deprived himself of income if such income would normally have been included in the financial assessment. Deliberate deprivation to reduce or avoid the charge does not have to be the main reason but must be a significant reason (CRAG, para.8.077). The timing of the disposal will be considered when deciding the purpose (CRAG, para.8.078). Where an income-producing asset is sold and converted to a capital asset, the previous income or the difference between the former income and the tariff income or increase in tariff income may be taken into account (CRAG, para.8.080). Case law on notional capital is applicable to notional income and is discussed at **para.5.2.5** and at **para.4.13.3**.

Income partially disregarded

Items of disregarded income other than earnings are set out in NAARR 1992, Sched.3. The main partial disregards are as follows.

- 50% of any occupational pension, personal pension or payment from a retirement annuity contract paid to a resident who has a spouse or civil partner so long as the resident pays at least 50 per cent of the pension to the spouse or civil partner for maintenance (CRAG, para.8.024A; NAARR 1992, Sched.3, para.10A);
- a £10 disregard on payments to victims of National Socialist persecution; civilian war injury pension; war disablement pension; war widows pension and war widowers pension (CRAG, para.8.021; NAARR 1992, Sched.3, para.11);
- annuity-based home income plans, where one of the annuitants is in occupation of the home (CRAG, paras.8.025–8.030; NAARR 1992, Sched.3, para.12);
- pension credit savings disregard – pension credit has two parts, i.e. 'guaranteed credit' and 'savings credit'. The guaranteed credit provides a minimum income for people aged 60 and over. The savings credit provides extra income to those people aged 65 and over who have modest savings and income. The savings disregards works to enable residents in receipt of savings credit to retain part or the entire sum, as it will not be taken into account for means testing.

Income fully disregarded

Many full income disregards apply to temporary residents so that they are not prevented from meeting their responsibilities. For more details on temporary residents, see below at **para.5.2.8**. Other notable disregards include Christmas bonus (CRAG, para.8.041; NAARR 1992, Sched.3, para.22); certain charitable and voluntary payments (CRAG, para.8.056; NAARR 1992, reg.22(7)); child tax credit; guardian's allowance; payments from the Macfarlane Trust, the Macfarlane (Special Payments) Trust, the Macfarlane (Special Payment) (No.2) Trust, the Eileen Trust, the Fund (payments to non-hemophiliacs infected with HIV), the Independent Living (Extension) Fund, and the Independent Living (1993) Fund (CRAG, para.8.042; NAARR 1992, Sched.3, para.24); income frozen abroad (CRAG, para.8.044; NAARR 1992, Sched.3, para.16); income in kind (CRAG, para.8.045; NAARR 1992, Sched.3, para.14); Social Fund payments (including winter fuel payments); war widows and widowers special payments (CRAG, para.8.046; NAARR 1992, Sched.13, para.25).

Personal expenses allowance

Section 22(4) of the National Assistance Act 1948 requires that the resident be allowed to retain a sum, after means testing, for his personal requirements. The sum changes each year by the National Assistance (Sums for Personal Requirements) Regulations 1993, SI 1993/462. The local authority has discretion to vary the personal expenses allowance, for example if a non-spouse partner or non-civil partner continues to live in the resident's former home, the personal allowance could be increased to pass an amount to the partner to meet domestic responsibilities.

5.2.4 Liable relatives

The local authority has no power under the National Assistance Act 1948 or NAARR 1992 to financially assess a couple according to their joint resources as it is the resident as the service user who is assessed. If the capital is held in a joint account there is a presumption that the account is owned in equal shares, unless it can be established otherwise, so the resident will be treated as owning his share of a joint account (NAARR 1992, reg.21(1); CRAG, para.6.010). However, under the 1948 Act, s.43 the local authority can enforce payment of a contribution towards care from a liable relative. The Government has on repeated occasions confirmed its intention to abolish the liable relative provisions and explicitly states in CRAG that 'in the interim, the Department would strongly encourage local authorities to exercise their discretion to NOT apply the liable relatives rule'.

A liable relative is a spouse or former spouse of a resident (National Assistance Act 1948, s.42). A 'liable relative' payment will only be sought when the resident cannot pay the full rate and the local authority decides that it is worth pursuing the spouse for a payment towards the shortfall. The remedy available is a complaint by the local authority to the magistrates' court, which determines how much payment (if any) should be made.

CRAG makes it clear that:

- the local authority cannot demand that the relative give details of his own finances (para.11.005);
- the basis for a contribution should be on discussion and negotiation (para.11.005A);
- the spouse should not be left in financial hardship as a result of making a liable relative payment and consideration should be given to the spouse's normal standard of living (paras.11.004 and 11.006);
- court action should only be considered as a last resort (para.11.006).

5.2.5 The resident's capital

The resident will not be assessed as being unable to pay for his accommodation if he has capital in excess of the prescribed capital limits (NAARR 1992, reg.20). Capital includes all land and buildings, savings and investments (unless disregarded). The value placed on the capital will depend on the nature of the capital and whether or not it needs to be realised. Part III of, and Sched.4 to, NAARR 1992 and section 6 of CRAG set out the capital rules.

Prescribed capital limits

A resident with capital of more than the prescribed upper limit (for 2006/07 this is expected to be £21,000) is liable to pay the full rate for the accommodation and will be treated as a self-funder. Capital including and under the prescribed lower limit (£12,750 for 2006/07) is fully disregarded. Income is of course still relevant and it could be that the resident has enough income to pay the full rate for the accommodation. The figures are higher in Wales. For every £250 of capital or part thereof held between the thresholds the resident is treated as having £1 per week of income (NAARR 1992, reg.28).

Guidance LAC (98) 19, LAC (2000) 11, and LAC (2001) 25 confirms that where a person's capital has reduced to the upper capital limit, as soon as reasonably practicable, the local authority should undertake an assessment and, if necessary, take over arrangements to ensure that the resident is not forced to use up capital below the upper capital limit. Once the local authority is aware of the circumstances, any undue delay in undertaking an assessment and providing necessary accommodation would mean that it has not met its statutory obligations and as such it may be liable to reimburse the resident for any payment which should have been met by the authority.

Disregard of the home during temporary stays

The usual residence is disregarded where the resident intends to return to his home which is still available for him or if the resident is taking reasonable steps to sell the property and buy another. Only one dwelling can be disregarded in these circumstances (CRAG, paras.3.008/7.002; NAARR 1992, Sched.4, para.1). A temporary resident is defined as a resident whose stay is unlikely to exceed 52 weeks, or in exceptional circumstances, unlikely substantially to exceed that period (NAARR 1992, reg.2(1)). If the stay initially was thought to be permanent but turns out to be temporary then the stay should be treated as being temporary from the start (CRAG, para.7.002; NAARR 1992, Sched.4, para.1).

Disregard of the home for the first 12 weeks of a permanent stay

The value of the resident's home should be disregarded for the first 12 weeks of a permanent admission to a care home, subject to:

(a) an assessment by the local authority which confirms the need for permanent residential care; and
(b) the resident not having sufficient income or other assets to cover the costs of care.

In the event of a delay in the assessment by the local authority, the resident should get the benefit of the disregard from the date he chooses to become permanent and not the date of the assessment. The resident may get the benefit of the property being disregarded during a temporary stay and a further 12 weeks, once the stay is confirmed as permanent. If the property is sold within the 12-week period the disregard ends from the date of the sale.

Where a person leaves residential care (where they have been living on permanent basis) before the end of 12 weeks and then re-enters on a permanent basis within 52 weeks they will be entitled to the remaining balance of the 12-week disregard. If a resident leaves permanent care and then re-enters more than 52 weeks later, he will qualify for the disregard again (LAC (2001) 10, para.12; NAARR 1992, Sched.4, para.2A; CRAG, para.7.003A–B).

Indefinite disregard of the home

Following permanent admission to a care home the resident's own home must be disregarded where it is occupied in whole or in part by the resident's partner or former partner (except where the resident is estranged or divorced from the partner or former partner); a lone parent who is the resident's estranged or divorced partner; a relative (as defined at CRAG, para.7.004) of the resident or member of his family (as defined at CRAG, para.7.004A) who is aged 60 or over, or is aged under 16 and is a child whom the resident is liable to maintain, or is incapacitated (CRAG, para.7.003; NAARR 1992, Sched.4, para.2).

Discretion to disregard property occupied by a third party

Local authorities can exercise their discretion to disregard the property in which a third party continues to live, such as a relative under 60 who is not incapacitated and who has given up his own home to care for the resident. The disregard does not have to continue indefinitely and would usually be taken into account if the third party were no longer in occupation of the property (CRAG, paras.7.007–7.008; NAARR 1992, Sched.4, para.18).

See *R* v. *Somerset CC ex p Harcombe* (1997) *The Times*, 7 May for an example of the application of such a disregard.

Valuation of joint beneficial ownership of property

Where a resident is a joint beneficial owner of property, it is the resident's interest in the property which is to be valued and not the asset itself. The value is governed by the resident's ability to reassign the benefit to someone else and there being a market for such an interest. If the market is limited to the other joint owner who is willing to buy the share, the value could be low and possibly nil (*Chief Adjudication Officer* v. *Palfrey* (1995) *Independent*, 10 April and NAARR 1992, reg.27(2); CRAG, paras.7.012–7.014A). In the case of *Wilkinson* v. *Chief Adjudication Officer* [2000] EWCA Civ 88, the Court of Appeal distinguished the case from *Palfrey* as the joint owner was not in occupation of the home and the property had not been obtained to provide a home for the claimant. As such it was likely that a claim for an order for sale under the Trusts of Land and Appointment of Trustees Act 1996, s.14 would have succeeded.

Jointly owned property is treated as being owned in equal shares unless there is contrary evidence, for example a trust deed that shows that the one owner has entirely funded the purchase. In *R (on the application of Kelly)* v. *Hammersmith and Fulham LBC* [2004] EWHC 435 (Admin), the resident purchased the property under a 'right to buy', which was funded entirely by her daughter, but no evidence by way of a trust deed was produced. The local authority registered a caution against the property to recover the cost of care of the mother. The court refused to remove the caution, as there was insufficient evidence to show that the mother had no beneficial interest in the property.

Partial capital disregards

The local authority has discretion to disregard the following for 26 weeks or longer.

- business assets owned (or part-owned) by the resident and for the purposes of which he was a self-employed worker, where he has stopped work but intends to take up work again when he is fit to do so (NAARR 1992, Sched.4, para.5);
- money for repairs to or replacement of the resident's home or personal possessions, provided it is used for that purpose (NAARR 1992, Sched.4, para.7);
- premises which the resident intends to occupy as his home where he has started legal proceedings to obtain possession (NAARR 1992, Sched.4, para.2);
- premises which the resident intends to occupy as his home where essential repairs or alterations are required (NAARR 1992, Sched.4, para.16);
- capital received from the sale of a former home, where the capital is to be used by the resident to buy another home (NAARR 1992, Sched.4, para.3);

- money deposited with a housing association which is to be used by the resident to purchase another home (NAARR 1992, Sched.4, para.7);
- grant made under a Housing Act which is to be used by the resident to purchase a home or pay for repairs to make the home habitable (NAARR 1992, Sched.4, para.17).

The date on when the 26-week period commences varies and further details are set out in para.6.029 of CRAG.

Other notable full capital disregards

These include:

- the value of any cashing-in options rights for an investment bond written as a life insurance policy are disregarded. In contrast, the surrender value of an investment bond without life assurance is taken into account. (See Income Support (General) Regulations 1987, SI 1987/1967, Sched.10, para.15; Social Security Commissioners decision R (IS) 7/98 and CRAG, para.6.002A–B);
- the surrender value of any life insurance policy (NAARR 1992, Sched.4, para.1) or annuity (NAARR 1992, Sched.4, para.9);
- payments in kind from a charity (NAARR 1992, Sched.4, para.17);
- any personal possession (NAARR 1992, Sched.4, para.8);
- any payment made by or derived from the Macfarlane Trust, the Macfarlane (Special Payments) Trust, the Macfarlane (Special Payment) (No.2) Trust, the Fund (payments to non-hemophiliacs infected with HIV), the Independent Living Fund, the Independent Living (Extension) Fund, or the Independent Living (1993) Fund (NAARR 1992, Sched.4, para.15);
- the value of funds held in trust or administered by a court which derive from a payment for personal injury to the resident (NAARR 1992, Sched.4, paras.10 and 19);
- the value of a right to receive income under an annuity, loan agreement (NAARR 1992, Sched.4, paras.9 and 13), payment under a trust where the funds derive from a personal injury (NAARR 1992, Sched.4, para.10), income under a life interest or a life rent (NAARR 1992, Sched.4, para.11), income payable in a country outside the UK which cannot be transferred to the UK (NAARR 1992, Sched.4, para.12), an occupational pension (NAARR 1992, Sched.4, para.15), or any rent (NAARR 1992, Sched.4, para.15);
- any Social Fund payment (NAARR 1992, Sched.4, para.13);
- any capital resource to which the resident has no rights as yet, but which will come into his possession at a later date, such as a contingent interest in a trust (NAARR 1992, Sched.4, para.4);
- age-related payments for pensioners over 70 years old (NAARR 1992, Sched.4, para.25);

- the value of any ex gratia payments made in consequence of a person's or person's spouse's imprisonment or internment by the Japanese during the Second World War (NAARR 1992, Sched.4, para.20);
- the value of any ex gratia payments from the Skipton Fund to people infected with hepatitis C as a result of NHS treatment with blood or blood products (CRAG, para.6.028);
- capital held outside the UK; the amount to be taken into account in the assessment of the resident's ability to pay will depend on the conditions for transfer to the UK (NAARR 1992, reg.24; CRAG, para.6.026). If the transfer is restricted, the local authority should take into account the value that a willing buyer would pay in the UK for the assets. This may be less than the market or surrender value in the foreign country (CRAG, para.6.020).

5.2.6 Treatment of trusts

A beneficiary of a trust will only be assessed on his interest in the trust in so far as he is entitled to it. Section 10 of CRAG sets out in detail how trust capital and income are to be treated. It can be summarised as follows.

1. Where a person has an absolute entitlement to income from a trust, the income he receives, or which would be available to him on an application, should be taken into account in full in the assessment.
2. The right to receive income from a trust has a value, but this is a capital asset, which is fully disregarded (NAARR 1992, Sched.4, para.11).
3. The reversionary interest in a trust should be disregarded (NAARR 1992, Sched.4, para.4).
4. Where payments are made wholly at the discretion of the trustees and there is no absolute entitlement to either capital or income, they should be treated according to the rules on voluntary payments (CRAG, paras.8.051–8.057).
5. Where the capital is held in court, in trust or part of a structured settlement, in consequence of a personal injury, both the capital and the capital value of any right to receive income are fully disregarded (NAARR 1992, Sched.4, paras.10 and 19).
6. Periodical payments from a trust, a structured settlement or from court whose funds are derived from a personal injury payment are fully disregarded if intended and used to pay for any item which was not taken into account when the standard rate was fixed for the accommodation provided. Otherwise, £20 is disregarded (NAARR 1992, Sched.4, para.10; CRAG, para.10.026).

5.2.7 Notional capital

A resident may be treated as possessing a capital asset even where he does not actually possess it. This is called 'notional capital' and can be added to actual capital to calculate if the resident has capital exceeding the prescribed capital limit.

Notional capital may be capital:

(a) which would become available to the resident if an application were made, but which has not yet been acquired and should only be treated as such from the date it could be acquired by the resident;
(b) which is paid to a third party in respect of the resident, such as being held in a bare trust on behalf of the resident; or
(c) of which the resident has deprived himself in order to reduce the amount of charge he has to pay (CRAG, paras.6.049–6.067; NAARR 1992, reg.25).

Questions of deprivation should only occur when the resident no longer possesses capital which would otherwise have been taken into account (CRAG, para.6.058). For example, if a person disposes of personal possessions before moving into a care home this should not be treated as a deprivation as personal possessions are disregarded in the financial assessment. However, if capital has been converted to a disregarded asset, such as personal possessions or investment bonds, the local authority will look carefully in case the conversion was a deliberate deprivation (CRAG, paras.6.061 and 6.065–6066).

Deliberate intention

The purpose of the disposal needs to be established. There may be more than one purpose for disposing of a capital asset, only one of which is to avoid a charge for residential accommodation. Avoiding the charge need not be the main motive but it must be a significant one (CRAG, para.6.062).

The timing of the disposal

The timing of the disposal will also be taken into account when considering the purpose. It would be unreasonable for the local authority to treat the transfer as a deliberate deprivation when the disposal took place at a time when the resident was fit and healthy and could not have foreseen the need for a move to residential accommodation (CRAG, para.6.064). The forseeability or immediacy of the need for care will therefore need to be established.

The subjective purpose test

In *Yule* v. *South Lanarkshire Council (No.2)* (2000) SLT 1249 the court held that there was no time limit in which the local authority could determine notional capital and that the true purpose of any transfer could be ascertained or inferred from the circumstances without any specific finding as to the state of knowledge or intention of the elderly person (**www.scotcourts.gov.uk/ index1.asp**).

In the only reported English case on notional capital, *Secretary of State for Health* v. *Beeson's Personal Representative* [2002] HRLR 15 and [2002] EWCA Civ 1812, Richards J in the High Court said that although *Yule* held that it is not necessary for the claimant to know of the capital limit and that no specific finding was required as to the exact state of knowledge or intention of the applicant, he did not see how an applicant could be found to have the relevant purpose unless he was aware of the possibility that he might be provided with accommodation and that he might be liable to pay for it (para.11). The correct test to be applied is to determine the subjective purpose of the disposal. There was evidence that funding of residential care did not come into Mr Beeson's thoughts and that the transfer took place at a time when he intended to live in and ultimately to die in his home. The local authority had failed to consider the reasons given for the gift and had focused solely on the general circumstances. Any decision to reject or accept the evidence required an overall assessment of that evidence.

Deprivation decided

Once the local authority decides that the resident has deliberately disposed of capital to avoid or reduce the charge, the local authority must decide whether to treat the resident as having notional capital and assess him accordingly. The authority will then need to decide whether to recover the assessed charge from the resident or use the Health and Social Services and Social Security Adjudications Act 1983 (the 1983 Act), s.21 to transfer the assessed charge liability to the recipient(s) of the transfer (CRAG, para.6.067 and **para.5.2.13** below).

Diminishing notional capital

Where a resident has been assessed as having notional capital, that capital will have to be reduced each week by the difference between the rate which he is paying for the accommodation and the rate he would have paid if he were not treated as possessing the notional capital (CRAG, para.6.068; NAARR 1992, reg.26). Once the resident's notional capital and actual capital falls to below the prescribed upper capital limit, the local authority will start making a contribution to the fees in the usual way.

5.2.8 Temporary residents

Admissions should be deemed temporary or permanent depending on the resident's needs and circumstances and not based on the local authority's or resident's resources. An admission will be temporary if it is intended to be time limited or there is uncertainty that permanent admission is required. An admission will be treated as permanent if the agreed intention is for the resident to remain in residential care. This should be put in writing (CRAG, paras.1.028/3.001A; LAC (2002) 11, para.25).

Temporary residents get the benefit of certain disregards:

- attendance allowance or disability living allowance (care component) which is disregarded for the first four weeks if relying on state-funded support (CRAG, para.3.014; NAARR 1992, Sched.3, para.3);
- that part of any income support/pension credit award which is paid in respect of home commitments as well as housing benefit (CRAG, para.8.039; NAARR 1992, Sched.3, paras.3 and 26);
- Supporting People payments made by the local authority to or on behalf of a resident for housing support charges of a kind falling within Sched.1B to the Housing Benefit (General) Regulations 1987, SI 1987/1971 (as in force immediately before 1 April 2003) (CRAG, para.3.010A; NAARR 1992, Sched.3, paras.28D and 28E, Sched.4 paras.22 and 23);
- a reasonable sum at the local authority's discretion, which will meet the extra costs of home commitments (NAARR 1992, Sched.3, para.27);
- income from sub-letting (whether paid by the sub-tenant or a third party) is disregarded where the resident occupies the dwelling of which part is sub-let as his home (NAARR 1992, Sched.3, para.12; CRAG, para.8.031);
- where a resident has income from a boarder for whom at least one cooked meal is provided (whether paid by the boarder or a third party) the first £20 of the income should be ignored plus half of any balance over £20 (NAARR 1992, Sched.3, para.13; CRAG, para.8.032);
- income from a mortgage protection insurance policy which is used to pay the loan where the purpose of the loan was to purchase or keep an interest in the occupied home or for repairs or improvements to the occupied home (CRAG, paras.8.033–8.035; NAARR 1992, Sched.3, para.19).

5.2.9 Less dependent residents

Before April 1993, local authorities had power to arrange residential accommodation under the 1977 Act, in addition to their power to arrange such accommodation under the National Assistance Act 1948. Local authorities were empowered to make a reasonable charge where appropriate, but were not required to assess the resident's ability to pay. Residents' remaining money for their personal use was not limited to the personal expenses allowance, as less dependent residents were encouraged to live as independently as possible and needed extra money for, e.g. the cost of food, household expenses or travel to work.

After April 1993 powers to provide accommodation under the 1977 Act were repealed by the National Health Service and Community Care Act 1990. From then on all adult residential accommodation placements, including those for people who are less dependent, are made under the National Assistance Act 1948, where the resident is subject to the usual charging regime. The normal charging rules are not always appropriate for less dependent residents because they will need to be left with more than the prescribed personal expenses allowance if they are to live as independently as possible. NAARR 1992, reg.5 enables local authorities to continue to treat less dependent residents differently where they consider it reasonable in the circumstances to do so, usually by increasing the personal expenses allowance.

5.2.10 Choice of accommodation and third party top up

Directions

Under the National Assistance Act (Choice of Accommodation) Direction 1992, and similar Directions made in Wales in 1993, where a person requires residential care, whether temporary or permanent, which is being provided under the National Assistance Act 1948 by the local authority, the proposed resident has the right to choose his accommodation subject to the following:

- there must be a place available;
- the accommodation must be suitable for the assessed needs;
- it must not cost more than the local authority would usually pay for such accommodation ('the usual cost'); and
- the home agrees to comply with local authority terms and conditions.

Guidance

Mandatory guidance has been issued in LAC (2004) 20 which replaced previous guidance and in Wales in WOC 12/93. References in this section relate to the relevant paragraph in the English guidance unless otherwise stated.

Third party top ups

If the proposed resident wishes to choose a more expensive home than the local authority will finance, it is possible for a third party to pay the difference (1.4). A third party can be a relative or friend but a liable relative who is making a contribution for the resident under the National Assistance Act 1948, s.42 cannot act as a third party, unless the top-up arrangements were agreed prior to 1 October 2001. The local authority will want to be satisfied that the third party is willing and able to meet the payments for the expected period of residency and may seek financial information from the third party. The third party is not under any obligation to provide such information. A resident cannot use his own resources to pay for more expensive accommodation and act as his own third party, except in limited circumstances (see below).

Market inadequacies and commissioning failures

The usual cost of care should be set at a level that is sufficient to meet the assessed care needs of supported residents (2.5.4), which should not be set arbitrarily so that residents are required routinely to seek assistance from third parties (2.5.7). They should be able to secure appropriate accommodation without having to rely on an additional payment (2.5.8). If this were to occur, it may indicate market inadequacies or commissioning failure by the local authority (2.5.5).

Accommodation in another local authority area

Choice is not limited by the local authority's boundaries as the proposed resident can choose a home anywhere in England and Wales (2.3). Local authorities can refer to their own usual costs when making placements in another area but if a local authority needs to place a person in a home at a higher rate in order to meet the person's needs it must meet the additional cost (2.4).

Changes in placement status

In some cases, individuals who move into a care home for an interim period may choose to remain there, even if a place in their originally preferred accommodation becomes available. If the cost of the interim care home is higher than the usual cost, once the resident has decided to stay, a third party or the resident could be approached to make the top up (2.5.14). For those who are already in a care home and subsequently require local authority provision the same rules apply. If the home costs more than the local authority usual rate and there is no third party who can pay the additional cost, it may mean that the resident has to move to another care home, unless, the assessed needs can only be met in the current accommodation. Where for any reason the local authority does not make a placement in the preferred home it must show a clear and reasonable justification for that decision, which should be in writing setting out the reasons (2.1).

Resident acting as own third party

A resident is able to make a top up out of his own resources for the cost of his care where the resident has accessed the 12-week property disregard or deferred payments agreement scheme (Health and Social Care Act 2001 (Commencement No.2) (England) Order 2001, SI 2001/3167; National Assistance (Residential Accommodation) (Additional Payments and Assessment of Resources) (Amendment) (England) Regulations 2001, SI 2001/3441). Similar regulations were issued in Wales in SI 2003/931 (W.121).

A resident subject to a 12-week disregard may top up from:

- earnings disregarded by CRAG;
- income disregarded by CRAG;
- capital disregarded by CRAG (with the exception of the value of the resident's home which is subject to the 12-week disregard);
- other capital resources, excluding his home, with the proviso that:
  - people can only top up to the value of the lower capital limit;
  - where the resources are used to top up by residents who have resources above the lower capital limit, the level of tariff income that applies during the 12-week period of topping up is the same as if it would be if the person were not using capital to top up.

Residents who have a deferred payment agreement may top up from:

- earnings disregarded by CRAG;
- income disregarded by CRAG;
- capital disregarded by CRAG;
- other capital resources, including the value of their home, which is subject to the deferred payment agreement, with the proviso that the resident must be left with the total capital resources under the means test to the value of the lower capital limit. When the value of the property is used as 'collateral' for top ups, the amount of the top up is added to the sum accruing under the deferred payment agreement (CRAG, para.8.019B).

5.2.11 Deferred payment agreements

Regulations made under the Health and Social Care Act 2001, s.55 created a power for the local authority to take a charge on land, instead of contributions towards the cost of care fees. People in accommodation provided under the National Assistance Act 1948, Part III or proposing to enter such accommodation, who would be liable to pay the full rate or any lower amount if the property were sold may instead enter into a deferred payment agreement (DPA) with the local authority. The National Assistance (Residential Accommodation) (Disregarding of Resources) (England) Regulations 2001, SI 2001/3067, and the National Assistance (Residential Accommodation)

(Relevant Contributions) (England) Regulations 2001, SI 2001/3069, have been issued. Similar regulations apply in Wales, i.e. SI 2003/969 (W.131) and the National Assistance (Residential Accommodation) (Additional Payments, Relevant Contributions and Assessment of Resources) (Wales) Regulations 2003, SI 2003/931 (W.121). Guidance has been published in LAC (2001) 25, LAC (2001) 29 and LAC (2002) 15, and in Wales in NAFWC 21/2003 (available from **www.wales.gov.uk**).

Local authorities have a discretion to offer a DPA, if the person entering or in permanent residential care has, after a financial assessment, been shown to have insufficient income and other assets, other than the value of his main or only home in which he has a beneficial interest, to meet the cost of his care and the person for whatever reason does not wish to sell his home or is unable to sell his home quickly enough to pay the care fees. Although local authorities have a discretion whether or not to offer the individual a DPA, they should operate such a scheme as failure to do so will amount to maladministration (LGO complaint against Manchester CC (04/C/04804). Local authorities will be cautious where there is an outstanding mortgage on the property and will only agree to a DPA if the resident can continue to meet the mortgage obligations and assessed contribution to care costs. The size of the weekly deferred contribution will be taken into account by the local authority when deciding whether to enter into an agreement. In the event that a resident has been refused a deferred payment, written reason should given to the resident with details of the complaints procedure.

The DPA does not apply during the mandatory 12-week disregard period as the property cannot be taken into account during the first 12-week stay following a permanent admission to a care home nor does it apply during temporary stays. Attendance allowance and the care component of disability living allowance still remains payable as the person is not being funded by the local authority as they will repay the sum owed at the end of the exempt period. Once the DPA has been entered into no payment is required until 56 days after the resident's death or a specified earlier date or if the property is sold in the meantime (the exempt period). The resident will be responsible for the cost of the Land Registry searches and legal fees. The total amount becomes payable at the end of the exempt period when interest will start to accrue.

5.2.12 Supporting People payments

From 1 April 2003, under 'Supporting People' arrangements, local authorities have power to make payments for housing support charges in respect of a resident's home address. Where a resident is paying part or all of the cost of housing support services under the Local Authorities (Charges for Specified Welfare Services) (England) Regulations 2003, SI 2003/907, the amount must be disregarded from the assessment of income and capital for residential care services (NAARR 1992, Sched.3, paras.28D and 28E, Sched.4, paras.22 and 23).

5.2.13 Enforcement

The local authority may seek to recover the cost of care. What route the local authority chooses will depend on whether the resident retains assets and the timing of any disposal.

Health and Social Services and Social Security Adjudications Act 1983, s.21(1)

The local authority can enforce proceedings against a third party under the 1983 Act, where a relevant asset has been transferred at an undervalue to that third party. The transfer must have occurred no more than six months before the resident entered local authority-funded accommodation and the local authority must be able to establish that the transfer was made knowingly and with the intention of avoiding accommodation charges. Section 21 does not apply to a resident who is self-funding in an independent home, and who has not been assessed or had his placement arranged through the local authority, although other enforcement routes could be used. Section 21 only applies to an asset which would have been taken into account in NAARR 1992 and so cannot apply to assets that would otherwise be disregarded. The value of the asset, other than cash, is the amount that would have been realised if the asset had been sold at the time of transfer on the open market by a willing seller (s.21(6)). The value should take into account any secured debts and 10 per cent of the value for expenses of sale (s.21(7)).

National Assistance Act 1948, s.56

This section gives local authorities the power to recover a civil debt with interest in a magistrates' court against the resident, within three years of the debt falling due. There is no reason why the local authority could not pursue the resident and seek payment from what little the resident may then financially possess, including assets that would be disregarded under CRAG. In practice this power is rarely used.

Transactions at an undervalue

Under the Insolvency Act 1986, ss.339–341 it is possible for a trustee in bankruptcy to apply to a court for an order to set aside a transaction at an undervalue. The transaction must have occurred within five years prior to the bankruptcy petition or within two years, if the individual concerned was insolvent at the time of the transaction or as a result of the transaction. A person is considered insolvent if he is unable to pay his debts as they fall due, or the value of his assets is less than the amount of his liabilities, taking into account contingent or prospective liabilities (s.341(3)). There are no reported cases of local authorities using this method to enforce payment, probably as the costs of bankruptcy proceedings are high with no guarantee of success.

Transactions to defraud creditors

Under the Insolvency Act 1986, ss.423–425, without the need for bankruptcy, the court has very wide powers either to set aside a transaction at an undervalue or to make such order as it thinks fit to protect the interests of people who are victims of the transaction and restore the position to what it would have been if the transaction had not been entered into. There is no applicable time limit, so the local authority could bring a claim irrespective of the time that has passed since the transfer; however, the longer the time elapsed the harder it may be to assess the purpose of the transfer.

The court has to be satisfied that the purpose of the transaction was to put assets beyond the reach of a creditor, potential creditor or to prejudice the interest of such creditors (s.423(3)). There is no need to prove dishonesty, only to prove avoidance of creditors (*Midland Bank Plc* v. *Wyatt* [1995] 1 FLR 696). Section 423(3) requires the claimant to show a dominant purpose to remove assets from the reach of actual or potential claimants or creditors, but this does not exclude the possibility that there might be other purposes behind the transfer. The purpose however has to be predominant (*Chohan* v. *Saggar* [1992] BCC 306). The test is not solely an objective one (*Royscott Spa Leasing Ltd* v. *Lovett* [1995] BCC 502). The onus is on the claimant to show the statutory purpose. It must be a real substantial purpose and it is not necessary for the claimant to establish that the purpose was the dominant one. The purpose will not be satisfied where it is a by-product of the transaction (para.25 of *Inland Revenue Commissioners v. Hashmi* (LTL 3/5/2002)).

The Court of Appeal in *Derbyshire CC* v. *Akrill* [2005] EWCA Civ 308 considered the application of s.423, which concluded that the section could apply where a person transferred his house by deed of gift to his children for the purposes of putting it beyond the reach of those who might have a claim in respect of the costs of his imminent residential care. However it is possible to raise as a defence an issue of public law that undermined the basis of that claim.

Placing a charge on land under Health and Social Services and Social Security Adjudications Act 1983, s.22

Where a resident has failed to pay the assessed charge for accommodation provided by a local authority, the local authority may at its discretion create a written charge in its favour on land in England or Wales in which the resident has a beneficial interest. The section applies to situations where residents are unwilling to pay their assessed contribution and a debt arises and recovery is being actively pursued. Those who are willing to pay their assessed contribution but do not wish to do so immediately should be offered a DPA (see **para.5.2.11** above). Interest on the charge does not start to accrue until after the resident's death at a reasonable rate determined by the local authority (s.24). The resident should always be advised or assisted to take independent legal advice (Appendix D of CRAG).

5.3 NON-RESIDENTIAL CARE SERVICES

5.3.1 Services that can be charged for

Section 17(1) of the 1983 Act (as amended) gives local authorities a discretionary power to make reasonable charges for services provided for adults under:

(a) National Assistance Act 1948, s.29 (welfare arrangements for people with disabilities);
(b) Health Services and Public Health Act 1968, s.45(1) (welfare of old people);
(c) National Health Service Act 1977, Sched.8 (care of mothers and young children, prevention of illness and care and after-care and home help and laundry facilities);
(d) 1983 Act, Sched.9, Part II, para.1, other than provision of services where payment may be required under the National Assistance Act 1948, ss.22 or 26;
(e) CDCA 2000, s.2.

In *Avon CC* v. *Hooper* [1997] 1 WLR 1605, Hobhouse LJ said at 1610b, that 'there is an overriding criterion of reasonableness which governs the local authority's exercise of the power which is given by subsection (1)'. That is, is it reasonable to make any charge? If there is to be a charge then that charge should be reasonable.

Although the 1983 Act does not specifically include services arranged under CSDPA 1970, s.2, in the case of *R* v. *Powys CC ex p Hambidge (No.1)* [1998] 3 FCR 190, the Court of Appeal held that there is nothing in the 1970 Act that has removed the right to charge for services provided under s.2, as such services are being 'provided under' the National Assistance Act 1948, s.29, which is listed in the 1983 Act, s.17(2). Charges for services provided can be in relation to local authority direct provision as well as provision arranged through direct payments. For more on direct payments see **para.4.9** and **para.15.8**.

5.3.2 Guidance

The Department of Health issued guidance to local authorities on charging policies for home care and other non-residential social services in LAC (2001) 32, which was updated in November 2003, to reflect changes brought about by the introduction of pension credit in October 2003. Practice guidance was issued in August 2002 (available from **www.dh.gov.uk**). Similar guidance has been issued in Wales in NAFWC 28/02, 17/2003, 32/2003 and 10/2004, although the National Assembly for Wales intends to make home care free. The guidance is mandatory, having been issued under LASSA 1970, s.7 and provides a broad framework to which local authorities can work. There is no compulsion to make a charge for non-residential care services, although most local authorities do charge. There is, however, scope for the local authority to reduce or waive the charge where it is not 'reasonably practicable' for the user to pay the full cost (1983 Act, s.17(3)). Automatic exemptions to charges applies to sufferers of any form of Creuzfeldt Jacob Disease and any payment made to hepatitis C infected persons as a result of NHS treatment blood products (LAC (2004) 9).

Charges for different types of services

Service users may receive a number of different types of service, for example, personal home care, day care, domestic help and transport. Each service should not be charged for in isolation from the other and the net impact on the service user needs to be taken into account, so as to prevent the user from falling below the basic levels of income support or the guarantee credit of pension credit plus a buffer of 25 per cent. It could mean that the service user does not pay for some of the services he receives. Local authorities may put a ceiling on what they expect a service user to pay so to prevent a service user being financially forced to move into residential care, as a cheaper option than funding the full cost of home care. Flat rate services are justified only where they are a substitute to ordinary living costs, such as meals on wheels service (para.9).

The local authority should not put an arbitrary ceiling on what it will fund for care at home, as it depends entirely on the service user's assessed community care eligible needs. If a service user requires 24–hour care and the residential care is the most appropriate type of provision for meeting the assessed needs, the local authority can choose the most cost-effective way to provide for those needs (*R* v. *Lancashire CC ex p Ingham and Whalley* (unreported) 5 July 1995, QBD). However, if residential care is not appropriate for the service user, for example the service user is young and the nature of the disability would mean that there is no suitable residential care home, the local authority may decide to choose the more expensive option for providing for his needs.

Welfare benefits advice

All service users should in receipt of the maximum state benefits and allowances before any means assessment is conducted and as such the local authority should ensure that appropriate advice is provided either from the authority's own benefit advisers or from independent advisers.

Effect of charges on user's income

Charges made for services should not reduce the service user's income to below 'basic' levels of income support, or guarantee credit of pension credit plus a buffer of not less than 25 per cent, to safeguard the user's independence (para.15 of policy guidance). As a result, anyone on the basic levels of those benefits should not be charged for home care services. In addition to this buffer, local authorities can choose to set a maximum percentage of disposable income over and above these basic levels, which would be available to pay towards home care costs, leaving some income on which to live (para.17).

Paragraph 20 makes it clear that users not in receipt of income support, the guarantee credit of pension credit or income-based jobseeker's allowance should be assessed to ensure that:

(a) those with income levels equal to the basic levels of income support, guarantee credit of pension credit or income-based jobseeker's allowance plus 25 per cent do not pay any charge; and
(b) users with higher income who are charged for services should not be reduced to incomes below those levels.

Local authorities may decide to include welfare benefits in the financial assessment. From 23 November 2001, no new financial assessment should take into account attendance allowance, disability living allowance, severe disability premium, constant attendance allowance or exceptionally severe disability allowance for the first time without as assessment of the service user's disability costs.

However, the following should be disregarded:

- earnings;
- working tax credit;
- child tax credit;
- savings credit of pension credit;
- mobility component of disability living allowance (DLA);
- war pensioner's mobility supplement;
- war widows supplementary pension;
- £10 per week of war disability pensions and war widows pensions;
- income received from the Independent Living (1993) Fund.

Local authorities have to be careful about including any benefit income for day care services where the benefit is payable for night care, unless of course night care is being charged for. In *R (on the application of Carton)* v. *(Coventry City Council* (2001) 4 CCLR 41, the High Court found that it was unlawful and unfair for the local authority to treat as income available for day care the amount of DLA paid for night care.

User's outgoings

Paragraph 21 states that it would be unfair for a service user to be charged for care, without taking into account some unavoidable expenses to minimise poverty. The following should be deducted from gross income:

- income tax;
- national insurance contributions;
- housing costs, such as rent or mortgage, which should be assessed net of any housing benefit or council tax benefit payable;
- council tax.

Local authorities have discretion to make allowances for home insurance and water rates.

Disability-related expenditure

Available income may be dramatically reduced by disability costs. Any item where the service user has little or no choice other than to incur the cost in order to maintain independence should be allowed to be deducted from assessable income and para.46 of both the practice and policy guidance provides that it may include:

- payment for any community alarm system;
- the cost of any privately arranged care services, including respite;
- the costs of any special item resulting from the disability such as:
  - specialist washing powder or laundry;
  - additional costs of special dietary needs of illness or disability;
  - special clothing or footwear if made, or the nature of the disability causes greater wear and tear;
  - additional costs of bedding, for example, because of incontinence;
  - any heating costs or metered water charges above average levels for the area or housing type, required by age, medical condition or disability;
  - reasonable costs of basic garden maintenance, cleaning or domestic help, if necessitated by the disability and not met by social services;
  - personal assistance costs, including any household or other necessary costs arising for the user;

- transport costs necessitated by illness or disability, including transport to day centres, over and above the mobility component of DLA (if it is paid for such);
- purchase, maintenance and repair of disability-related equipment, including equipment or transport needed to enter or remain in work, including the reasonable cost of equipment if waiting for supply of equipment from the local authority.

The local authority may not allow costs where there is a reasonable alternative available at a lower cost, such as the private purchase of incontinence pads as they are free on the NHS. In addition, the local authority must not fetter its discretion in considering whether money paid to a carer should be disregarded (*R (on the application of Stephenson)* v. *Stockton on Tees BC* (2005) *The Times*, 5 September).

Savings and capital

Savings may be taken into account to calculate tariff income on the same basis as set out in CRAG. Local authorities may treat capital owned (which is not otherwise to be disregarded) over the lower prescribed limit but under the upper prescribed limit as creating an income of £1 per week for every £250 of capital held. Users with more than the upper capital limit may be asked to meet the full charge for the service. The guidance does not specifically say (although it is implied) that capital under the lower prescribed limit should be fully disregarded (para.58).

There are a limited number of capital disregards, which are specifically mentioned in paras.59 and 60 and these are:

- the value of a main residence occupied by the user;
- any ex gratia payments made to former Far Eastern prisoners of war;
- any payment made under the Vaccine Damage Payment Scheme.

Many of the capital disregards contained within CRAG are not specifically mentioned and may create the impression that any disregards are limited to those singled out. Paragraph 59 states that 'other forms of capital may be taken into account as set out in CRAG' and has in practice created ambiguity as to whether it was subject to the disregards attached to such capital. It has been clarified in LAC (2003) 8, para.8 which provides that 'savings and capital should be treated no less generously than the rules for assessing residential care charges'. Local authorities should mirror the relevant CRAG disregards as relevant within their charging policies. Failure to include these disregards in particular in charging policies could mean that the user has to challenge the local authority through the courts on the grounds of the authority being unreasonable and a misunderstanding of the guidance.

Partner's income and savings

As with financial assessments for residential care, charges arising under the 1983 Act, s.17 are restricted to assessing reasonable charges against the individual. However, if the local authority has some reason to believe that the service user has means other than those disclosed, it can reasonably make a request for the user to arrange for the user's partner to disclose his relevant resources. In the event of non-disclosure (by whoever), the local authority may consider that it is not satisfied that the user has insufficient means to pay the charge for the service.

Financial assessment of carers

Paragraph 83 provides that when undertaking an assessment for carers' services local authorities should take into account certain expenditure incurred by informal carers, such as:

- private purchase of care, for example, to allow short breaks from caring, or where this is needed to enable the carer to maintain employment or to fulfil obligations as a parent;
- additional transport or other costs, e.g. taxis, which may arise unavoidably because the carer cannot long be absent from home;
- range of additional costs for cleaning, clothing, laundry, etc. where these are met by the carer.

5.4 FAILURE TO PAY CHARGES

The assessment of need for care should not be confused with a financial assessment. Once a service user has been assessed as needing a service, that service should not be withdrawn because the service user does not pay the charge. The Department of Health's Policy Guidance *Caring for People: Community Care in the Next Decade and Deyond* (1990) clearly states at para.3.31 that 'the provision of services, whether or not the local authority is under a duty to make provision, should not be related to the ability of the service user or their families to meet the costs . . . The assessment of financial means should, therefore follow the assessment of need and decisions about service provision'. Local authorities should provide or continue to provide the service, while pursuing the debt. Section 56 of the National Assistance Act 1948 provides for recovery for a civil debt (see **para.5.2.13** above), although a debt could be pursued through the usual county court/High Court route.

5.5 COMPLAINTS PROCEDURE

General but clear information about charges and how service users are assessed should be available for users and carers in accordance with local 'Better Care, Higher Standards' Charters. Paragraph 70 of the FACS policy guidance makes it clear that specific written details of charges should be promptly given which show how the fee has been assessed and calculated.

Section 17(3) of the 1983 Act gives the user a right to seek a review of the assessed charge for non-residential care services if the user cannot afford to pay the charge, or users may make a formal complaint about the level of charge levied by a local authority, subject to the usual social services complaints procedures. For reviews of residential care charges, the resident may pursue the matter through the complaints procedure.

PART III

Responsibility for the provision of health care

CHAPTER 6

Provision of aids/appliances

6.1 COMMUNITY EQUIPMENT SERVICES

6.1.1 Guidance on community equipment services

The need for an integrated system between health and social services was identified in the Audit Commission's report *Fully Equipped: The Provision of Equipment to Older and Disabled People by the NHS and Social Services in England and Wales* (2000). Guidance on the provision of community equipment services has been issued in HSC 2001/8, LAC (2001) 13, which applies to all age groups, including children. Guidance entitled *Guide to Integrating Community Equipment Services* was simultaneously published by the Department of Health. As such, all health and local authorities in England should have in place community equipment services, so that certain equipment can be provided irrespective of which public body has responsibility for provision. Associated documentation is available in HSC 2001/01, LAC (2001) 1. Guidance can be obtained from the Department of Health's website (**www.dh.gov.uk**).

6.1.2 Community equipment defined

Community equipment is defined in para.7 of the guidance as being 'equipment for home nursing usually provided by the NHS, such as pressure relief mattresses and commodes, and equipment for daily living such as shower chairs and raised toilet seats, usually provided by local authorities'. It includes, but is not limited to:

- minor adaptations, such as grab rails, lever taps and improved domestic lighting;
- ancillary equipment for people with sensory impairments such as liquid level indicators, hearing loops, assistive listening devices and flashing doorbells;
- communication aids for people with speech impairments;
- wheelchairs for short-term loan, but not for permanent wheelchair users, as these are prescribed and funded by different NHS services;

- telecare equipment such as fall alarms, gas escape alarms and health monitoring for people who are vulnerable.

6.1.3 Funding of community equipment

The service must be unified by joint funding (Health Act 1999, s.31), a single operational manager, although advised by a board from health and social services and unified stock so that the distinction between NHS and social services stock is removed.

As a result of the Community Care (Delayed Discharges etc.) Act 2003, local authorities are no longer able to charge for any community equipment that the individual is assessed as needing, to bring them into line with NHS provision and ensure better integration (Community Care (Delayed Discharges etc.) Act (Qualifying Services) (England) Regulations 2003, SI 2003/1196 and LAC (2003) 14).

Minor adaptations should not be charged for if the cost of making the adaptation is £1,000 or less, which sum includes the cost of buying and fitting. Where the adaptation is over £1,000 then local authorities have discretion to make a charge (1983 Act, s.17).

There is no similar guidance on community equipment services in Wales, and it is fragmented, with services being provided by health and social services as well as housing and the voluntary sector. A centralised policy is needed.

6.2 THE ROLE OF THE GP IN ASSISTING WITH COMMUNITY CARE SERVICES AND PROVISION OF EQUIPMENT

GPs can prescribe items from an approved list, which include elastic stockings, appliances for colostomies, some types of trusses or wound dressings, urinary catheters, pressure-relieving cushions, and mattresses and continence pads. The approved list is available online (see **www.ppa.org.uk**) and is updated monthly.

The GP can also refer the patient to specialist services for other kinds of health equipment, such as wheelchairs and walking aids, hearing and vision aids, artificial limbs, and surgical appliances and communication aids. The referral can be to the occupational therapist, who may be employed by the PCT/LHB, hospital trust, social services or a joint appointment, or a physiotherapist, who may be employed by the PCT/LHB or the hospital trust for an assessment of the needs for aids and/or equipment. Guidance should not be used to restrict the GP's duty to provide necessary medical services (*R* v. *Secretary of State for Health ex p Pfizer Ltd* (1999) *The Times*, 17 June).

The GP may also refer the patient to social services for the assessment of community care services. The new GP contract no longer makes it specifically obligatory for GPs to give advice to enable patients to avail themselves of services provided by social services; however, in practice many GPs will still refer where they consider it appropriate (National Health Service (General Medical Services Contracts) Regulations 2004, SI 2004/291 and in Wales SI 2004/478 (W.48)). GPs must, where appropriate, refer the patient for other NHS services, so arguably the obligation may still apply but be limited to referrals for community care services that could be provided under the 1977 Act (see **para.2.5.2**).

6.3 THE ROLE OF THE HOSPITAL CONSULTANT IN THE PROVISION OF EQUIPMENT AND APPLIANCES

Hospital doctors employed by the hospital may prescribe any drug, appliance or piece of equipment, which are felt to be clinically necessary for the patient. The contract that the doctor has with the hospital may specifically restrict their ability to prescribe expensive items without prior agreement with the hospital managers. The hospital doctor may refer the patient to an occupational therapist, physiotherapist, stoma or continence nurse to be assessed for relevant aids and equipment. Many stoma nurses although employed by the hospital are sponsored by the appliance company. The hospital may supply walking sticks, zimmer frames or crutches on loan for short-term use, often requiring a returnable deposit. For long-term use, the patient will usually be referred to the community equipment services.

6.4 THE ROLE OF THE PCT/LHB IN THE PROVISION OF AIDS AND APPLIANCES

The PCT and LHB commission a number of community services, such as continence services, specialist medical and nursing equipment (see **paras.8.5** and **8.6**). In addition other local services are the home oxygen and wheelchair services.

Home oxygen service

Ambulatory oxygen is now available on prescription as part of an integrated (i.e. cylinder, concentrator and ambulatory oxygen) service delivered under a new service contract. Specialist teams can assess and authorise oxygen therapy, which is delivered directly to patients in their own homes. GPs will continue to prescribe oxygen where a patient has short-term needs. If the patient requires long-term or ambulatory oxygen, the GP can refer patients to the specialist team to assess and prescribe. The service will be provided under contract from the PCT/LHB.

Wheelchair services

Following discharge from hospital, if required the patient may be loaned a wheelchair on a temporary basis until an assessment has been undertaken. An occupational therapist, a physiotherapist or a consultant will assess the patient's need for a wheelchair. The assessment may take place at home, in hospital or at the local NHS wheelchair service as a general medical service (1977 Act, s.29). NHS wheelchairs are provided on loan for as long as they are needed, although for short-term use wheelchairs are available from voluntary or charitable organisations such as the Red Cross. The NHS will pay for repairs as long as they are not caused by misuse or neglect (1977 Act, Sched.12, para.1(d)). Powered wheelchairs will only be supplied if the professional assessment recommends it. HSG (96) 34 'Powered indoor/outdoor wheelchairs for severely disabled people', states at para.8 that eligibility is determined by the patient being severely disabled and:

- unable to propel a manual chair outdoors;
- able to benefit from the chair through increased mobility leading to an improved quality of life;
- able to handle the chair safely.

The NHS in England operates a wheelchair voucher scheme (HSG (96) 53: Wheelchair voucher scheme). The voucher is worth the same amount as a standard wheelchair and can be used towards the cost of a more expensive wheelchair, although it cannot be used for powered wheelchairs. Where this occurs the patient owns the vehicle and is fully responsible for its maintenance, unlike the loan scheme.

National minimum standards for wheelchairs have been issued by the wheelchair managers forum and are available from their website (**www.wheelchairmanagers.nhs.uk**).

6.5 THE ROLE OF SOCIAL SERVICES IN NOTIFYING THE NHS OF A HEALTH NEED

Under the National Health Service and Community Care Act 1990, s.47(3) if during the assessment of needs under the Act it appears to the local authority that the individual may be in need of health services by the PCT/LHB or health authority, then the local authority must notify the relevant body and invite it to assist, to such extent as is reasonable in the circumstances. The local authority must take into account any likely available services which the relevant body is likely to provide for the individual when assessing and deciding service provision.

6.6 RATIONING AND MEDICAL PRESCRIPTIONS

The Prescribing Pricing Authority, which is a Special Health Authority, compiles on behalf of the Department of Health for England and Wales, the NHS Drug Tariff, which lists those drugs that doctors are allowed to prescribe. It is updated monthly (reg.56(1) of the National Health Service (Pharmaceutical Services) Regulations 2005, SI 2005/641 (as amended), National Health Service (Pharmaceutical Services) Regulations 1992, SI 1992/662 (as amended)). Subject to this, the PCT/LHB and health trusts can ration the amount of drugs that can be prescribed at any one time or indeed have a policy where certain drugs cannot be prescribed unless certain criteria are met. To assist local NHS providers to use resources effectively, the National Institute for Health and Clinical Excellence (NICE) produces best practice guidance. The local NHS bodies are expected to make drugs available throughout England and Wales where NICE advises that they are clinically and cost effective. The NHS bodies are able to ration provision within local priorities and resources (*R* v. *Secretary of State for Social Services ex p Hincks* (1980) 1 BMLR 93). See also *R* v. *Cambridge District Health Authority ex p B (No.1)* [1995] 1 FLR 1056; *R* v. *Central Birmingham Health Authority ex p Walker* (1987) 3 BMLR 32.

CHAPTER 7

Discharge from hospital

7.1 THE NHS RESPONSIBILITY FOR ARRANGING AND FUNDING HOSPITAL IN-PATIENT CARE

7.1.1 The duty to provide in-patient care

In England, hospitals are managed by Acute Trusts or Foundation Trusts, and in Wales, by Hospital Trusts, which provide hospital care to those in clinical need. NHS bodies have a wide general power as to the services they provide under the 1977 Act, s.3. The following in-patient services can be provided as are considered necessary to meet all reasonable requirements:

- hospital and other accommodation;
- medical, dental, nursing and ambulance services;
- facilities for the care of expectant and nursing mothers and young children;
- facilities for the prevention of illness, care of people who are ill and after-care services; and
- other services required for the diagnosis or treatment of illness.

Services can be provided within NHS hospitals, private hospitals or other private facilities (1977 Act, s.23) or from outside England and Wales (1977 Act, s.3(1A)). Guidance on securing treatment abroad has been issued and is available on the Department of Health's website (**www.dh.gov.uk**). Treatment in private facilities or abroad will usually occur where there is a waiting list for the treatment needed, there is undue delay in receiving the necessary treatment, and the service cannot be secured elsewhere (*R (on the application of Watts)* v. *Bedford Primary Care Trust* [2004] EWCA Civ 166).

7.1.2 Limits on resources

The NHS does not have to meet all health needs. Under the 1977 Act, s.1(1), there is a general duty to 'continue to promote a comprehensive health care service'; as such, it is not an absolute duty to provide, since a comprehensive health care system will never be achieved owing to limits of human and financial resources (*R* v. *North and East Devon Health Authority ex p Coughlan* [2001] QB 213, [2000] 3 All ER 850, paras.22–24).

NHS Trusts receive funding through contracts for services with the PCT/LHB. All NHS bodies have limited resources and will operate policies to manage their resources. However, the level of service provision must be justifiable within local priorities and resources (*R* v. *Secretary of State for Social Services ex p Hincks* (1980) 1 BMLR 93; *R* v. *Cambridge District Health Authority ex p B (No.1)* [1995] 1 FLR 1056; *R* v. *Central Birmingham Health Authority ex p Walker* (1987) 3 BMLR 32). The NHS bodies should not operate a policy that does not allow for exceptional circumstances and so fetter their discretion (*R* v. *North West Lancashire Health Authority ex p A* [2000] 1 WLR 977). They should also follow circular guidance (*R* v. *North Derbyshire Health Authority ex p Fisher* (1997–98) 1 CCLR 150).

7.2 DISCHARGE FROM HOSPITAL

7.2.1 Discharge guidance

Once a patient is determined as clinically fit to be discharged and has been assessed as not requiring NHS continuing in-patient care, the patient does not have the right to occupy an NHS bed indefinitely. The patient can however refuse to be discharged from NHS care to, say, a care home. The hospital would need to work with the patient, their family or carer(s) to resolve the matter or implement the delayed discharge procedure (see **para.7.3** below).

The Department of Health has published a best practice guide *Discharge from Hospital: Pathway, Process and Practice* (the Pathway Guidance) (January 2003), a Safe Discharge Protocol *Definitions – Medical Stability and 'Safe to Transfer'* (June 2003) and a toolkit *Achieving Timely 'Simple' Discharge from Hospital'* (August 2004). These are all available from the Department of Health's website (**www.dh.gov.uk**). Less extensive guidance has been issued in Wales, as the *Hospital Discharge Planning Guidance* (NAFWC 17/2005, WHC (2005) 035, available from **www.wales.nhs.uk**).

The Pathway Guidance builds on the *Hospital Discharge Workbook* published in 1994 and applies to all patients. Additional guidance on the needs of children has been included within Part 1 of *National Service Framework for Children, Young People and Maternity Services – Standard for Hospital Services* (available from **www.dh.gov.uk**).

The Pathway Guidance at para.1.4 sets out the key principles for effective discharge and transfer of care, so that:

– unnecessary admissions are avoided and effective discharge is facilitated by a 'whole system approach' to assessment processes and the commissioning and delivery of services;

- the engagement and active participation of individuals and their carer(s) as equal partners is central to the delivery of care and in the planning of a successful discharge;
- discharge is a process and not an isolated event. It has to be planned for at the earliest opportunity across the primary, hospital and social care services, ensuring that individuals and their carer(s) understand and are able to contribute to care planning decisions as appropriate;
- the process of discharge planning should be co-ordinated by a named person who has responsibility for co-ordinating all stages of the 'patient journey'. This involves liaison with the pre-admission case co-ordinator in the community at the earliest opportunity and the transfer of those responsibilities on discharge;
- staff should work within a framework of integrated multidisciplinary and multi-agency team working to manage all aspects of the discharge process;
- effective use is made of transitional and intermediate care services, so that existing acute hospital capacity is used appropriately and individuals achieve their optimal outcome;
- the assessment for, and delivery of, continuing health and social care is organised so that individuals understand the continuum of health and social care services, their rights and receive advice and information to enable them to make informed decisions about their future care.

The Welsh guidance contains similar but differently worded principles at para.22.

7.2.2 Planning and consultation prior to admission

For a planned admission to hospital there is scope to anticipate and plan for likely problems. Pre-admission clinics have a role in planning ahead. For those in receipt of packages of support prior to admission, their community care coordinator or key worker should be fully involved to ensure that admission is as short as possible and that necessary support is in place on discharge. This would avoid the need for proceedings under the Community Care (Delayed Discharges etc.) Act 2003. With emergency admissions, planning ahead is unlikely.

The admission process provides an opportunity to explain to patients and their family and/or carer(s) what to expect and involve them in key decisions, particularly for anticipated discharge. They should be kept fully informed by regular reviews and updates of the care plan. Appendix 4 of the Pathway Guidance contains useful carer's checklists, leaflets and care plans. All communication must take account of the individual's ability to understand and consider information, and should be provided in a suitable format. Consideration should also be given to involving an advocate, where appropriate, for example where the patient does not have any relatives or lacks mental capacity.

7.2.3 Procedure to be followed before discharge from hospital

The Safe Transfer Protocol sets out three criteria for making the decision to discharge, which should occur at the same time, namely:

1. A clinical decision has been made that the patient is ready for transfer.
2. A multidisciplinary team decision has been made that the patient is ready for transfer.
3. The patient is safe to discharge/transfer.

The decision to discharge a patient can be made by the patient's consultant (or his delegated representative) or another doctor who has clinical responsibility for the patient. Nurse-led discharge occurs in some hospitals for specific conditions, such as those with deep vein thrombosis, in accordance with agreed protocols. For more information see *Developing Key Roles for Nurses and Midwives – A Guide for Managers* (November 2002, available from **www.dh.gov.uk**).

Alternatively, the individual can self-discharge, for example when the patient is discharging himself against medical advice, provided he has sufficient mental capacity to make such decision.

7.2.4 The ward-based care coordinator

Once the patient is admitted to hospital, a ward-based care coordinator (in Wales, the term care coordinator is used) should be designated to coordinate care and ensure a smooth discharge planning process. The role is usually undertaken by nurses, although can be undertaken by others such as a social worker, provided they have an understanding of the discharge planning process. Paragraph 5.4.2 of the Pathway Guidance sets out the key tasks of the ward-based care coordinator as:

- Co-ordinating patient assessment, care planning and daily review of the care pathway.
- To discuss with the patient a potential transfer/discharge date usually within 24 hours of admission and recorded in the patient's notes.
- Ensure that timely referrals are made, results are received and any delays followed up.
- Identify, involve and inform the patient about all aspects of care planning, ensuring that the special needs of young carers are identified.
- Engage the carer and make arrangements for carer assessment if appropriate. Make arrangements to see the carer separately regarding their own needs.
- Keep the patient's documentation up to date.
- Liaise with specialist nursing service and other specialist services as appropriate.
- Finalise the transfer/discharge arrangements 48 hours before discharge and confirm with the patient and carer/family.
- On the day of transfer/discharge ensure the patient's condition remains as expected and confirm follow up arrangements.

7.2.5 Discharge planning teams

The discharge planning team consists of professionals and support workers who assist in the discharge planning of an individual who will require community health and social care services on leaving hospital. They support the ward-based care coordinator and the wider multidisciplinary team in planning the discharge of the patient.

The team will comprise the following members.

1. The liaison/discharge planning nurse will advise on community nursing services, assessment for NHS continuing care, Registered Nursing Care Contribution determinations, assistance for self-funding patients to find an appropriate care home placement, home nursing equipment through the integrated equipment services and available continence services.
2. Hospital-based social workers will be involved in the assessment of the patient and any carers, organise care management, adaptations to the home, community equipment and facilitate housing issues that may arise.
3. The clinical team will be involved in screening patients, investigating delays and resolving issues relating to hospital efficiency and bed management.

The assessment

A joint health/social services assessment of the patient's needs should be conducted, where appropriate, for those with continuing health and social care needs. Such an assessment falls within the unified/single assessment process (see **Chapter 3**). The multidisciplinary assessment should be proportionate to the individual's presenting needs. Consideration should be given to:

- the potential for rehabilitation and recuperation;
- whether the patient's need is primarily one of health, which indicates that the patient qualifies for continuing NHS health care (see **Chapter 8**);
- identifying the nature (complexity, intensity or unpredictability) of health care needs, which are the areas that determine eligibility for continuing health and social care needs;
- the need for intermediate care;
- the need for support at home;
- the need for support at home with a care package of health and social care;
- the need for admission to a care home that does not provide nursing care;
- the need for admission to a nursing home;
- the need for admission to a hospice;
- the need for the provision of equipment;
- the need for aids, such as continence aids;

- the need for medicines;
- the need to refer the person for very sheltered housing or other model of housing with care.

Once the plan for future care has been agreed, the local eligibility criteria should be applied and settled as to which agency and/or person is providing the care. A date for a review should also be set, which will usually be within the following three months.

7.2.6 Transport from hospital

PCTs have responsibility for commissioning transport across their geographical area for those who meet their eligibility criteria for transport for outpatient appointments. Transport from hospital may be arranged by the hospital trust using the ambulance service. Local agreements should be developed as to when the transport service should be used.

7.3 BED BLOCKING AND THE ROLE OF SOCIAL SERVICES UNDER THE COMMUNITY CARE (DELAYED DISCHARGES ETC.) ACT 2003

7.3.1 The statutory framework

The reason for the Act

Prior to the introduction of the Community Care (Delayed Discharges etc.) Act 2003 (the 2003 Act), 4,000 people at any one time in England were using acute NHS beds but were ready to be discharged. The Government believed this was because social services had either not assessed the patients or they were waiting for services to be put in place. The majority of NHS in-patients are older people and as such they are often the subject of the delayed discharge process.

The 2003 Act introduced a financial incentive for local authorities with social services responsibilities to provide community care services for the individual and/or his carer that are needed for the individual's safe transfer to a more appropriate setting.

Legislation, guidance and directions on the Act

The 2003 Act is fully in force in England although the Welsh Assembly has no intention to implement it. The following regulations are in force: the Delayed Discharges (England) Regulations 2003, SI 2003/2277 and the Delayed Discharges (Mental Health Care) (England) Order 2003, SI 2003/2276. Guidance and Directions have been issued in LAC (2003) 21, HSC 2003/009 and the Delayed Discharges (Continuing Care) Directions

2004. The Department of Health has also issued additional information, such as checklists and model notification forms, on its website under 'reimbursement'.

7.3.2 Consultation under the Community Care (Delayed Discharges etc.) Act 2003

Prior to serving notice under the 2003 Act, the NHS body should consult the patient and his carer(s) (if any) (2003 Act, s.2(4)). This is to allow patients who want to arrange their own care to do so and also prevents the NHS initiating assessments that are not required.

7.3.3 Application of the Community Care (Delayed Discharges etc.) Act 2003

If the patient is deemed by the NHS body to be 'likely in need of community care services', it can serve a 'section 2 notice' on social services to assess the patient and then put into place services to meet the assessed needs. The serving of the notice is the start of the discharge process (the assessment notification). Usually, at the same time, notice is given under the 2003 Act, s.5, of the proposed date for discharge (the discharge notification). Failure to comply with this may cause the social services department to be charged for each day the resident is in an acute hospital bed when they are ready to be discharged. If any aspect of the delay is related to NHS responsibility, then the charge does not arise; this includes waiting for an assessment for Registered Nursing Care Contribution (RNCC) (see **para.8.7**).

7.3.4 Hospitals to which the Community Care (Delayed Discharges etc.) Act 2003 applies

The patient must be in an NHS hospital or an independent hospital under arrangements made by an NHS body and in receipt of acute or geriatric medical care provided in a general and acute hospital (2003 Act, s.1(1)). The Act does not extend to mental health care, palliative care, intermediate care, recuperation or rehabilitation care or maternity care services (SI 2003/2277, reg.3). Delays in children's services are not covered, as children under 18 do not receive community care services under the Act, although carers' services provided under CDCA 2000 are covered. Acute care is determined by the patient and the services needed by that individual and not the bed occupied. LAC (2003) 21, HSC 2003/009 contain detailed explanation of what is or is not acute care.

7.3.5 When can the notice be given?

Consideration must also be given to whether the person meets the criteria for continuing NHS health care before notice is served. The notice should include a statement that the NHS body has considered whether or not to provide the patient with continuing NHS care and of the result of that consideration (SI 2003/2277, reg.4(3)(e)). The notice is given no earlier than eight days before the day of expected admission (2003 Act, s.2(3)(b)). The admission day itself is counted in this eight-day period. This enables social services to use the period before admission, where possible, or following admission but before discharge, to assess the need for community care services and to plan the required services.

7.3.6 Duties arising where a notice under s.2 has been given

Once the notice has been served, social services must then assess and, in consultation with the NHS body, determine what community care services it will provide for the patient and/or his carer (2003 Act, s.4). The assessment is irrespective of whether the person has previously been subject to an assessment of their needs, under the National Health Service and Community Care Act 1990, s.47. Social services will have a duty to assess most patients, irrespective of the issue of funding care. However, if the patient is to arrange and fund the care himself, social services responsibility (and any charge) will be limited to the period of the assessment. The duty arising under s.4 is cancelled if the s.2 notice is withdrawn or ceases to have effect, for example where the patient's health deteriorates and he is no longer fit for discharge or the patient discharges himself (SI 2003/2277, reg.4(4)–(5)).

7.3.7 How long do social services have to arrange services?

The local authority has a minimum of two days to put together a discharge plan in consultation with the relevant NHS bodies and determine which services it will provide to the patient on discharge (SI 2003/2277, reg.6). In the event that social services have not started or completed an assessment of the patient's and carer's needs or discharge is not possible because social services have not provided a service they had decided to provide, then social services will be charged for each day the patient stays in the acute bed. The charge is set at £120 in London, the Home Counties and parts of the South East and £100 elsewhere (SI 2003/2277, reg.7). The delayed discharge period ends on the date social services notify the NHS body that they have assessed the patient and determined what services they will provide and that they have made those services available (2003 Act, s.6).

7.3.8 Dispute resolution between the NHS and social services

The NHS body must identify the responsible social services department, which will be the one for the area in which the patient is ordinarily resident when the notice of likely need is given (see **para.2.5.4**). For those of no fixed abode, the local authority responsible is identified by the postcode of the place where the patient was admitted. Paragraphs 65–70 of LAC (2003) 21, HSC (2003) 9 contain details of how this is determined.

The SHA must establish dispute panels, where the NHS body and social services cannot reach agreement (2003 Act, s.9). The panel's role is advisory and as such its recommendations cannot be formally binding. The Regulations provide for the form and jurisdiction of the panel.

7.3.9 Adjustments between social services departments

Social services are required to accept a s.2 notice, even though it may not be the correct social services department to be notified for that particular patient (2003 Act, s.10(1)). If another social services department is subsequently found to be responsible for the patient, it must take over responsibility (SI 2003/2277, reg.18(2)). The incorrect social services department can recover any sums paid out in respect of care from the correct social services department (SI 2003/2277, reg.18(4)).

7.3.10 Choice of accommodation

Where the social services department has assessed an individual as needing care in a care home but there is no suitable home in the area or the preferred choice of home has no space, the person may be placed in another care home or interim services put into place until a suitable home or the home of choice becomes available. Local authorities must take all reasonable steps to gain an individual's agreement to an interim care home or care package, which should include reasonable efforts to take account of the individual's desires and preferences. All relevant facts should be ascertained including the person's relevant circumstances. The individual (and his family or carers) should be told of the consequences of failing to come to an agreement, which the local authority must ensure they understand.

Where the patient unreasonably refuses to agree to the care package, whether interim or permanent, social services can be discharged from the statutory duty to provide community care services and may then inform the individual, in writing, that he will need to make his own arrangements (*R* v. *Kensington and Chelsea RLBC ex p Kujtim* [1999] 4 All ER 161). (See 2.5.9–2.5.15 of the *Guidance on National Assistance Act 1948 (Choice of Accommodation) Directions 1992* (LAC (2004) 20) and paras.97–102 of LAC (2003) 21, HSC (2003) 9.) Local authorities should not move a patient who objects to being moved as it may amount to a tortious and/or criminal act, such as common assault.

7.4 REVIEW OF THE DECISION TO DISCHARGE

Under the Delayed Discharges (Continuing Care) Directions 2004, before a s.2 notice is served the NHS body must carry out an assessment of the patient's continuing care needs, in consultation, (where appropriate) with social services. In doing so it must consult with the patient and any carer. The NHS body must then decide whether the patient's needs call for the provision by an NHS body of continuing care. The NHS body must notify the patient of the decision and record the decision in its notes. The patient must be informed of the review process if dissatisfied with the outcome. If a patient asks for a review of the decision it should occur within 14 days. During this period the patient should remains the responsibility of the NHS. For full details of the review process see **para.8.10**.

CHAPTER 8

Continuing health care

8.1 WHAT IS CONTINUING CARE?

'Continuing care' or 'long-term care' is a general term that describes the care people need over an extended period of time as a result of disability, an illness or accident. The term covers both physical and mental health needs (LAC (2001) 18, para.5, HSC 2001/15, WHC 2004/54, para.6, NAFWAC 2004/41). The individual may need 'continuing health and social care', which describes a package of care provided by the NHS and social services. The term also covers people who require 'continuing NHS health care', which is a package of care arranged and funded solely by the NHS. Continuing care may be provided in a hospital, a care home, hospice, sheltered accommodation or the person's own home.

The range of services which all PCTs/LHBs are expected to arrange and fund to meet health care needs at home or in a care home setting include:

- primary health care, including community nursing (other than district nursing if the care is in a nursing home setting), nursing advice;
- assessment by doctors and registered nurses;
- rehabilitation and recovery (other than intermediate care (see **para.8.4** below));
- physiotherapy, occupational therapy, speech and language therapy, dietetics and podiatry;
- respite health care (see **para.8.3** below);
- community health services;
- specialist health care support;
- palliative care (see **para.8.3** below);
- health care equipment, continence pads, nursing aids and related equipment (see **Chapter 6** and **paras.8.5** and **8.6** below);
- access to hospital care;
- specialist transport services.

In addition for those in nursing homes, the PCT/LHB is responsible for arranging specialist medical and nursing equipment, such as feeding equipment that is normally only available through hospitals (see **para.8.6** below).

8.2 POLICY ON CONTINUING CARE

The National Assistance Act 1948 and the 1977 Act do not specifically make any reference to 'continuing care', although it forms part of nursing and after-care services under the 1977 Act, s.3. Care provided by the NHS is usually free at the point of delivery whilst care provided by social services will usually be subject to a means test. **Chapters 5** and **10** cover charging in detail.

The NHS and social services experienced a cultural shift with the introduction of the so-called internal market, outlined in the 1989 White Paper, *Working for Patients: The Health Service – Caring for the 1990s*, which was passed into law as the National Health Service and Community Care Act 1990. Between 1 April 1993, when social services became responsible for funding care beds, and 1 April 2003, local authorities' responsibilities to provide nursing home care coexisted with the NHS's duty to provide under the 1977 Act, s.3 in addition to s.23 which gave health authorities power to buy beds outside the NHS, often in nursing homes.

By shifting the responsibility from the NHS to social services the financial burden also passed. Problems have occurred as to which body is responsible for commissioning the care and the implications for the service user and the public body are great. Unfortunately, as will be highlighted below, long-term care is, and has been, a long-term problem.

8.2.1 The Leeds case E62/93–94

The Health Service Commissioner (Ombudsman) published a report into an investigation in 1994, which involved a man who suffered from a neurological condition. He was doubly incontinent, could not eat or drink without assistance, could not communicate, had a tumour in his kidney, cataracts in both eyes and occasional epileptic fits. It was accepted that he did not need active medical treatment but that he needed substantial nursing care. At the time Leeds Health Authority had made no provision for such patients. His family met the cost of his care but pursued a complaint to the Health Service Commissioner who found that in failing to make available long-term care beds within the NHS for the man, the authority had acted unreasonably and such action constituted a failure in service provision.

8.2.2 The 1995 guidance

In response to the publication of the Leeds case, the Department of Health published *NHS Responsibilities for Meeting Continuing Health Care Needs* (HSG (95) 8, LAC (95) 5, WOC 16/95, WHC (95) 7 in Wales (which have all since been repealed and replaced: see **para.8.2.5** below)), which set out a national framework of conditions which all health authorities should meet in drawing up local policies and eligibility criteria for continuing health care. It made it clear that those with medical or specialist nursing needs should be cared for at the expense of the NHS. It also required health authorities to develop and publish policies and eligibility criteria from April 1996.

8.2.3 The *Coughlan* judgment

The Court of Appeal considered whether a local authority could lawfully provide nursing care for a chronically ill patient in the case of *R* v. *North and East Devon Health Authority ex p Coughlan* [2001] QB 213. Pamela Coughlan was involved in a road traffic accident in 1971. As a result she was a tetraplegic; doubly incontinent; required regular catheterisation; was partially paralysed in the respiratory tract, with consequential difficulty in breathing; suffered headaches caused by an associated neurological condition and subject to the problems of her mobility, required personal care. As such, her care included nursing care but was not confined to it.

The guidance and policy published by the health authority sought to make distinctions between specialist and general nursing care, with the effect that those with general nursing care needs would become the responsibility of the local authority. The local criteria were criticised in the judgment as the health authority had listed 'non-specialist services' that it would expect a care home to provide which were arguably specialist services, such as general physical and mental nursing care, artificial feeding, continuous oxygen therapy, wound care, pain control, administration of drugs and medication, catheter care, bladder wash-outs, suction, tracheotomy care, and tissue viability (para.13).

At para.41, Lord Woolf MR said:

> Where the issue is whether the service should be treated as the responsibility of the NHS, not because of their nature or quality, but because of the quantity or continuity with which they are provided, the distinction between general and specialist services is of less assistance. The distinction does not provide an exhaustive test. The distinction does not necessarily cater for the situation where the demands for nursing attention are continuous and intense. In that situation the patient may not require in-patient care in a hospital under the new policy, but the nursing care which is necessary may still exceed that which can be properly be provided as part of a social services care provision.

The notion of specialist nursing services is at times therefore, elusive (para.13).

The court held that there could be no precise legal line drawn between those nursing services that are, and those that are not, capable of being treated as included in a package of care services. The distinction between those services that can and cannot be provided is one of degree, which in a borderline case will depend on a careful appraisal of the facts of the individual case. As a very general indication as to where the line is to be drawn, whether it was unlawful depended on whether the nursing services were:

(a) merely incidental or ancillary to the provision of the accommodation which a local authority is under a duty to provide; and
(b) of a nature which it can be expected that a local authority could be expected to provide.

The first part of the test is focusing on the overall quantity of the services and the second part on the quality of the services provided. The judge confirmed that where the individual's care was primarily one of health, the full cost of care was the responsibility of the NHS. Miss Coughlan needed services of a wholly different category.

8.2.4 *Coughlan* – follow up guidance

Follow up guidance was issued under HSG 1999/180, LAC (1999) 30 recommending that health authorities satisfy themselves that their continuing and community care policies, eligibility criteria and other procedures were in line with the then current guidance and the *Coughlan* judgment. Where criteria were revised, health authorities were advised to consider what action they needed to take to reassess the eligibility of service users against their revised criteria.

8.2.5 The 2001 guidance

The 1995 guidance was cancelled and substituted by *Continuing Care: NHS and Local Councils' Responsibilities* (HSC 2001/15, LAC (2001) 18). Similar guidance has been issued in Wales (WHC (2004) 54, NAFWC 41/2004, which is supported by the *All-Wales Continuing NHS Health Care: Framework for Implementation in Wales*, published at the same time). Supplementary guidance on NHS-funded nursing care in England was issued under HSC 2003/06, LAC (2003) 7.

The guidance relates to adult services, although it is targeted at older people. The NHS continues to have responsibility for children, people with learning disabilities and mental health patients (see **Chapters 11** and **12**). Appendix C of the 2001 guidance sets out the key issues to consider when establishing continuing NHS health care criteria, which should be agreed by the SHAs with their local authorities.

1. The eligibility criteria or application of rigorous time limits for the availability of services by a health authority should not require a local authority to provide services beyond those they can provide under the National Assistance Act 1948, s.21.

2. The nature or complexity or intensity or unpredictability of the individual's health care needs (and any combination of these needs) require regular supervision by a member of the NHS multidisciplinary team, such as the consultant, palliative care, therapy or other NHS member of the team.
3. The individual's needs require the routine use of specialist health care equipment under supervision of NHS staff.
4. The individual has a rapidly deteriorating or unstable medical, physical or mental health condition and requires regular supervision by a member of the NHS multidisciplinary team, such as a consultant, palliative care, therapy or other NHS member of the team.
5. The individual is in the final stages of a terminal illness and is likely to die in the near future.
6. A need for care and supervision from a registered nurse and/or a GP is not, by in itself, sufficient reason to receive continuing NHS health care.
7. The location of care should not be the sole or main determinant of eligibility. Continuing NHS health care may be provided in an NHS hospital, a nursing home, hospice or in the individual's own home.

In addition to the above, the Welsh guidance includes provision for those that are at risk to themselves or others, which covers those with a mental disorder, including dementia. It also includes clarification of what is 'regular' (weekly or more frequent); 'near future' (six to eight weeks) and 'input' (assessment, intervention or monitoring).

8.2.6 The Health Service Commissioner's (Ombudsman) Special Report on NHS funding long-term care: February 2003 and further report of June 2003

The February 2003 report into NHS funding of long-term care contained the results of four investigations into complaints about the way health authorities set and applied their eligibility criteria for NHS funding for continuing care of older and disabled people. In all the cases the criteria had been applied over-restrictively and were not *Coughlan* compliant.

The cases included failure to provide for continuing NHS health care in a care home setting (the former Dorset Health Authority and Dorset Healthcare NHS Trust case no. E.208/99–00 and the former Berkshire Health Authority case no. E.814/00–01); a requirement for clinical or constant supervision or management by a consultant (the former Dorset Health Authority and Dorset Healthcare NHS Trust case no. E.208/99–00); a need for specialist nursing/clinical intervention (the former Wigan and Bolton Health Authority and Bolton Hospitals NHS Trust case no. E.420/00–01); and complex and difficult care needs requiring skilled health care staff to look after the patient around the clock (Birmingham Health Authority case no. E.1626/01–02).

In the June report, similar issues arose but in addition it highlighted flaws in the assessment tools used and the criteria's application, in particular how area-wide criteria were inconsistently applied (the former Shropshire Health Authority cases no. E.2119/01–02 and E.5/02–03 and Suffolk Health Authority case no. E.2339/01–02).

The Ombudsman recommended that the Department of Health provide clearer national guidance, including detailed definitions of terms used with examples of cases likely to satisfy the criteria for funding, as the current wording has contributed to the problems. It is doubtful as to whether the 2001 guidance is *Coughlan* compliant, in that although it provides for the nature, intensity, complexity or unpredictability of care, it also provides that the person requires regular supervision from a member of the NHS multidisciplinary team. This is at odds with the *Coughlan* judgment in that it is possible to qualify on the quantity of care alone. In *R (on the application of Grogan)* v. *Bexley NHS Care Trust* [2006] EWHC 44, the judge concluded that the 2001 guidance was 'far from being as clear as it might have been'. The claimant was a multiple-sclerosis sufferer aged 65 years, doubly incontinent, immobile with some cognitive impairment. She challenged a decision by Bexley NHS Trust that she was not entitled to continuing NHS funding. The judge held that the trust had used flawed criteria as it failed to set out a test of how to identify those who had a primary health care need and the quantity and quality factors of those needs that would identify those that fall within the criteria. Most criteria, if not all, currently in existence do not set out such tests and will need to be reviewed in the light of this case. The overlap between continuing NHS health care and registered nursing care is considered below at **para.8.7.4**.

As a result of the Ombudsman's report, the Department of Health responded by asking SHAs and PCTs to review their criteria and the way they were applied since 1996, taking into account the *Coughlan* judgment, the 2001 guidance and the Ombudsman's findings. Patients or their estates should be reimbursed money spent on the cost of care. They should also attempt to identify any patients in their area who may wrongly have been made to pay for their care in a home and make appropriate recompense to them or their estates. The DWP has issued guidance on the effect of NHS payments for continuing care on means-tested benefits. The effect is that past payments are not affected; however, future benefits may be affected. See *Jobseekers Allowance and Income Support – Continuing Care Provided by the NHS* and *State Pension Credit – Continuing Care Provided by the NHS* (available from **www.dwp.gov.uk**).

The independent report *Continuing Health Care: Review, Revision and Restitution* commissioned by the Department of Health (December 2004) explored progress made by SHAs in the review process of such cases. At the same time the Health Service Ombudsman published *NHS Funding for Long-term Care: Follow-up Report*, which recommended that the Department of

Health should establish national minimum eligibility criteria. This led to the Health Minister Stephen Ladyman announcing plans to develop a national framework for assessment for continuing care funding. This has been followed by an update Newsletter in June 2005, and a letter to SHAs in November 2005, to remind assessors of the correct process to be applied for assessing those in the high band of RNCC against criteria for continuing NHS health care.

8.2.7 The Pointon case – eligibility in own home

In February 2004, the Health Service Ombudsman reported and upheld a complaint against the former Cambridgeshire Health Authority and South Cambridgeshire PCT (Malcolm Pointon) (case no. E.22/02–03). The Ombudsman upheld a complaint that the assessment should have taken note of the *Coughlan* requirement to judge both the amount and the type of nursing care required and that the care given by the spouse was equal to that of a registered nurse. There had also been a failure to consider the patient's psychological problems, in the criteria, policy guidance, assessment and in the tools used. The criteria did not provide for care in one's own home, which may not be compliant with the 2001 guidance.

8.2.8 Rationing and choice of accommodation

The PCTs/LHBs can choose how to meet the health care needs within their available resources (*R* v. *Secretary of State for Social Services ex p Hincks* (1980) 1 BMLR 93; *R* v. *Cambridge District Health Authority ex p B (No.1)* [1995] 1 FLR 1056; *R* v. *Central Birmingham Health Authority ex p Walker* (1987) 3 BMLR 32). The PCT/LHB may arrange and fund a place in a care home, a specialist ward or hospital. Where nursing care is needed in the patient's own home, the PCT/LHB will usually arrange this via primary care services, such as practice and district nurses. For more substantial care, it may be possible for the PCT/LHB to use partnership arrangements with local authorities under the Health Act 1999 to fund care (see **para.2.6.2**). In *Gunter* v. *South Western Staffordshire Primary Care Trust* [2005] EWHC 1894 (Admin) the High Court held that the PCT had power under the 1977 Act to do what appeared necessary to achieve the provision of services which could involve the use of a voluntary organisation, such as an independent user trust as the supplier.

The National Assistance 1948 (Choice of Accommodation) Directions 1992 (LAC (2004) 20) and the 1993 Directions in Wales (WHC (2004) 066), which apply to local authority provision, do not apply to NHS-funded placements. This means that, providing the care the NHS is offering is clinically suitable, patients do not have the right to choose where they receive the care. Problems can emerge for those already in a care home when they qualify for continuing NHS health care as the resident may have to move to another care setting.

8.2.9 The role of social services assessments for continuing NHS health care

The Local Government Ombudsman has upheld a complaint against Hertfordshire County Council (00/B/16833), for a failure of the social worker to apply for continuing NHS health care funding when a person is assessed for nursing care. It was established that the person would have qualified at the time of the assessment. The case recognises the role of social services in notifying the NHS of a person with continuing NHS health care needs under the National Health Service and Community Care Act 1990, s.47(3). Unusually the health authority was involved in the investigation and agreed to reimburse the cost of care jointly with the local authority.

Many local authorities are funding care, albeit means testing the service user, where arguably the person is the responsibility of the NHS. In such cases the local authority is acting ultra vires as it is exceeding its powers. Although local NHS bodies and their local authority partners should agree their eligibility criteria so that there is no gap in service provision, it seems that many have not been agreed, an issue highlighted in the Select Committee's report (see **para.8.7.5** below).

8.3 PALLIATIVE AND RESPITE HEALTH CARE SERVICES

Local eligibility criteria for continuing NHS health care can be applied to palliative care, where the person is likely to die in the near future, and health respite care services. Alternatively, respite can be arranged by the local authority, in which case there may be a charge, subject to the nursing care by a registered nurse element being met by the PCT/LHB.

The timescale of providing care can vary between the remainder of the individual's life and episodes of care. The number of episodes will by their nature be unpredictable, so applications of time limits are not appropriate (2001 guidance, para.18; Welsh guidance, para.23). Executive Letter (1993) 14, annex A, para.4 states that terminally ill people 'are those with an active and progressive disease for which curative treatment is not possible or not appropriate, and whose death can reasonably be expected within 12 months'. PCTs/LHBs often interpret the guidance in respect of palliative care restrictively, in that individuals will often meet the criteria based on the length of their life expectancy being a period of weeks, rather than months. This approach is inappropriate, as it does not allow for any flexibility.

The Health Select Committee's Inquiry into Palliative Care (22 July 2004), recommended that there should be national criteria for continuing NHS health care, including palliative care (para.47). In response to the inquiry in September 2004, the Department of Health stated:

> patients who receive palliative care should meet the local criteria for fully funded NHS continuing care, in which case their personal care should remain the responsibility of the NHS.

Little is said in the 2001 guidance on the provision of health respite care other than that the NHS has important responsibilities for respite health care, including for people who, during a period of respite, require or could benefit from rehabilitation (which may include a package of intermediate care) (para.25).

8.4 REHABILITATION AND RECOVERY SERVICES

Rehabilitation services should be able to promote the recovery and maximise the independence of patients who, for example, have had a heart attack, a stroke or suffered an acute episode of a chronic illness. Services can range from residential rehabilitation, rehabilitation provided in a day hospital or day centre and supported discharge, where short-term support to aid recovery is given at home. The period for rehabilitation and recovery, with the exception of intermediate care services, is unlimited in time and will depend on the clinical need of the patient.

8.4.1 Intermediate care

Some patients have in the past been discharged too early from hospital which has either prevented their recovery or delayed it. As a result, the English *NHS Plan* (2000) and *Improving Health in Wales* (2001) set out government policy for vulnerable adults, by way of intermediate care. It can be generally identified as either intensive rehabilitation services, which are often provided in a hospital setting, or recuperation facilities, which may be provided in a care home setting or in the person's own home.

Paragraph 14 of the guidance on Intermediate Care (HSC 2001/1, LAC (2001) 1) sets out the range of services that can be provided. It does not preclude the individual from receiving additional or dovetailed services (see para.6.1 of the Pathway Guidance (January 2003)).

The guidance defines intermediate care which should:

- be targeted at people who would otherwise face unnecessary prolonged hospital stays or inappropriate admission to acute in-patient care, long-term residential care or continuing NHS in-patient care;
- be provided on the basis of a comprehensive assessment, resulting in a structured individual care plan that involves active therapy, treatment or opportunity for recovery;

- be planned with an outcome of maximising independence and typically enabling the user/patient to resume living at home;
- be time limited up to a period of six weeks;
- involve cross-care professional working, with a single framework, single professional records and shared protocols.

If social service are providing services as part of a package of intermediate care services, there should be no charge for six weeks (Community Care (Delayed Discharges etc.) Act (Qualifying Services) (England) Regulations 2003, SI 2003/1196 and CRAG, para.3.015, and also LAC (2001) 1 and LAC (2003) 14). The National Assembly for Wales has a similar policy, which is contained in *Community Care: Six Weeks Support At Home For Vulnerable People* (NAFWC 05/02, WHC (2002) 128, NAFWC 43/2002).

8.5 CONTINENCE SUPPLIES

Continence supplies include catheters, sheaths, leg bags and other drainage bags as well as pads and sheets and should be provided free of charge by PCTs (paras.23 and 29 of the 2001 continuing care guidance). An assessment of continence needs should be included in the joint assessment and also as part of the registered nursing care assessment. If appropriate, an assessment by a continence adviser should also be carried out (HSC 2001/17, LAC (2001) 26, paras.11–15, and Department of Health guidance entitled *Good Practice in Continence Services* (April 2000)). Care homes should not charge for the supplies as they should work with PCTs to ensure that they receive enough supplies for residents.

8.6 SPECIALIST MEDICAL AND NURSING EQUIPMENT

The 2001 guidance makes clear that PCTs are responsible for arranging specialist medical and nursing equipment, such as specialist feeding equipment (para.23). However, it is expected that nursing homes, as part of their facilities, will provide some standard items of equipment for residents' needs, including hoists, wheelchairs for occasional use, bath and shower seats, and grab rails. Other items can be provided in the same way as if the person were in their own home (Appendix 5.3.1 *Discharge from Hospital* guidance (January 2003) and paras.8–9 of HSC 2001/17, LAC(2001) 26).

8.7 NURSING CARE BY A REGISTERED NURSE

8.7.1 Health and Social Care Act 2001

In response to the Royal Commission's report *With Respect to Old Age* (Cm 4192, TSO), the Government in England in its *NHS Plan* (July 2000) proposed to make nursing care provided by a registered nurse free to everyone who needs it. This was enacted in the Health and Social Care Act 2001, which applies to England and Wales (see guidance LAC (2001) 26, HSG 2001/17 and LAC (2003) 7, HSC 2003/06; for guidance in Wales see NAFWC 25/2004, WHC 2004/024 (the Welsh guidance)).

'Nursing care by a registered nurse' is defined in the Health and Social Care Act 2001, s.49(2) as 'any services provided by a registered nurse and involving the provision of care, or the planning, supervision or delegation of the provision of care, other than any services which, having regard to their nature and the circumstances in which they are provided, do not need to be provided by a registered nurse'. This definition does not include time spent by non-nursing staff, such as care assistants (although it does cover the nurse time spent in monitoring or supervising care that is delegated to others). Neither does it cover personal or social care costs nor the costs of accommodation to residents, which are means tested. Social services are able to provide nursing care placements under the National Assistance Act 1948, s.21 as a 'community care service', although they cannot arrange nursing care provided by a registered nurse.

8.7.2 The nursing assessment

The Department of Health has produced a Practice Guide and Workbook on *NHS Funded Nursing Care* (August 2001) to ensure nurses follow the same procedures when conducting assessments. The Welsh Assembly published a similar Workbook in December 2001. An assessment is made by a trained nurse to determine that nursing care is appropriate. In Wales, the resident's contribution is a flat rate of £107.63 (2005/06) per week, irrespective of how great the needs are. In England the level of care provided by a registered nurse is determined where each person is allocated into a particular band which triggers the level of funding to be met by the NHS, known as 'the Registered Nursing Care Contribution' (RNCC).

Despite what happens in practice, guidance makes it clear that registered nursing care by a registered nurse should only be considered once other care options have been considered, including rehabilitation, reablement, intermediate care, support at home and continuing NHS health care (English Practice Guide and Workbook, 2.9; Welsh guidance, Sched.3.11).

The bands of care

The bands are:

(a) low (minimal nurse input);
(b) medium (multiple care needs, that are stable and predictable and need a registered nurse, at least daily); or
(c) high (complex needs that require frequent mechanical, technical and/or therapeutic interventions by a registered nurse throughout a 24-hour period, and where physical/mental health state is unstable and/or unpredictable).

There is strong argument that, because of this definition, anyone on the high band should qualify for continuing NHS health care as they will have substantial care needs that need to be provided by a registered nurse and would satisfy the *Coughlan* quantity/quality test.

Discretionary payments

There is also a discretion to pay a sum between the low and medium band, where appropriate (and a sum in excess of the high band, where the person has exceptional long-term needs for nursing care, both in amount and type, yet which do not meet local criteria for continuing health care (Appendix 6 of HSG 2001/17, LAC (2001) 26)). Arguably anyone who is to receive this additional payment over and above the high band should qualify for continuing NHS health care as they satisfy the *Coughlan* quantity/quality test.

When assessments occur

A joint NHS/social services assessment of needs should be undertaken before an assessment for NHS-funded nursing care is carried out (LAC (2003) 7, para.8, Welsh guidance, Appendix 3.1). In Wales, the assessment should occur within two weeks, whereas no set time limit is applicable in England (Welsh guidance, Sched.3.9). The NHS will be responsible for the funding of the nursing care aspect but will only have to conduct a full assessment if the stay is likely to last more than six weeks.

The assessment, where appropriate, should form part of the Unified/Single Assessment Process where a holistic approach should be followed and consideration given to the totality of information gained from the domains of the assessment and the care plan (see **para.3.4.1**).

Decisions should be recorded and a copy of the summary of the determination should be given to the patient, which should explain without jargon how the nurse has reached the decision.

Reviews

Anyone entering a care home should have his registered nursing care needs reviewed after three months and every 12 months thereafter or if there has been significant change to his health status. Reviews outside these times, such as if the patient's condition worsens or if he is in disagreement with the decision, should be channelled through the nursing/care home coordinator based at the PCT/LHB.

8.7.3 How funds are paid

The PCT/LHB appoints a nursing/care home coordinator and lead nurse who manage the budget and monitor the quality and consistency of nursing determinations of care by a registered nurse. These personnel manage reviews, appeals, disputes, information provision, contracts and payments. They are also responsible for liaising and providing advice to care homes. The NHS-funded nursing care contribution is paid by the PCT/LHB to the proprietor of the care home.

Where nursing is provided, the care home should set out in its contract with the resident the fee payable for accommodation and food, personal care and nursing care (Care Homes (Amendment No.2) Regulations 2003, SI 2003/1703 and in Wales, SI 2003/1004 (W.144)). In practice the resident will contract for the gross fees including the contribution towards registered nursing care, which sum will be deducted from the amount payable. As a result of this system, the greater the nursing care needs, the less the resident will pay for accommodation and personal care and as such it creates an incentive for dependency.

Retainers

Where the resident needs to be admitted to hospital the nursing contribution is not paid by the PCT/LHB. This has caused problems as some residents or their families have been asked to meet the shortfall by the care home to ensure their rooms are still available to them upon their discharge from hospital. PCTs can make a payment of a retainer equivalent to the value of the RNCC (para.23 of HSC 2003/06, LAC (2003) 7). Paragraph 38 of the Welsh guidance provides for retainers payable for up to six weeks.

8.7.4 Relationship with continuing health care

Terminology within the nursing care guidance is at times very similar to the guidance for continuing NHS health care. The terms 'complex, unpredictable, unstable, frequent intervention' appear in both sets of guidance. Although Appendix 6 of HSG 2001/17, LAC (2001) 26 says the use of similar terminology should not be confused with similar terminology in the guidance for continuing care, it is impossible to see how it cannot be confused. Both the Health Service Ombudsman's reports and the Health Select Committee's report (April 2005) confirmed the confusion in the two systems and the need for clarification (see **para.8.7.5** below).

An individual may qualify for NHS-funded care even though his care needs can be undertaken in the main by someone other than a registered nurse or medic. The problem with the incompatibility between registered nursing care (RNC) and continuing NHS health care assessments is apparent, as partial funding for the former is dependent on RNC input, but full funding of the latter is not dependent on the care being provided by a registered nurse. Indeed it is unlikely Pamela Coughlan would have qualified for anything other than the middle band based on the current definitions.

In *R (on the application of Grogan)* v. *Bexley NHS Care Trust* [2006] EWHC 44, the judge considered the overlap and the approach to be taken when undertaking an assessment. In determining whether a person's care needs are continuing NHS health care needs, consideration should be given to whether all the nursing needs in the accommodation, including the nursing provided by a registered nurse as part of RNC, could have lawfully been provided by the local authority prior to the enactment of the Health and Social Care Act 2001, s.49. If the assessor concludes that the care could not legally have been provided by a local authority (because the care is more than ancillary and incidental to the provision of accommodation, which the local authority is under a duty to provide), this should be taken into account when determining the question whether or not the person qualifies for continuing NHS health care. It does not automatically follow that if the local authority is not responsible then the NHS would be, as there is scope for gaps in the system – hence the need for consideration of eligibility and not an automatic conclusion.

8.7.5 The Government's response to the Health Select Committee's Report

The Health Committee's Report on NHS Continuing Care, Sixth Report of Session 2004–2005 (April 2005), made recommendations along similar lines to the Health Service Ombudsman's recommendations. In response, the Government has confirmed (July 2005, Cm 6650) that there should be a national framework, after public consultation, which should include:

- the establishment of a single set of national criteria for continuing care, which takes into account psychological and mental health needs as well as physical, and which must be *Coughlan* compliant;
- consideration of the establishment of national standard assessment tools to ensure assessments against national criteria are carried out consistently

across the country, supported by better and consistent training to ensure more uniformity of assessments;
- clarification on the implementation issues surrounding assessment for RNCC and continuing NHS health care;
- guidance on reviews and dispute procedures to provide greater clarity;
- consideration of greater flexibility in funding for NHS continuing care, to enable people to be cared for more easily in their own homes, where that is their preference;
- consideration of how to identify and reward care homes with a track record of improving independence, rather than rewarding dependency, as the system currently does;
- confirmation that people should not be denied fully funded continuing care at home because the people providing care are not registered nurses, as it is the nature of care that is crucial. Decisions on full funding should not be based on definitions of nursing.

8.8 BOUNDARY DISPUTES: ESTABLISHING THE RESPONSIBLE COMMISSIONER

8.8.1 Responsible commissioner for registered nursing care

Arguments can arise as to which NHS body is responsible for commissioning care, for example when the patient moves from one area to another area, whether on a temporary or permanent basis. The Department of Health has attempted to resolve the problem in *Establishing the Responsible Commissioner – Guidance for PCT Commissioners on the Application of the Legal Framework on PCT's Secondary Care Commissioning Responsibilities* (October 2003) (available from **www.dh.gov.uk**). No similar guidance has been issued in Wales, although the *NHS Funded Nursing Care in Nursing Homes* guidance (WHC 2004/24, NAFWC 25/04) sets out the commissioning arrangements in para.42.

Patients registered with a GP are the responsibility of the PCT with which the GP practice is associated, even if resident in another PCT or SHA area. The PCT has responsibility for funding health care for those not registered with a GP in their locality, provided they are usually resident in the area. In Wales, it is the LHB where the resident is registered with a GP that determines the responsible commissioner.

Where a person is permanently resident in a care home and the placement is not fully funded by the PCT, for example, being entitled to RNCC, the PCT responsible is determined by the GP with whom the patient is registered.

If the patient wishes to move to a care home away from where he currently lives, the receiving PCT will be responsible for paying for the RNCC. The

PCT in which the patient currently lives should undertake the assessment and notify the receiving PCT of the band it considers appropriate.

8.8.2 Responsible commissioner for continuing NHS health care

The National Health Service (Functions of Strategic Health Authorities and Primary Care Trusts and Administration Arrangements) (England) (Amendment) Regulations 2006, SI 2006/359, ensure that the placing PCT will remain responsible for commissioning the health care services even if the patient changes his GP to one in the new PCT area. In the meantime, PCTs have been advised to ensure that no patients are denied the services they are assessed as needing.

LHBs in Wales and local authorities are expected to work together to agree commissioning arrangements for continuing NHS health care (Welsh guidance, paras.9–10).

8.8.3 Moves between England and Wales

A protocol between the Welsh Assembly and the Department of Health for placements between England and Wales has been agreed for registered nursing care by a registered nurse. The basic principle is that the arrangements for and level of funding applicable in the receiving PCT/LHB will apply (para.2.28, *NHS-Funded Nursing Care in Nursing Homes* guidance, WHC 2004/24, NAFWC 25/04; available from **www.wales.nhs.uk**).

Care in the person's own home is governed by the *Procedure for Cross-Border Healthcare Commissioning between England and Wales* (WHC (2005) 12). The principle is that the commissioning arrangements applicable will depend on where the person is registered with a GP, although legal responsibility will depend on where the person is resident. The protocol will run until 31 March 2006, after which time commissioning responsibility will revert to the residency-based responsibility.

8.9 ASSESSING FOR CONTINUING CARE

Adequate consideration should be given to whether the person is eligible for continuing NHS health care, which may form part of the Single Assessment Process for older people or the Unified Assessment Process in Wales. A joint NHS/social services assessment of needs should be undertaken before an assessment for NHS-funded nursing care is carried out (para.8 of LAC (2003) 7, HSC 2003/06). Paragraph 17 of the Welsh guidance makes it clear that all adults going into a care home and those who are likely to qualify for continuing NHS health care should receive a multidisciplinary assessment. Before the RNCC is determined, the nurse should consider whether the person qualifies for continuing NHS health care. The Government's response to the Health Select Committee on continuing care confirmed that it would reinforce this process within the proposed national eligibility criteria.

8.9.1 Assessment under the Delayed Discharges (Continuing Care) Directions 2004

The Delayed Discharges (Continuing Care) Directions 2004 provide that before giving notice to discharge a patient, under the Community Care (Delayed Discharges etc.) Act 2003, the NHS body must assess for continuing care needs, in consultation with social services (if appropriate) (para.2(2)). It must consult the patient and any carer (para.2(3)), notify the patient of the decision, record it in the notes, inform the patient of how the decision was made and how to obtain a review (para.2(5)).

8.9.2 Assessment under the Continuing Care (NHS Responsibilities) Directions 2004

For other cases, the Continuing Care (NHS Responsibilities) Directions 2004 give a discretion to the NHS body to assess persons who may be in need of continuing care services or variation of services (para.3). Where an assessment is carried out the PCT must inform the person of the decision made, record the decision and provide details of the review process (para.3(2)).

8.9.3 Failures in assessment

The NHS body should inform the patient, family or any carer of the outcome of the assessment, record the decision and inform those involved of how to ask for a review. Failure to do so could amount to maladministration. The Health Service Ombudsman, Anne Abraham, in her *Special Report on Long Term Care* was critical of some NHS bodies, and said (para.16):

> Too often I receive complaints of patients' and relatives' views not being taken into account in multi-disciplinary assessments, of little or no written information being provided and of criteria and procedures not being explained adequately.

In identifying the reason why this occurred she went on to say (para.17):

> It is usually trust staff who carry out clinical assessments of patients' needs against the criteria, sometimes with little or no guidance on the practical application of the criteria. Also they are not always sufficiently well informed to discuss the wider issues of eligibility, for instance the review procedure, with patients and relatives.

Further Ombudsman cases have been reported highlighting similar issues (Central Manchester PCT and Central Manchester and Manchester Children's University Hospital NHS Trust case no. E.629/01–02 and the former Gloucester Health Authority case no. E.112/02–03).

8.10 CONTINUING CARE REVIEW PANELS

The patient can ask for a review (which is distinct from NHS complaints) of the decision that he does not meet the eligibility criteria for continuing NHS health care or the nursing care band assessed as needed. The review process cannot be used where the criteria content is being challenged, in which case the matter should progress through the NHS complaints procedure (see **Chapter 18**) or judicial review should be sought (**Chapter 23**). The purpose of the review is to ensure that proper procedures have been followed in reaching the decision and eligibility criteria have been properly and consistently applied.

Details of the review process are contained in HSC 2001/015, LAC (2001) 18 and the Continuing Care (NHS Responsibilities) Directions 2004, and in Wales in Annex F of WHC 04/54 and NAFWC 41/04. The 2004 Directions are applicable to all SHAs/PCTs in England and create a duty on the SHA to produce one set of eligibility criteria from which all PCTs in its area must follow (para.2(2)). This problem does not occur in Wales, as the LHBs set the eligibility criteria.

8.10.1 Informal review stage

The patient, his family or carer may ask the manager with responsibility for continuing NHS health care or the nursing care coordinator of the PCT/LHB to review the decision. The outcome of this review, including an explanation of the reasons for its conclusions, should be conveyed to the patient, relative or carer by the PCT/LHB. Most PCTs operate an additional lengthy review panel process, prior to going for an independent review.

During the review period the patient should be allowed to remain in hospital while the process is conducted. As such, it may be appropriate to challenge a decision whilst the patient is still in hospital. Once the patient is discharged, the delays in the review process can be considerable.

8.10.2 Independent review stage

The SHA must establish a standing panel consisting of a chair (and a reserve chair), a member of each PCT and each local authority within its area. In the event that the matter has not been resolved informally and the patient, relative or carer wishes for the case to be reviewed, the SHA can refer the matter to the review panel drawn from the standing panel. The PCT and local authority representatives must not sit on panels concerning reviews of their own criteria. In Wales, the LHB establishes the standing panel.

The review panel should comprise an independent chair and nominated panel representatives from the PCT/LHB and local authority. The procedure and operation of the panel is a matter for the chair, subject to existing guidance. Legal representation is not prohibited in the English guidance but is in Wales, although most chairs appear to exercise their discretion to exclude lawyers, unless the lawyer is of course acting as a Court of Protection appointed receiver or an attorney, in which case he acts as a statutory agent. All NHS bodies should ensure that there are proper records of discussions and recommendations and that consideration is limited to relevant issues and that relatives should be allowed to attend in person if they wish (*R (on the application of Goldsmith)* v. *Wandsworth LBC* [2004] EWCA Civ 1170).

The review panel's role is advisory and has no legal status; however, in all but exceptional circumstances the decisions of the panel should be accepted by the PCT/LHB. The PCT/LHB must send its decision in writing, with reasons, to the patient and to the chair of the panel. All relevant parties should also receive the information.

The review should be completed within two weeks of the request for a review being received. The period starts once any action to resolve the case informally has been completed and should be extended only in exceptional circumstances.

If at the end of the review process the patient is still dissatisfied, the matter can be referred through the NHS complaints process. However, the Ombudsman has said that if the case relates to a period prior to April 2004, the matter can be passed to the Health Service Ombudsman without the need to go through the whole NHS complaints process.

8.10.3 No panel

The panel will not be convened if the patient clearly falls outside the eligibility criteria or where it is clearly not appropriate for the panel to consider. If this occurs, the NHS body should give a full written explanation of the basis of the decision with details of the NHS complaints procedure.

8.11 CLOSURE OF NHS CARE HOMES

Moving older and frail persons, particularly if they have been in a long-stay hospital for many years, may bring about their premature death or destabilise their health. The NHS Executive issued good practice guidance in April 1998 for the procedure for transferring frail older NHS patients to other long-stay settings under HSC 1998/48. It is arguably applicable to all vulnerable people.

The guidance makes it clear that there need to be wide consultation, a flexible project plan and individual assessments with a care plan for each patient. In the event that the patient is medically unfit to move the transfer should be delayed or halted until the patient is well enough to move.

The human rights issues in moving vulnerable people are considered further in **Chapter 13** on the vulnerable adult.

CHAPTER 9

Community health services

Community health services are varied and may be commissioned by the PCT/LHB or hospital trust independently but increasingly they will be commissioned jointly with social services. The provision of community equipment is dealt with separately in **Chapter 6**.

9.1 GENERAL PRACTITIONERS

9.1.1 The GP contract for medical services

General practitioners are central to the provision of community health services as they provide and act as referrers for patients who need additional services. Section 16CC of the 1977 Act (as inserted by the Health and Social Care (Community Health and Standards) Act 2003, s.174), creates a duty on each PCT and LHB to commission or provide primary medical services to the extent that it considers necessary to meet all reasonable requirements. Arrangements under the 1977 Act, s.29 have been replaced by new contract arrangements (1977 Act, s.28Q–28R).

The National Health Service (General Medical Services Contracts) Regulations 2004, SI 2004/291 (as amended), and in Wales SI 2004/478 (W.48), set out essential services that must be given to patients who are:

(a) ill, with conditions from which recovery is generally expected;
(b) terminally ill; or
(c) suffering from chronic disease,

which are to be delivered in the manner determined by the practice in discussion with the patient and include:

- provision of advice in connection with the patient's health, including relevant health promotion advice;
- offering consultation and, where appropriate, physical examination for the purpose of identifying the need, if any, for treatment or further investigation;

- the making available of such treatment or further investigation as is necessary and appropriate, including the referral of the patient for other NHS services and liaison with other health care professionals involved in the patient's treatment and care (reg.15).

The PCT/LHB may also contract with GPs to provide minor surgery, maternity medical services, child health surveillance, vaccinations and immunisations, contraceptive services and cervical screening as additional services (SI 2004/291, reg.16 and Sched.2). The Regulations specifically provide for patients aged 75 and over to be offered an annual assessment and if appropriate a home visit (SI 2004/291, Sched.6, para.6).

Out-of-hours care may be managed by the GP practice, a deputising service, a cooperative or directly by the PCT/LHB. It may be that the GP's emergency telephone number will initially refer the caller to NHS Direct which will then determine if the patient should go to hospital, be given advice and information, or advised to make an appointment with a GP.

9.1.2 Referral for community care services

The new contract no longer makes it specifically obligatory for GPs to give advice to enable patients to avail themselves of services provided by social services. Referrals are limited to other health care professionals involved in care and treatment of the patient and other services provided under the 1977 Act, which should include but not be limited to community care services available under Sched.8, which covers elderly people, expectant mothers, those misusing drugs and alcohol and certain ill people. See **para.2.5.2** for further detail. Although there is no longer an obligation on GPs to refer, this does not prevent them from making a referral to social services where they consider it appropriate.

9.1.3 Medical certificates

Regulation 21 of, and Sched.4 to SI 2004/291 confirm the GP's role in providing medical certificates free of charge to the patient or his personal representative for a variety of purposes, but in particular for claiming social security benefits, council tax exemptions or discounts and to support exemption applications from charges for drugs, medicines and appliances.

9.1.4 Prescription by GPs

The GP can prescribe any drugs, medicines or appliances that are needed for the treatment of any patient, other than those that are not allowed to be prescribed (SI 2004/291, Sched.6, para.39). However, GPs have restrictions placed on them when prescribing buprenorphine or other controlled drugs as specified in Sched.2 to the Misuse of Drugs Regulations 2001, SI 2003/1432 (as amended), which are aimed at preventing and controlling abuse. The Prescription Pricing Authority produces a weekly list of items that may be prescribed and the 'drug tariff' is available online (**www.ppa.org.uk/ppa/edt_intro.htm**). Some appliances form part of community equipment, which is covered in **Chapter 6**.

The National Health Service (General Medical Services Contracts) (Prescription of Drugs etc.) Regulations 2004, SI 2004/629, and in Wales SI 2005/366 (W.32), restrict the prescription of items that are commonly available over the counter from a pharmacy.

9.1.5 General practitioners and nurses with special interests

Practitioners with special interests may be recruited by PCTs to help reduce waiting times in primary care and extend the range of services available under the 'Wider Range of Services in Primary Care' programme. Such practitioners may undertake outpatient appointments, undertake advanced procedures, or develop services, but do not provide a full consultant service. The scheme is to be extended to allied health professionals, such as physiotherapists, counsellors and occupational therapists.

9.2 THE ROLE OF THE HOSPITAL

Doctors working within an NHS hospital trust can prescribe any drug, appliance or equipment considered by the doctor to be clinically necessary for the patient's treatment. This is subject to the doctor's contract, which may restrict prescription of certain treatments. Doctors may also refer patients to community health services as appropriate, such as physiotherapists, occupational therapists, continence advisers, and speech and language therapists.

9.3 DISTRICT NURSES

District nurses, also known as community nurses, provide nursing care for patients in non-hospital settings. They may work in patients' own homes, GP surgeries, health centres and care homes that are registered to provide only personal care. They are usually employed by the PCT or LHB to provide nursing care such as palliative care, wound dressing and administering medication in a variety of settings. They work closely with GPs, health visitors, social workers, school nurses, occupational therapists and midwives. Amendments have been made to the Medicines Act 1968, which now allow district as well as practice nurses, midwives and health visitors who undertake specialist training to prescribe but only from the items listed in the Nurse

Prescribers' Formulary (Medicines Act 1968, s.58(d)). The full list is available on the Department of Health's website under 'nurse prescribing'.

9.4 COMMUNITY PSYCHIATRIC SERVICES

Community psychiatric nurses and community mental health nurses are nurses with specialist mental health training, and may be employed by a PCT/LHB or hospital trust. Access to the service is either by a referral from the GP or from a psychiatrist who may be community or hospital based. Their role is to assess, counsel, manage and support people in the community who have mental health problems and support their family and carer(s) in providing care. They also assist with monitoring and administering psychiatric drugs to patients in the community. For children and adults with mental health and behavioural problems, including those with autism spectrum disorders and attention deficit hyperactivity disorder, services may be provided through the Child and Adolescent Mental Health Service, which are commissioned by the PCT/LHB.

9.5 PREGNANCY SERVICES

The GP, where contracted, must provide all necessary maternity medical services throughout the antenatal period, which extend to babies throughout the postnatal period (14 days after the birth). Women who have miscarried or have aborted or seek a termination must be provided with all necessary medical care unless, in the event of a termination, the GP has a conscientious objection, in which case he should refer the patient to another GP who does not hold such views (SI 2004/291, reg.16, Sched.2, para.7). Community services include provision of midwifery services.

9.6 SERVICES FOR DISABLED CHILDREN

Some social services departments may operate joint health and social care teams for disabled children and can assess and refer to the appropriate community health service. Occupational therapists can advise on modifications or equipment that may be useful at home to increase the independence and mobility of a person with a disability. They can be accessed through a GP or social services. The PCT/LHB may have commissioned a paediatric home care nursing team who can provide nursing care at home for children up to the age of 16. A paediatric physiotherapist may also be able to assist with problems that disabled children have with movement.

9.7 SERVICES FOR THOSE WHO ARE LEARNING DISABLED

Speech and language therapists can help not only with communication difficulties but also with eating and swallowing difficulties. They may be accessed through the GP or hospital service as well as social services. Community learning disability nurses may also be able to provide support ranging from advocacy to behaviour management.

CHAPTER 10

Charging for health care

Section 1(2) of the 1977 Act provides that NHS services 'shall be free of charge except so far as the making and recovery of charges is expressly provided for by or under any enactment, whenever passed'. The 1977 Act also provides that the Secretary of State can make regulations for charges for drugs and appliances (s.77), dental and optical appliances and treatment (ss.78–79) for private patients (s.58) and for patients who are not ordinarily resident in the UK (1977 Act, s.121 as amended by Health and Medicines Act 1988, s.7(12) and (14)). See HSC 1999/199 on NHS charges.

When a person is an in-patient then no charge applies (1977 Act, Sched.12). This covers any premises where the person is receiving care arranged by the NHS, and includes an NHS hospital, a private hospital or a nursing home.

10.1 ITEMS THAT CAN BE CHARGED FOR

Charges can be made for drugs and appliances including surgical/abdominal supports, wigs, surgical brassieres, elastic hosiery and oxygen cylinders (National Health Service (Charges for Drugs and Appliances) Regulations 2000, SI 2000/620 (as amended)). In addition, charges can be made for eye tests, glasses and contact lenses (National Health Service (Optical Charges and Payments) Regulations 1997, SI 1997/818 (as amended) and the National Health Service (General Ophthalmic Services) Regulations 1986, SI 1986/975 (as amended)), and dental treatment and appliances (National Health Service (Dental Charges) Regulations 1989, SI 1989/394 (as amended)). The regulations also provide for exemptions from charges. Directions in respect of optical charges were issued in August 2005 under the 1977 Act, Sched.12, para.2(1), and are available from the Department of Health's website (**www.dh.gov.uk**).

10.2 ITEMS THAT CANNOT BE CHARGED FOR

10.2.1 Oxygen concentrators

Patients who need regular oxygen, such as those with chronic lung disease, may be provided with portable, domiciliary machines for the provision of long-term home oxygen therapy. The most cost-effective way in which the NHS can provide oxygen is through concentrator machines. There should be no charge for such oxygen concentrators where they are used for long periods of time (SI 2000/620, reg.3(d)).

10.2.2 Replacement and repairs

The patient cannot be charged for the replacement or repair of an item which is defective (1977 Act, Sched.12, para.1(d)) but if the repair or replacement is due to an act or omission of the patient then the NHS can make a charge (1977 Act, s.82 and National Health Service (Charges for Appliances) Regulations 1974, SI 1974/284 (as amended)).

10.3 INDIVIDUALS WHO ARE EXEMPT FROM CHARGES

10.3.1 Exemption from prescription charges

Individuals should not be charged, if at the time the prescription is dispensed they:

(a) are aged under 16 or under 19 and in full-time education*;
(b) are aged 60 or over;
(c) are pregnant or have had a baby within the last 12 months and have a valid exemption certificate;
(d) have a valid exemption certificate and have one or more of the following conditions:

- permanent fistula (including caecostomy, colostomy, laryngostomy or ileostomy) requiring continuous surgical dressing or an appliance;
- the following disorders for which specific substitution therapy is essential:
  - Addison's disease and other forms of hypoadrenalism for which specific substitution therapy is essential;
  - diabetes insipidus and other forms of hypopituitarism;
  - diabetes mellitus (except when treated by diet alone);
  - hypoparathyroidism;
  - myasthenia gravis;
  - myxoedema or other conditions which require supplemental thyroid hormone;

- epilepsy requiring continuous anti-convulsive therapy;
- a continuing physical disability, which prevents the patient from leaving his residence without the help of another person;

(e) are (or their partner is) in receipt of income support; income-based jobseeker's allowance or pension credit guarantee credit and hold Form HC2*;
(f) have an NHS tax credit exemption certificate*;
(g) have a valid war pension exemption certificate issued for the supply of drugs and appliances for the treatment of the accepted disablement*;
(h) are named on a valid HC2 certificate*.

In Wales, prescriptions are also free to those under 25 years. Those marked with an * also qualify for free wigs and fabric supports.

10.3.2 Exemption from optical fees

Individuals do not have to pay for eyesight tests if they are:

(a) under 16, or under 19 and in full-time education*;
(b) aged 60 or over*;
(c) registered blind or partially sighted;
(d) diagnosed as having diabetes or glaucoma;
(e) 40 or over with a first degree relative with glaucoma, or the patient has been advised by an ophthalmologist that he is at risk of glaucoma;
(f) prescribed a complex lens*;
(g) in receipt of income support or income-based jobseeker's allowance; pension credit guarantee credit* (or their partner is);
(h) entitled to a NHS tax credit exemption certificate*;
(i) named on a valid HC2 certificate*.

Those marked with an * also qualify for free glasses or contact lenses.

10.3.3 Exemption from charges for NHS dental treatment

The following are exempt from charges if when the treatment starts they are:

(a) aged under 18;
(b) aged 18 and in full-time education;
(c) pregnant, or have had a baby in the 12 months before treatment starts;
(d) an NHS hospital dental service outpatient or a community dental service patient, in which case charges can be made for dentures and bridges;
(e) an individual or their partner in receipt of income support; income-based jobseeker's allowance; pension credit guarantee credit;

(f) entitled to, or named on, a valid NHS tax credit exemption certificate; or
(g) named on a valid HC2 certificate.

In Wales, free dental examinations also apply to those under 25 or 60 or over.

10.4 HELP WITH NHS CHARGES

10.4.1 NHS Low Income Scheme

Those who would usually have to pay NHS charges may be able to get help with health costs under the NHS Low Income Scheme, which is based on a comparison between an individual's income and requirements at the time that a claim is made or a charge was paid. There are no restriction on who can make a claim, provided that they do not have capital which exceeds the capital limit. The capital limits for 2005/06 are as follows:

- £20,500 for those permanently living in a care home;
- £12,000 for those aged 60 or over;
- £8,000 for everyone else.

These figures are increased in line with capital disregards for income support and local authority means-testing purposes.

See HSG 96(49) on the Low Income Scheme. The scheme is administered through the Patients' Services Team at the Prescription Pricing Authority. Claim forms and further details can be obtained from the Prescription Pricing Authority's website (**www.ppa.org.uk**).

10.4.2 DWP exemptions certificates

Patients can get help on age or medical grounds or by being in receipt of one of the exempting benefits or tax credits. No help is available if a person has capital in excess of the prescribed limit. Application is made by the completion of form HC1, available from Jobcentre Plus offices, local DWP offices, main post offices and NHS hospitals. If eligible, patients will receive form HC2 for full exemption, or HC3 if they qualify for partial exemption.

10.4.3 Hospital Travel Costs Scheme

Financial assistance is available under the Hospital Travel Costs Scheme (HTCS) to those patients who do not have a medical need for ambulance transport and who cannot meet the cost of travel to hospital. The scheme is operated under the National Health Service (Travelling Expenses and Remission of Charges) Regulations 1988, SI 1988/551 (as amended). Patients will qualify if they or their partner are in receipt of income support, pension credit guarantee credit or income-based jobseeker's allowance. War disablement pensioners will also qualify. Application is made by completion of form HC1 available from local DWP offices, and submitting it to the local hospital trust. Updated guidance was issued in May 2005 and can be found on the Department of Health's website (**www.dh.gov.uk**).

10.5 OVERSEAS VISITORS

10.5.1 Basis for charging overseas visitors

The National Health Service (Charges to Overseas Visitors) Regulations 1989, SI 1989/306 (as amended) and the National Health Service (Charges to Overseas Visitors) (Amendment) Regulations 2004, SI 2004/614 provide for the making and recovery of charges in respect of certain services provided under the 1977 Act to overseas visitors. Similar regulations were made by the Welsh Assembly in SI 2004/1433 (W.146). GP services, however, can be accessed in the same way as for UK residents at the discretion of the GP practice.

Best practice guidance *Implementing the Overseas Visitors Hospital Charging Regulations – Guidance for NHS Trust Hospitals in England* was issued by the Department of Health in April 2004, with similar guidance being issued in Wales in May 2004.

The Regulations provide that the NHS must determine whether the regulations apply to any overseas visitor treated. Where the person is not ordinarily resident in the UK, the NHS must make reasonable enquiries into the circumstances of that person to ascertain if he is exempt or liable to pay charges. In the event that the individual is liable to pay, the NHS must make and recover payment. In *R* v. *Hammersmith Hospitals NHS Trust ex p Reffell* (2001) 4 CCLR 159, the Court of Appeal held that NHS hospital trusts had the power to require advance payment of those charges and had a discretion as to whether to continue treatment in the absence of advance payment.

See *R* v. *Barnet LBC ex p Shah (Nilish)* [1983] 1 All ER 226 on establishing 'ordinarily resident' and also **para.2.5.4**.

10.5.2 Exempt NHS services

The following NHS services are exempted from charge, regardless of the status of the patient:

- treatment provided in an accident and emergency department, casualty department or walk-in centre providing services similar to those given in an accident and emergency department. The exemption stops when the overseas visitor is admitted to a ward or given an outpatient appointment;

- treatment given elsewhere than a hospital (other than a walk-in centre), or treatment given by someone who is not employed by or under the direction of the NHS Trust;
- family planning services;
- treatment for acute encephalitis, acute poliomyelitis, amoebic or bacillary dysentery, anthrax, cholera, diphtheria, food poisoning, leprosy, leptospirosis, malaria, measles, meningitis, meningococcal septicaemia (without meningitis), mumps, ophthalmia neonatorum, paratyphoid fever, plague, rabies, relapsing fever, rubella, salmonella infection, relapsing fever, severe acute respiratory syndrome, scarlet fever, smallpox, staphylococcal infections, tetanus, tuberculosis, typhoid fever, typhus, viral haemorrhagic fevers, viral hepatitis, whooping cough or yellow fever;
- treatment in or as a referral from a sexually transmitted disease clinic, but in respect of HIV/AIDS it is limited to diagnosis and associated counselling;
- treatment given to people detained under MHA 1983;
- treatment given for mental health problems as part of a court probation order.

10.5.3 Exempt individuals

If either a husband or wife is exempt then that individual's spouse and any children under 16 or 19 if in full-time education are also exempt if they are in the UK with the exempt person for the duration of their stay or live permanently with the exempt person in the UK on a settled basis, such as to work.

The exemptions apply to a person who is:

- engaged in employment with an employer which has its principal place of business in the UK, or is a UK-registered branch of an overseas company, or who is self-employed working in the UK;
- working as a volunteer, providing services similar to health or social services;
- studying full time in the UK on a course lasting at least six months, or if less than six months, which is funded in the main by the UK government;
- taking up permanent residence in the UK;
- living lawfully in the UK for 12 months preceding the need for treatment, except where the person has been given leave to enter the UK specifically for private medical treatment or given special leave to enter the UK on humanitarian grounds;
- a refugee or an asylum seeker who has made a formal application with the Home Office which is still to be determined;
- working on a ship registered in the UK;
- receiving a UK war pension;
- a diplomat posted to the UK;

- a member of her Majesty's UK forces;
- a UK civil servant or a person working abroad for the British Council or the Commonwealth Grave Commission who was recruited in the UK;
- working abroad for less than five years provided he has lived lawfully in the UK for 10 continuous years at some point;
- working abroad, where his post is financed in part by the UK Government in agreement with another government or public body;
- working abroad in another European Economic Area (EEA) country or Switzerland who pays compulsory national insurance contributions in the UK;
- from other EEA country or Switzerland who has been referred to the UK for treatment;
- in receipt of a UK pension and spends at least six months of the year living in the UK and resides in the UK and in another EEA member state;
- a prisoner;
- from one of the countries with which the UK holds bilateral health care agreements and who is in the UK to receive specific treatment with the agreement of his home country.

10.6 CHARGES FOR ROAD TRAFFIC ACCIDENTS

The Road Traffic (NHS Charges) Regulations 1999, SI 1999/785 (as amended) provide for the recovery from insurers and individuals charges in connection with the treatment of road traffic casualties by the NHS. The charge is payable where a traffic casualty received NHS treatment. Different amounts apply depending on whether or not the casualty was admitted to hospital. A daily rate applies to those admitted to hospital up to a maximum prescribed figure.

10.7 THE NURSING/SOCIAL CARE DIVIDE

Some nursing services can be provided by social services and so will be subject to a means test rather than provision by the NHS, which is free at the point of delivery. However, this will be limited to those nursing services which are legitimately provided as part of a social service package of care. The nursing care must be ancillary or incidental to the provision of accommodation and of a type that the local authority is under a duty to provide under the National Assistance Act 1948, s.21 (*R* v. *North and East Devon Health Authority ex p Coughlan* [2001] QB 213). Social services are however prohibited from arranging nursing care provided by a registered nurse, which is specifically excluded by the Health and Social Care Act 2001, s.49. It is in practice very difficult to determine what will amount to nursing services and what will amount to social care services as this will depend on a careful appraisal of the facts of each case and the quantity and quality of the care provided. There will be a point where care which is generally regarded as social care, such as managing the personal care and all activities of daily living for an individual, amounts to nursing care due to the intensity of care needs.

PART IV

Particular groups affected by community care

CHAPTER 11

Children and young adults

11.1 LEGISLATIVE BACKGROUND

Children can be entitled to and often do receive 'community care services'. Unlike in other areas of community care law, where the provision has been introduced piecemeal over a number of years, the basic framework for community care support for children and young adults and their families can be found in the 1989 Act, as amended by the CDCA 2000, the Children (Leaving Care) Act 2000 and the Adoption and Children Act 2002. New duties, many of which have yet to be subject to guidance or scrutiny by the courts, are also found in the Children Act 2004.

11.2 *EVERY CHILD MATTERS* AND CHILDREN'S TRUSTS

11.2.1 The Government agenda

The Government agenda *Every Child Matters: Change for Children* is a cross-departmental approach to meeting the needs of all children from birth to age 19. It involves both legislation and lots of new guidance, practices and approaches to dealing with children. Central to the aim of the Government is to create a new, inter-agency way of working with children, so that all agencies work together. Much of the agenda emerged from the Climbie Inquiry. The Government is currently piloting organisations known as 'Children's Trusts' around the country, which is a new approach to the well-being of children and young people from birth to age 19 (see the Green Paper *Every Child Matters*, para.5.14). It is designed to construct a multi-agency approach which cuts across government departments and which also fully takes into account the views of children and young people themselves. Full details of the strategy can be found on the Department for Education and Skills website (**www.dfes.gov.uk/everychildmatters**) and see further *Every Child Matters* at para.5.23.

11.2.2 The Children's Commissioner

Chapter 22 deals with the Children's Commissioner who was appointed in March 2005 to give young people a voice in government and public life. The Commissioner's role is partly investigative, but he is also expected to explore and put forward the views of vulnerable young people in society and will promote their involvement in organisations whose decisions and actions affect them.

11.2.3 The creation of Children's Trusts

The major local authority vehicle for inter-agency working is the creation of the role of a children's services department and the construction of a Children's Trust. Most areas should have a Children's Trust by 2006 and the Government's *Every Child Matters* agenda expects that all areas will have a Children's Trust by 2008.

A number of authorities have been piloting Children's Trusts in 30 different areas since 2003/04. These authorities are called pathfinders and all are operating different schemes depending on local circumstances. Children's Trusts will not, however, be legal entities and there is no duty in the Children Act 2004 to create such a structure. They will form part of the local authority. Details of the pilot areas and schemes are available online (see **www.everychildmatters.gov.uk**).

11.2.4 Inter-agency working and structural changes to social provision following the Children Act 2004

As already partially explored at **para.2.7.4**, the Children Act 2004 was a response to the findings of Lord Laming in the Climbie Inquiry (**www.climbieinquiry.gov.uk**). It is designed to integrate services pertaining to children into one organisational framework, so that children cannot slip through the system.

Director of children's services

The Children Act 2004 establishes the post of director of children's services (s.18), who is to be an officer of the local authority charged with exercising the functions of the local authority in respect of education, social services (as far as they relate to children), care leavers and the well-being power and functions of the PCT (so far as they relate to children) under the Health Act 1999, s.31, from April 2005 onwards. The posts of director of social services, as it relates to children, and chief education officer are abolished. Section 19 provides for the creation of a cabinet post for a councillor of lead member for children's services (not yet brought into force) but the expectation is that by

2008 each authority will have such a lead member. The roles and responsibilities of both posts are outlined in *Statutory Guidance on the Roles and Responsibilities of the Director of Children's Services and Lead Member for Children's Services* (DoES, 2005). Further guidance is found in the revised *Working Together to Safeguard Children: A Guide to Inter-agency Working to Safeguard and Promote the Welfare of Children* (April 2006).

Duty to cooperate

The central duty is to be found in the Children Act 2004, s.10, which took effect in April 2005. This provides that every children's services authority must make arrangements to promote cooperation between itself and its partners or any other body which is involved in providing activities in relation to children in the area of the authority (s.10(1)). These arrangements are to be made (s.10(2)) 'with a view to improving the wellbeing of children in the authority's area' in relation to:

- physical and mental health and emotional well-being;
- protection from harm and neglect;
- education, training and recreation;
- the contribution made by the children to society;
- social and economic well-being.

These arrangements must have regard to the importance of parents and other people caring for children. Relevant partners are set out at s.10(4) and include the police, probation boards, PCTs and the Learning and Skills Council. These partners must cooperate with the authority in the making of arrangements.

Power is given for the authority to provide staff, goods, services, accommodation or other resources and establish and maintain a pooled fund (s.10(6)). The pooled fund comprises contributions made by both the authority and relevant partners, and payments can be made from it when carrying out the discharge of the authority's functions under the Children Act 2004 (s.10(7)). The authority must have regard to local authority guidance given by the Secretary of State when exercising its functions (s.10(8)). Guidance is available on the website (**www.everychildmatters.gov.uk**) on this duty.

The need to safeguard and promote the welfare of children

Section 11 of the Children Act 2004 provides that all children's services authorities, PCTs, NHS Trusts, NHS Foundation Trusts, police authorities, probation boards, prison governors and further education providers must make arrangements to ensure that their functions are discharged having regard to the need to safeguard and promote the welfare of children and any services are made having regard to that need. This duty took effect on 1 October 2005.

Statutory guidance has been issued concerning these duties (*Statutory Guidance on Making Arrangements to Safeguard and Promote the Welfare of Children under Section 11 of the Children Act 2004* (August 2005) and *Statutory Guidance on Inter-agency Co-operation to Improve the Well-being of Children: Children's Trusts*. These are both available from the Every Child Matters website (**www.everychildmatters.gov.uk**)).

The target duty

The duty under the Children Act 2004, ss.10 and 11 is mandatory in nature, but its purpose is broad, and although it has not yet been subject to judicial scrutiny, it is potentially a 'target duty', i.e. not available to be used in judicial review at the suit of an individual (see *R (on the application of A)* v. *Lambeth LBC* [2003] UKHL 57), but may be used by agencies to compel others to work with them (*R (on the application of T, D and B)* v. *Haringey LBC* [2005] EWHC 2235 (Admin)).

Information databases

Information databases are due to be set up under the Children Act 2004, s.12, which will provide one route by which all information about children can be put in one place. However their format is currently under consultation by the Government and it is unlikely that these will come into force much before 2007/2008.

Local Safeguarding Children Boards

The Children Act 2004 also sets up Local Safeguarding Children Boards (s.13), which will include representatives of each local authority, NHS Trusts and the police, etc., and which have to be in place by April 2006. They are to coordinate what is done by each body for the purposes of safeguarding and promoting welfare and ensure the effectiveness of what is done by each body. They are meant to work as a semi-independent check and balance system for ensuring that inter-agency working is effective. Regulations and guidance on their functions were published in April 2006 as part of the revised *Working Together* guidance.

Children and Young People's Plans

The last new framework put in place by the Children Act 2004 is the Children and Young People's Plans, which must be provided by every authority by

April 2006, pursuant to s.17. Authorities have to consult all bodies involved in discharging duties under ss.10 and 11, and the relevant regulations provide that children, young people, parents, carers and local schools should be consulted at an early stage and given equal opportunities to participate in the development of the plan (paras.2.28–2.30 of the *Guidance on the Children and Young People's Plan*, to be found at **www.everychildmatters.gov.uk**).

It should be a single, overarching plan for all services affecting children and young people, which should be reviewed annually. The relevant regulations (Children and Young People's Plan (England) Regulations 2005, SI 2005/2149) set out the scope of the plan, which is intended to cover improvements that the authority intends to make, the assessment of needs, priorities, resources, and the arrangements for cooperation. Complaints and failure to consult relevant partners could lead to judicial review by disgruntled groups or complaints under the 1989 Act, s.26.

11.3 THE NATIONAL SERVICE FRAMEWORK FOR CHILDREN AND YOUNG PEOPLE

As part and parcel of this approach, in October 2004 the Government published a National Service Framework for Children, Young People and Maternity Services. This is a 10-year programme to promote improvement in young people's health and well-being. The heart of the Framework is a 'fundamental change in thinking about health and social care services'. It is intended to lead to a cultural shift, resulting in services which are designed and delivered around the needs of children and families using those services.

There are five 'core' services which are:

1. A coordinated programme to promote and deliver health and well-being to all children.
2. Supporting parenting.
3. Creating high quality services which are coordinated around the individual and family needs and take into account their views.
4. Age appropriate services.
5. All agencies are to work to safeguard children.

Children and young people with specific needs

The Government has also created standards involving specifically children and young people who are ill, in hospital, disabled or with complex health needs and who have mental health problems and disorders (Standards 6–11). The Framework Guidance (see **www.dh.gov.uk**) provides extensive guidance concerning good practice in this area.

The guidance regarding those who are disabled and have complex health needs provides:

> Children and young people who are disabled or who have complex health needs should receive co-ordinated, high quality child and family centred services which are based on assessed needs, which promote social inclusion and where possible, which enable them and their families to live ordinary lives.

It provides extensive guidance and good practice to ensure that local authorities react responsively and provide good quality services which are transparent and clear.

11.4 COMMON ASSESSMENT FRAMEWORK

As part of the Government's focus certain areas will from 2005–06 be piloting a common assessment framework, which will then be implemented by all areas between 2006 and April 2008. This is a framework to shift the focus from dealing with the consequences of difficulties to trying to promote early identification of needs and provide a simple and non-bureaucratic process. There is a guide for all managers and assessment guidance available on the Every Child Matters website (**www.everychildmatters.gov.uk**). It is meant to be used in health and education situations to identify and tackle problems before they become serious. It is also meant to streamline relationships. In that context, one individual should be the lead professional providing assistance and a single point of contact.

11.5 ASSESSING CHILDREN FOR COMMUNITY CARE SERVICES

11.5.1 Assessing under the community care legislation

Under the new assessment and cooperation regime, children may already have been through a 'common assessment framework' or had input from a number of agencies before a 'formal' assessment by children's services is required. Children can be assessed by the children services department for their social care needs using the National Health Service and Community Care Act 1990, s.47 and the 1989 Act, s.17 and receive services under the 1977 Act, Sched.8, para.3 and CSDPA 1970, s.2 (*R* v. *Bexley LBC ex p B* (2000) 3 CCLR 15).

11.5.2 Assessing under the Children Act 1989

Section 17 of the 1989 Act is the statutory foundation stone which enables social services to provide community care services for children. It provides that it is the 'general' duty of every local authority to safeguard and promote the welfare of children within its area who are in need, and, so far as is consistent with that duty, to promote the upbringing of such children by their families, by providing a range and level of services appropriate to meeting their needs. Such services are wide in breadth and can include assistance in kind, in cash or in accommodation (s.17(6)).

11.5.3 When is a child to be assessed for community care services?

Children should be assessed for community care services when they present as requiring such, pursuant to the National Health Service and Community Care Act 1990, s.47 (i.e. CSDPA 1970, s.2 or 1977 Act, Sched.3 (1989 Act, Sched.2, para.3)) or when they are a child 'in need' under the 1989 Act.

Children in need defined

Children 'in need' are defined in the 1989 Act, s.17(10) as those:

(a) who are unlikely to achieve or maintain, or to have the opportunity of achieving or maintaining, a reasonable standard of health or development without the provision for them of services by a local authority; or
(b) whose health or development is likely to be significantly impaired or further impaired without the provision of such services by the local authority; or
(c) who are disabled.

Disabled child defined

Section 17(11) defines who is a disabled child:

> a child is disabled if he is blind, deaf or dumb or suffers from mental disorder of any kind or is substantially and permanently handicapped by illness, injury or congenital deformity or such other disability as may be prescribed and in this Part –
>
> 'development' means physical, intellectual, emotional, social or behavioural development; and
>
> 'health' means physical or mental health.

There is no definition within the statute of what amounts to a 'mental disorder' and so assistance when determining that question may need to be sought from other statutory contexts (for example, Disability Discrimination Act 1995, s.1 or MHA 1983).

Identifying children in need

Paragraph 1 of Sched.2 to the 1989 Act provides that it is the duty of the local authority to take reasonable steps to identify the extent to which there are children in need in that area. This therefore requires the authority to identify and assess the need of each child who is found to be in its area. The 'threshold' for requiring assessment is quite low. The House of Lords in *R (on the application of A)* v. *Lambeth LBC* [2003] UKHL 57 did intimate, although it was not stated as part of the ratio of the case, that it is implicit in this provision that the local authority will assess the needs of the child, whenever it is necessary to do so.

11.5.4 The requirement to follow statutory guidance

This assessment should follow, or at the very least good reasons should be given for not following the *Framework for Assessment of Children in Need and their Families* (DOH, April 2000) (the Framework Assessment), which provides statutory guidance under LASSA 1970, s.7(1). The authority must 'have regard' to such guidance when carrying out its duties. Having regard to such guidance indicates that the guidance should be followed by a local authority, unless there are good reasons for deviating from it (see *R* v. *Islington LBC ex p Rixon* (1997–98) 1 CCLR 119). In *R (on the application of AB)* v. *Nottingham City Council* [2001] EWHC Admin 235, it was found (following *R* v. *Lambeth LBC ex p K* (2000) 3 CCLR 441 at 444) that the legislative framework requires that the assessment follows the general guidance set out by the Secretary of State.

11.5.5 The assessment

In order to carry out an assessment lawfully, a systematic process must be undertaken in which the needs of the disabled child and any appropriate carers are first assessed, a care plan is then written, and identified services are subsequently provided. In *R (on the application of J)* v. *Newham LBC* [2001] EWHC Admin 992 the court compelled the authority to carry out a lawful s.17 assessment. The assessment should use the framework tools to consider the child's needs in various areas and a set of common assessment tools have been produced and can be downloaded to create consistency.

An initial assessment is an opportunity to see the child and determine whether or not the child is in need, the nature of any services required and whether or not a more detailed core assessment is necessary. A core assessment is an in-depth assessment which addresses the central aspects of the needs of a child and the capacity of the child's parents to respond appropriately to these needs within a wider family and community context.

11.5.6 The child in need plan

Paragraph 4.21 of the Framework Assessment provides that the key aspects underlying any considerations and planning for children in need are:

- ensuring that the child is safe;
- remembering that a child cannot wait indefinitely to have its needs met;
- ensuring that the child's learning be maintained.

The Framework Assessment sets out (at paras.4.35–4.37) that the following areas require clarification and identification within a child in need plan, with objective outcomes for regular reviews:

(a) the objective of the plan;
(b) the services to be provided;
(c) the timing and the nature of professional contact; and
(d) the purpose of the contact.

A child in need plan should be produced after a core assessment. The guidance indicates that such a plan should identify a child's difficulties and the services to meet those difficulties. The guidance also suggests that a review should occur once every six months.

11.5.7 Timescale for the assessment

The guidance sets out as good practice that:

- within one working day of a referral being made, there should be a response as to what response is required;
- within seven days there should be an initial assessment;
- if felt necessary, there should be within 35 working days a core assessment of a child's needs.

11.6 PROVISION OF COMMUNITY CARE SERVICES UNDER THE CHILDREN ACT 1989

The authority can provide such services as are appropriate to safeguard and promote the welfare of children (1989 Act, s.17(1)). Authorities can make such provision as they see fit for any person to act on their behalf and can provide services in cash, in kind or including accommodation (1989 Act, s.17(5) and (6)).

11.6.1 Provision of services

The 1989 Act, Sched.2, Part I provides that every local authority must design services to minimise the effect on disabled children within its area of their disabilities and to give such children an opportunity to lead lives which are as normal as possible. Paragraph 8 of Sched.2, Part I provides that the local authority must make such provision as it considers appropriate for the following services to be available for children in need in its area:

- advice, guidance and counselling;
- occupational, cultural and recreational activities;
- home help;

- assistance with travel;
- assistance to enable a child to live with a family.

The range of services to be provided should be wide enough to allow children's services to meet their obligations under the 1989 Act and the Children Act 2004.

11.6.2 Resources and the nature of the duty to provide

In *R (on the application of A)* v. *Lambeth LBC* [2003] UKHL 57, the House of Lords set out the nature of the duty to assess and provide services for children in need under the 1989 Act, s.17. This series of cases involved the provision of accommodation for children in need. One set of children had been housed in unsuitable accommodation for their disabilities (they were autistic and would run out on to the road), and posed severe disadvantages for the children's health and well-being. A core assessment found that they should be rehoused away from the road. The mother sought to compel the social services authority to provide suitable accommodation in line with the assessment of needs of the children. In another case, an intentionally homeless mother (who was a person from abroad) and her children asked that social services provide her and her children with temporary accommodation. In both cases, the authority refused to provide accommodation, arguing that pressure on resources prevented it from so doing.

The House of Lords recognised that the question behind these appeals was the intractable problem of lack of resources: some of money, and some of resources such as trained staff. Local authorities have a strictly limited amount of money. They decide where the priorities lie, and those decisions are accountable through elections. It is only where a local authority is exercising a statutory duty, as opposed to a power, that it has no choice how it spends its money. The House of Lords indicated that identifying the nature of the duty owed in social welfare law is not easy. Generally, the more specific and precise the obligation, the more readily an obligation is imposed.

The court decided that the 1989 Act was designed to bring together the child protection legislation with the 1977 Act and CSDPA 1970. The intention of the Government in creating the legislation was to ensure that the children concerned should receive the standard of care and protection and professional review appropriate to their needs. Local authorities were given a broad umbrella power to provide services to promote the care and upbringing of children.

The court found that s.17(1) provides a general duty to provide such safeguards as is reasonable. This duty is not imposed, however, upon the needs of an individual child, and is not absolute or near absolute. It is a general duty, which must be exercised, however, within a reasonable way (see para.30 of the speech of Lord Nicholls). The authority therefore has considerable latitude as to what services it provides, and the way in which these are provided.

Lord Hope of Craighead found that the purpose of the 1989 Act was to create a consistent code for child law (para.66), and the purpose of s.17 was to assist families by the provision of support services designed to avoid the necessity to accommodate these children in a compulsory manner. It was designed to reflect Britain's obligation signed under Art.18(2) of the United Nations Convention on the Rights of the Child to render appropriate assistance to parents and guardians in their performance of child-rearing responsibilities.

The House of Lords found that s.17 gave authorities a wide power to do anything (which includes in exceptional circumstances providing cash, or assistance in kind), but the House of Lords found that it is impossible for the authority to fulfil every conceivable need, and a judgement has to be exercised as to how needs may best be met, given the available resources. The House of Lords found that a local social services authority is not obliged to meet every need which has been identified by an assessment of the needs of each individual child in need within its area. As such, there is no duty to provide such services.

There is however, a duty, under the 1989 Act, s.17(2) for the authority to have the specific powers and duties set out in Sched.2, Part I to that Act. This imposes a duty on the local authority to take reasonable steps to identify the extent to which there are children in need in its area, which will involve the assessment of children in need (1989 Act, Sched.2, para.3). There is a discretion so that an individual does not have an absolute right to the provision of services under s.17(1) of the Act. It is up to the local authority to make a decision as to the priority to be given within the resources available to it.

The House of Lords further accepted the argument set out in *R (on the application of AB)* v. *Nottingham City Council* (2001) 4 CCLR 295, that assessment under s.17 must be done systematically, and that failure to do so can mean that the court can impose a mandatory order to do so (see paras.32 and 94 of the speeches of their Lordships).

This decision of the House of Lords therefore provides that whilst a mandatory order can be made to compel assessment, if services are to be provided to children, the claimant must point to a specific duty to take the step imposed elsewhere in the Act (or in other legislation) or must invalidate the local authority's decision to decline to take the step on the usual reasonableness and proportionality grounds available in judicial review (see para.135).

Some commentators (Clements *Community Care and the Law*, 3rd Edn (LAG, 2004) at pp.481–2) have argued that, in cases where an individual wishes to rely on the 1989 Act, s.17 it could be argued that it is fact specific, as the *Lambeth* case concerned services which were not provided under the 1989 Act, Sched.2 and had not been assessed as necessary by the local authority, and so if individuals could bring themselves within Sched.2 there is an argument that this creates a specific law duty.

11.6.3 Provision of accommodation

Section 20 of the 1989 Act imposes a mandatory duty on the authority to provide accommodation to children who have no one for whom parental responsibility could be accepted, or where the child is lost or abandoned, or where a person who has been caring for the child is prevented, on a temporary or permanent basis, from providing the child with suitable accommodation or care. The authority is also empowered to provide such care even if a person who has parental responsibility for the child is able to provide the child with accommodation, if the authority considers that to do so would safeguard or promote the child's welfare. Such accommodation may not be provided by the authority if someone has parental responsibility for the child, is willing and able to provide or arrange such accommodation, and that person objects. Individuals with parental responsibility for the child can remove the child at any time and the parent retains a right to decide where the child should live (*R* v. *Tameside MBC ex p J* [2000] 1 FLR 942).

11.7 PROVISION UNDER THE CHRONICALLY SICK AND DISABLED PERSONS ACT 1970, S.2

Section 2 of CSDPA 1970 provides that a local authority is under a duty to provide domiciliary and community services for disabled children by virtue of s.28A. Section 2 of CSDPA 1970 provides as follows:

> (1) Where a local authority are satisfied . . . that it is necessary in order to meet the needs of that person for that authority to make arrangement for all or any of the following matters, namely –
>
> (a) the provision of practical assistance for that person in his home;
> (b) the provision for that person of, or assistance to that person in obtaining, wireless, television, library or similar recreational facilities;
> (c) the provision for that person of lectures, games, outings or other recreational facilities outside his home or assistance to that person in taking advantage of educational facilities available to him;
> (d) the provision for that person of facilities for, or assistance in, travelling to and from his home for the purpose of participating in any services provided under any arrangements made by the authority, in any services provided otherwise than as aforesaid which are similar to services which could be provided under such arrangements;
> (e) the provision of assistance for that person in arranging for the carrying out of any works of adaptation in his home or the provision of any additional facilities designed to secure his greater safety, comfort or convenience;
> (f) facilitating the taking of holidays by that person, whether at holiday homes or others, and whether provided under arrangements made by the authority or otherwise . . .

> Then, it shall be the duty of the authority to make those arrangements in exercise of their functions.

This duty is mandatory in nature (*R* v. *Islington LBC ex p Rixon* (1997–98) 1 CCLR 119). In cases involving severely disabled children, services could be provided under CSDPA 1970, s.2, or the 1989 Act. In *R* v. *Bexley LBC ex p B* (2000) 3 CCLR 15, the court found that where services could be provided under either statute, but where the 'reality of the situation' means that services could properly be provided under CSDPA 1970, s.2(1) (by virtue of CSDPA 1970, s.28A and the National Health Service and Community Care Act 1990, s.47) then services will be provided under that statute and not under the more general 1989 Act duties (at 22E–22C).

11.7.1 Children and health care services

More severely disabled children will often receive services primarily through the NHS trust, sometimes as part of a pooled service under the Health Act 1999, s.31.

Unlike adults, a local authority could provide nursing provision to children under CSDPA 1970, s.2 (*R (on the application of Spink)* v. *Wandsworth LBC* [2005] EWCA Civ 302), as it is not specifically excluded by the Health and Social Care Act 2001, s.49. However, respite care for a child with complex medical needs requiring 24-hour care was not held to be care under CSDPA 1970, s.2 or the Children Act 1989, s.17 (*R (on the application of T, D and B)* v. *Haringey LBC* [2005] EWHC 2235) as nursing care should primarily be provided by the NHS, for the reasons set out in *R v. North and East Devon Health Authority ex p Coughlan* [2001] QB 213. The duties owed by the NHS trust to provide medical services for children are target duties (NHS Act 1977, ss.1 and 3). However, these duties can crystallise into mandatory duties if to fail to provide such services is a breach of the Human Rights Act 1998 (*R (on the application of T, D and B)* v. *Haringey LBC* above at paras.104–144).

11.8 CARERS AND DISABLED CHILDREN ACT 2000

11.8.1 Right to an assessment of the carer

People with parental responsibility for a disabled child are entitled to an assessment of their needs as carers under CDCA 2000, s.6. In practice, most authorities indicate that this assessment is encompassed within any core assessment of a disabled child; however, it is often the case that these core assessments ignore the full difficulties and/or do not fully explore the difficulties with the caring role experienced by many parents. In these circumstances, a separate carer's assessment could be requested.

The local authority is under a duty to consider the assessment and decide:

- whether or not the carer has needs in relation to the care which the carer provides or intends to provide;
- if so, whether the community care needs could be satisfied by services which the local authority may provide; and
- whether or not to provide services to the carer (CDCA 2000, s.2).

Such services are any services which will in the local authority's view help the carer care for the person cared for. A service may be provided to the carer, even if it takes the form of a service delivered to the person cared for (CDCA 2000, s. 2(3)(a)). The local authority must take this assessment into account when deciding whether or not to provide services for the disabled child under Part III of the 1989 Act (CDCA 2000, s.6(5)).

11.8.2 Guidance

Mandatory combined policy guidance on CDCA 2000 and the Carers (Equal Opportunities) Act 2004 was issued in August 2005 under LASSA 1970, s.7(1). **Paragraph 15.5.2** sets out in further detail the guidance issued under these Acts. The Carers (Equal Opportunities) Act 2004 creates a duty on authorities to inform carers of their right to an assessment, and must take into account the wish of a carer to work or participate in education and training. Furthermore, the Carers (Equal Opportunities) Act 2004 provides that where a local authority requests another public authority, such as education or health, to provide assistance in planning services for a carer, then the authority must give due consideration to that request. Paragraphs 71–90 deal with the needs of those caring for disabled children. The previous guidance (*Policy Guidance on Carers and Disabled Children* (DOH, March 2001)) was more detailed than that now issued and may be useful to set the context within which the legislation should work. In particular, the Carers (Equal Opportunities) Act 2004 and guidance makes it clear that the authority should not assume that a carer will continue to care, and must take account of a parent's wish to work or undertake education or training. For more detail on the Carers (Equal Opportunities) Act 2004, see **para.15.6**.

11.9 DIRECT PAYMENTS

Section 17A of the 1989 Act provides that local authorities may make direct payments to those with parental responsibility for a disabled child or to a disabled child if aged 16 or 17. Much of the law concerning direct payments for parents of disabled children is similar to that relating to carers in general and reference should be made to **para.15.8** and **para.4.9** for detailed guidance about the direct payment services.

The Government has published guidance on direct payments in both 2001 and 2003. These are the *Direct Payments for Young Disabled People Policy Guidance and Practice Guidance* (March 2001) which sets out the rationale behind such payments and the need for appropriate assessment. Further guidance can also be found in *Direct Payments Guidance: Community Care, Services for Carers and Children's Services (Direct Payments) Guidance England 2003* (September 2003) available from the Department of Health's website (**www.dh.gov.uk**) and the *Carers and Disabled Children Act 2000 and Carers (Equal Opportunities Act) 2004 Combined Policy Guidance* (published August 2005, and available from **www.dh.gov.uk**).

11.10 VOUCHER SCHEMES FOR SHORT-TERM BREAKS

Section 17B of the 1989 Act (as inserted by CDCA 2000, s.7(1)), enables local authorities to provide vouchers for those with parental responsibility of disabled children. A voucher is a document whereby if the authority agrees with the individual with parental responsibility that it would help to care for the child if that person had a break from caring, then the temporary provision of services under the 1989 Act, s.17 can be secured. Further detail on the operation of the voucher scheme, regulations and guidance issued are contained in **para.15.7**.

11.11 YOUNG CARERS

An individual can receive a carer's assessment under the Carers (Recognition and Services Act) 1995 at any age. Very often, young adults may be 'young carers' either for siblings or for older family members. Such individuals would also be considered 'children in need' under the 1989 Act (see further Vol.6 of the Department of Health guidance *Working Together* (to be revised sometime in 2006) headed 'Children with Disabilities'). The *Framework for the Assessment of Children in Need and their Families* (DOH, 2000) provides guidance on the assessment and needs of young carers (see paras.3.61–3.63 of the Framework Assessment) as does the *Carers and Disabled Children Act 2000 and Carers (Equal Opportunities Act) 2004 Combined Policy Guidance* at paras.9–14). Young carers are children in need for whom the local authority may provide services. The assessment and service provision is to be made for them as for other children. **Paragraph 15.4** contains additional detail.

11.12 HOMELESSNESS AND DISABLED CHILDREN

Section 17 of the Children Act 1989 provides a power for children to be provided with accommodation by children's services. However, the 1989 Act cannot be used to jump the queue if children have been assessed as requiring more suitable accommodation as there is no mandatory duty to provide such accommodation (see *R (on the application of A)* v. *Lambeth LBC* [2003] UKHL 57). However the 1989 Act, s.17(6) makes it explicitly clear that social services have the power to provide accommodation to such families if required. In LAC (2000) 13 the government guidance on this issue indicates that such accommodation can be provided to families or to lone children.

If a disabled child resides with someone who would usually be eligible for assistance as that person is homeless or threatened with homelessness, then they would be assessed as in priority need for such housing. Under the Housing Act 1996, s.213A the housing authority should refer all cases involving individuals under the age of 18 to social services. The *Homelessness Code of Guidance* (issued in 2002) provides that the housing authority can provide advice and assistance such as help locating suitable accommodation but the authority does not have to ensure that accommodation becomes available. **Chapter 14** provides further detail on this issue.

11.13 YOUNG ADULTS

11.13.1 Statutory provision for transition to adulthood

Transition from child to young adult is often a time of difficulty for parents with disabled children and children in need, as most social services departments divide their social work responsibility into children's and adult services. In order to prevent these difficulties, children's services have a series of statutory provisions to endeavour to ensure a smooth handover of responsibility.

The Children (Leaving Care) Act 2000 and the Children (Leaving Care) (England) Regulations 2001, SI 2001/2874 and the Welsh equivalent regulations in SI 2001/2189 (W.151), amend ss.22 and 23 of the 1989 Act and extend the duties owed to those 'accommodated' under s.20 or in care after a compulsory care order. Detailed guidance is provided and should be had regard to by local authorities on the duties owed. Although the Act is not retrospective, the Government has indicated that it should be administered to all care leavers, irrespective of when they entered the care system (*Children Act 1989: Guidance and Regulations*, Vol.3, Chapter 9: 'Family – After care: advice and assistance' and Vol.3, Chapter 7, Vol.6, Chapter 16: 'Children with Disabilities' and the 'Children Leaving Care Act Guidance' (Welsh Assembly – September 2001)).

11.13.2 The principles of the Children Act 1989

Any preparation for leaving care should take into account the principles of the 1989 Act in that:

- services for young people should take into account the lengthy process from childhood to adulthood;
- young people should be fully involved in discussions of their future;
- well before a young person leaves care, a continuing care plan should be formulated and parents or foster parents should be invited to help formulate the plan;
- preparation for leaving care should help develop a young person's capacity to make satisfactory relationships, develop his self-esteem and enable him to acquire the necessary practical skills for independent living;
- young people should be helped to develop socially and culturally;
- religious persuasion, racial origins and cultural background should be taken into account;
- multi-agency planning should be take place.

The guidance (*Children Act 1989: Guidance and Regulations*, Vol. 3 and Vol. 4 and *Working Together*) provides that the nature of preparation for leaving care is in order to enable young people to:

(a) build relationships;
(b) develop self-esteem; and
(c) teach practical skills.

11.13.3 The responsible authority

The responsible local authority is the authority where the child was looked after (*National Protocol: Interauthority Arrangements for Negotiating Support for Care Leavers Resident outside of their Responsible Authority* (LASSL (2004) 20).

11.13.4 Eligible children

Children under care orders leave care at 18, although very often care leavers will leave the care or accommodation system at 16. There is power to accommodate children up to the age of 21 if needed (1989 Act, s.20(5)). The authority is under a duty to advise, assist and befriend a child (1989 Act, Sched.2, para.19A) if the child is an 'eligible child' (i.e. the child is age 16 or 17 and has been looked after for a period of 13 weeks which started after the child's fourteenth birthday and ended after the child reached 16 (barring short-term placements of up to four weeks). In *R (on the application of Berhe)* v. *Hillingdon LBC* [2003] EWHC 2075, the court found that the test of eligibility is satisfied if the claimants are provided with accommodation under ss.20 or 17 of the 1989 Act. If they are eligible, then:

- they must have an assessment of their needs with a view to determining what advice, support and assistance they require;

- a pathway plan must be prepared and reviewed regularly (1989 Act, Sched.2, para.19B(5));
- a personal adviser must be arranged (1989 Act, Sched.2, para.19C).

11.13.5 Relevant children

Relevant children are those who are 16 and 17 and were looked after until the age of 16 or 17, unless they have lived with their parents for at least five months. The authority has a duty to do the following in this case:

- keep in touch and consider how to re-establish contact;
- appoint a personal adviser;
- carry out a needs assessment to determine what advice and assistance is necessary;
- prepare a pathway plan and review it regularly;
- maintain children and provide them with suitable accommodation.

A pathway plan must be prepared in line with the Children (Leaving Care) (England) Regulations 2001, SI 2001/2874 and must include a written statement.

11.13.6 Former relevant children

A former relevant child is an individual between 18 and 21 who would have been either a relevant or an eligible child under the age of 18. The full leaving care provision applies after 1 January 2002. If someone became a former relevant child on or before 1 January 2002, the authority is under a duty to prepare a pathway plan and keep in touch and appoint a personal adviser. This may include giving assistance, to the extent that the individual's welfare requires it by contributing to expenses incurred by that person in living near the place where employment is sought (1989 Act, s.23C(4)(a)) and to give assistance to the extent that the individual's welfare and educational and training needs require it by contributing to expenses incurred living near such education, or by making a grant to that person, or by giving assistance, including cash (1989 Act, s.23C(4)(c) and (7)).

11.13.7 Children with statement of SEN

The education department has to consult with social services to determine if an individual over the age of 14 who has a statement of special educational needs (SEN) pursuant to the Education Act 1996 (EA 1996), s.324 (see below) is likely to require support when that person leaves school (Disabled Persons (Services, Consultation and Representation) Act 1986, ss.5 and 6). The social services department should contribute to a transition plan at age 14 (pursuant to EA 1996, s.328 and the Education (Special Educational

Needs) (England) Regulations 2001, SI 2001/2216, and Welsh equivalent SI 2002/152 (W.20)). At this stage, the Connexions service is also required to attend a transition review and to prepare an appropriate transition plan.

If children are neither looked after nor have statements of SEN, then, even under the general *Children Act 1989: Guidance and Regulations* (para.5.4 of Vol.6) and the FACS guidance (LAC (2002) 13) there should be transitional arrangements for those entering adulthood.

Under the Learning and Skills Act 2000, s.140 all those with statements of SEN in their last year of school who are likely to transfer into the further education sector should be provided with assessments of their learning difficulties by the Learning and Skills Council. The role of the Connexions service in transition planning and delivery is set out at paras.9:51–9:58 of the SEN Code of Practice on Special Educational Needs.

The Connexions service provides support for all young people aged 13–19. Most children's educational needs will, after the age of 16, be met by the Learning and Skills Council operating under the Learning and Skills Act 2000. Connexions, through its personal advisers, often plays a large role in guiding children into appropriate educational placements after the age of 16.

11.14 EDUCATION

Children's services have responsibility for identifying those children with learning difficulties who live in the local authority's area under EA 1996, s.321. Those with learning difficulties are those who have a significantly greater difficulty in learning than the majority of children of their age or whose difficulty hinders them from making use of facilities generally provided in schools in the area by the local education authority (EA 1996, s.312(2)). Special educational provision is defined under s.312(4) as that which is additional to or different from educational provision made in mainstream LEA schools for those over the age of two, and for those under the age of two, 'educational provision of any kind'.

The LEA can provide a statutory assessment of a child's special educational needs if the LEA concludes that the child has, or probably has, SEN and that it is necessary to determine the child's SEN (EA 1996, s.323). Such assessment can lead to the issue of statement of SEN (under EA 1996, s.324). There is a detailed code for the procedures to be followed in this instance (the Education (Special Educational Needs) (England) (Consolidation) Regulations 2001, SI 2001/3455, and the SEN Code of Practice). The vast majority of children with SEN will have their needs met within schools, which are under duties to secure appropriate provision for children in school (EA 1996, ss.317–318) either at 'School Action' or 'School Action Plus'. A school must tell a parent if a child is on the SEN register (EA 1996, s.317A).

Parents have rights of appeal at various stages within the statutory process including:

(a) when there has been a refusal to make a statutory assessment (under EA 1996, ss.328 and 329);
(b) when there has been a refusal to issue a statement of SEN after a statutory assessment (EA 1996, s.325);
(c) against the contents of a statement of SEN (EA 1996, s.326);
(d) against a decision to cease to maintain a statement (EA 1996, Sched.27, para.11(2)(b));
(e) against the refusal of the LEA to change the name of a maintained mainstream school in a statement of SEN to another (EA 1996, Sched.27, para.8(3)(b)).

For further information about the SEN process, refer to Jackman, Hay and Wilkins *Practical Education Law* (Law Society Publishing, 2005), Richard McManus *Education and the Courts* (Jordan Publishing, 2004), and Oliver *Special Educational Needs and the Law* (Jordan Publishing, 2002).

11.15 CHARGING FOR CHILDREN'S SERVICES

Section 29 of the 1989 Act provides that the authority can recoup monies from users for services provided under ss.17 and 18 but not for advice, guidance and counselling (s.29(1)) (*R (on the application of Spink)* v. *Wandsworth LBC* [2005] EWCA Civ 302). That is, for those under the age of 16, their parents, and for those over the age of 16, the children themselves and if services are provided to a family member, then those family members (s.29(4)), will be financially assessed. No person can be charged if that person is in receipt of income support, family credit or income-based jobseeker's allowance (s.29(3)) or where the individual's means are insufficient to pay for the charge (s.29(2)). This is similar to the charging provision for adults and is considered in more detail in **Chapter 5**.

The only situation in which young adults may need to worry is if they have sufficient capital themselves, which may mean that they could not receive the appropriate benefits.

Schedule 2, Part III of the 1989 Act empowers the local authority to charge for the cost of accommodating children. The rules for such charges are the same as for services under the 1989 Act, s.17, save that the local authority cannot charge a sum greater than the sum that it would normally be prepared to pay if a similar child had been placed with local foster parents.

CHAPTER 12

The mentally ill

12.1 SECTION 117 OF THE MENTAL HEALTH ACT 1983

Services can be provided for certain mentally ill individuals in receipt of after-care under MHA 1983, s.117. Section 117(2) creates a joint duty on the PCT or health authority and social services to provide, in cooperation with relevant voluntary agencies, after-care services for certain mentally ill people, until such time as they are both satisfied that the after-care service is no longer required.

Detention occurs under MHA 1983 under prescribed procedures, although most people receive care and treatment in hospital on a voluntary or informal basis. All classes of person to whom s.117 extends are exceptionally vulnerable and must have been detained under one of the following sections, and cease to be detained and (whether or not immediately after so ceasing) leave hospital. The relevant sections of the MHA 1983 are as follows:

(a) s.3, which provides for the compulsory admission of a patient suffering from any mental disorder to hospital for treatment;
(b) s.37, where a 'hospital order' is made by the Crown Court or magistrates' court for a patient suffering from any mental disorder, who has been convicted of an imprisonable offence ordering the person to be detained in a hospital, or the court has placed the person under the guardianship of social services or a person approved by social services;
(c) s.45A, where the Crown Court has made a 'hospital direction' to transfer the person to a named hospital for treatment instead of a term of imprisonment. The individual must be suffering from a psychopathic disorder;
(d) a 'transfer direction' made under ss.47 or 48 by the Secretary of State to transfer the person who is in prison, on remand, a civil prisoner or detained under the Immigration Act 1971. The individual must be suffering from any mental disorder under s.47 or from a mental illness or severe mental impairment under s.48.

12.2 MENTAL HEALTH (PATIENTS IN THE COMMUNITY) ACT 1995

The Mental Health Act 1983 was amended by the Mental Health (Patients in the Community) Act 1995, with the insertion of ss.25A–25J. The aim was to ensure that mentally ill patients living in the community were subject to supervision after their discharge from detention under MHA 1983, which is known as 'supervised discharge'. *Guidance on Supervised Discharge (After-care under Supervision) and Related Provisions* has been issued (HSG (96) 11, LAC (96) 8, WHC (96) 11). Chapter 28 of the *Code of Practice to the Mental Health Act* (1999) contains detailed guidance on supervised discharge and states that its purpose is to help ensure that the patient receives after-care services under MHA 1983, s.117 (see **para.12.3.3** below). It is available for patients suffering from any form of mental disorder but is primarily intended for those with severe mental illness, to prevent substantial risk of serious harm to themselves or other people, or of serious exploitation, and who must have been detained under ss.3, 37, 47 or 48 (28.2–28.3 of the Code). Whilst the patient is under supervised discharge that individual must receive after-care services (s.117(2)). The health authority/PCT must ensure that the patient has a community 'responsible medical officer' (RMO) and a professionally qualified supervisor to ensure that the patient receives the after-care services (s.117(2A); 28.4 of the Code). After-care under supervision ends completely if the patient is admitted to hospital under ss.3 or 37, and there are special rules on suspension of after-care (28.8 of the Code).

12.3 SERVICES AND ACCOMMODATION

12.3.1 What are 'after-care services'?

There is no definition of the term 'after-care services' in MHA 1983. In *Clunis* v. *Camden and Islington Health Authority* [1998] QB 978, 992 Beldam LJ commented 'They would normally include social work support, support in helping the ex-patient with problems of employment, accommodation or family relationships, the provision of domiciliary services and the use of day centre and residential facilities.' It falls on the appropriate authority to determine what are after-care services, within the framework of the care plan, which should occur before discharge (27.10f). In *R* v. *Ealing District Health Authority ex p Fox* [1993] 3 All ER 170, the court held that health authorities and social services must take reasonable steps to identify appropriate after-care facilities for a patient before actual discharge from hospital. The duty of the health authority is to use its best endeavours to procure compliance with conditions laid down by the Mental Health Review Tribunal in respect of a supervised discharge (*R (on the application of IH)* v. *Secretary of State for the Home Department* [2004] 1 All ER 412).

12.3.2 Care Programme Approach and after-care

The *National Service Framework for Mental Health: Modern Standards and Service Models for Mental Health* (HSC 1999/223 and published in Wales in April 2002) addresses the mental health needs of adults up to the age of 65. It sets out national standards and service models, local action and programmes for implementation with milestones to assure progress, with performance indicators to support effective performance management. It also includes an organisational framework for providing and commissioning services.

Standard 2 sets out that service users who contact their primary health care team should have their mental health needs identified and assessed. They should be able to make contact round the clock with the local services necessary to meet their needs and receive adequate care (Standard 3). All mental health service users should be assessed using the Care Programme Approach (CPA).

The after-care arrangements should be drawn up as part of the discharge planning process, following the principles of the CPA. The CPA was introduced in 1991 to provide a framework for assessing, planning and implementing effective mental health care. It is embodied in Circular HC (90) 23, LASSL (90) 11, and in the Welsh Office Mental Illness Strategy (WHC (95) 40). The most recent guidance was published in January 1999 in England entitled *Effective Care Co-ordination in Mental Health Services: Modernising the Care Programme Approach – A Policy Booklet* and in Wales *Mental Health Policy Wales Implementation Guidance: The Care Programme Approach for Mental Health Service Users* (February 2003) and *Adult Mental Health Services in Wales: Equity, Empowerment, Effectiveness, Efficiency: A Strategy Document* (2001). The Welsh guidance is broadly the same as the English guidance, although they aim to be integrated within the Unified Assessment Process.

The 1999 guidance sets out four main elements of the CPA.

1. Systematic arrangements for assessing the health and social needs of people accepted into specialist mental health services.
2. The formulation of a care plan which identifies the health and social care required from a variety of providers.
3. The appointment of a key worker to keep in close touch with the service user and to monitor and coordinate care.
4. Regular review and, where necessary, agreed changes to the care plan.

There are two levels of CPA set out in paras.57–58 of the guidance.

Those on the standard CPA will include some of the following characteristics.

1. They require the support or intervention of one agency or discipline or they require only low key support from more than one agency or discipline.

2. They are more able to self-manage their mental health problems.
3. They have an active informal support network.
4. They pose little danger to themselves or others.
5. They are more likely to maintain appropriate contact with services.

Those on the enhanced CPA are likely to have some of the following characteristics.

1. They have multiple care needs, including housing, employment, etc. requiring inter-agency coordination.
2. They are only willing to cooperate with one professional agency but they have multiple care needs.
3. They may be in contact with a number of agencies (including the criminal justice system).
4. They are likely to require more frequent and intensive interventions, perhaps with medication requirements.
5. They are more likely to have mental health problems coexisting with other problems such as substance misuse.
6. They are more likely to be at risk of harming themselves or others.
7. They are more likely to disengage with services.

Those on supervised discharge should be on the enhanced level of CPA.

CPA and the Single Assessment Process

For older people to whom the CPA is applicable, the Single Assessment Process for older people (SAP) is the multidisciplinary assessment required under the CPA, but the care coordinator will usually be a mental health professional unless there is another person who is better placed to undertake this role. In Wales the CPA is integrated into the Unified Assessment Process. (See **Chapter 3** on assessments.) The Department of Health issued a clarification note *Care Management for Older People with Serious Mental Health Problems* (July 2002) which provides:

1. The CPA should be applied to older people with severe mental illness due to schizophrenia or other psychosis. The assessment of their needs should be based on the SAP.
2. SAP plus critical aspects of the CPA should be applied to other older people with severe functional or organic mental health problems, who were they younger would be provided for under CPA.
3. When individuals subject to CPA reach old age, switches to SAP are not inevitable, and should only be made in the best interests of individuals and the continuity of their care.

The responsible authorities

The health authority and the social services authority responsible for the after-care is determined by the area in which the patient is resident or to which the individual is sent on discharge by the hospital in which he was detained (MHA 1983, s.117(3)). In *R* v. *Mental Health Review Tribunal ex p Hall* [2000] 1 WLR 1323 the Court of Appeal confirmed that the health and social services authorities where the patient was resident at the time of admission to hospital have legal responsibility for providing after-care under s.117.

12.3.3 After-care and the MHA Code of Practice

The Secretary of State issued guidance on MHA 1983 in a Code of Practice (April 1999), which is also contained in LAC (99) 11, HSC (99) 50. The Code should be followed unless there is good reason not to (*R (on the application of Munjaz)* v. *Mersey Care NHS Trust* [2005] UKHL 58). Chapters 27 and 28 of the Code relate to s.117.

The Code makes it clear that the purpose of after-care is to equip patients to cope with life outside hospital and function there successfully without danger to themselves or other people and so avoid unnecessary readmission (27.1). The RMO (in consultation with relevant parties) should ensure that the patient's needs for health and social care are fully assessed and the care plan addresses them (27.5). The issues that should be considered in agreeing after-care services are set out in 27.10, including the need for daytime activities or employment; appropriate accommodation; outpatient treatment; counselling and personal support; assistance in welfare rights and managing finances and a contingency plan in case the patient relapses. Any care plan should be in writing and reviewed regularly (27.11 and 27.12). The Code sets out who should be involved in consideration of the patient's after-care needs. They arguably should also be consulted for any discharge from s.117. Consultees include the patient, if the patient wishes, and/or a nominated representative; the patient's RMO; a social worker/care manager specialising in mental health work; and a community psychiatric/mental health nurse (27.8). Owing to the statutory obligation all patients who are subject to s.117 should be identified and records kept of them (27.3).

In respect of supervised discharge, the RMO must consult with the current and the proposed future care team about the arrangements for after-care and the requirements to be imposed. They should ensure that agreement about a care plan is reached. Details of the after-care services must be attached to the supervision application with a list of the imposed requirements, which also names the supervisor and RMO (28.7).

12.3.4 Unlawful charging

The Department of Health has consistently taken the view that health authorities and social services should not charge for services provided under MHA 1983, s.117 (*Advice Note for Use by Social Services Inspectorate* (January 1994)); however, despite this the majority of social services have charged. The House of Lords confirmed that local authorities have no statutory basis to charge for such services and the cost should be met by health and social services. (See *R* v. *Redcar and Cleveland BC ex p Armstrong; R* v. *Manchester City Council ex p Stennett; R* v. *Harrow LBC ex p Cobham* [2002] 4 All ER 124.) The effect of HSC (2000) 3, LAC (2000) 3, para.3, is that the authorities must have an agreed policy and criteria showing which authority will finance each after-care service.

12.3.5 The end of s.117 funding

After-care services do not have to continue indefinitely. They should continue until, after a joint assessment, the health authority and social services are satisfied that the person is no longer in need of after-care services. It is for the authority providing the particular services to take the lead in deciding when those services are no longer required. The patient, the patient's carer and other agencies should always be consulted (MHA 1983, s.117(2); LAC/HSC (2000) 3, para.4).

Funding can end if the patient is no longer in need of mental health care but, in practice, this is believed to affect very few patients. In *R* v. *Richmond upon Thames LBC ex p Watson* (1999) *The Times*, 15 October, Sullivan J said:

> There may be cases where, in due course, there will be no need for aftercare services for the person's mental condition, but he or she will still need social service provision for other needs, for example, physical disability. Such cases will have to be examined individually on their facts, through the assessment process provided for by section 47 [of the National Health Service and Community Care Act 1990]. In a case such as Mrs Watson where the illness is dementia, it is difficult to see how such a situation could arise in practice.

It is always worthwhile obtaining medical opinion from the RMO as it is often found that the RMO has not been consulted in the decision to end funding. In the event that the patient is still in need of mental health care, even though the patent is stable and settled, then arguably the patient should still be in receipt of the after-care service.

12.3.6 Retrospective reviews

Following the *Stennett* case, the Local Government Ombudsman investigated a number of complaints where social services were retrospectively assessing individuals and removing them from s.117. (See the special report on s.117 cases at **www.lgo.org.uk/special-reports.htm** (July 2003).) The special report contained the following general advice.

1. Social services should not carry out retrospective assessments purporting to remove a person from s.117 after-care as from an earlier date.
2. Any retrospective assessments should be reviewed.
3. Where previous assessments to end s.117 after-care were not properly made, then restitution is appropriate until a proper assessment is undertaken.
4. People who have paid for s.117 after-care should receive financial restitution with interest.
5. Mechanisms should be put in place to identify those persons improperly charged, or improperly deprived of financial assistance, and establish arrangements for reimbursing them or their estates.
6. No general cut-off date should be used when calculating repayments.

12.4 THE MENTAL HEALTH BILL

The Government plans to reform MHA 1983 and has published a draft Mental Health Bill, which has gone through the process of pre-legislative scrutiny. A new Code of Practice will underpin the legislation. The definition of mental disorder will be simpler but wider. Section 117 will be repealed with no equivalent provision made. Limited provision is available in clause 68 of the Bill, as for the first six weeks after discharge from hospital the patient will not be charged for services he receives. This is in line with the provision of intermediate care services (see **para.8.4.1**).

12.5 OTHER COMMUNITY CARE PROVISIONS

An individual suffering from a mental health problem, although not eligible for assessment under the CPA, is still entitled to an assessment for community care services under the National Health Service and Community Care Act 1990, s.47 (*R (on the application of HP)* v. *Islington LBC* (2005) 82 BMLR 113). Non-residential services can be provided under CSDPA 1970, s.2 and the 1977 Act, Sched.8. Residential services can be provided under the National Assistance Act 1948, s.21.

12.6 THE BOURNEWOOD GAP

12.6.1 What is the Bournewood gap?

R v. *Bournewood Community and Mental Health NHS Trust ex p L* [1999] 1 AC 458 has had a major impact on the detention of compliant but mentally incapable individuals for the purposes of consenting or objecting to mental health treatment. The case concerned an autistic man ('L') who was taken to hospital and detained without formal compulsion procedures, as these were felt by the treating doctor to be unnecessary as L was compliant, did not resist admission or make any attempt to leave. As such he was admitted as an 'informal patient' under MHA 1983, s.131 in his best interests under the common law doctrine of necessity.

L's carers were denied the ability to visit him and were told that he would be released only when the health care professionals deemed it appropriate. He was kept under continuous observation. Without formal detention neither L nor his representatives were afforded the right to appeal and have the protection of MHA 1983.

A relative sought judicial review of the decision and following the Court of Appeal's decision that L was unlawfully detained, he was formally detained. L was released six weeks later, once it was established that his mental disorder was not of a nature or degree to warrant continued detention in hospital, nor necessary for his health or safety or for the protection of others. The House of Lords overturned the earlier judgment enabling compliant people such as L to be informally detained but without any ability to challenge it, so creating the 'Bournewood gap'.

The case was taken to the European Court of Human Rights which held that L had been deprived of his liberty in breach of Art.5(1) of the European Convention on Human Rights. The absence of procedural safeguards failed to protect against arbitrary deprivations of liberty on grounds of necessity and so there had been a violation of Art.5(1), and there was no available procedure to review the decision, which was a breach of Art.5(4).

The judgment relates to deprivation of liberty and not treatment generally of incapacitated people and its impact will depend on the circumstances of each case. Deprivation of liberty is determined by considering the type of deprivation (such as being detained in hospital), the duration, its effects (such as a decline in mental health) and the manner in which the detention is implemented. The distinction between a deprivation of, and restriction upon, liberty is one of degree or intensity and not one of nature or substance (see para.89 of the judgment). L was deprived of his liberty as the health care professionals had exercised complete and effective control over him.

12.6.2 The Bournewood gap and the Mental Capacity Act 2005

Interim advice was given by the Department of Health in December 2004 (available from **www.dh.gov.uk**). It announced the Government's intention to bring forward plans to close the gap. The aim was that the Mental Capacity Act 2005 would fill this gap but it is doubtful whether it will provide the solution, particularly as the 2005 Act is not planned to be brought into force until spring 2007, at the earliest.

The Act allows the Court of Protection to determine questions of where an incapacitated individual should live as well as any medical treatment that person should or should not receive. An Independent Mental Capacity Advocate (IMCA) may be appointed in limited situations when doctors are proposing 'to provide serious medical treatment' (such term to be defined in later Regulations), or when the NHS or social services intend to provide a change of accommodation and the individual is unbefriended (see **para.16.8**). If the individual concerned has another person interested in his care and treatment, such as a family member or friend, then the IMCA cannot act.

It will be left to families and friends to challenge any proposed decision, although unlike appeals to the Mental Health Review Tribunals, legal aid is not automatic and many families may be put off from funding a case, particularly those who have limited assets. It is unclear how emergency applications will be dealt with and there may be delays in bringing any matter to the court. During this time the individual may need decisions to be made without agreement of what is in the patient's best interest.

Although the Act has power for the court to request reports, there are no safeguards, which currently exist in MHA 1983, for second clinical opinions sought in the event of the planned use of specified serious treatment, such as electro-convulsive therapy. The Court of Protection will wherever possible make single orders and the process does not allow for the monitoring of care and treatment in hospital or when planning discharge and future care.

The Department of Health has consulted on its proposals for closing the gap and at the time of writing no response has been published. The proposals centre on either extending guardianship under MHA 1983 and/or creating a status of 'protective care', governed by the Mental Capacity Act 2005.

CHAPTER 13

The vulnerable adult

The title of this chapter, 'the vulnerable adult', is intended to cover the wide-ranging disabilities and frailties that affect the general population, including older people, learning disabled, physically disabled, drug and alcohol misusers and those suffering from AIDS. Although other chapters of this book focus on specific groups such as those suffering from mental illnesses, asylum seekers and carers, this chapter expands on aspects of health and service provision that will affect all vulnerable adults.

13.1 NATIONAL SERVICE FRAMEWORKS

National Service Frameworks (NSFs) are part of the Department of Health's and the Welsh Assembly's long-term agenda to improve specific areas of care, so that regional variations are reduced. The NSF commonly set national standards and identify key interventions for a defined service or care group. The English NSFs are available on the Department of Health's website (**www.dh.gov.uk**) and in Wales at the Welsh NHS website (**www.wales.nhs.uk**).

There are now a number of NSFs which relate to vulnerable adults, in particular the following.

1. 'Mental health' sets out how mental health services are to be planned, delivered and monitored until 2009. It lists seven standards that set targets for the mental health care of adults aged up to 65. These standards span five areas: health promotion and stigma; primary care and access to specialist services; the needs of those with severe and enduring mental illness; carers' needs; and suicide reduction.
2. 'Older people' sets eight national standards and service models of care across health and social services for all older people, whether they live at home, in a care home or are being cared for in hospital. The aim is to root out age discrimination, create systems of person-centred care, improve general hospital care, improve prevention and care in relation to strokes, falls and mental health, promote good health and an active life in older age and promote access to intermediate care services.

3. 'Long-term conditions' was published in England on 10 March 2005. The aim of the NSF is to improve the lives of people who live with neurological and other long-term conditions by providing them with better health and social care services.

An NSF exists for children, which sets standards for children's health and social services, and the interface of those services with education. There is no NSF for people with learning disabilities; however, there are a number of important strategy and policy documents that have been published in England.

1. The White Paper *Valuing People: A New Strategy for Learning Disability for the 21st Century* (Cm 5086, March 2001).
2. Mandatory implementation guidance issued in HSC 2001/16, LAC (2001) 23, which sets out the responsibility of Learning Disability Partnership Boards within each local authority area which has responsibility for overseeing and advising on implementing the White Paper's proposals of 'rights, independence, choice and inclusion'. It makes it clear that those with Asperger's Syndrome or higher functioning autism should not be excluded from services, where appropriate.
3. Additional guidance issued in December 2001 *Planning with People – Towards Person-centred Approaches: Guidance For Partnership Boards* and *Guidance for Implementation Groups*.

More information can be obtained from the Valuing People website (**www.valuingpeople.gov.uk**).

13.2 ACCOMMODATION UNDER S.21 OF THE NATIONAL ASSISTANCE ACT 1948

Consideration of when this duty arises and in respect of which client group an individual might fall within is covered separately at **para.2.5.1**. The position of asylum seekers is considered in detail in **Chapter 14**.

13.2.1 The nature of the accommodation that can be provided

Section 21(1)(a) of the National Assistance Act 1948 provides that a local authority is under a duty, by virtue of directions made by the Secretary of State to provide residential accommodation for those who are aged 18 or over who by reason of age, illness, disability or any other circumstances are in need of care and attention which is not otherwise available to them (LAC (93) 10). Usually such accommodation is provided in a care home setting, although it can be provided in ordinary housing, which could otherwise be provided under the housing legislation. In *R* v. *Newham LBC ex p Medical*

Foundation for the Care of Victims of Torture (1997–98) 1 CCLR 227, the High Court held that the word 'residential' meant no more than 'accommodation where a person lives'. Accommodation without board or services may be provided, which will depend on the circumstances of the case, but can be provided when it would be the answer to a need which would otherwise have to be met by other community care services (*R* v. *Bristol City Council ex p Penfold* (1997–98) 1 CCLR 315). Indeed, a refusal for accommodation under the housing legislation does not preclude the individual from being provided residential accommodation under the National Assistance Act 1948, s.21 (as in the *Penfold* case). As a consequence there have been a number of cases where individuals who had previously been denied accommodation under the housing legislation have used the community care legislation as a means to obtain the accommodation sought (*R* v. *Kensington and Chelsea RLBC ex p Kujtim* [1999] 4 All ER 161; *R* v. *Wigan MBC ex p Tammadge* (1997–98) 1 CCLR 581 and *R* v. *Islington LBC ex p Batantu* (2001) 4 CCLR 445). However in all these cases there still needs to be established that the person has an eligible community care need, which the local authority is under a duty to meet. For example, in the *Batantu* case, the claimant had an existing mental health problem. If social services refer the matter to the housing department for provision, the duty to provide remains with social services to make arrangements to meet the eligible needs (as in the *Batantu* case). If there is to be a delay in provision, social services must make interim arrangements which will meet the assessed need. There is an exclusion from accommodation being available under s.21(1)(a) for asylum seekers, which is considered further in detail in **Chapter 14** (s.21(1A)).

13.2.2 Care and attention

The term 'care and attention' is not defined in the legislation, although the courts appear to interpret it widely. In *R* v. *Hammersmith and Fulham LBC ex p M; R* v. *Lambeth LBC ex p P and X; R* v. *Westminster City Council ex p A* (1997–98) 1 CCLR 85, the Court of Appeal held that s.21(1)(a) of the National Assistance Act 1948 was not a safety net on which anyone who was short of money or accommodation could rely. However, the applicants who were all refused asylum and were destitute qualified under s.21(1)(a) because of the effect on them of the problems under which they were labouring. In addition to their lack of food and accommodation was their inability to speak the language, their lack of knowledge of Britain and the fact they had been subject to the stress of coming to Britain in circumstances that involved contending they were refugees.

Section 21(1A) of the National Assistance Act 1948 provides that where a person to whom the Immigration and Asylum Act 1999, s.115 applies (exclusion from benefits), he is precluded from the provision of residential accommodation where the need for care and attention has arisen solely because he is destitute or because of the physical effects, or anticipated physical effects, of being destitute. This should be construed so that where the need for care and attention is to any material extent made more acute by some circumstance, other than the mere lack of accommodation and funds, then, subject to an assessment of needs, the individual should qualify for assistance (*R* v. *Wandsworth LBC ex p O; R* v. *Leicester City Council ex p Bhikha* [2000] 1 WLR 2539; *R (on the application of Mani)* v. *Lambeth LBC* [2003] EWCA Civ 836; *R (on the application of M)* v. *Slough BC* [2004] EWHC 1109 (Admin). A failed asylum seeker who satisfies the criteria of s.21(1) and (1A) will be entitled to accommodation provided by the local authority to avoid a breach of the individual's rights under the European Convention on Human Rights (*R (on the application of AW)* v. *Croydon LBC;* [2005] EWHC 2950, QB). Further consideration of asylum seekers is set out at **para.14.5**.

Section 21 requires a need for care and attention which would only be met if the accommodation were provided. In *R (on the application of Wahid)* v. *Tower Hamlets LBC* [2002] EWCA Civ 287, the court defined the need for care and attention as meaning needing to be 'looked after' and it can take the form of food and a home. Needing to be looked after is not in itself reason to qualify; however if the claimant is likely to require care and attention because of lack of housing which could make him ill or disabled, then he could qualify.

13.2.3 Not otherwise available

The obligation for social services to provide accommodation only arises when the care and attention that a person needs is not otherwise available to that person and is a duty of last resort (*Steane* v. *Chief Adjudication Officer* (1997–98) 1 CCLR 538, HL). In deciding whether a person is in need of care and attention that is not otherwise available to him, the local authority must disregard so much of the person's capital as does not exceed the capital limit for the purposes of the National Assistance Act 1948, s.22 (s.21(2A)): *R* v. *Sefton MBC ex p Help the Aged* [1997] 4 All ER 532). Having in excess of the prescribed limit is considered at **para.4.13**.

13.2.4 Types of care homes

Social services can make residential accommodation arrangements provided by themselves or another local authority (s.21(4)), a voluntary organisation (s.26(1)) or a 'provider for reward' (s.26(1)). The majority of provision is now made in private care homes and, to a lesser extent, voluntary care homes (Laing & Buisson's annual update: *Care of Elderly People – UK Market Report 2005*).

Care homes still refer to themselves as residential, nursing, or mental nursing homes although the Care Standards Act 2000 (CSA 2000) refers to all such homes as 'care homes', which have different conditions attached to their registration. A care home is defined as such under CSA 2000, s.3(1) if it provides accommodation with nursing or personal care for persons:

(a) who are or have been ill;
(b) who are or have had a mental disorder;
(c) who are disabled or infirm; or
(d) who are or have been dependent on alcohol or drugs.

All care homes are regulated by the CSCI in England and the CSIW in Wales. **Chapter 17** contains more information about the Commission and the regulation of care homes. Choice of accommodation and charging for care homes is covered at **para.5.2**.

13.3 CLOSURE OF CARE HOMES

13.3.1 Reasons for home closures

Capacity across all care home sectors is 100,000 places lower than the peak in 1996. An estimated 582 independent sector care homes with 12,792 places closed during the year to 1 April 2005 – about the same rate as in the previous year, but well below the peak of 800 closures (17,000 places) in 2000 (Laing & Buisson, 2005). This has had an impact on choice of accommodation for both the self-funding client and for those funded by the State.

The reasons for home closures are complex, but care homes are struggling with increased regulation, problems in recruitment and retention of staff, increase in overheads and restrictions in what local authorities will pay for care beds. Attempts to challenge the fees that the local authority will pay have not been successful in the courts (*R* v. *Coventry City Council ex p Coventry Heads of Independent Care Establishments* (1997–98) 1 CCLR 379 and *R (on the application of Birmingham Care Consortium)* v. *Birmingham City Council* (2002) 5 CCLR 600).

Bed occupancy is running at nearly 92 per cent (Laing & Buisson, 2005) and so as demand exceeds supply in some areas, it restricts choice. In a home that only takes self-funding residents, an increase in demand would usually result in an increase in the charge for the bed, and for this reason proprietors are known to ask residents to leave once their assets fall to be means tested if the local authority will not pay a higher rate for the care bed. Alternatively, they may only accept local authority assisted residents who have the benefit of a third party willing to make a financial contribution towards the cost of care. Some care homes charge one rate for self-funding clients and another lower rate for local authority funded residents – in effect it is a cross-subsidy, which enables care homes to continue to operate.

Demand has reduced for care homes with a greater emphasis on supported living and the provision of non-residential care services. However, care home demand may start increasing again. The Government Actuary's recent long-term population projection indicates demand across all sectors increasing from 439,000 residents in 2005 to 1,100,000 residents by the middle of the 21st century (**www.gad.gov.uk/Population/Index.asp**).

13.3.2 Moving vulnerable residents

Moving vulnerable people, in particular those who are old and frail, who have been in a care home for some years, may cause at best extreme stress, or at worse their premature death. There have been a number of well-publicised cases of this happening and reference should be made to the Gloucestershire Council's report *Scrutiny Inquiry into Care Homes* following the death of Violet Townsend (23 July 2003), which made recommendations to the Department of Health to alert them to the reasons for home closures (available on their website **www.gloucestershire.gov.uk**).

There is no guidance for social services on this type of situation but the NHS Executive issued Good Practice Guidance in April 1998 on the procedure for transferring frail older NHS patients to other long-stay settings (HSC 1998/048). This is available from the Department of Health's website (**www.dh.gov.uk**). Social services can follow the HSC but they are not bound to have regard to it (*R (on the application of Dudley)* v. *East Sussex CC* [2003] EWHC 1093 (Admin)).

Prior to any move there should be wide consultation, a flexible project plan and residents should be assessed individually, with a care plan drawn up. Ideally, moves should not take place in winter or at the weekend and friends should be moved together. If residents are unfit to move, then the transfer should be delayed or halted until such time as they are fit. The Gloucestershire Inquiry recommended introducing realistic timetables for moves, and communicating with and providing comprehensive advice and information to family members and carers. This should enable them to be kept up to date with the situation, and ensure that they have information on the complaints procedure and availability of advocacy services.

13.3.3 The need to consult and assess residents

Before the local authority makes the final decision to close one of its care homes it must adequately consult residents. Concern has been raised about areas where there are no longer any council-run homes. The local authority only has to ensure that there is adequate provision in its area, irrespective of which organisation is providing the care (*R* v. *Wandsworth LBC ex p Beckwith (No.1)* [1996] 1 All ER 129). The consultation should occur when proposals are at a formative stage, and it must include reasons, adequate time for responses should be allowed, and these responses should be taken into account in the final decision (*R* v. *Brent LBC ex p Gunning* (1986) 84 LGR 168). The decision to close a home without consultation of residents on the closure and the move to a new home may render the decision unlawful (*R* v. *Devon CC ex p Baker; R* v. *Durham CC ex p Curtis* [1995] 1 All ER 73). A specialist assessment is not necessary when deciding to close a home, unless the residents are particularly vulnerable, such as those who are learning disabled (*R (on the application of Phillips)* v. *Walsall MBC* (2002) 5 CCLR 383 and *R* v. *Merton, Sutton and Wandsworth Health Authority ex p P* [2001] Lloyds Rep Med 73).

13.3.4 Legitimate expectation of a home for life

In *R* v. *North and East Devon Health Authority ex p Coughlan* [2001] QB 213, the Court of Appeal held that the health authority had made a promise to the resident which induced a legitimate expectation of a substantive right or benefit, in that the home would be the resident's for life. The promise could be broken only if an overriding public interest required it (para.52). The decision to close the home and so frustrate the resident's expectation was so unfair that it amounted to an abuse of power, which was in breach of Art.8 (the right to family life) of the European Convention on Human Rights. As such, the promise bound the health authority. Whether a statement amounts to a promise depends on what the ordinary resident would think that the promise was trying to convey (*R (on the application of B)* v. *Camden LBC* [2002] 63 BMLR 154). The promise should however be 'clear and unequivocal' (*R (on the application of Phillips)* v. *Walsall MBC* (2002) 5 CCLR 383).

However in *R (on the application of C)* v. *Brent, Kensington and Chelsea and Westminster Mental Health NHS Trust* [2002] Lloyd's Rep Med 321, *R (on the application of Cowl)* v. *Plymouth City Council* [2002] 1 WLR 803, *R (on the application of Dudley)* v. *East Sussex CC* [2003] EWHC 1093 (Admin), the homes closed as there had been consultation with representation of residents, assessments and care plans occurred and there was no finding of a promise of a home for life being substantiated by evidence. In the *Cowl* case the Court of Appeal held that the courts should not permit, except for good reason, proceedings for judicial review to go ahead if a significant part of the issues between the parties could be resolved outside the litigation process. The lawyers on both sides were under a heavy obligation to resort to litigation only if it was really unavoidable.

13.3.5 Independent home closures

Independent home closures are not usually amendable to judicial review as was highlighted in the cases of *R (on the application of Heather)* v. *Leonard Cheshire Foundation* [2002] 2 All ER 936 and *R* v. *Servite Houses ex p*

Goldsmith [2001] BLGR 55. These cases are distinguished from *R (on the application of A)* v. *Partnerships in Care Ltd* [2002] 1 WLR 2610, where the decision of the managers of a private psychiatric hospital to alter the care and treatment of a patient was held to be an act of a public nature and as such was susceptible to judicial review.

13.3.6 Human rights issues

Closure of a home may evoke challenges of infringement of human rights under the European Convention on Human Rights, in particular, the right to life (Art.2), the right not to be subjected to torture, inhuman or degrading treatment (Art.3) and right to family life (Art.8). Arguments of Art.8 infringement have been more successful in the courts (*R* v. *North and East Devon Health Authority ex p Coughlan* [2001] QB 213 and *R (on the application of Madden)* v. *Bury MBC* [2002] EWHC 1882 (Admin)).

Articles 2 and 3 arguments have not been successful (*R (on the application of Dudley)* v. *East Sussex CC* [2003] EWHC 1093 (Admin)). In *R (on the application of Haggerty)* v. *St Helens Council* (2003) *The Times*, 30 April the High Court held that there was no evidence that the risk to the claimants' lives by the planned move would reach the level needed to engage Art.2. There was a high threshold to be reached before Art.3 was engaged. The obligation on the public authority to take measures to protect citizens from breaches of Arts.2 and 3 is limited, in that the obligation must not impose an 'impossible or disproportionate obligation on the authorities' (*Osman* v. *UK* (2000) 29 EHRR 245). The public body's financial resources are an important element to be considered in the balancing exercise required in the application of Art.8(2).

13.4 HEALTH AND SAFETY ISSUES

There are health and safety risks for users of health and social care services, and for those that provide care for them. The legislative framework is aimed at protecting the employee, with guidance being aimed at the service user. Both, however, focus on balancing the risk with the need to undertake the work while limiting safety concerns.

13.4.1 The legislative framework

Employers, whether proprietors of care homes or community-based services have a general duty to ensure, so far as is reasonably practicable, the health, safety and welfare at work of their employees and others who may be affected by their work activities (Health and Safety at Work etc. Act 1974). There are a number of Regulations which impact on the issue of health and safety of staff.

1. The Manual Handling Operations Regulations 1992, SI 1992/2793, require employers to avoid hazardous manual handling operations, so far as is reasonably practicable. Manual handling is defined in reg.2 as 'any transporting or supporting of a load (including the lifting, putting down, pushing, pulling, carrying or moving thereof) by hand or by bodily force'. In the event that manual handling cannot be avoided, employers should assess the hazard involved in the task and take measures to reduce the risk, so far as practicable (reg.4).
2. The Management of Health and Safety at Work Regulations 1999, SI 1999/3242, require employers to assess the risks to employees and others who may be affected by the work they are required to carry out.
3. The Control of Substances Hazardous to Health Regulations 2002, SI 2002/2677, require employers to prevent or control exposure to hazardous substances at work. Hazardous substances include cleaning chemicals and potentially harmful biological agents contained in clinical waste or soiled laundry.

13.4.2 Guidance for health and social care providers

The Health and Safety Executive has produced various guidance.

Scalding risks

Scalding Risks from Hot Water in Health and Social Care guidance is available from the Health and Safety Executive website (**www.hse.gov.uk**).

Social inclusion and elective risk

Social Services: Social Inclusion and Elective Risk advice in SIM 07/2000/08 explains the priorities which social services have for promoting social inclusion of clients into the community and the need for such clients to be allowed to take elective risks (available from **www.hse.gov.uk**).

General health and safety issues in care homes

Guidance in *Health and Safety in Residential Care Homes* (HS(G) 104), is available from HSE Books, PO Box 1999, Sudbury, Suffolk CO10 2WA. Tel: 01787 881165. The guidance is extensive and is beyond the remit of this book.

Manual lifting and handling

Guidance on the 1992 Regulations has been published in the HSE booklet *Manual Handling: Guidance on Regulations* (ISBN 071762823X). In addition, the following useful guides have been produced: *Manual Handling: Solutions You Can Handle* (ISBN 0717606937); *Manual Handling in the Health Services* (ISBN 0717612481); and *Handling Home Care: Achieving Safe Efficient and Positive Outcomes for Care Workers and Clients* (ISBN 0717622282).

13.4.3 Manual lifting and handling

The competing interests between local authorities or care agencies which may inform staff that they should restrict performing any manual lifting and handling operations and those of disabled people who need such assistance was consider in detail in the High Court in *R (on the application of A)* v. *East Sussex CC* (2003) 6 CCLR 194. The court held that the legislation was aimed to avoid hazardous manual lifting, so far as was reasonably practicable and commensurate with the best interests of the disabled person, his dignity and the promotion of his independence and human rights. An employee whose job is to lift people may have to accept a greater degree of risk than one who is employed to move inanimate objects; the court also recognised that an employee cannot be exposed to an 'unjustifiable risk' (para.58). In some situations, some manual handling is an inherent and inescapable feature of the task that the employee is employed to do (para.63). However it was also recognised that the needs of the disabled person could mean that it was not reasonably practicable to avoid a particular risk or to reduce it, as much as might otherwise be appropriate (para.64). In assessing what was reasonably practicable the relevant factors were:

- the possible methods of avoiding the risk;
- the context – frequency and duration;
- the risks to the employee; and
- the physical, emotional, psychological and social impact upon the disabled person (para.128).

Once the impact on both the carer and the disabled person of the range of alternatives had been assessed, the employer had to balance the two impact assessments against each other. Once the balance had been struck, if it came down in favour of manual handling, then the employer had to make appropriate risk assessments and take all appropriate steps to minimise the risks (para.130).

13.5 PROVISION OF ACCOMMODATION UNDER OTHER ENACTMENTS

In addition to accommodation being provided under the National Assistance Act 1948, s.21, accommodation can also be provided under:

(a) National Assistance Act 1948, s.29(4)(c) (hostel accommodation for disabled people engaged in workshops provided by the local authority) (see **para.2.5.1**);

(b) MHA 1983, s.117 (see **para.12.3.2**);
(c) LGA 2000, s.2 (see **para.2.5.1**) and
(d) 1977 Act, where the NHS owes a duty to the individual to provide continuing NHS health care. **Chapter 8** sets out at length the responsibility on the NHS for providing such care.

13.6 SERVICES IN THE HOME

Non-residential services can be provided under:

(a) National Assistance Act 1948, s.29 (**para.2.5.2**);
(b) CSDPA 1970, s.2 (**para.2.5.2**);
(c) 1977 Act, s.21 and Sched.8, para.2(1) (**para.2.5.2**);
(d) 1977 Act, Sched.8, para.3(1) (**para.2.5.2**);
(e) Health Services and Public Health Act 1968, s.45 (**para.2.5.2**);
(f) Health and Social Services and Social Security Adjudications Act 1983, Sched.9, Part II (**para.2.5.2**);
(g) MHA 1983, s.117(2) (**para.2.5.2**); and
(h) LGA 2000 (**para.2.5.2**).

Non-residential services can also be provided where individuals qualify for NHS continuing care services in their own homes (**Chapter 8**).

13.7 PROTECTION POWERS FOR VULNERABLE ADULTS

There are a number of protection powers that may be used to assist vulnerable adults, although some are rarely used due to concerns about human rights infringement. In addition to these, all local authorities should have in place procedures for dealing with abuse of vulnerable adults in line with the English *No Secrets* and the Welsh *In Safe Hands* guidance (available from **www.dh.gov.uk** and **www.wales.gov.uk**) respectively. The organisation Solicitors for the Elderly has produced a signposting strategy guidance for lawyers in identifying, preventing and dealing with abuse, which is available from its website (**www.solicitorsfortheelderly.com**).

13.7.1 Removal order under the National Assistance Act 1948

Section 47 of the National Assistance Act 1948, as amended by the National Assistance (Amendment) Act 1951, authorises the local authority's 'Proper Officer' (who will be from the Environmental Health Department) to remove a person to a place of care where that a person:

- is suffering from a grave chronic disease or, being aged, infirm or physically incapacitated, is living in unsanitary conditions, and
- is unable to devote to him/herself, and is not receiving from other persons, proper care and attention, and
- refuses to go into hospital or an institution even though a bed is available.

Social services will be closely linked in the application, as will a GP. They must have tried without success to obtain the person's agreement to receive help and assistance. The application is made by the Proper Officer in writing with medical support to the magistrates' court certifying that the Proper Officer is satisfied after a thorough inquiry and consideration that it is necessary to remove the person from the premises in which he is residing because it is in that person's interests, or it is necessary to prevent injury to the health of, or serious nuisance to other persons. The order can last up to three months and is renewable with no right of appeal. Alternatively in an emergency it is possible to obtain immediate removal without giving notice to any person involved, which lasts only three weeks, provided it is established by the Proper Officer that it is in the person's interest (National Assistance (Amendment) Act 1951). As with less urgent applications, there is no appeal and it is doubtful if this procedure is compliant with the European Convention on Human Rights.

13.7.2 Duty to protect property under the National Assistance Act 1948, s.48

The local authority is under a duty to take reasonable steps to prevent or mitigate loss or damage to the person's property when the individual has been admitted to residential accommodation under s.21 or removed under s.47 powers. The local authority can enter the premises to take steps to protect it. Any reasonable expenses incurred in doing such are recoverable from the person concerned.

13.7.3 The common law doctrine of necessity and the inherent jurisdiction of the High Court

The common law the doctrine of 'necessity' provides a defence to conduct which would otherwise be a tort, and may be a defence when making decisions in the best interests of a vulnerable person. The Family Division of the High Court has inherent power to grant declaratory relief, where a person is incapable of making his own medical and/or welfare decision (*Re F (Adult: Courts Jurisdiction)* [2000] 3 WLR 1740). The Court of Protection will be able to make such welfare and medical declarations on behalf of adults without capacity once the Mental Capacity Act 2005 is in force in Spring 2007.

13.7.4 Entry and inspection of premises by an approved social worker

Under MHA 1983, s.115 an approved social worker can enter and inspect any premises occupied by a mentally disordered person, if the social worker believes that the person is not receiving proper care. The social worker cannot use force to break in, and has no power under the Act to remove the person. If it is thought that removal is necessary then a warrant under s.135 (see **para.13.7.5** below) should be obtained. Anyone refusing entry to the approved social worker would be committing an offence under s.129.

13.7.5 Place of safety orders under the Mental Health Act 1983

Section 135 orders

Section 135 of MHA 1983 enables an approved social worker to apply to a magistrate for a warrant which will allow a police officer to enter premises where it is thought that a person who is suffering from a mental disorder is residing and that person is being (or has been) ill-treated, neglected, or not kept 'under proper control', or that the person may be living alone and unable to care for himself.

An approved social worker and a doctor should accompany the police officer who is to execute the warrant, which is valid for 28 days. They can break into the premises if appropriate, and where necessary the person can be removed and taken to a place of safety. A place of safety can be a police station, a hospital, a care home or other suitable place.

The section lasts for up to 72 hours from the time that the person arrives at the place of safety. The person should be assessed during this period and once a decision is made as to the treatment or care required, then the section ceases. There is no right of appeal.

Section 136 orders

Section 136 of MHA 1983 enables a police officer to remove a person to a place of safety, if the officer finds that person in a public place, and he appears to be suffering from a mental disorder, is in need of care and control and such removal is in the interest of that person or for the protection of others. Detention can be up to 72 hours, during which time an assessment would take place for any necessary arrangements for care to be made, with no right of appeal. Once this has been done the section ceases to be in effect.

Section 7 orders

The Mental Health Act 1983 enables a guardianship order to be made (s.7). To be received into guardianship the person must be suffering from a mental illness, a severe mental impairment, a psychopathic disorder or a mental impairment, of a nature or degree which warrants the order and it is necessary in the interests of that person, or for the protection of other people. The order may specify where he must live, that he must attend a place or at a time for medical treatment, occupation, education, and training or that a doctor, an approved social worker or anyone else the guardian specifies must have access to see the person (s.8). The guardianship lasts for six months and is renewable for a further six months and then for a year at a time under s.20. There is a right of appeal to the Mental Health Review Tribunal.

13.8 DRUG AND ALCOHOL MISUSE

13.8.1 The strategy for tackling misuse

In 1998, the Government published its strategy paper *Tackling Drugs to Build a Better Britain* which was updated in 2002. The aim is to create a coordinated approach to dealing with the problems that drug misuse presents to individuals and to society generally. The Home Office has overall responsibility to manage drug misuse in England. Drug teams exist in the nine National Treatment Agency (NTA) Offices, which support Drug Action Teams, or in some areas known as Drug and Alcohol Action Teams (DATs) by assessing performance and providing guidance and best practice advice. DATs receive their funding from central government and local funding, such as from the local authority and PCT. NTA is a Special Health Authority, established in 2001 to ensure that there is more, better and fairer treatment, available to all those who need it (**www.nta.nhs.uk**).

DATs comprise representatives from health services, social services, police, probation services, local education authorities, youth services, social housing providers and voluntary sector service providers. DATs have responsibility for commissioning services from the NHS as well as voluntary organisations, and monitor and report on performance and communicate with stakeholders. In some places, DATs have merged with Crime and Disorder Reduction Partnerships (CDRPs), to make the best use of available resources and reduce bureaucracy.

There are similar CDRPs in Wales, which have responsibility for implementation of the Welsh Substance Misuse Strategy. See *Tackling Substance Misuse in Wales – A Partnership Approach* (May 2000).

The 'A to Z of Substance Misuse Guidance and Publications' is available at the Department of Health's website (**www.dh.gov.uk**).

13.8.2 NHS responsibilities

The NHS is responsible for the health care element of any package of care and has an overlapping responsibility for rehabilitation and recovery with local authorities. As such, the guidance makes it clear that local authorities should work with their NHS partners and draw up agreements as to arrangements for funding treatment and rehabilitation (para.7).

According to the White Paper *Tackling Drugs Together* (Cm 2846, HMSO 1995) and *Purchasing Effective Treatment and Care for Drug Misusers* (DOH, 1997), the NHS has responsibility in particular for:

- detoxification and rehabilitation, which includes provision in hospital units;
- urgent assessments and acute care;
- community drug dependency services;
- needle and syringe exchange schemes;
- methadone reduction programmes;
- hospital and outpatient community-based clinics;
- advice and counselling; and
- after-care and support services.

GPs also have a role to identify and counsel misusers (*Drug Misuse and Dependence* (DOH, 1999)).

13.8.3 Social services responsibilities

Local authorities have the following responsibilities for arranging and funding the social care of alcohol and drug misusers:

- assessing the needs of the local population for alcohol and drug services and including this information in various strategic plans (see **para.2.4.2**);
- assessing the social care needs of individual alcohol and drug misusers;
- arranging appropriate packages of care.

However, in practice the assessment and provision role is carried out by DATs.

Provision of residential accommodation

Social services are authorised by the Secretary of State in LAC (93) 10, Appendix 1 at para.2(6) to provide residential accommodation under the National Assistance Act 1948, s.21 to alcoholics and drug dependent users, where they are ordinarily resident in the local authority area and are assessed as being in need of care and attention that is not otherwise available to them. The local authority has an additional duty to arrange residential accommodation where a person is in their area but has no settled residence (National Assistance Act 1948, ss.24(3)(a) and 32) or if the person is ordinarily resident outside the local authority's area but is in urgent need of residential care (National Assistance Act 1948, s.24(3)(b)). Residential treatment programmes are commonly provided under s.21.

Provision of non-residential services

The local authority has a specific discretionary power under Sched.8, para.2(1) to the 1977 Act to provide services for alcoholics or drug dependent persons (LAC (93) 10, Appendix 3, para.3(3)). Service provision may also be provided under CSDPA 1970, s.2, but only if the person were to be so affected by the problem that he is considered by the local authority to be disabled (National Assistance Act 1948, s.29).

Services that can be provided include advice and counselling, day care and residential rehabilitation and presentation and harm minimumisation (1990 policy guidance *Caring for People: Community Care in the Next Decade and Beyond*).

13.8.4 Guidance

Guidance to local authorities has been issued in LAC (92) 3, on providing community care services for adults assessed under the 1990 Act, who misuse alcohol and/or drugs (available from **www.dh.gov.uk**). Assessment and provision for those under 18 is governed by the 1989 Act.

Assessment and care management of misusers

Paragraphs 12–27 set out in detail how the local authority should assess misusers. They highlight the need for the local authority to:

- offer a programme of care that will help the misusers make positive changes in their lives;
- ensure that their assessment systems take full account of the different ways in which alcohol and drug misusers present for services, their different characteristics and their particular needs;
- ensure that standard assessment procedures and documentation include consideration of substance misuse;
- provide assessment and care management which are flexible, rapid and proportionate to the needs of misusers, to allow misusers to access services they need in a way that meets their special circumstances;
- use eligibility criteria which are sensitive to the circumstances of alcohol and drug misusers, including those of transient residence.

Delegation of assessment to third parties

There are a range of organisations and professionals, often within the independent sector, who deal frequently with alcohol and drug misusers. As such, they have a substantial number of experienced professionals with skills to undertake an appropriate assessment. Local authorities will have arrangements with all the agencies in their area to which misusers are likely to present for help, which will enable those agencies to initiate the assessment procedures (para.14). These may extend to rapid assessment procedures (also known as 'fast track assessments'), where for example the individual needs immediate residential care (paras.21–22). Arrangements for assessments by third parties should be included in the contract that the local authority has with those organisations to provide a service. When conducting an assessment, the third party must be aware of other potential needs for which the local authority has a responsibility. The local authority is however, ultimately responsible for the decision to commit resources (para.17).

Out-of-area referrals

Arrangements should be in place for assessments to be conducted on behalf of another local authority, where the person concerned is ordinarily resident in that authority's area. There will be a need to liaise and have systems in place with that authority to establish responsibility for funding the care package (paras.18 and 24).

Where a person is ordinarily resident in the area of the local authority undertaking the assessment, there may be a benefit, subject to the individual choice, in referring to a residential service away from the area in which the person is experiencing their alcohol and drug problems. Resources should be identified for such placements (para.23).

13.8.5 Provision and commissioning of services

In practice, DATs assess and commission services based on the NTA and the Department of Health guidance *Models of Care: Treatment for Adult Drug Users – Framework for Developing Local Systems of Effective Drug Misuse in England* (2002) (available from **www.nta.nhs.uk**). It is currently in the process of being updated.

Service users may receive a number of different treatments simultaneously, which can be grouped into four broad bands or tiers. Paragraph 4.2 of the guidance sets out the tiers, which can be summarised as follows.

Tier 1: Non-substance misuse specific services – the role includes the provision of screening and referral to local drug and alcohol treatment services by organisations that have contact with misusers. It may also include assessment, services to reduce drug-related harm, and liaison or joint working with tier 2 and 3 specialist drug and alcohol treatment services.

Tier 2: Open access drug and alcohol treatment services – the aim of the treatment in tier 2 is to engage drug and alcohol misusers in treatment and reduce drug-related harm. There is a low threshold for accessing services. Services include needle exchange, drug (and alcohol) advice and information services, assessment of social care needs and ad hoc support not delivered in the context of a care plan.

Tier 3: Structured community-based drug treatment services – requires the misusers to receive a drug assessment and to have a care plan which is agreed between the service provider and client.
Structured non-residential services – include psychotherapeutic interventions (e.g. cognitive behavioural therapy, motivational interventions, structured counselling, methadone maintenance programmes, community detoxification, or day care provided either as a drug- and alcohol-free programme or as an adjunct to methadone treatment). Also included in tier 3 services are community-based after-care programmes for drug and alcohol misusers leaving residential rehabilitation or prison.

Tier 4: Residential services for drug and alcohol misusers – aimed at individuals with a high level of presenting need.

Tier 4a: Residential drug and alcohol misuse specific services – includes in-patient drug and alcohol detoxification or stabilisation services; drug and alcohol residential rehabilitation units; and residential drug crisis intervention centres.

Tier 4b: Highly specialist non-substance misuse specific services – includes specialist liver units that treat the complications of alcohol-related and infectious liver diseases, forensic services for mentally ill offenders, specialist liaison services such as specialist hepatitis nurses, HIV liaison clinics, genito-urinary medicine.

Owing to the nature of misuse, individuals are highly likely to fail a number of times to complete treatment successfully, before they break their dependency. Because of the cost implications, guidance has been issued as *Purchasing Effective Treatment and Care for Drug Misusers – Guidance on Commissioning Better Services for People with Drug Related Problems* (DOH, 1997), which sets out guidance on commissioning better services for drug misusers and highlights the need for a coordinated approach to avoid unnecessary waste. The guidance considers needs assessment, the identification of resources, joint commissioning, contracting effective interventions, and the needs of young people, those with mental health problems, ethnic minorities, women with children and pregnant drug misusers. Copies can be obtained from the Department of Health, as there are no electronic versions available.

13.8.6 Dual diagnosis

Diagnosis, care and treatment for someone with a mental health illness and substance misuse problems are more difficult, with service users being at higher risk of relapse, readmission to hospital and suicide. There are often a number of agencies involved in the care of a person with dual diagnosis and as a result gaps can occur.

The *Mental Health Policy Implementation Guide: Dual Diagnosis Good Practice Guide* (2002) provides a framework for cooperation between the various agencies for those with severe mental health problems and substance misuse. It is available at the Department of Health's website (**www.dh.gov.uk**). Its objective is that those who are duel diagnosed should be cared for within mental health services, with the support, consultancy and training from specialist drug and alcohol agencies. The guidance sets out advice on assessment, mapping planned care and commissioning of services. Local implementation teams for mental health services should take the lead role in ensuring that commissioning is coordinated across PCTs and DATs.

13.9 HIV AND AIDS

The community care legislation and directions do not make specific reference to those infected with HIV or suffering from AIDS. However, services may be provided if the person has needs that fall within the scope of the statutory provision for social care (**paras.2.5** and **13.2.2** above) or that person's health care needs fall within the responsibility of the NHS (**Chapter 8**). HIV key documents aimed at health professionals, issued by the Department of Health can be accessed on the Department of Health's website (**www.dh.gov.uk**).

CHAPTER 14

Asylum seekers, housing and homelessness

14.1 INTRODUCTION

This topic, more than any other in community care, has been subject to amendment by statute and frequent intervention by the courts over the past 10 years. This chapter is designed to be a broad overview of the complex and ever-changing law in this area. More specialist reference should be made to Knafler, Willman and Pierce, *Support for Asylum Seekers*, 2nd edn (LAG, 2004), and *McDonald's Immigration Law and Practice*, 6th edn (Butterworths, 2005).

14.2 THE LEGISLATIVE FRAMEWORK FOR ASYLUM SEEKERS

The regime operates in two different ways: primary responsibility for asylum seekers until their asylum claims have been determined lies with the National Asylum Support Service (NASS). However, after their claims have been determined or in certain other situations they may have a claim for community care services pursuant to the National Health Service and Community Care Act 1990.

14.2.1 Who is an asylum seeker?

The Immigration and Asylum Act 1999 (IAA 1999) provides that individuals are asylum seekers or are dependants of asylum seekers if they are people over the age of 18 who have made an undetermined claim for asylum (s.94(1)), or if they are a spouse or child/dependant under the age of 18 (s.95(1)). Where the household includes a dependent child, then even after the claim for asylum has been determined, the claimant is treated as an asylum seeker whilst he has a dependent child under the age of 18 and they are in the UK (s.94(5)). As such they are covered by NASS.

14.2.2 Who is an asylum seeker but does not receive NASS assistance?

Under ss.54 and 55 of the National Immigration and Asylum Act 2002 (NIAA 2002) an individual is not covered by NASS if they have not claimed asylum as soon as is reasonably practicable after their arrival within the United Kingdom. The Asylum and Immigration (Treatment of Claimants, etc.) Act 2004 enables those with dependent children to be excluded from community care and NASS services in certain circumstances once their asylum claim has been determined. The practical effect of this is that NASS and local authorities have no responsibility for adults or children in that situation, although the local authority will have a residual duty to care for the children (but not their parents) under the 1989 Act (ss.17 and 20) (*G* v. *LB of Barnet* [2003] UKHL 57).

14.2.3 Residual rights under the European Convention on Human Rights

NASS has to provide individuals with support if it is necessary to prevent a breach of a right under the European Convention on Human Rights (Art.3 (inhuman and degrading treatment) pursuant to NIAA 2002, s.55(5). The House of Lords considered the circumstances in which a destitute asylum seeker may meet the criteria under s.55 in *R (on the application of Limbuela)* v. *Secretary of State for the Home Department* [2005] UKHL 66, where the asylum seekers in question were without food, housing or the most basic necessities of life.

14.3 WHO IS EXCLUDED FROM ACCESSING COMMUNITY CARE SERVICES?

14.3.1 Healthy, able-bodied asylum seeking adults with children

Healthy, able-bodied asylum seeking adults with children receive accommodation and essential living needs from NASS under IAA 1999, s.95 and the Asylum Support Regulations 2000, SI 2000/704. This applies even if the children are disabled or have special educational needs. Such individuals are still eligible for asylum support even after the refusal of an asylum claim so long as this individual has dependent children under the age of 18 (IAA 1999, s.94(5)). However, under the Asylum and Immigration (Treatment of Claimants etc.) Act 2004, s.9 such families can be certified as having not taken steps to leave the UK voluntarily and therefore the adults will be excluded from community care services and can be deported. Their children will still be eligible for community care services, which would usually involve either being taken into accommodation pursuant to the 1989 Act, s.20 or being taken into care pursuant to s.31 (*R (on the application of G)* v. *Barnet LBC* [2003] UKHL 57).

14.3.2 Healthy, able-bodied destitute adult asylum seekers without dependent children

Healthy, able-bodied destitute adult asylum seekers without dependent children also receive support from NASS under IAA 1999, s. 95 and SI 2000/704, which continues until a final decision is made on their application for asylum. After that, accommodation may be available for them in limited cases under the hard cases support.

14.3.3 EEC citizens, refugees and failed asylum seekers

Adults who are citizens of other EEA countries, or who have been granted refugee status by other EEA countries or who are failed asylum seekers who have failed to cooperate with removal directions or who are present in the UK in breach of immigration laws are excluded (NIAA 2002, s.54 and Sched.3).

14.3.4 Unaccompanied asylum seeking young adults who were previously unaccompanied asylum seeking children

Unaccompanied asylum seeking children who have reached the age of 18 should be dealt with by NASS (NASS Bulletin 29: Transition at the Age of 18) if they are still asylum seekers, but duties may well be owed by the local authority as well under s.23A *et seq.* of the 1989 Act.

14.3.5 Dependent children of adults who may receive community care services

The Court of Appeal held in *R (on the application of O)* v. *Haringey LBC* [2004] EWCA Civ 535 that where an asylum seeker with dependent children is owed a duty by a local authority under s.21(1)(a) of the National Assistance Act 1948 by reason of illness or disability, the authority's duty is limited to providing accommodation to the asylum seeker. NASS is responsible for the asylum seeker's children (IAA 1999, s.95). It may mean that the authority provides accommodation to the whole family but receives a financial contribution from NASS in respect of the children.

14.4 WHO CAN STILL RECEIVE COMMUNITY CARE SERVICES?

14.4.1 Unaccompanied asylum seeking children under the age of 18

The local authority has a duty to provide for such children under the 1989 Act. The services received by these children will generally involve a duty to accommodate them (s.20). A local authority should presume that accommodation should be provided unless an assessment under s.17 provides that a child does not wish to enter the system and the child is old enough to be considered to be competent to make such decisions and have other possible support (*R (on the application of Berhe)* v. *Hillingdon LBC* [2003] EWHC 2075 and LAC 2002 (13)).

14.4.2 Young adult asylum seekers who have been in care

Young adults who have been in care by reason of their asylum seeker status are entitled to support on leaving care; this includes those who have either been declared to be asylum seekers or have not yet been excluded under Sched.3 to NIAA 2002 – i.e. their asylum claim has not yet been refused (s.23A *et seq.* of the 1989 Act and the Children (Leaving Care) (England) Regulations 2001, SI 2001/2874). Young adults who are disabled would, by virtue of their disability, receive accommodation under the National Assistance Act 1948, s.21 irrespective of their asylum seeker status.

14.4.3 Destitute asylum seekers with community care needs

Adult asylum seekers and other persons from abroad who are not just destitute, but fall into one of the categories provided under the National Assistance Act 1948, s.21 (i.e. pregnant or nursing, old, disabled or suffering from a physical or mental illness) and some other community care categories under the National Assistance Act 1948, s.29 or CSDPA 1970, s.2 may be entitled to receive services. Details of the type of services that can or must be provided are set out in **para.2.5**.

14.4.4 Asylum seekers who have been subject to compulsory treatment under the Mental Health Act 1983

Those who have been discharged from mental hospital after treatment pursuant to MHA 1983, s.3 are entitled to after-care services under s.117. Section 117 is proposed to be abolished under the planned Mental Health Bill. More detail on s.117 is contained in **Chapter 12**.

14.4.5 Humanitarian protection, discretionary leave or refugee status

Those who have been granted refugee status or humanitarian protection or discretionary leave to remain in the UK would qualify for community care services irrespective of their asylum status and/or if the individual's needs cannot yet be met by the UK benefit system because their papers have not yet arrived.

14.4.6 Dependent children without NASS support

Dependent children of failed asylum seeking adults who no longer receive NASS support may be entitled to children's services (see **para.14.6** below).

14.5 WHEN ARE ADULT ASYLUM SEEKERS CONSIDERED TO REQUIRE COMMUNITY CARE SERVICES?

14.5.1 Ordinarily resident

Adult asylum seekers will not be treated as ordinarily resident in an area where residence has not been adopted voluntarily, for example where NASS has required them to live in a particular location or where there has been no settled purpose in living in a particular residence (*Al-Ameri* v. *Kensington and Chelsea RLBC* [2004] UKHL 4). As such although an asylum seeker is resident in a certain area it does not follow that the asylum seeker is 'ordinarily resident'.

Once an asylum seeker is considered to be ordinarily resident, then if that person is moved to accommodation under the National Assistance Act 1948, s.21 in another local authority area, the local authority cannot discharge its duty under s.21 (National Assistance Act 1948, s.24(5)). The relevant date for considering whether an asylum seeker is ordinarily resident in an area is the date that the individual made his application for assistance (*R (on the application of Mani)* v. *Lambeth LBC* [2002] EWHC 735 (Admin)). Furthermore, under s.21 a local authority has a duty to provide accommodation for those who are not ordinarily resident in its area but are in its area when the need arises and those who are in urgent need (National Assistance Act 1948, s.24(3); LAC (93) 10). In most circumstances. therefore, those who present themselves to an authority will require assessment, as they will be in 'urgent need'. In any event, even if there is a dispute about residence, government circulars indicate that an authority should still assess and then sort out the financial dispute later (LAC (93) 7 'Ordinary Residence').

14.5.2 Uncertainty as to the status of the individual

It may not be clear if someone is subject to immigration control or is an asylum seeker. In those circumstances, it may be appropriate to carry out an assessment of that individual's asylum status/immigration status to determine if that person requires services. In any event, the individual may need to be assessed for community care services to ensure there is no breach of the Human Rights Act 1998 by not providing such services (see **para.14.2.3** above).

14.5.3 Persons subject to immigration control

Persons subject to immigration control (PSICs) are excluded from the National Assistance Act 1948, s.21, Health Services and Public Health Act 1968, s.45 and 1977 Act, Sched.8, para.2, pursuant to IAA 1999, ss.116–117. This exclusion only arises for those individuals who are defined as a person subject to immigration control under IAA 1999, s.115. A PSIC is an individual who is not an EEA national and who:

(a) requires leave to enter or remain in the UK but does not have it, which includes asylum seekers;
(b) requires leave to enter or remain in the UK given as a result of a maintenance undertaking (someone has undertaken to look after that person);
(c) has leave to enter or remain which is subject to a condition that the individual does not have recourse to public funds; or
(d) has leave to enter or remain only as a result of leave having been extended whilst that individual appeals against a refusal to grant leave.

The exclusion from eligibility is for all those who do not have recourse to public funds: they are people whose need for the service in question arises solely because they are destitute or because of the physical effects of their destitution (IAA 1999, s.116).

The law was tightened again in 2002 under NIAA 2002, s.54 and Sched.3, as local authorities cannot provide community care services at all for those who are failed asylum seekers or individuals who are unlawfully in the UK and/or those who are lawfully or unlawfully here but with breaches of the immigration laws who are not asylum seekers, or nationals of other EEA states, refugees granted asylum in other EEA states, or those with dependent children who failed without excuse to leave voluntarily.

The services excluded to such asylum seekers are:

(a) National Assistance Act 1948, ss.21 and 29;
(b) 1977 Act, s.21 and Sched.8;
(c) 1989 Act, ss.17 and 23C *et seq.*; and
(d) LGA 2000, s.2.

Services cannot be provided to an individual unless that person is also a British citizen, a child or included by virtue of the regulations (s.54). However, the prohibition on the provision of accommodation for these individuals does not apply where the failure to provide assistance would breach the rights of an individual under the European Convention on Human Rights or the EC Treaty. The Department of Health has determined that EEA nationals, their families and students should be provided with such social care services in order to protect their freedom of movement (DOH Note of Clarification, para.13).

14.5.4 Withholding and withdrawing support

For these purposes the Secretary of State has made regulations and guidance which deal with how a local authority is meant to deal with individuals who do not quality for community care services (Withholding and Withdrawal of Support (Travel Assistance and Temporary Accommodation) Regulations 2002, SI 2002/3078 and NIAA 2002, s.54 and Sched.3). This enables local authorities to give EEA refugees with children money to travel to the EEA state from whence they came and accommodate them until the Secretary of State has determined that they had failed to comply with the removal directions (reg.3) (*R (on the application of M)* v. *Islington LBC* [2004] EWCA Civ 235 and *R (on the application of G)* v. *Barnet LBC* [2003] UKHL 57).

The local authority may be under an obligation to provide services to avoid a breach of a human right, as was considered in *R (on the application of Q)* v. *Secretary of State for the Home Department* [2003] EWCA Civ 364 and *R (on the application of S)* v. *Secretary of State for the Home Department* [2003] EWCA Civ 1285, where it was found that if an individual would or is likely to be subject to inhuman and degrading treatment, which has been defined as 'actual bodily injury or intense physical or mental suffering . . . or humiliates or debases their human dignity' (*Pretty* v. *UK* (2002) 35 EHRR 1) so that Art.3 of the European Convention on Human Rights is breached, then residential accommodation has to be provided. For example, in the case of S, a duty under the National Assistance Act 1948, s.21 was held to be owed to an individual who was found to have psychological disturbance and considerable malnutrition and who was sleeping rough. He was unable to eat more than a few mouthfuls of food. In *R (on the application of Limbuela)* v. *Secretary of State for the Home Department* [2005] UKHL 66 the court, although dealing with whether or not NASS had a right to provide support gave guidance on when an individual's destitution would be in breach of Art.3 of the Convention. It will be analogously used to determine whether or not an authority may be required to provide community care services in order to avoid such a breach. It provides that the State has an absolute obligation to refrain from inflicting inhuman and degrading treatment.

The decision by the Secretary of State to withdraw support from someone which would then lead to their destitution was an intentionally inflicted act for which the Secretary of State would be responsible under the Convention for the inhuman and degrading treatment which followed. Withdrawing support was not inhuman and degrading treatment in and of itself, but it would be inhuman and degrading once the individual was at risk of or was suffering inhuman and degrading treatment under Art.3. The threshold for meeting Art.3 might be crossed if the entire package of restrictions and deprivations that surrounded him was so severe that it could properly be described as inhuman and degrading pursuant to Art.3, e.g. if someone who had no means, no alternative source of support and could not by law support himself by employment was then, by deliberate action of the State, denied shelter, food or the most basic necessities. As soon as an asylum seeker made it clear that that there was an imminent prospect of a breach of Art.3, the Secretary of State had the duty under the Human Rights Act 1998 to avoid it.

14.5.5 Need for care and attention under the National Assistance Act 1948, s.21

However, apart from the above restrictions, the courts have found destitute asylum seekers and PSICs to be entitled to residential accommodation under the National Assistance Act 1948, s.21, if the major component of their need for care and attention is illness, disability, old age or pregnancy (*R* v. *Wandsworth LBC ex p O* [2000] 1 WLR 2539). In the *Wandsworth* case, the court found that if the individual's need for care and attention is made more acute by some circumstance other than mere destitution, then, despite being subject to immigration control, the individual should qualify for assistance. The court has found that the individual should apply to the social services department of the local authority and not NASS in these situations (*R on the application of Westminster City Council)* v. *National Asylum Support Service* [2002] UKHL 38).

This has meant that the courts have held that individuals who may well be excluded under the immigration legislation may obtain residential accommodation if, for example:

- they are infected with HIV (*R (on the application of J)* v. *Enfield LBC* [2002] EWHC 432; *R (on the application of H)* v. *Kingston upon Thames RLBC* [2002] EWHC 3158; *R (on the application of M)* v. *Slough BC* [2004] EWHC 1109 (Admin); *R (on the application of O)* v. *Haringey LBC* [2004] EWCA Civ 535);
- they suffer from chronic depression (*R* v. *Wandsworth LBC ex p O* [2000] 1 WLR 2539);
- they are disabled (*R (on the application of Westminster City Council)* v. *NASS* [2002] UKHL 38; *R (on the application of Mani)* v. *Lambeth LBC* [2002] EWHC 735 (Admin); *Murua* v. *Croydon LBC* (2002) 5 CCLR 51;
- they are subject to serious domestic violence (*R (on the application of Khan)* v. *Oxfordshire CC* [2004] EWCA Civ 309).

Asylum seekers or those subject to immigration control will therefore qualify if they are persons who would, if they were UK citizens, require accommodation under the National Assistance Act 1948, s.21. Asylum seekers should have the same type of assessments and be provided with the same services as non-asylum seekers (see **Chapters 3** and **4**).

14.6 SERVICES FOR ASYLUM SEEKING NON UK NATIONAL CHILDREN

There is a distinction between services to be provided for those who are unaccompanied or arriving with adults. If children arrive with adults, then, in most cases, NASS will be responsible for looking after them. Dependent children will also be provided with support under the Children Act 1989 if NASS is not providing support to them because of the status of their parents or because the Secretary of State certifies that the family has failed to take reasonable steps to return to the country under the Asylum and Immigration (Treatment of Claimants) Act 2004, s.9. The House of Lords in *R (on the application of G)* v. *Barnet LBC* [2003] UKHL 57 effectively approved of the fact that, contrary to the position in respect of children of UK nationals or those who are here legally, children and their parents can be separated under the 1989 Act for support to be provided under ss.17 or 20 and there is no duty to provide accommodation for an entire family under the legislation.

Those who are to be assessed are those who are physically present within the area of the local authority and will be eligible for assessment if they are children in need under the 1989 Act, s.17(10). The question of ordinary residence does not arise in the case of children.

Unaccompanied children are immediately the responsibility of the local social services department who have to provide them with assistance under the 1989 Act in the same ways as for UK children who are in care.

In cases where the age of the child is in dispute (which is common), the case of *R (on the application of B)* v. *Merton LBC* [2003] EWHC 1689 provides guidance for local authorities. The local authority is under a duty to make an independent decision about the age of the child and not just follow a decision of the Home Office. The age of a child should not be determined solely on the basis of appearance, and social services should also look at the family circumstances, education background, ethnic and cultural information. Social services can look at previous statements that an individual claimed to be over 18 and can test the credibility of such individuals, but must offer adequate reasons for the decision as to whether or not an individual is a child.

Where unaccompanied asylum seeking children become adults, they are subject to the leaving care regime (1989 Act, Sched.2, para.19A *et seq.* and ss.23A and 24B *et seq.*).

14.7 HOUSING AND COMMUNITY CARE

Paragraph 2.8 provides details of when the housing authority and the social services authority may be required to cooperate and collaborate in providing services for homeless adults who may require community care services.

14.7.1 What general duties are owed by the housing authority?

Local housing authorities are under a duty to consider and have regard to the needs of chronically sick and disabled people when providing housing stock in their local area (CSDPA 1970, s.3). They are also under a duty not to evict individuals who have a disability by virtue of the Disability Discrimination Act 1995. A disabled person cannot be treated less favourably than someone who is not similarly disabled unless the treatment is justified under Disability Discrimination Act 1995, s.24 (*North Devon Homes Ltd* v. *Brazier* [2003] EWHC 574; *Manchester City Council* v. *Romano* [2004] EWCA Civ 834).

14.7.2 Section 21 of the National Assistance Act 1948 and the residual duty to provide accommodation

Homeless people are no longer part and parcel of the community care regime per se, although there is still a duty under s.21(1)(a) of the National Assistance Act 1948 to provide residential accommodation for adults who are in 'urgent need' which could cover an emergency situation. Otherwise, in order to be provided with accommodation, the individual would have to come within the definition under s.21, i.e. an expectant or nursing mother, someone who is old, disabled, or due to other circumstances requires care and attention which is not otherwise available, and/or who is in urgent need of accommodation.

The requirement for care and attention under the 1948 Act, s.21 has been broadly defined by the courts, and is not encompassed in a single definition. It is primarily for the local authority to determine whether or not an individual requires care and attention, but that attention does not necessarily imply a need for accommodation in and of itself (*R* v. *Hammersmith and Fulham LBC ex p M* (1997–98) 1 CCLR 85 at 92K–93C and *R (on the application of Mani)* v. *Lambeth LBC* [2003] EWCA Civ 836 (both cases involving destitute asylum seekers)). The nature of and qualification for accommodation under s.21 is covered in more detail in **para.13.2** and for classes of people who qualify see **para.2.5.1**.

14.8 HOUSING UNDER THE HOUSING ACT 1996

14.8.1 Priority need

Other than through the National Assistance Act 1948, s.21, the Housing Act 1996 provides a single route to obtain social housing accommodation for all individuals. Housing Act 1996 (HA 1996), Part VI sets up an allocation scheme for social housing (including nominations of housing to social landlords, the vast majority of whom now only house individuals who have been allocated to them by a local authority), including determining priority between individuals (HA 1996, s.167(1)). This ensures that reasonable preference is given to those who are in priority need and can receive accommodation under HA 1996, Part VII but preference is also given to the following:

(a) those who may have been intentionally homeless but are in priority need because:

- they have dependent children;
- they have been flooded out or subject to fire;
- they are vulnerable because of old age, mental illness, handicap, physical disability or other special reason;
- they are pregnant or reside with a pregnant woman (HA 1996, s.189);
- they are care leavers;
- they have been in the armed forces;
- they have been in prison; or
- they had to leave the home because of violence or domestic violence;

(b) people occupying unsanitary or overcrowded conditions or living in unsatisfactory housing conditions;
(c) people who need to move on medical or welfare grounds;
(d) people who need to move to a particular locality in that authority's area, where a failure to meet that need would cause hardship to themselves or others.

This scheme can be framed to give additional preference to those who have an urgent housing need (HA 1996, s.176(2)). Therefore those who may well require community or health care services have a right of preference when being allocated housing by a local authority.

14.8.2 Homeless individuals

Housing Act 1996, Part VII provides an exhaustive route for local authority housing for those who are homeless. This is defined in the legislation as those who have no accommodation for their use in the UK in which they can claim a legal interest (HA 1996, s.175), or where they cannot occupy accommodation along with members of their family or those who might be expected to reside with them (HA 1996, s.176). The term 'family' is defined in the legislation under s.178 as relatives, cohabitants and children.

Those individuals who are homeless are given priority need if they have dependent children or are vulnerable because of old age, mental illness, handicap or physical disability or other special reasons, or they are pregnant (HA 1996, s.175(4)). In England, individuals can also have priority need if they are care leavers, or have previously been accommodated or fostered, or have been in prison or the armed forces (Homelessness (Priority Need for Accommodation) (England) Order 2002, SI 2002/2051).

14.8.3 The Homelessness Code of Guidance

The Government has published a *Homelessness Code of Guidance*, available from the Department for Communities and Local Government, for local authorities to which both social services and the housing authority must have regard (Homelessness Act 2002, s.1(2)). Chapter 8 of the Code provides extensive guidance on who should have priority need (see the 'homelessness' section of the website **www.odpm.gov.uk**).

14.8.4 The duty to provide housing

There is a duty to house in permanent accommodation individuals who are unintentionally homeless and in priority need, i.e. by providing a local authority tenancy or social landlord tenancy (HA 1996, s.193). Under HA 1996, s.195, those who are intentionally homeless and in priority need should be provided with secure temporary accommodation whilst they secure their own accommodation.

Further information about homelessness duties can be found in Arden and Hunter *Homelessness and Allocations* 6th Edn (LAG, 2003) and Butterworths *Housing Encyclopaedia*).

14.9 DISABLED FACILITIES GRANTS

Disabled facilities grants (DFGs) are paid by the local housing authority to eligible disabled claimants to provide facilities and adaptations to assist the disabled person to live independently and are made pursuant to the Housing Grants, Construction and Regeneration Act 1996 (HGCRA 1996). Guidance was issued by the Department of the Environment in Circular 17/96 (ISBN 0117533440) although further guidance is available from the Department for Communities and Local Government website (**www.odpm.gov.uk**). Separate guidance has also been issued by the Department of Health in LAC (90) 7 as *House Adaptations for People with Disabilities* (available from **www.dh.gov.uk**).

14.9.1 Eligibility

Disabled occupants

DFGs are payable in respect of disabled occupants (National Assistance Act 1948, s.29). Referrals may be made by the social services department following an assessment of the disabled person's community care needs.

The applicant

Although the disabled occupant is usually the applicant, it is possible for a landlord to apply on behalf of a disabled occupant. The applicant does not have to be the owner-occupier and as such tenants and licensees can apply (HGCRA 1996, s.19(5)). The applicant must be an exiting tenant and so those planning to move into a new tenanted property are ineligible until they are in situ.

Mandatory grants (a maximum £25,000 in England (Disabled Facilities Grants and Home Repair Assistance (Maximum Amounts) (Amendment No.2) (England) Order 2001, SI 2001/4036) or £30,000 in Wales (SI 2002/837 (W.99)) can be awarded and used towards (HGCRA 1996, s.23(1)):

- provision of disabled access;
- a bedroom, toilet or bathroom;
- making the property safe;
- food preparation facilities;
- enabling the use of power and light;
- suitable heating;
- providing free movement around the house.

Minor adaptations under £1,000, which sum includes the cost of buying and fitting, can be provided by the local authority without the individual being subject to a means test. Further information is set out in **para.6.1**.

The work is necessary and appropriate

Once the housing authority is satisfied that the applicant is eligible under s.23(1), it must then be satisfied that the following two criteria are fulfilled:

(a) that the relevant works are necessary and appropriate to meet the needs of the disabled occupant; and
(b) that it is reasonable and practicable to carry out the relevant works having regard to the age and condition of the dwelling, qualifying houseboat, qualifying park home or building (HGCRA 1996, s.24(3); *R (on the application of B) v. Calderdale MBC* [2004] 1 WLR 2017).

The housing authority must consult with social services over whether the works are necessary and appropriate, although it is ultimately the decision of the housing authority (HGCRA 1996, s.23(3)(b)).

14.9.2 The administrative process

The timescale

Decisions should be given within six months and work should be completed within 12 months from the date of the application (HGCRA 1996, ss.34(1) and 36). Once eligibility has been determined, the housing authority cannot refuse to pay on the grounds of lack of funds (*R* v. *Birmingham City Council ex p Mohammed* [1999] 1 WLR 33). It is not uncommon however for considerable delays to occur, particularly before the application has been submitted due to waiting for occupational therapists reports (Local Government Ombudsman's Complaints against Middlesbrough DC (case no. 94/C/0964) and Cleveland CC (case no. 94/C 0965)).

The means test

Eligibility for DFGs is subject to a means test which is applied to disabled persons and their spouse or partner (HGCRA 1996, s.30). In respect of a disabled child, the parents will be subject to the means test. This is determined by the Housing Renewal Grants Regulations 1996, SI 1996/2890, which are updated annually and follow similar means testing regulations, such as those for income support and housing benefit.

14.9.3 Social services residual duty

Although the applicant may not meet the eligibility criteria for a DFG, the social services department may still owe a duty to the disabled person to meet the assessed eligible need under CSDPA 1970, s.2.

14.10 DISCRETIONARY ASSISTANCE

The Regulatory Reform (Housing Assistance) (England and Wales) Order 2002, SI 2002/1860, gives local authorities power to provide discretionary assistance, which can take the form of low cost loans, equity release, grants to private homeowners and others to help them to renovate, repair or adapt their home. The Office of the Deputy Prime Minister (now the Department for Communities and Local Government) issued guidance in Circular 05/2003 (available from **www.odpm.gov.uk**).

14.11 SUPPORTING PEOPLE PAYMENTS

The Supporting People Programme was launched in April 2003 to provide housing-related support services as part of an agreed package of services to vulnerable people in need of those services. Funds are paid to the administering authorities from central government. There is a distinct assessment and means testing regime for services provided under the programme, which is separate from community care services. The range of services that can be provided under the programme is wide and is tailored to the individual's specific needs. Examples of housing-related support services include ensuring the person has the correct skills to maintain a tenancy, advising on home improvements, accessing a community service alarm, or provision of an on-site full-time support worker.

The following guidance has been issued (available from **www.spkweb.org.uk**):

(a) Supporting People (England) Directions 2003;
(b) Supporting People Programme Grant and Grant Conditions;
(c) Supporting People Grant (England) Guidance 2003;
(d) Local Authorities (Charges for Specified Welfare Services) (England) Regulations 2003, SI 2003/907.

CHAPTER 15

Carers

15.1 WHO IS A CARER?

The 2001 Census showed that there are 5.2 million people (which equates to one in ten of the population) providing informal care in England and Wales. Over 1 million people provide more than 50 hours of care each week and of those, nearly a quarter are in poor health themselves and well over half are over 55 years of age. Many carers do not automatically recognise that they are carers, as they define themselves by their relationship to the person who, because of age, physical or learning disability, accident or illness, including mental illness, needs support. They may see themselves as a spouse, parent, partner, other relative, or friend rather than a carer. Carers can act on an informal basis, such as relatives and friends, or they may have a formal role, such as a paid care worker or a volunteer for a voluntary organisation. A carer may be an adult or a minor. Statutory provision for carers' services is aimed at informal carers.

15.2 WHAT SERVICES ARE PROVIDED FOR THE CARER?

Support and services for carers are varied and are determined by the locality where the carer and cared for person live, as well as their specific needs. Services may be provided through social services, the NHS, and voluntary or charitable organisations. Local authorities have since April 1999 had a ring-fenced Carer's Special Grant from central government to create diverse and flexible provision for breaks for carers or direct services to carers to support them in their caring role. Some local authorities use grant funds to pay voluntary or charitable organisations to provide services direct to carers.

Support may also be provided in the workplace, such as allowing flexible working arrangements, as well as through carers' support services and networks, for example, the Princess Royal Trust for Carers or the 'Ring Around Carer' telephone scheme, run jointly by the charity Community Network and the BBC. For information on services and equipment see *A Practical Guide for Disabled People or Carers where to Find Information,*

Services and Equipment (DOH, April 2003). There is no equivalent publication in Wales, but although the information in the guide mainly relates to services in England, some contact details are given for Wales.

Services can be provided by social services for:

(a) the cared for person as part of 'community care services' (see **para.15.4** below);
(b) the disabled child as 'children's services' (see **para.15.4** below); or
(c) for the carer as 'carers' services' (see **para.15.5** below).

It is up to the local authority to decide what provision it will make and this will depend on whether the cared for person and/or carer meet its eligibility criteria and, in the case of children, whether the service safeguards and promotes the welfare of the child. The Department of Health's *Practice Guidance on the Carers and Disabled Children Act 2000* (March 2001) emphasises however, that it is not the type of services provided by social services but the outcome for the carer and the person cared for that is important, to allow flexibility (paras.45–48).

General types of services that may be provided can be distinguished and are set out below.

15.2.1 Help at home

Provision can range from help with personal care, such as assistance with getting up in the morning, and getting dressed and washed, through to help such as to preparation of meals, sitting services that allow the carer to run essential errands, or a direct payment for the carer, for example to allow the carer to employ someone to do the ironing.

15.2.2 Day care

Day care services may be provided to give the carer a break, but may also be for the primary benefit of the cared for person, for example by providing the opportunity to learn a new skill, undertake a hobby or participate in organised events and activities.

15.2.3 Aids and equipment

There are a range of aids and equipment that help individuals with disabilities and their carers to get on with everyday living. They can range from grab rails to hoists and much more inbetween. For more details on community equipment services see **para.6.1**. The Disabled Living Foundation has information about aids and equipment. There are a number of local Disabled Living Centres or Independent Living Centres throughout the country, which provide advice and information about a range of aids and equipment with displays and demonstrations of equipment: contact the Disabled Living Centres Council (see Appendix 3).

15.2.4 Home adaptations

Grants may be available to assist with the cost of repairing, adapting or improving the home to allow easier care management. See **Chapter 14** for more details.

15.2.5 Care homes

The cared for person may need either temporary or permanent care in a care home.

15.2.6 Carers' services

Carers' services are not defined but are services given to carers to assist them in their caring role or to help them maintain their own health and well-being. Services can range from counselling to deal with the stress to facilitating adult education.

15.2.7 Health services

Health services provided through primary care services, such as the GP, health visitor, pharmacist and palliative care teams may assist the carer and cared for person with both emotional and practical support.

15.2.8 Young carers

The Department for Education and Skills now has responsibility for policy development of young carers. See **Chapter 11** for more details.

15.3 DISABLED PERSONS (SERVICES, CONSULTATION AND REPRESENTATION) ACT 1986, S.8

Where a disabled person lives at home and receives a substantial amount of care on a regular basis from a person (not employed) and it falls on the local authority to consider the disabled person's needs under the Disabled Persons (Services, Consultation and Representation) Act 1986 (DPSCRA 1986), s.4, in deciding the needs the local authority should have regard to the carer's ability to continue to care on a regular basis. Although this is not an assessment of a carer, it takes into account the carer's ability to continue to care and applies even though the carer has not asked to be assessed. The terms 'substantial' and 'regular' are not defined in the Act but have been defined in guidance (see **para.15.5.5** below). The definition of a carer under DPSCRA 1986 includes voluntary organisation volunteers. Department of Health guidance on DPSCRA 1986 has been issued in LAC (87) 6.

The local authority can provide services under the National Assistance Act 1948, Part III, CSDPA 1970, s.2 or the 1977 Act, Sched.8 (s.16) but cannot make provision for services under the Health Services and Public Health Act 1968 or MHA 1983. If an assessment is undertaken under the Carers (Recognition and Services) Act 1995 (CRSA 1995), DPSCRA 1986 cannot be used (CRSA 1995, s.1(5)).

15.4 CARERS (RECOGNITION AND SERVICES) ACT 1995

15.4.1 Carer's assessment linked to assessment for service user

Section 1 of CRSA 1995 provides that at the time when a local authority assesses a person's needs for community care services, under the National Health Service and Community Care Act 1990, s.47(1)(a) (CRSA 1995, s.1(1)), or assesses the needs of a disabled child, for the purposes of the 1989 Act, Part III or CSDPA 1970, s.2 (CRSA 1995, s.1(2)), individuals who provide or intend to provide a substantial amount of care on a regular basis for that person have the right to request an assessment of their ability to provide or continue to provide care. The authority must take that assessment into account when making any decision about services for the cared for person or to meet the needs of the disabled child. Policy and practice guidance on CRSA 1995 was issued in LAC (96) 7 (although this is no longer current), and in Wales in WOC 16/96 and WHC (96) 12.

The carer must be an informal carer and unlike DPSCRA 1986, CRSA 1995 does not cover voluntary organisation carers (s.1(3)). The meaning of substantial and regular is covered at **para.15.5.5** below.

15.4.2 How does a carer get an assessment under the Carers (Recognition and Services) Act 1995?

The carer can be an adult or a minor child and provision can be made regardless of the age of the person cared for. The carer does not have to be living with the person cared for, nor does the carer have to be the sole carer. Services provided under this Act are for the cared for person as 'community care services' or a disabled child as 'children's services' and as such it is the service user, not the carer who is financially assessed (see **para.15.5.8** below.) If the carer is finding it difficult to cope because, for example the cared for person's or the carer's health is deteriorating, the carer should approach social services for an assessment of the cared for person or, if previously assessed, for a reassessment and at this time ask for a carer's assessment.

15.4.3 Where the wishes of the service user and carer are in conflict

The 1995 Act is silent on the situation where the wishes of the service user and the carer conflict; however if, for example, the carer wants a service that the cared for person does not wish to receive, the local authority's primary duty is to the cared for person and so it will have to try to resolve the conflict. The carer could ask for an independent assessment under the Carers and Disabled Children Act 2000 (CDCA 2000) (see **para.15.5** below).

15.5 CARERS AND DISABLED CHILDREN ACT 2000

15.5.1 The right to request an independent carer's assessment

The Carers National Strategy document *Caring about Carers*, which was developed in association with carers and carers' organisations, published in February 1999, highlighted the need for legislation to enable local authorities to provide services direct to carers.

Sections 1 and 6 of CDCA 2000 give carers the right to request an assessment independent of any assessment of the cared for person. This is particularly useful where the cared for person has refused a needs assessment under CRSA 1995. It also gives local authorities power to provide carers' services to meet the carer's needs and help the carer to care. Carers' services are not specifically defined in the Act, although they are any service which helps the carer in their caring role (s.2(2)).

15.5.2 Guidance on the Carers and Disabled Children Act 2000

The Department of Health has issued mandatory practice guidance and *A Practitioner's Guide to Carers' Assessments under the Carers and Disabled Children Act 2000* (March 2001, available from **www.carers.gov.uk**) and *Carers and Disabled Children Act 2000 and Carers (Equal Opportunities) Act 2004 Combined Policy Guidance* (August 2005, available from **www.dh.gov.uk**). Similar guidance has been issued in Wales entitled *Guidance on the 2000 Act* and *Practitioners Guide to Carers' Assessments* (August 2001) and is obtainable from the Welsh Assembly. The guidance should be read alongside the *Framework for the Assessment of Children in Need and their Families* (published by the Department of Health in 2000 and the Welsh Assembly in 2001); the *Single Assessment Process for Older People* (HSC 2002/001, LAC (2002) 1); the *Fair Access to Care Services: Guidance on Eligibility Criteria for Adult Social Care* (LAC (2002) 13); and in Wales, *Creating a Unified and Fair System for Assessing and Managing Care* (UFSAMC) (WHC (2002) 32, NAFWC 09/02).

15.5.3 Who is entitled to an assessment under the Carers and Disabled Children Act 2000?

The carer's right to an assessment applies to carers aged 16 or over, who provide or intend to provide a substantial amount of care on a regular basis for another individual aged 18 or over, or for a disabled child for whom the carer has parental responsibility ('parent carer'), and who ask a local authority to carry out an assessment of their ability to provide and to continue to provide care for the person cared for. The local authority must carry out such an assessment if it is satisfied that the person cared for, whether adult or child, is someone for whom it may provide or arrange the provision of community care services (s.1) or children's services (s.6).

The carer does not have to be living with the person cared for, nor does the carer have to be the sole carer in order to ask for an assessment. There may be more than one carer providing substantial and regular care in the household, each of whom is entitled to an assessment under CDCA 2000.

Parent carers

Those with parental responsibility for a disabled child will usually receive an assessment for services for their family under the provisions of the Children Act 1989. The assessment should follow the *Framework for the Assessment of Children in Need and their Families*. 'Parental responsibility for a disabled child' is defined in s.3 to include all the rights, powers, authority and duties of parents in relation to the child and his property.

Although it is unlikely that the parent carer will seek a separate assessment, provision is made for this under CDCA 2000, s.6. The assessment must be taken into account by the local authority, when deciding what services, if any, to provide to the child or the child's family under the 1989 Act, s.17. Services may be provided to a member of the child's family if they are provided with a view to safeguard or promote the welfare of the child. It may be that providing services that meet the needs of parents is the most effective way of promoting the welfare of the disabled child (policy guidance, para.76).

Young carers aged 16 and 17 years

Any assessment of 16 and 17-year-old carers should be child centred and follow the guidance set out in the *Framework for the Assessment of Children in Need and their Families* to ensure that they are not adversely affected by their caring responsibilities which could undermine their own education, training or work needs.

CDCA 2000 is rarely used by local authorities assessing the needs of 16 and 17-year-old carers, although the local authority could decide that it would be more helpful to a young person to be assessed and receive services under the provisions of CDCA 2000, where it is satisfied that even though caring is on a substantial and regular basis, the child's welfare can still be promoted and safeguarded (Practice Guidance, paras.75–79).

15.5.4 The assessment

A carer's assessment under CDCA 2000 is carried out at the request of the carer to determine:

- whether the carer is eligible for support;
- the support needs of the carer; and
- if those needs can be met by social or other services.

The assessor may be from social services but it could be that the local authority has asked NHS staff to undertake the assessment as an agreement under the Local Government Act 1972, s.113.

If a carer does not wish to be assessed under CDCA 2000, the package of care for the cared for person could still reflect the carer's need for a break and as such may include additional services delivered to the cared for person under CRSA 1995 which enable the carer to rest (see Practice Guidance, para.52).

If carers do not want the cared for person to be approached it will be difficult for a full assessment to take place and as such carers may deny themselves support under the Act (see Practice Guidance, paras.53–58).

The carer should have the chance to discuss with the assessor their ability to provide or continue to provide care, and the assessment should be focused on what the carer identifies as the best possible outcome which will depend on how the impact of caring affects the carer. It should never be assumed that the carer wants or is expected to continue to provide care. Nor should it automatically be assumed that the cared for person wants to continue to receive care from this carer.

15.5.5 Substantial and regular care

There is no definition in CRSA 1995 and CDCA 2000 of 'substantial and regular care'. It is for the assessor to identify the impact of the caring role on the carer, in light of the carer's age, health, employment status, interests and other commitments. The Practice Guidance at para.68 provides that in deciding the impact of the caring role on the carer, the practitioner will need to address the following questions:

- Is the caring role sustainable?
- How great is the risk of the caring role becoming unsustainable?

15.5.6 Sustainability

The *Practitioner's Guide to Carers' Assessments* (para.17 and in Wales, para.2.2.4) sets out some key questions to identify the level of risk to the sustainability of the caring role, which may include the following.

- How long has the carer been caring?
- How much help does the carer get?
- How often does the carer get a full night's sleep?
- How much physical impact does the caring role have?
- How much emotional impact does the caring role have?
- Does the carer understand the nature of the cared for person's condition?
- How much time does the carer have when the carer feels 'off duty'?
- How appropriate is the role for someone of the carer's age or in that particular relationship to the cared for person?
- How appropriate is the role for someone of the carer's culture, religion and gender?
- How many other roles (parent, employee, carer for someone else) impact on the carer?
- How does the caring role impact on the carer's other relationships and community networks?
- How sustainable does the carer's role appear?
- Does the cared for person want the carer to continue in this role?
- How far does the carer gain any sense of satisfaction/reward from caring?

The extent of risk to the sustainability of the caring role is the degree to which a carer's ability to sustain that role is compromised or threatened either in the present or in the foreseeable future by the absence of appropriate support. The Practice Guidance at para.70 sets out that local authorities must consider the level at which they fix eligibility for services in relation to sustainability of the caring role in the light of the following bands of risk:

Critical risk to sustainability of the caring role arises when:

- their life may be threatened;
- major health problems have developed or will develop;
- there is, or will be, an extensive loss of autonomy for carers in decisions about the nature of tasks they will perform and how much time they will give to their caring role;
- there is, or will be, an inability to look after their own domestic needs and other daily routines while sustaining their caring role;
- involvement in employment or other responsibilities is, or will be, at risk;
- many significant social support systems and relationships are, or will be, at risk.

Substantial risk to sustainability of the caring role arises when:

- significant health problems have developed or will develop;

- there is, or will be, some significant loss of autonomy for carers in decisions about the nature of tasks they will perform and how much time they will give to their caring role;
- there is, or will be, an inability to look after some of their own domestic needs and other daily routines while sustaining their caring role;
- involvement in some significant aspects of employment or other responsibilities is, or will be, at risk;
- some significant social support systems and relationships are, or will be, at risk.

Moderate risk to sustainability of the caring role arises when:

- there is, or will be, some loss of autonomy for the carer in decisions about the nature of tasks they will perform and how much time they will give to their caring role;
- there is, or will be, some inability to look after their own domestic needs and other daily routines while sustaining their caring role;
- several social support systems and relationships are, or will be, at risk.

Low risk to sustainability of the caring role arises when:

- there is, or will be, some inability to carry out one or two domestic tasks while sustaining their caring role;
- one or two social support systems and relationships are, or will be, at risk.

15.5.7 Services of an intimate nature

Services provided under CDCA 2000 may be delivered to the cared for person, with the cared for person's agreement, although provided to the carer, but cannot be of an intimate nature, such as lifting, washing, grooming, feeding, dressing, bathing, toileting, administering medicines or otherwise having physical contact with the person cared for or assistance to do these tasks. The reason for this is that if the cared for person was willing to receive intimate services, they would be receiving them as community care services (CDCA 2000, s.2(3)(b); Carers (Services) and Direct Payments (Amendment) (England) Regulations 2001, SI 2001/441, reg.2; Carers (Services) and Direct Payments (Amendment) (Wales) Regulations 2001, SI 2001/2186 (W.150), reg.2).

However, it is possible to provide an intimate service at the request of the cared for person or in circumstances where the cared for person is believed by the service provider to be at risk of imminent serious personal harm if the service is not provided and the cared for person is unable to give consent to the necessary task (reg.2(2)).

In the case of children, care services of an intimate nature can be provided but as the child matures the child's own views should be taken into account.

15.5.8 Financial assessment of carers

The CDCA 2000 gives local authorities power to charge carers for carer's services they receive under the Health and Social Services and Social Security Adjudications Act 1983, s.7. In the event that services are provided for children under the 1989 Act, then a financial contribution can only be recovered when the local authority considers it reasonable to do so, but not from any individual who is in receipt of income support, working families tax credit or disabled person's tax credit under the Social Security Contributions and Benefits Act 1992, Part VII or of income-based jobseeker's allowance.

Carers should not be charged for community care services provided to the people they care for. Under the 1983 Act, s.17, local authorities have a wide discretion to make reasonable charges for any non-residential services they provide in line with mandatory guidance, LAC (2001) 32, entitled *Fairer Charging Policies for Home Care and Other Non Residential Social Services*, and updated in September 2003 and in Wales under NAFWC 28/02, 17/03, 32/03, and 10/2004 (see **Chapter 5**).

In contrast, it is the cared for person and not the carer who is financially assessed when provision is made under CRSA 1995 for community care services. If both the cared for person and carer are being assessed for a charge for their respective services, they may choose to be separately or jointly assessed for any charges. Charges for any service should only be made once the service has been supplied. In the event that the financially assessed person is unhappy with the charge made, they can ask for a review under the 1983 Act, s.17(3).

All carers and those that they care for should ideally have a welfare benefits check to maximise their income, which can be arranged through local authorities' social services departments or Citizens Advice Bureaux.

15.6 CARERS (EQUAL OPPORTUNITIES) ACT 2004

Often the nature of caring prevents carers from seeking timely help and support. One of the objectives of the Carers (Equal Opportunities) Act 2004, which extends to England and Wales and came into force on 1 April 2005 and 18 April 2005 respectively, requires local authorities to inform carers that they may be entitled to a carer's assessment.

15.6.1 Duty to inform carers of right to assessment

Section 1 of the Carers (Equal Opportunities) Act 2004 inserts provisions into CRSA 1995 and CDCA 2000 which require a local authority to inform carers that they may be entitled to an assessment under those Acts. It means that when a local authority is carrying out an assessment of a person's community care needs or the needs of a disabled child, or would be required to carry out a carer's assessment, if asked, and it appears to the authority that an individual may be entitled to request an assessment of his ability to care (but has not done so), the local authority must inform the carer of this right before it goes on to make any decision about services.

The local authority does not need to inform the carer of this right where, in relation to the cared for person or the disabled child, the local authority has already carried out a carer's assessment, or made an assessment under the Community Care (Delayed Discharges etc.) Act 2003, s.4(3) or informed the carer of this right (CDCA 2000, s.6A(3) and (4)).

15.6.2 Recognition of carer's own life

Section 1 of both CRSA 1995 and CDCA 2000 have been amended with the effect that an assessment of a person's ability to care must include consideration of whether the carer works or wishes to work, or is undertaking or wishes to undertake, any education, training or leisure activity. As such the local authority must ask the carer about these activities during the assessment, and take them into account when making a decision as to whether the needs of the carer, cared for person or the disabled child, call for the provision of any services by the authority.

15.6.3 Cooperation between authorities

There is now a formal basis for cooperation between local and other authorities, such as any other local authority, any local education authority, any local housing authority, and certain NHS bodies, including any PCT, any NHS Trust or NHS Foundation Trust, and any LHB (s.3).

Where a local authority asks such an authority for assistance in planning of (s.3(1)), and/or provision of services (s.3(3)) to a person who is entitled to an assessment under CRSA 1995, s.1 or CDCA 2000, ss.1 or 6 or for whom that individual provides, or intends to provide, regular and substantial care, the authority must give due consideration to the request and make a decision about whether to provide the assistance or the services. The types of services are not specified in the Act, but can include services for either the carer or the person cared for.

Due consideration means that appropriate thought should be given to the request. What this means will vary from case to case, but the authority to which the request is made cannot fail to consider it, dismiss it arbitrarily, or have a blanket ban on considering certain types of requests (para.36 of the Policy Guidance).

15.7 VOUCHER SCHEMES FOR SHORT-TERM BREAKS

Sections 3(1) and 7(1) of CDCA 2000 provide for the Secretary of State to make regulations to enable local authorities to issue vouchers to parent carers, disabled adults, and their carers, as a simple and flexible way of providing short-term breaks, as an alternative to direct provision by the local authority or direct payments (see **para.15.8** below). As CDCA 2000 creates only a power to issue vouchers some local authorities do not operate the scheme.

The Carers and Disabled Children (Vouchers) (England) Regulations 2003, SI 2003/1216 apply in England, whilst regulations have not yet been introduced in Wales, although pilot schemes have been operating for a while. Mandatory policy and practice guidance entitled *Carers and Disabled Children Act 2000: Vouchers for Short Term Breaks* was published in July 2003 (see **www.carers.gov.uk**).

15.7.1 Who can have vouchers?

Vouchers can only be issued for community care or children's services and not for carers' services. Carers may instead benefit from breaks which are part of community care services, which are provided to the disabled person.

The recipient must be able to manage vouchers and his consent to the voucher scheme should be obtained unless, in the case of an adult, he lacks the mental capacity to do so, in which case the local authority must be satisfied that the outcome is in the person's best interest.

Local authorities do not generally give vouchers to young carers aged 16 and 17 years of age as the operation of the scheme could add to their responsibilities; however flexibility has been built in to the regulations for situations where it would be more helpful to the young carer to receive vouchers instead of direct provision.

Certain categories of people cannot be issued with vouchers. These people are the same as the specified categories who are not allowed to have direct payments as set out in the Community Care, Services for Carers and Children's Services (Direct Payments) (England) Regulations 2003, SI 2003/762 (see **para.4.9.2**).

15.7.2 How the voucher scheme works

Local authorities call the schemes by different names as the term 'voucher' may imply a restriction on individual choice, whereas the aim is to increase flexibility. Each local authority runs the scheme slightly differently as the authority has discretion as to its format. The administration procedure is usually simple, such as vouchers being in the format of a letter, which prevents the need for security printed vouchers. The vouchers should be monitored and evaluated by care managers who should know which voucher holder is redeeming the vouchers, for what services and at what frequency, as it may indicate problems such as a rapid deterioration of the cared for person, a decrease in the carer's ability to provide care, or that the carer does not fully understand how the scheme operates.

Vouchers take the form of 'time value' or 'money value' vouchers but not both (SI 2003/1216, reg.3(1)). Time value vouchers are redeemed for specific services delivered by specific suppliers with whom the local authority already has a contract or with whom it has arranged contracts (SI 2003/1216, reg.3(2)). Time value vouchers can be given to the carer of a disabled adult, either because they wish the carer to have the vouchers or they do not have capacity to give consent and the local authority feels it is in the best interests of the disabled adult to do so (SI 2003/1216, reg.4(1)).

Money value vouchers do not specify the service provider or the specific service and so the recipient can choose to spend the voucher on non-residential care services or a type of residential care. Money vouchers cannot be given to the carer of a disabled adult (SI 2003/1216, reg.4(2)).

The recipient of the voucher agrees when and how he wants to take advantage of the service provided with the service provider. The service provider can be the issuing local authority, another local authority or an independent provider (SI 2003/1216, reg.5(3)). All vouchers have a defined period of validity with a maximum period of one financial year, which will not be carried over to the next financial year. For accounting purposes a voucher is considered redeemed on the day of the service. If the disabled person moves local authority area, all unused vouchers should be returned and the individual should be reassessed by the receiving local authority for care services.

15.7.3 Top ups

Where the holder of a voucher wishes to receive extra services in addition to, or more expensive than, those which the voucher will meet, it is possible for a third party to pay for the extra cost. The third party is defined in the regulations as someone other than the service user, the parent carer or issuing local authority (SI 2003/1216, reg.6(3)). Top-up payments may be made direct to the provider. For children's services, top ups should only be used to acquire services which on the basis of the assessment are deemed to safeguard and promote the welfare of the child.

15.7.4 Residential care

A voucher may not be used to arrange residential accommodation for a single placement of more than 28 days at a time or a total duration of placements in excess of 120 days each year (SI 2003/1216, reg.7).

15.8 DIRECT PAYMENTS FOR CARERS' AND CHILDREN'S SERVICES

Direct payments can be made by the local authority as an alternative to direct provision. In doing so, the service user has day-to-day control of the money and commissions the care package directly with the provider, which creates greater choice and control in the type and delivery of care. Direct payments for community care services are dealt with more fully in **para.4.9**. This section deals with direct payments for carers' or children's services only.

15.8.1 Who can receive direct payments?

Local authorities are under a duty to offer direct payments to certain prescribed people who are assessed as needing children's services or carers' services, whether short term or long term, including adults, parent carers or 16- and 17-year-old carers providing they are satisfied that the direct payment can be used to secure services to meet the eligible needs. (See the Health and Social Care Act 2001, s.57; the Community Care, Services for Carers and Children's Services (Direct Payments) (England) Regulations 2003, SI 2003/762 and the Community Care, Services for Carers and Children's Services (Direct Payments) (Wales) Regulations 2004, SI 2004/1748 (W.185).) The local authority is prohibited from offering direct payments to certain prescribed individuals (see **para.4.9.2**).

15.8.2 Managing direct payments

When preparing the care plan for the carer, the local authority must specifically consider direct payments, which should be recorded in the care plan (see the *Fair Access to Care* guidance (LAC (2002) 13)). The local authority must be satisfied that the carer, or in the case of a disabled child, the person with parental responsibility, is able to consent and be capable of managing a direct payment, either alone or with assistance (SI 2003/762, reg.2(1)(a)). The Green Paper on social care *Independence, Well-being and Choice* (Cm 6499, March 2005) proposes to extend direct payments to those who lack capacity and those who are unable to manage even with assistance. Direct payments can be made for services provided by close relatives or a cohabitee living in the same household only where the local authority is satisfied that it is necessary to meet the eligible needs and in the case of a child is necessary for promoting the welfare of the disabled child (SI 2003/762, reg.6(1) and (2)). **Paragraphs 4.9.3** and **4.9.4** explain what help is available in setting up direct payments and how the system operates.

15.9 CONSULTING CARERS AND RIGHTS TO INFORMATION UNDER THE DATA PROTECTION ACT 1998 AND FREEDOM OF INFORMATION ACT 2000

Consultation of carers with service users should be an integral part of any assessment and care planning for health and social care services. Efforts have been made to make such consultation part of the legal framework.

15.9.1 Consulting carers under the Mental Health Act 1983

A nearest relative of a patient detained under MHA 1983 has a number of specific rights and powers under the Act. Prior to an approved social worker making an application for a patient to be subject to a s.2 order (for an assesment) or s.3 order (for treatment), the social worker must consult, if reasonably practical, the person whom the social worker believes to be the patient's nearest relative (MHA 1983, s.26). The nearest relative must be living permanently in the United Kingdom and be the person who is closest to the patient according to the following list:

- husband or wife (or cohabitees living together as husband and wife for at least six months);
- son or daughter;
- father or mother;
- brother or sister;
- grandparents;
- grandchild;
- uncle or aunt;
- nephew or niece;
- someone, not being a relative, with whom the person concerned normally resides, and has done so for at least five years.

Relatives of the full blood take precedence over half-relatives of the same category. If the person concerned has been living with a relative who has been caring for him, then that relative will take precedence. People who have been living together 'as husband and wife' count as husband or wife, where they have been living together for at least six months. Same-sex partners are not regarded as living together 'as husband and wife' even if their relationship has been registered under the Civil Partnership Act 2004, so they would only be considered the nearest relative if they fell into the last category in the list above and if there were no relatives in the other categories.

15.9.2 Consultation with patient and carer under the Community Care (Delayed Discharges etc.) Act 2003

Prior to notification under the delayed discharges legislation, the NHS body should consult fully the patient and his carer(s) (if any) (see **Chapter 7**). This is to allow those that want to arrange their own care to do so and prevents the NHS from initiating assessments that are not required. See the Delayed Discharges (England) Regulations 2003, SI 2003/2277 and the Delayed Discharge (Continuing Care) Directions 2004.

The Welsh Assembly has no foreseeable plans to bring into force the delayed discharge legislation.

15.9.3 Community Care Assessment Directions 2004

Under these Directions, when assessing an adult for community care services, the local authority must consult with the assessed person, as well as any carer, and to take reasonable steps to agree services. Information should be given to the assessed person, and if appropriate any carer, of charges for the cost of care services. The Directions have been published in LAC (2004) 24 and apply to England only.

15.9.4 Cared for person consents to disclosure of information

If the cared for person, including young people aged 16 or 17, wants the carer to be given information about assessments, services, health treatment and care, this should be made clear to the professionals involved, who should respect the cared for person's wishes. However, if the cared for person has capacity and does not want the carer to be kept informed, the carer has no right to information, unless it is in the public interest, is required by law (such as the person having a notifiable disease), or there is a court order requiring the information to be given.

Guidance has been published by the Department of Health to the NHS and NHS-related organisations on patient information confidentiality, as *Confidentiality: NHS Code of Practice* (July 2003) (available from **www.dh.gov.uk**). A similar code has been published by the Welsh Assembly for health and social care services (August 2004) (available from **www.wales.gov.uk**).

15.9.5 No capacity to consent to information disclosure

In respect of people who lack capacity to consent to or refuse disclosure, a balance has to be reached between the public interest and the individual's private interests in maintaining confidentiality and the public and private interest in disclosing. Guidance was given on this point in the case of *R (on the application of S)* v. *Plymouth City Council* [2002] EWCA Civ 388), which established '. . . a clear distinction between disclosure to the media with a view to publication to all and sundry and disclosure in confidence to those with a proper interest in having the information in question' (at para.49).

It is up to the health or social care team involved to consider whether it is in the best interests of the cared for person to discuss relevant matters with the carer. A balance needs to be struck between the individual's right to confidentiality and the rights of carers to be able to exercise their responsibilities.

15.9.6 Data Protection Act 1998

Individuals have the right to see most information stored about them on any relevant filing system, which includes electronic and manual data. The Data Protection Act 1998 establishes eight principles relating to the processing of information, which must be:

- fair and lawful;
- for specified purposes;
- adequate, relevant and not excessive;
- accurate;
- kept for no longer than is necessary;
- processed in accordance with the Act;
- protected by appropriate measures to safeguard against unauthorised or unlawful access, accidental loss, destruction or damage;
- not transferred to countries without adequate protection.

The Information Commissioner has issued legal guidance on the Data Protection Act 1998 (available from **www.ico.gov.uk**).

The Department of Health has also issued guidance as LASSL (2000) 2 *Data Protection Act 1998 – Guidance to Social Services*, with similar guidance issued in Wales (June 2000). The NHS has issued guidance as HSC 2000/009 *Data Protection Act 1998: Protection and Use of Patient Information* (March 2000) and *Guidance for Access to Health Records Requests under the Data Protection Act 1998* (June 2003). Access to non-personal information under the Freedom of Information Act 2000, held by public bodies, is covered in **para.1.7.2**.

The Information Commissioner keeps a register of data controllers who hold personal information. Information can be obtained by making a written request to the data controller and payment of a fee. The individual is entitled to be given a copy of the information in an intelligible and permanent form, unless this would involve 'disproportionate effort'. The data controller must comply with the request for access as soon as possible and, in any event, within 40 days of the request.

The mere fact that a person has been named in documents does not entitle that person to the information. It must go beyond the recording of the putative data' subjects involvement in the matter or an event that has no personal connotations and the information should have the putative data subject as its focus (*Durant* v. *Financial Services Authority* [2003] EWCA 1746). The Data Protection Act 1998 does not allow information to be disclosed which at common law could not lawfully be disclosed because it is confidential, unless there is a common law or statutory exception available (ss.29–37). If information relates to an identifiable third party, that person's consent is required prior to disclosure unless it is reasonable in all the circumstances to not require consent. Dissatisfied applicants can complain to the data controller, the Information Commissioner and finally the court. The Act should not be used however as a misguided attempt as a means of third party discovery with a view to litigation (*Durant* v. *Financial Services Authority*, above).

Third party access

Where an application is made on behalf of a child or an incapacitated adult, the data controller may withhold any information that was provided on the understanding that it would not be disclosed to the person requesting the information. The third party must have legal authority to act on the data subject's behalf, such as a person acting under an order of the Court of Protection or acting within the terms of a registered enduring power of attorney (Data Protection Act 1998, s.7).

Exemption from disclosure of health and social care records

Access to health records of living individuals may be refused or limited access be given, after consulting the 'appropriate health professional' by the data controller, where disclosure would be likely to cause serious harm to the physical or mental health or condition of the data subject or another person, or where giving access would disclose information relating to or provided by a third person who had not consented to the disclosure (Data Protection Act 1998, s.10(1)). The appropriate health professional is the person with the most recent responsibility for the patient's clinical care in connection with the subject matter of the request (Data Protection (Subject Access Modification) (Health) Order 2000, SI 2000/413).

Access to health records relating to deceased individuals is covered by the Access to Health Records Act 1990.

Similar provisions exist in relation to social work records, although the decision rests with the social work authority alone, with no obligation to consult any other professional (Data Protection (Subject Access Modification) (Social Work) Order 2000, SI 2000/415 (as amended)).

CHAPTER 16

Capacity

16.1 PRESUMPTION OF CAPACITY

Every adult is presumed to have the mental capacity to make his own decisions and the burden of proof is on those who assert to the contrary on the 'balance of probabilities' (*Simpson* v. *Simpson* [1989] Fam Law 20). This common law presumption is now embodied in the Mental Capacity Act 2005 (MCA 2005), s.1(2), which is planned to come into force in Spring 2007. Statutory guidance will be given in supporting Codes of Practice and underpin the objectives of the Act. The common law also presumes that once incapacity has been established the condition continues until it is proved that the individual is no longer incapacitated, although the individual may have capacity during periods of lucidity.

16.2 CAPACITY IS ISSUE SPECIFIC

There is no single test of capacity but it will depend on whether the individual understands the nature and effect of the transaction or decision. The legal capacity required depends on whether there is a particular legal test of capacity applicable to the decision and on the complexity of the information relevant to that decision. The capacity to get married (*In the Estate of Park* [1954] P 89), make a will (*Banks* v. *Goodfellow* (1869–70) LR 5 QB 549), make a gift (*Re Beaney (Deceased)* [1978] 1 WLR 770), enter into a contract (*Boughton* v. *Knight* (1872–75) LR 3 PD 64), litigate (*Masterman-Lister* v. *Brutton & Co and Jewell* [2003] 3 All ER 162), grant an enduring power of attorney (*Re K (Enduring Powers of Attorney), Re F* [1988] Ch 310), consent to medical treatment (*Re MB (Medical Treatment)* [1997] 2 FLR 426) are established in common law and are all issue specific: does the individual understand the nature and quality of that transaction?

The level of understanding required is relative to the transaction which it is to effect, for example a person may have the capacity to get married but not make a will (*In the Estate of Park* [1954] P 89). It does not matter that the decision is an unwise decision, so long as the individual has the necessary legal capacity to make that decision (*Bird* v. *Luckie* (1850) 8 Hare 301). As such someone with capacity may make an unwise decision, but such a decision may be a symptom of a person who lacks capacity. It follows that the ability of the individual to weigh up the issues is crucial in determining capacity.

Section 2(1) of MCA 2005 provides that 'a person lacks capacity in relation to a matter if at the material time he is unable to make a decision for himself in relation to the matter because of an impairment of or a disturbance in the functioning of the mind or brain', and so makes the test of incapacity both issue specific and time specific. The aim is to empower those with compromised capacity so that they can make those decisions that they are able to and not remove from them all decision-making power. For example, a person may have the capacity to manage a bank account with limited funds but not capacity to manage a substantial share portfolio. In effect, incapacity is not necessarily a continuous state.

16.3 BEST INTERESTS

Under common law, once lack of capacity is established then the person authorised or purporting to act must act in the best interests of the incapacitated person. The High Court's jurisdiction to grant declarations in the best interests of a mentally incapable person was confirmed in *Re F (Adult: Court's Jurisdiction)* [2000] 3 WLR 1740). The task in each case is to balance all the relevant factors, by way of a balance sheet of advantages and disadvantages to decide what is in the best interests of the incapacitated person (*Re A (Medical Treatment: Male Sterilisation)* [2000] 1 FLR 549 at 560).

Section 4 of the MCA 2005 has codified the common law. The decision maker must when making his decision about what is in the incapacitated person's best interests, consider the circumstances and whether the person will at some point have capacity. If possible, the individual without capacity should participate and regard should be given to his past and present wishes and feelings, beliefs, values and factors that would influence the decision in hand. The decision maker should consult carers, an attorney, deputy or other person named by the person without capacity to be consulted, as to what would be in the person's best interest. When determining best interest in relation to life-sustaining treatment, the decision maker must not be motivated by a desire to bring about his death (s.4(5)).

The General Medical Council issued guidance in August 2002, entitled *Withholding and Withdrawing Life-prolonging Treatments: Good Practice in Decision-Making* (available from **www.gmc-uk.org**) which contains guidance for doctors on determining best interests for mentally incapable patients. The patient cannot direct a doctor to give him treatment which the doctor believes would be futile or harmful (*R (on the application of Burke)* v. *GMC* [2005]

EWCA Civ 1003). Guidance contained in a booklet on establishing best interests, aimed at family and friends is available from the Department for Constitutional Affairs called *Making Decisions: Helping People who Have Difficulty Deciding for Themselves* and can be obtained from its website (**www.dca.gov.uk**).

16.4 CAPACITY TO MANAGE PROPERTY AND AFFAIRS

16.4.1 Receiverships

The Court of Protection has jurisdiction under MHA 1983, Part VII over the property and affairs of a person (referred to in MHA 1983 as 'the patient') where it is satisfied that the person is 'incapable by reason of mental disorder of managing his property and affairs' (s.94(2)). The court will require medical evidence to support any application. The court is supported in its work by the Public Guardianship Office (PGO), which is an executive agency of the Department for Constitutional Affairs and acts as the administrator for the court.

'Mental disorder' is defined by s.1(2) as 'mental illness, arrested or incomplete development of mind, psychopathic disorder and any other disorder or disability of mind' and psychopathic disorder means 'a persistent disorder or disability of mind (whether or not including significant impairment of intelligence) which results in abnormally aggressive or seriously irresponsible conduct on the part of the person concerned'. Such definition excludes people with certain personality disorders and temporary conditions, but these will be covered by the wider definition in MCA 2005, s.2(1). This is qualified by MCA 2005, s.3, by the person being unable:

(a) to understand the relevant information including information about the reasonably foreseeable consequences of deciding one way or another, or failing to make the decision;
(b) to retain that information;
(c) to use or weigh that information as part of the process of making the decision; or
(d) to communicate his decision (whether by talking, using sign language or any other means).

The court's powers are currently limited to the patient's property and affairs, which means his 'business matters, legal transactions, and other dealings of a similar kind' (*F* v. *West Berkshire Health Authority* [1989] 2 All ER 545, at 554d). It does not include personal decisions such as where to live or questions of medical treatment. Under MCA 2005, a new Court of Protection will be established as a superior court of record which will take over the work undertaken by the present Court of Protection on financial matters and will also deal with health and welfare matters that presently come before the High Court to determine by virtue of its inherent jurisdiction (*Re F (Adult: Court's Jurisdiction)* [2000] 3 WLR 1740).

Under MHA 1983 the judge has wide powers to make such orders, directions and authorities as appear to him as necessary or expedient for the maintenance or other benefit of the patient, patient's family, other persons or purposes for whom or which the patient might be expected to provide or otherwise for administering the patient's affairs. In the event that the patient's estate is over £16,000, a receiver is appointed by the court to manage the patient's property and affairs in the manner directed by the court, for example by giving authority to collect all income, pay bills and debts, dispose of furniture and sell a property. Where the assets are under £16,000, a one-off 'short order' can be made authorising a named person to do such tasks as directed by the court.

Once MCA 2005 is in force, the court will appoint a deputy (instead of a receiver) in cases where there is a need for on-going decision-making powers, although the court will be expected, wherever possible, to make a single order to resolve the matter. Any order that is made will be limited both in its scope and in duration. Supervision of deputies will be undertaken by the Public Guardian, a role currently undertaken by the PGO (MCA 2005, s.58).

Assessing a patient's capacity to manage and administer his property and affairs is a subjective functional test and may depend on the extent of the patient's property and affairs and the degree that it needs to be managed (*Re CAF* (unreported) 23 March 1962); the ability of the person to obtain appropriate advice, consider it and act upon it (*White* v. *Fell* (unreported) 12 November 1987), as well as the extent to which the patient may be vulnerable to abuse.

The Court of Appeal in *Masterman-Lister* v. *Brutton & Co and Jewell* [2003] 3 All ER 162 confirmed that it does not follow that because a person may be a patient for litigation purposes that he is also a patient for Court of Protection purposes (paras.12 and 19 of the judgment). When considering the subjective functional capacity test for litigation purposes, the court had to consider the nature and extent of the property and affairs that an individual had to administer and the extent to which the person in question would be likely to seek, understand and act on appropriate advice where needed, as well as the person's family background and the degree of support from family and others. Unlike the Court of Protection's jurisdiction, the purpose of the High Court's jurisdiction was not to protect the individual from the consequences of a wrong or imprudent decision but to remove the decision-making function where the person did not have sufficient capacity to understand, absorb and retain information that would enable him to make decisions based on that information.

16.4.2 Mental Health Act 1983, s.142

Section 142 of MHA 1983 provides that any pay, pensions or other periodical payments due from the Government to a person who is, by reason of mental disorder, unable to manage his affairs, may be paid to the institution or person having care of the patient for his benefit. Similar arrangements apply to local authority pensions. The authority must be satisfied after considering medical evidence that the person to whom the money is payable is incapable by reason of mental disorder of managing and administering his property and affairs.

16.4.3 Attorneyships

A person with capacity ('the donor') may grant a power of attorney to another person or persons ('the attorney') by virtue of the Powers of Attorney Act 1971 to enable the attorney to manage his property and affairs as set out in that power. Such power, known as an 'ordinary power' will cease to have legal validity on the onset of the donor's mental incapacity.

The Enduring Powers of Attorney Act 1985 (EPAA 1985) allows for the creation of a prescribed power, known as an 'enduring power' to continue to have legal validity not withstanding the donor's incapacity, provided it is registered with the Court of Protection on the onset of incapacity. The attorney has a duty to register the enduring power when the attorney has reason to believe that the donor is or is becoming mentally incapable of managing his property and affairs (s.4). There is no automatic requirement to provide evidence of incapacity at the point of registration. During the registration period the attorney has limited powers to maintain the donor and do such acts to prevent a loss to his estate (s.1(2)). Once registered the attorney has power to continue to act in accordance with the terms of the power.

The level of capacity to grant an EPA is not set out in the EPAA 1985, but shortly after the Act came into force, the Court of Protection received a number of applications to register enduring powers soon after they had been created. This raised doubts as to whether the donors had been mentally capable when they created the powers. The problem was resolved in the test cases *Re K (Enduring Powers of Attorney), Re F* [1988] Ch 310. To grant a power the donor must be capable of understanding:

- if such be the terms of the power, that the attorney will be able to assume complete authority over the donor's affairs;
- if such be the terms of the power, that the attorney will be able to do anything with the donor's property which the donor could have done;
- that the authority will continue if the donor should be or should become mentally incapable; and
- that if the donor should be or should become mentally incapable, the power will be irrevocable without confirmation by the Court of Protection.

As such, the donor does not have to have capacity to manage his property and affairs, only the capacity to grant an EPA and so an EPA can be granted during a period of lucidity. It will need to be registered as soon as possible after it has been granted.

The Mental Capacity Act 2005 creates a new type of power, the lasting power of attorney (LPA), which will enable a person, aged over 18 years, whilst capable, to appoint a person(s) to act for him in relation to finances and/or health and/or welfare decisions. The health and welfare LPA will only be effective in the event that the donor is incapacitated, whereas the finance LPA can be used where the donor still has capacity and so the attorney should take instructions from the donor when acting.

The LPA may authorise the restraint of the incapacitated person if the attorney believes that it is necessary in order to prevent harm and it is a proportionate response to the likelihood of suffering harm and the seriousness of harm. The restraint cannot however deprive the person of his liberty within the meaning of Art.5(1) of the European Convention on Human Rights (s.11(6)).

An LPA will need to be registered with the Court of Protection prior to use, and must contain a certificate of capacity signed by a prescribed person. It will also need a certificate that no fraud or undue pressure was used to induce the donor to create the power (MCA 2005, Sched.1, para.2(1)(e)). Once MCA 2005 is in force, no new EPAs will be able to be created, although existing EPAs will still be valid. The EPAA 1985 will be revoked but it is replicated in Sched.4 to MCA 2005, with some minor changes and will apply to EPAs made before the introduction of the 2005 Act. As such there will be parallel systems of attorneyships depending on when the relevant power was created.

16.4.4 Social security agents

For claimants who are unable or unwilling to use an account to receive their benefits or pensions directly from the Department for Work and Pensions, cheques are issued to the claimant's home address on a regular basis to match the frequency of their payments under a cheque-based payment scheme. Third parties are able to cash the cheque if the claimant signs the back of the cheque in the appropriate place to indicate that he has asked someone else to cash it on their behalf. The person who is actually cashing the cheque also signs a declaration on the back of the cheque to indicate that it is being cashed on behalf of the claimant. The Post Office requires the person cashing the cheque to produce evidence of both his own and the claimant's identities. The third party is only authorised to collect the money and not to spend it and the claimant must have sufficient capacity to manage the money.

16.4.5 Social security appointees

If the claimant is 'unable for the time being to act' and a receiver has not been appointed by the Court of Protection or an attorney appointed under a registered EPA, an 'appointee' can be named to claim any benefits on the claimant's behalf (Social Security (Claims and Payments) Regulations 1987, SI 1987/1968, reg.33). The appointee can collect, deal with and spend the money for the sole benefit of the claimant but his powers do not extend beyond handling the social security benefit. An appointee does not have authority to deal with the capital or other income belonging to the incapacitated person. Unspent pension and benefits may constitute capital, even if held in the name of the appointee. The appointee may not have full legal authority to deal with it and as such it may be necessary to obtain a 'short order' from the Court of Protection.

16.5 CAPACITY TO CONSENT TO MEDICAL TREATMENT

The doctor has responsibility to obtain the consent of the patient before treatment commences (unless in an emergency where treatment is necessary and reasonably required in the best interests of the patient) (*Re F (Mental Patient: Sterilisation)* [1990] 2 AC 1). The doctor must determine whether the patient has the capacity to consent and explain in simple terms the benefits and risks of the proposed treatment with possible alternatives.

Thorpe J in *Re C (Adult: Refusal of Medical Treatment)* [1994] 1 FLR 31 at 36, described three stages of the decision-making process, 'first, comprehending and retaining treatment information, second, believing it and, third, weighing it in the balance to arrive at choice.' In *Re MB (Medical Treatment)* [1997] 2 FLR 426), Butler-Sloss LJ did not consider the second stage of 'belief' as necessary in establishing capacity but confirmed that the person must be able to:

(a) understand and retain the information relevant to the decision in question, especially as to the likely consequences; and
(b) use that information and weigh it in the balance as part of the process of arriving at a decision.

The level of capacity required to make a medical decision is proportionate to the gravity of the decision, so that where more complex treatment is proposed, greater capacity is required (*Re T (Adult: Refusal of Treatment)* [1992] 4 All ER 649).

In the event that the patient does not have capacity then the prior sanction of the Family Division of the High Court by virtue of its inherent jurisdiction (*Re F (Adult: Court's Jurisdiction)* [2000] 3 WLR 1740), is required for the following cases:

(a) sterilisation cases, where this is proposed to be done for contraceptive purposes (*Re B (A Minor) (Wardship: Sterilisation)* [1988] AC 199 and *Re F (Mental Patient: Sterilisation)* [1990] 2 AC 1);
(b) the discontinuance of artificial nutrition and hydration for a patient in a permanent vegetative state (*Airedale NHS Trust* v. *Bland* [1993] AC 789);
(c) where there are disputes as to capacity or what is in the patient's best interest.

The British Medical Association has issued a Code of Practice on Advance Statements in 2000 to assist doctors treating patients who no longer have mental capacity and who have made an advance statement about their medical treatment.

The MCA 2005 has codified the common law requirements relating to advance refusals of medical treatment, which clarifies their status once the patient has lost mental capacity to make medical decisions. The advance refusal to withdraw life-sustaining treatment must be made in writing by a person aged over 18, signed by the patient or by another person in his presence and by his direction and witnessed (s.25(6)). Any withdrawal or alteration does not need to be in writing (s.24(3) and (4)).

A personal welfare LPA will be subject to any existing advance decision to refuse treatment and can extend to the giving or refusing of consent to carry out or continue medical treatment, although it will not cover consent to give or refuse life-sustaining treatment unless the LPA contains express provision (s.11(7) and (8)). This express provision is not the same as an advance decision as the latter only applies to refusals of specified medical treatment in specified circumstances. Where the LPA has been created after an advance decision was made and confers the same authority as that advance directive, then the advance decision will not be treated as valid (s.25(2)). There is concern about the operation of an LPA where it gives express power to consent or refuse life-sustaining treatment, as it is wider than an advance decision as it does not set out the circumstances in which it is to be used.

16.6 CAPACITY TO MAKE WELFARE DECISIONS

Where there are disputes as to capacity or what is in the person's best interest, the High Court can grant declaratory relief (*Re F (Adult: Court's Jurisdiction)* [2000] 3 WLR 1740). It is accepted that the test of capacity in *Re MB* (see **para.16.5** above) can be used for decisions relating to personal welfare, family and personal relationships (*Practice Note (Official Solicitor: Declaratory Proceedings: Medical and Welfare Decisions for Adults who Lack Capacity)* [2001] 2 FLR 158, available on the website of the Official Solicitor (**www.offsol.demon.co.uk**)).

Carers through necessity without any legal authority take most day-to-day personal and medical decisions, ranging from activities such as getting the individual dressed to giving medication. If challenged, the decision maker would have to rely on the common law doctrine of necessity, which can create uncertainty for professionals and carers. The MCA 2005, s.5 will allow the decision maker to undertake acts in connection with the care or treatment on behalf of someone who lacks capacity without incurring any liability, providing that the decision maker is acting in the person's best interests. Most health and welfare decisions are covered by s.5, including performing operations and undertaking diagnostic tests.

16.7 WHO DETERMINES CAPACITY?

The Court of Appeal in *Masterman-Lister* v. *Brutton & Co and Jewell* [2003] 3 All ER 162 upheld the High Court's finding that it was for the court and not the medical profession to decide whether or not a person had capacity (*Richmond* v. *Richmond* (1914) 111 LT 273). The court will need medical evidence to guide it, which may not necessarily be given greater weight than other relevant evidence. In practice, few cases go to court on the issue of capacity but nevertheless any expert asserting capacity must be prepared to stand by his opinion in court. As establishing capacity is not always easy, a multidisciplinary approach is best adopted to form a consensus of opinion. For further reading see *Assessment of Mental Capacity: Guidance for Doctors and Lawyers* 2nd Edn (BMJ, 2004).

16.8 INDEPENDENT MENTAL CAPACITY ADVOCATE SERVICE

Sections 35–41 of MCA 2005 creates a new scheme to provide the input of an Independent Mental Capacity Advocate (IMCA), where 'serious medical treatment' is to be provided by an NHS body or long-stay accommodation is to be provided by the NHS or local authority for vulnerable people who lack capacity and who have no family or friends who may be consulted about the decision. Serious medical treatment is defined in the Act as 'treatment which involves providing, withholding or withdrawing treatment of a kind prescribed by regulations' (s.37(6)). 'Long stay accommodation' means a stay of more than 28 days in hospital accommodation or more than eight weeks in a care home (ss.38–39). If there is an LPA in force, even if it is limited to financial decisions, the IMCA will not be appointed, as the attorney can be consulted. Deputies who have been appointed can return to the Court of Protection for a one-off order to be made.

Regulations are yet to be made, so presently it is unclear how the scheme will work, although it will be independent of the NHS or local authority (s.35(4)). The eventual regulations are unlikely merely to list specific treatment as this is likely to be found to be too prescriptive and it may be difficult to draft a list that fits all situations. As such, the regulations are likely to include characteristics of the decision to be made, for example where the benefit versus the risk is finely balanced or treatment would be irreversible.

16.8.1 Functions of the IMCA

The functions of the IMCA are:

- providing support to the person so that he may participate as fully as possible in the decision;
- obtaining and evaluating relevant information;
- ascertaining the person's wishes, feelings, beliefs and values that would influence the person if he had capacity;
- ascertaining if there is an available alternative course of action;
- obtaining a further medical opinion where treatment is proposed. (s.36(2)).

The decision maker will be under a duty to take into account the opinion formed by the IMCA but the decision maker does not have to follow it (MCA 2005, s.38(5) and (6)).

16.8.2 Access to the person and his records

The IMCA must be able to meet the person concerned in private and see that person's relevant health, social services and care home records, to be able to properly represent and support the person who lacks capacity (s.35(6)).

PART V

Surveillance, complaints and judicial remedies

CHAPTER 17

Health and Social Care Commissions

17.1 CARE STANDARDS ACT 2000

17.1.1 The regulatory framework

The Care Standards Act 2000 (CSA 2000) brought about changes to the registration and regulation of residential and nursing homes, which was previously managed under the Registered Homes Act 1984. It also created a regulation system for establishments that were previously unregulated, such as domiciliary care agencies. Part VI of CSA 2000 inserts Part XA into the 1989 Act in respect of children's services.

Regulation in England

In England, the National Care Standards Commission took over the role previously undertaken by local and health authorities in the regulation of care homes. No sooner than the Commission was up and running, the Government announced that it was to be replaced by two inspectorates: the Commission for Social Care Inspection (CSCI) and the Commission for Healthcare Audit and Inspection (known as the Healthcare Commission), which were formed by Part 2 of the Health and Social Care (Community Health and Standards) Act 2003 (HSC(CHS)A 2003).

The Healthcare Commission also took over the work of the Commission for Health Improvement, the national NHS value for money work of the Audit Commission, and when the Mental Health Bill is passed, the aim is that the Healthcare Commission will take over the work of the Mental Health Act Commission, which will then be abolished. The CSCI also incorporates the work formerly done by the Social Services Inspectorate and the Audit Commission Joint Review Team. In the Budget of March 2005, the Government announced its intention to merge the CSCI and the Healthcare Commission by 2008.

Regulation in Wales

In Wales, the Care Standards Inspectorate for Wales (CSIW) regulates social care and independent and voluntary health care services under the delegated authority of the National Assembly for Wales. The Social Services Inspectorate for Wales undertakes inspection of social service provision, and the Healthcare Inspectorate for Wales is responsible for inspection and investigation of Welsh NHS bodies, both of which are accountable to the Assembly.

17.1.2 Regulated establishments and agencies

Although the registration organisations are independent they act under guidance from the Department of Health or the National Assembly for Wales (CSA 2000, ss.6, 7 and 8) and have the responsibility of enforcing regulations made under CSA 2000, s.22 and minimum standards issued under CSA 2000, s.23.

The CSA 2000 regulates the following establishments and agencies:

- children's homes (s.1), which include community homes (1989 Act, Part VI), secure homes (s.4 as amended by HSC(CHS)A 2003, s.107), voluntary homes (1989 Act, Part VII) and registered children's homes (1989 Act, Part VIII);
- childminders (ss.79D(1)(a), (b) and 79F);
- day care centres (ss.79C, 79E(3) and 79F);
- independent acute and mental health hospitals, clinics and medical agencies (s.2(2)–(3), (4) and (5) as amended by HSC(CHS)A 2003, s.106);
- care homes (s.3(1)–(2)) where the accommodation, personal and/or nursing care is provided to persons who are ill, have a mental disorder, who are disabled or infirm, or who are recovering alcoholics or drug addicts;
- residential family centres (s.4(2));
- domiciliary care agencies (s.4(3));
- fostering agencies (ss.4(4) and 110);
- nursing agencies (s.4(5));
- local authority adoption and fostering services (inspection only) (s.45);
- boarding schools, residential special schools and further education colleges (1989 Act, s.87) (inspection only) (registration is with the Department for Education and Skills for independent schools or the local education authority for LEA maintained schools); if a college of further education provides personal or nursery care to more than 10 per cent of the students who are resident and boarding schools providing or arranging accommodation for any child over 295 days per year it must be registered (s.1(6));
- voluntary adoption agencies (s.4(7)).

17.2 HEALTHCARE COMMISSION

The Healthcare Commission has the general function of encouraging improvement in the provision of health care by and for NHS bodies in England and Wales (HSC(CHS)A 2003, s.48(1)). In England only, this includes regulation of the independent health care sector.

The Healthcare Commission's functions relate to the provision, quality, effectiveness and efficiency of health care and information about health care (Chapter 3 of HSC(CHS)A 2003). It also has functions in relation to the need to safeguard and promote the rights and welfare of children (HSC(CHS)A 2003, s.48(2)). Details of what they regulate are contained in the Private and Voluntary Healthcare (England) Regulations 2001, SI 2001/3968 (as amended).

The Healthcare Commission's functions include the following:

- publishing information about the state of health care across the NHS and independent sector;
- publishing annual performance ratings for all NHS organisations and producing annual reports to Parliament on the state of health care;
- regulating the independent health care sector through annual registration and inspection, taking into account any minimum standards set by the Secretary of State;
- independently assessing the performance of health services from patients' perspectives, using standards set out by the Secretary of State;
- aligning inspections of health care provided by the NHS and the independent sector;
- collaborating with other relevant organisations, including the CSCI (see **para.17.3** below);
- identifying how effectively funds are used within health care;
- carrying out the independent review function of the NHS complaints process (see **Chapter 18** for more detail);
- investigating and reporting on serious failures in health care services.

17.3 COMMISSION FOR SOCIAL CARE INSPECTION

The CSCI is the independent inspectorate for all social care services in England with the primary function to promote improvements in social care, which includes the regulation of care homes, covering those providing nursing care, domiciliary care and nurses agencies. Its role is set out in Chapter 5 of HSC(CHS)A 2003.

Its functions include the following:

- registration, inspection, assessment, reviews and reports on public social, private and voluntary care services taking into account national minimum standards set by the Secretary of State;

- inspection of boarding schools, residential special schools and further education colleges with residential students aged under 18.;
- providing the local authority with details of the number and quality of private and voluntary care services in its local area;
- dealing with complaints about care service providers. It will eventually undertake the independent review stage of complaints about local authority social services departments (see **Chapter 18** for more detail);
- assessment of how local authorities deliver social services functions and use their resources; annual collation of this evidence to form an overall assessment about the state of social care services nationally;
- using the information to inform policy makers of the impact of national and local policies on people who use social care;
- reporting annually to Parliament on the state of social care in England, how resources are being used and how the reform of social care is progressing;
- carrying out research and studies into social care;
- commenting on social care research by other organisations.

17.4 CARE STANDARDS INSPECTORATE FOR WALES

The CSIW regulates a range of settings against Regulations and national minimum standards set by the National Assembly for Wales. The CSIW registers, inspects and deals with complaints, investigation and enforcement for:

- adult care services, including care homes and adult placements;
- children's day care services for children under eight, including day nurseries, childminders, playgroups, out-of-school clubs, crèches and play schemes;
- other children's care services, including children's homes, fostering and adoption services, boarding schools, further education colleges, residential family centres; and
- health services including private and voluntary health care and nurses' agencies and domiciliary care agencies.

Chapter 4 of HSC(CHS)A 2003 contains provision as to the health care functions of the National Assembly for Wales. The CSA 2000 also established a Children's Commissioner for Wales with powers to safeguard and promote the rights and welfare of children (CSA 2000, Part V). **Chapter 22** contains details of the Children's Commissioner.

17.5 REGULATING AND INSPECTING CARE SERVICES

17.5.1 Registration

The Registration Authority is responsible for formally approving and granting registration to persons or organisations providing or managing the establishment or agency. The registration requirements are set out in CSA 2000, Part II. Applicants must provide various documentation and statements, and be able to demonstrate that they are suitable to provide or manage the service and that the proposed service is suitable to meet the needs of those who will be using it. A fee is charged by the Registration Authority, which is governed by regulations.

The Registration Authority looks at the fitness of person or persons applying, the fitness of the premises and the fitness of services and facilities. A criminal records check is undertaken on the person applying and the registered person will have to undertake such checks on all staff employed (see **www.crb.gov.uk**).

Registration will not occur unless minimum standards are satisfied and regulation requirements for registration are complied with. Registration can be granted unconditionally or subject to any reasonable condition (CSA 2000, s.13(3)). The Registration Authority has power to vary, impose new or remove conditions (CSA 2000, s.13(5)). Once registered the establishment will receive a registration certificate, which must be displayed. Running an unregistered establishment or agency is a criminal offence (CSA 2000, s.11(1)).

17.5.2 De-registration

Where an establishment or agency wishes to de-register because it has become a supported living scheme it must show that it is no longer an establishment as defined under CSA 2000, s.3(1). This was considered in *Alternative Futures* v. *National Care Standards Commission* [2002] EWHC 3032. Alternative Futures was a registered charity providing accommodation and care services for people with mental health needs in a number of registered care homes. The charity changed its arrangements and created tenancies for the residents and provided the services through two separate companies. Both companies were part of the Alternative group. It argued that as such it was providing supported living accommodation and no longer needed to be registered. The Court of Appeal considered the situation, which is reported as *R (on the application of Moore)* v. *Care Standards Tribunal* [2005] EWCA Civ 627. The court held that an 'establishment' included a group of companies which owned houses in which they provided accommodation together with nursing and personal care to persons with a mental disorder. As such the accommodation could not be de-registered as a care home. The crucial consideration was whether the establishment provided the accommodation together with nursing or personal care, which will be a question of fact.

17.5.3 Minimum standards

The Secretary of State has published the following minimum standards under CSA 2000, s.23(1) which are taken into account by the Registration Authority when making decisions:

- Care Homes for Older People;
- Care Homes with Adult Placements;
- Care Homes for Adults 18–65;
- Adult Placement Schemes;
- Domiciliary Care;
- Nurses Agencies;
- Children's Homes;
- Residential Family Centres;
- Adoption;
- Fostering Services;
- Boarding Schools;
- Residential Special Schools;
- Accommodation of Students under Eighteen by Further Education Colleges.

These standards are all available from the Department of Health's website (**www.dh.gov.uk**). Similar standards have been issued in Wales (see **www.wales.gov.uk**).

17.5.4 Inspection and investigation

The Registration Authority undertakes regular inspections to assess the quality of care provided by the establishment or agency (CSA 2000, s.32). The national minimum standards and regulations are used as the basis for each inspection, which will assess to what extent service providers exceed, meet, or fail to meet each individual standard. The Authority aims to work together with the registered person to identify problems and help them agree an action plan within a timescale to enable the registered person to comply with the standards. An inspector has power to enter and inspect any premises and seize and remove any document or material that he believes may show evidence of a failure to comply with a condition or requirement. If the inspector is obstructed in his work, it is a criminal offence. Inspection reports will be produced and usually published. Copies will be given to the establishment or agency. In addition to inspection, the registered person must submit to the Registration Authority an annual return to maintain the establishment or agency registration (CSA 2000, s.33).

17.5.5 The Concordat

The Healthcare Commission and CSCI are part of a voluntary Concordat, spearheaded by the Healthcare Commission, to make sure their approach to inspecting, regulating and auditing health care is coordinated. Although the CSCI does not regulate health care, it is recognised that patients and service users often receive care or support from several agencies and that the effective delivery of social care is an important aspect of their overall care. As part of its duty to cooperate, the CSCI ensures that arrangements are developed for social care services that are consistent with the Concordat's principles.

The Concordat commits each organisation to a set of principles, which aim to support improvement in health services while minimising disruption and duplication, to ensure that information is shared appropriately and to encourage joint inspections.

17.6 COMPLAINTS AND ENFORCEMENT POWERS

17.6.1 Complaints

The Registration Authority has established a complaints procedure through which service users can lodge complaints about the establishment or agency. It is expected that all complaints, if appropriate, will be made initially to the registered establishment or agency, through their internal complaints procedure. The Registration Authority will investigate complaints and concerns raised, and will try to secure improvements where regulations and national minimum standards are not being met.

17.6.2 Enforcement

The Registration Authority must make sure that the requirements of CSA 2000, associated regulations, and national minimum standards are met. CSA 2000 gives extensive powers which enable the Registration Authority to take enforcement action against registered service providers that consistently fail to meet the level of service provision set out in the legislation. This could lead to prosecution and ultimately, the cancellation of registration.

17.6.3 Cancellation

The Registration Authority will cancel registration if a person has been convicted of a relevant offence, or an offence in relation to the establishment or agency, or the establishment or agency has not complied with relevant requirements of the CSA 2000 and regulations, or the person or premises are 'unfit' or where registration has been cancelled on an urgent application granted by a magistrates' court. A relevant offence is one where there has been: a failure to comply with any conditions (CSA 2000, s.24); contravention of any regulation (CSA 2000, s.25); a false description given of an establishment or agency (CSA 2000, s.26); a false statement provided in a registration application (CSA 2000, s.27); failure to display a registration certificate (CSA 2000, s.28); obstruction of an inspector during a visit or inspection (CSA 2000, s.31); contravention of the regulations made under the Adoption and Children Act 2002; and any offence or breach of regulations made under the 1989 Act.

For urgent cases the Registration Authority can apply to the magistrates' court for cancellation of registration. The court must be satisfied that there would be a serious risk to a person's life, health or well-being is suffering, or in the case of a childminder, the child is likely to suffer significant harm (CSA 2000, ss.20 and 79K). The application can be without notice, although this is unlikely, so as to avoid arguments that the Registration Authority has breached Art.6 of the European Convention on Human Rights.

17.6.4 Appeals

In the event that registration is refused or granted with disputed conditions, the applicant can first ask the Registration Authority to review the decision. Ultimately, the applicant can appeal to the Care Standards Tribunal (CSA 2000, s.21). The Protection of Children and Vulnerable Adults and Care Standards Tribunal Regulations 2002, SI 2002/816 (as amended) govern the procedure of the Tribunal. The appeal must be brought before the expiry of 28 days after notice was served of the decision or order (CSA 2000, s.21(2)). Appeals are in relation to decisions made by the Registration Authority under CSA 2000, Part II and decisions made under ss.20 or 79K by a magistrates' court. The Tribunal has an excellent user-friendly website (**www.carestandardstribunal.gov.uk**). The Tribunal's decisions are subject to appeal on points of law to the Administrative Court (Tribunals and Inquiries Act 1992) and the decision-making process is amenable to judicial review.

CHAPTER 18

Complaints

18.1 USING THE COMPLAINTS PROCEDURE

What happens in practice and what *should* happen are frequently different things. Health and social service employees may not always have adequate knowledge of the legal and policy framework in which they work. Those acting at the coalface can make mistakes that can often be resolved relatively quickly through the internal complaints procedure, which is simple and inexpensive and may very often achieve the desired outcome.

18.2 COMPLAINTS ABOUT NHS SERVICES

18.2.1 The statutory framework

The Health and Social Care (Community Health and Standards) Act 2003, s.113, gives the Secretary of State and the Welsh Assembly power to make regulations for handling and considering complaints concerning the function of an NHS body and the provision of health care by or for such body. It also includes the provision of services by an English or Welsh NHS body or cross-border Special Health Authority under a partnership arrangement made by it under the Health Act 1999, s.31 in relation to the exercise of the health-related functions of a local authority (s.113(1)). As such, a person receiving both health and local authority services from an NHS body under a partnership arrangement can complain to that health body even if the complaint is about the local authority services that it provides.

Regulations have been made in England as the National Health Service (Complaints) Regulations 2004, SI 2004/1768 (NHS Complaints Regulations 2004). Guidance to support implementation of the NHS Complaints Regulations 2004 was issued in August 2004 (available from **www.dh.gov.uk**). NHS Foundation Trusts have their own process for handling complaints at local level, which may differ from the 'local resolution' procedure outlined in the NHS Complaints Regulations 2004, in which case complainants will need to make contact with the relevant Foundation Trust for details. The independent review stage operated by the Healthcare Commission does apply to NHS Foundation Trusts, which are also covered by the Health Service Ombudsman.

The NHS Complaints Regulations 2004 do not apply to the handling of complaints by primary care practitioners at local resolution (GPs, dentists, opticians and pharmacists). Pending the outcome of the report from the Shipman Inquiry, amended regulations should be issued sometime in 2006. In the meantime, the following regulations set out the statutory framework for the handling of complaints at a local level by primary care practitioners and about personal medical services:

(a) National Health Service (Pharmaceutical Services) Amendment Regulations 1996, SI 1996/698;
(b) National Health Service (General Dental Services) Amendment Regulations 1996, SI 1996/704;
(c) National Health Service (General Ophthalmic Services) Amendment Regulations 1996, SI 1996/705;
(d) National Health Service (General Medical Services Contracts) Regulations 2004, SI 2004/291;
(e) National Health Service (Personal Medical Services Agreements) Regulations 2004, SI 2004/627;
(f) General Medical Services and Personal Medical Services Transitional and Consequential Provisions Order 2004, SI 2004/865.

The Welsh Assembly has yet to issue regulations, although in April 2003 it published *Complaints in the NHS: A Guide to Handling Complaints in Wales* (available from **www.wales.nhs.uk**). References throughout relate to the detailed English regulations and guidance.

18.3 SCOPE OF DECISION MAKING USING THE NHS COMPLAINTS PROCEDURE

18.3.1 Who can complain?

A complaint can be made by the patient or his representative (such as a person with parental responsibility of a child under 16 years of age, the personal representatives of a deceased patient, the attorney or receiver of someone who lacks mental capacity or someone who has the written consent of the patient). Relatives or other persons who have sufficient interest in the welfare of the patient may also act as his representative, for example, where physical incapacity prevents the patient acting in person (NHS Complaints Regulations 2004, reg.8). If the complaints manager decides that the representative is not suitable to act, full information should be provided which outlines the reason for the decision (Guidance, para.3.29).

18.3.2 Excluded matters

Regulation 7 of the NHS Complaints Regulations 2004 sets out the matters that are excluded from the NHS complaints process, which include the following:

- complaints to one NHS body about another NHS body;
- grievances from employees or disciplinary proceedings against employees;
- a complaint which is being or has been investigated by the Health Service Commissioner (Ombudsman);
- a complaint arising out of an NHS body's alleged failure to comply with a data subject's request under the Data Protection Act 1998 or a request for information under the Freedom of Information Act 2000, where the complaint should be referred to the Information Commissioner;
- a complaint about which the complainant has stated in writing that he intends to take legal proceedings. The complaints manager should not infer that the complainant has decided to take legal action, even if the letter is from his instructed solicitor (para.3.13).

18.3.3 The time limit

Complaints should be made within six months of the incident forming the basis of the complaint or within six months of the complainant becoming aware of the incident. If the complainant had good reasons for not making the complaint in the time limit, it may still be investigated (NHS Complaints Regulations 2004, reg.10(2)). The discretion to vary the time limit should be used flexibly and with sensitivity (Guidance, para.3.37). Complaints made out of time can in any event be pursued through the Healthcare Commission (NHS Complaints Regulations 2004, reg.14(1)(c) and Guidance, para.3.38).

18.4 THE NHS COMPLAINTS PROCESS

Each NHS body should publish its complaints procedure, a copy of which must be given to any person who requests one. It must also appoint a complaints manager who manages the complaints process at local level (NHS Complaints Regulations 2004, reg.3(3) and (5)). Complaints are initially made to the NHS body or health care provider, which is the subject of the complaint, where an attempt should be made to investigate and resolve the matter locally. If this is not possible, the second stage will involve consideration by the Commission for Healthcare Audit and Inspection (the Healthcare Commission) in England. In Wales, the Independent Review Secretariat conducts the independent review stage.

18.4.1 Stage 1 – local resolution

The primary purpose of stage 1 is to resolve the complaint satisfactorily. The procedure should be open, fair, flexible and conciliatory, which should encourage communications on all sides (Guidance, para.3.1). Complaints should also be conducted in an impartial open-minded manner (Guidance, para.3.44). Local resolution of the complaint may occur with a meeting between both parties, although it may be preferable to formalise the complaint in writing (including electronically) to the complaints manager of the relevant NHS body. The complaints manager should acknowledge the complaint in writing within two working days of the date when the complaint was made and must include information about the right to assistance from the independent advocacy services, which provide conciliation and mediation services (NHS Complaints Regulations 2004, reg.11(4) and Guidance, para.3.32). The acknowledgement letter may also indicate when a full response will be provided (Guidance, para.3.39).

Independent Complaints Advocacy Services (ICAS)

ICAS have been set up in every PCT to provide an advocacy service for those making a formal complaint about NHS services (Health and Social Care Act 2001, s.12). The service is confidential and ICAS is not required to account to the NHS body. This role was previously offered by Community Health Councils. ICAS are in the main run through Citizens Advice Bureaux but for exact details see the Department of Health's website (**www.dh.gov.uk**). In Wales this role is fulfilled by the Community Health Councils (see **www.wales.nhs.uk**). The service can be accessed directly by patients or their representatives, or via the Patient Advice and Liaison Service, based in every NHS Trust.

The investigation

Disclosure of patient information should be confined to matters that are relevant to the investigation of the complaint and such matters should only be disclosed to those people who have a need to know for the purpose of investigating the complaint (Guidance, para.3.40). The manner of investigation will depend on the nature of the complaint. In any event, the complainant should be kept informed of progress and given a proper opportunity to talk to the investigating officer, who may not be the same person as the complaints manager (Guidance, para.3.46).

The response

A written response to the complaint should be received within 20 working days. If the time limit cannot be met, then the response should be sent as soon as reasonably practicable (NHS Complaints Regulations 2004, reg.13(3)). The response should be clear, accurate, balanced, simple, fair and easy to understand. It should summarise the nature and substance of the complaint, describe the investigation, summarise the conclusions made and set out the outcome, or explanation of planned action (NHS Complaints Regulations 2004, reg.13 and Guidance, para.3.55). It should also explain that if the complainant is unhappy, the matter could be pursued to the Healthcare Commission (NHS Complaints Regulations 2004, reg.13(4)). The response can then be shared with those involved in the investigation and named in the complaint (NHS Complaints Regulations 2004, reg.13(5)).

18.4.2 Stage 2 – independent review

Making a complaint to the Healthcare Commission

A complaint can be made to the Healthcare Commission where the complainant remains dissatisfied with the outcome of the local resolution; if the complaint has not been resolved within six months; or the complaints manager has decided not to investigate the complaint on the ground of it being out of time (NHS Complaints Regulations 2004, reg.14(1)). The Healthcare Commission cannot consider a complaint where the complainant has stated in writing that he intends to take legal proceedings (NHS Complaints Regulations 2004, reg.15(3)(a)). The Healthcare Commission also has remit to investigate complaints against independent service providers, where the NHS body has arrangements with them for the provision of services for NHS patients. The complainant would be expected to make a complaint to the independent provider using the provider's own complaints process before the matter was pursued to the Healthcare Commission.

The time limit

The complaint to the Healthcare Commission can be made either orally or in writing (including electronically) within two months of, or as soon as reasonably practicable after, the date on which the response letter from the NHS body (or independent provider, if appropriate) was sent to the complainant (NHS Complaints Regulations 2004, reg.14(3)). As a minimum, the complainant should send to the Healthcare Commission a request for the review, the case file from the original investigation, consent forms for the release of confidential information, any relevant medical records, and any other relevant documentation.

The initial review

On receipt of the complaint, a case manager will carry out an initial assessment of the nature and substance of the complaint and decide how it should be handled (NHS Complaints Regulations 2004, reg.16). The case manager may contact the complainant, the independent provider, any person complained against, or the NHS body to clarify details before reaching a decision. The case manager may also take advice from an expert adviser. The case manager will make and notify the complainant of his decision, which can relate to all or each part of the complaint and can decide any of the following:

- to take no further action;
- to make recommendations to the NHS body or the health care provider as to what action might be taken to resolve the matter, such as giving more information to the complainant, carrying out further investigation or taking remedial action;
- to carry out a full investigation of the complaint;
- to investigate the complaint further by establishing a panel to consider it;
- to refer the complaint to another body for further action or investigation such as the General Medical Council or the Health Service Ombudsman;
- to refer the complaint for action by another section of the Healthcare Commission.

Notification of the decision with reasons must be sent to any person who or body which is the subject of the complaint (NHS Complaints Regulations 2004, reg.16(3)(a) and (c)). The Healthcare Commission has discretion to inform any other body which it considers has an interest in the complaint (NHS Complaints Regulations 2004, reg.16(3)(b)). If complainants are unhappy with the outcome of the initial review, they will be able to complain about the decision to the Health Service Ombudsman (NHS Complaints Regulations 2004, reg.16(3)(d)).

Investigation by the Healthcare Commission

In the event of the decision to investigate the complaint, the case manager will send to the complainant and the complained against its proposed terms of reference for its investigation within 10 working days of the decision notice or as soon as reasonably practicable thereafter (NHS Complaints Regulations 2004, reg.17(1)).

If the case manager decides not to investigate certain parts of the complaint, he should provide reasons. Both the complainant and complained against are able to comment on the draft terms of reference within 10 days thereafter (NHS Complaints Regulations 2004, reg.17(2)).

The investigation can be conducted in any appropriate manner, which may include obtaining independent expert advice, medical or legal advice, or advice from someone who can give a patient or public interest perspective. Documentation and information may also be obtained from those complained against (NHS Complaints Regulations 2004, reg.17(4)). The case manager may also decide to interview people connected with the complaint.

The report of the investigation

When the investigation is completed, a draft report is prepared and distributed for comment on factual accuracy. The report summarises the nature and substance of the complaint; the investigation and its conclusions; the Healthcare Commission's opinion of those findings with reasons and recommendations on what action should be taken and by whom to resolve the complaint; and identifies what other action, if any, should be taken and by whom (NHS Complaints Regulations 2004, reg.19(1)). The report is then finalised and sent to the complainant, the patient (if the patient was not the complainant), the complained against person, independent provider or NHS body (in which case the chief executive of the relevant NHS organisation will receive notification) and the Strategic Health Authority (NHS Complaints Regulations 2004, reg.19(3)). The complainant should be told in writing of his right to take the complaint to the Health Service Ombudsman if he is unhappy with the conclusions and recommendations (NHS Complaints Regulations 2004, reg.19(3)(a)).

The panel

The Healthcare Commission may decide to appoint a panel from a list of independent lay people to hear and consider the complaint (NHS Complaints Regulations 2004, regs.17(3) and 18(1)). An independent lay person cannot be a member or an employee of an NHS body or a person who is or has at any time been a health care professional or an employee of a health care professional (NHS Complaints Regulations 2004, reg.18(2)).

The panel will consist of three people selected from the list, one of whom must be appointed to be the chairman (NHS Complaints Regulations 2004, reg.18(3)). The case manager and chair will agree the terms of reference for the panel, taking into account comments made by the parties involved. A panel coordinator will then take over organising the panel and producing the report. The panel may consider a complaint in any manner and adopt any procedure as it considers appropriate (NHS Complaints Regulations 2004, reg.18(4)). In the event of disagreement the majority view prevails (NHS Complaints Regulations 2004, reg.18(7)).

The panel should ensure that the participants are kept generally informed and in particular informed about the composition of the panel, the date and time of any hearing, and the names of any person whom the panel proposes to interview or from whom it proposes to take advice or evidence (NHS Complaints Regulations 2004, reg.18(5)).

A participant before a panel may be accompanied or represented by a friend or advocate, but may not be represented by a legal representative acting as such (NHS Complaints Regulations 2004, reg.18(6)). A lawyer acting as an attorney or receiver should however be allowed, as they are acting in the capacity of agent.

As with an investigation without a panel hearing, all parties involved will have a chance to check the draft report for factual accuracy before it is finalised and distributed. The panel's report should contain the same information as the investigation without panel (see above).

Independent Review Secretariat in Wales

The Independent Review Secretariat, which is independent of the NHS, manages the independent review stage. A letter sent by the local NHS body should inform the complainant of the results of the local resolution, making it clear that it is the end of the local stage and providing information of the next stage. The request for an independent review must be made to the Independent Review Secretariat within 28 days of receiving this final letter.

The complaint will be initially assessed by an independent reviewer who is a lay person who can:

(a) decide to take no further action;
(b) refer the matter back for further action by the local NHS body, if it is felt that a resolution could still be achieved;
(c) refer the matter outside the NHS complaints procedure to a relevant professional body; or
(d) set up an independent review panel which will investigate the complaint.

The composition and process of the panel is broadly the same as in England. If the complainant is still not happy with the outcome he can take the matter to the Health Service Commissioner for Wales, which from 1 April 2006 will be under the umbrella of the Public Services Ombudsman for Wales.

18.5 COMPLAINTS ABOUT SOCIAL SERVICES

Section 7B of LASSA 1970 gives the Secretary of State power to require local authorities to establish a complaints procedure. Such procedure is required of all local authorities under the Local Authority Social Services (Complaints Procedure) Order 1990, SI 1990/2244. Directions and practice guidance have been issued which set out the procedure to be adopted (Complaints Procedure Directions 1990 and *The Right to Complain: Practice Guidance on Complaints Procedures in Social Services Departments* (HMSO, 1991, ISBN

011 3214340). Aspects of the 1990 policy guidance *Caring for People: Community Care in the Next Decade and Beyond* also contain detail of the complaints procedure. If the complaint relates to children's services provided under the 1989 Act, a separate but similar procedure exists under Part III of the Children Act 1989 (Representations Procedure (Children) Regulations 1991, SI 1991/894; Advocacy Services and Representations Procedure (Children) (Amendment) Regulations 2004, SI 2004/719; and Welsh equivalent SI 2004/1448 (W.148)). The Welsh Assembly has issued the Social Services Complaints Procedure (Wales) Regulations 2005, SI 2005/3366 (W.263), which come into force on 1 April 2006).

18.6 SCOPE OF DECISION MAKING USING THE SOCIAL SERVICES COMPLAINTS PROCEDURE

Anyone can make a complaint if social services have either a power or a duty to provide or secure the provision of a service to him and the need for that service has come to the department's attention (LASSA 1970, s.7B(2)). As such, people for whom social services have no power or duty to provide a service are excluded from being able to complain. In addition, the complaint must relate to the discharge of or failure to discharge social services functions that relate to the individual concerned (LASSA 1970, s.7B(1)). Despite these restrictions, the local authority still has discretion to deal with complaints that fall outside the criteria (*Caring for People: Community Care in the Next Decade and Beyond*, para.6.5, 1990 policy guidance). Disciplinary or grievance procedures relating to staff are dealt with separately to the complaints process (1990 policy guidance, para 6.12). Housing- or education-related complaints do not fall to be considered under the social services complaints procedure, unless the complaint relates to the discharge of a social services function, for example a complaint concerning adaptations to a home. Social services may have referred the matter to the housing department for consideration of an application for a disability facilities grant. It may be unclear whether the complaint should be made to the housing or social services department. Failure by the local authority to have a system in place to deal with such cases will amount to maladministration (LGO complaint against Kirklees MC (01/C/00627)).

18.7 THE SOCIAL SERVICES COMPLAINTS PROCESS

Local authorities must appoint a complaints coordinator to advise them of all aspects of the complaints procedure and must ensure all staff are familiar with the procedure (Direction 4(1) and (2)). In practice this role is carried out by a person of a senior position, who should not have any conflict of interest in the investigation (LGO complaint against Bury MBC (97/C/1614)). All written complaints are registered by the coordinator and all failures to comply with time limits which are set out in the directions must be recorded (Direction 9).

18.7.1 The informal stage

The initial complaint can be made in writing or verbally and efforts should be made to resolve the complaint informally (Direction 5(1)). This informal approach should not however be treated as casual (*Right to Complain*, para.4.3). Although there is no statutory timetable for dealing with such complaints, many local authorities will set out target times in their published procedure. In relation to complaints concerning children leaving care, a 14-day time limit applies for the informal resolution stage (Children (Leaving Care) (England) Regulations 2001, SI 2001/2874 and Welsh equivalent SI 2001/2189 (W.151)). The complainant should be advised by the local authority of his right to pursue the matter to the next stage if he remains unhappy (LGO complaint against Waltham Forest (97/A/2464)). There is no requirement to use the informal stage and it is possible to progress to the formal stage immediately (*Right to Complain*, para.4.9).

18.7.2 The formal stage

Where the complaint has not been resolved through the informal stage, social services must give or send the complainant details of the formal or review stages and ask him or someone on his behalf (*Right to Complain*, para.4.10) to make a written complaint (Direction 5(2)). Assistance and guidance on the complaints procedure should be offered to the complainant, or he should be given information as to where help can be obtained, which can be provided through advocacy services (Direction 5(3)). Where appropriate, the local authority may arrange for the investigation into the complaint to be overseen by an independent person (*Right to Complain*, para 4.12), and for expert advice to be sought (para.3.16). Under the Children's Complaint Procedure an independent person must be involved. The complaints manager can postpone or stop the decision, which is subject to the complaint from being made or taken (*Right to Complain*, para.3.10).

A reply should be given within 28 days, although if this is not possible then the complainant must be informed of the reason for the delay and when a reply can be expected (Direction 6(1)). In any event, a full response should be made within three months. The local authority should send the decided outcome to the complainant, his representative and anyone else with sufficient interest (Direction 7(1)).

18.7.3 The review stage

If the complainant remains unsatisfied with the decision of the local authority, he has 28 days from the date of being notified of the outcome of the formal stage to request in writing a review by a panel (Direction 7(2)). Complainants should be given 10 days' notice of the hearing and be told who is on the panel and their status (1990 policy guidance, Chapter 6 Annex A, para.5). The complainant has the right to make oral and written submissions to the panel and is entitled to bring someone with him who can speak on his behalf, but this should not be a solicitor or barrister acting in a professional capacity. This would not prevent a professional from acting as the complainant's agent if he were appointed as the complainant's attorney or receiver by the Court of Protection. Likewise, local authority solicitors should also not be present. The panel must meet to hear the complaint within 28 days of receipt of the request (Direction 7(3)).

The panel comprises three people, at least one of whom must be independent of the local authority (Direction 2(1)). The independent person will act as chair, whilst the other members will usually be connected to the local authority, as either a councillor or an officer of the authority. In *R (on the application of Beeson)* v. *Dorset CC* [2002] EWCA Civ 1812, the Court of Appeal held that such a composition of the panel did not infringe Art.6(1) of the European Convention on Human Rights, as the complaints procedure, coupled with the availability of judicial review would usually be sufficient to satisfy the Art.6 standard of a right to a fair trial. The panel meeting should be conducted as informally as possible. The chair should explain the purpose of the meeting and the procedure to be adopted. The complainant or his representative should make his oral submission before the local authority submission. Evidence given by others should be agreed by the panel first and witnesses should only be in attendance during that part of the meeting (1990 policy guidance, Chapter 6, Annex A, para.6).

The panel will consider the evidence relating to the previous decision, evaluate it and arrive at a recommended conclusion. A majority decision prevails, but in the event that one member disagrees, the decision should record that member's view and his reasons for it (1990 policy guidance, Chapter 6, Annex A). The decision must be recorded in writing within 24 hours after the hearing (Direction 8(1)). A copy of the recommendation with reasons should be sent by the panel to thc complainant, his representative, the local authority and anyone else with sufficient interest (Direction 8(2) and (3)).

On receipt of the recommendation, the local authority has 28 days in which to decide whether to accept the recommendation, what action to take and to inform with reasons the complainant, his representative, and anyone else with sufficient interest. The local authority does not have to accept the recommendations but departure from them will require full rational reasons (*R* v.

Islington LBC ex p Rixon (1997–98) 1 CCLR 119; *R* v. *North Yorkshire CC ex p Hargreaves* (1994) *The Times*, 9 November).

18.7.4 Remedies

One of the roles of the panel is to fact find and to make recommendations based on those facts, such as recommending a certain course of action. It can also recommend that compensation be awarded (LGA 2000, s.92(1)), where for example delayed action has resulted in injustice and no practical action could provide a full and appropriate remedy, or loss or suffering has been caused. The panel can also recommend that the local authority review policy, practices and procedures or suggest improvements. The Local Government Ombudsman has produced some helpful good practice guidance on remedies (available from **www.lgo.org.uk/pdf/remedies.pdf**).

18.8 REFORM OF SOCIAL SERVICES COMPLAINTS PROCEDURE

Proposals for reforming social services complaints procedure received parliamentary approval in Chapter 9 of HSC(CHS)A 2003. Draft regulations were issued by the Department of Health in England during the consultation process on implementation (available from **www.dh.gov.uk**). The Welsh Assembly manages the Welsh equivalent and has also published final regulations in December 2005 (see **www.welshconfed.org**). These are to come into force in April 2006.

The Department for Education and Skills has produced draft regulations during its consultation regarding social services complaints in respect of children (available at **www.dfes.gov.uk**).

Key features of the reforms are:

(a) greater cooperation in dealing with complaints that may overlap with the NHS (s.115(6), as at present it may necessitate a complaint being made to both bodies);
(b) introduction of a duty on the local authority that receives a complaint which relates (in part or in full) to services provided under the Care Homes Regulations 2001, SI 2001/3965, to refer the complaint to the registered provider and inform the complainant within two working days of receiving the complaint. If the complaint relates to elements relating to its social services functions, then the local authority will be under a duty to cooperate with the provider so that one response is given;
(c) introduction of a 12-month time limit to make a complaint, as there is currently no time limit (the Welsh Regulations continue not to impose a time limit);

(d) requirement for the local authority to appoint a complaints manager (in Wales referred to as a complaints officer) whose function will be to resolve and investigate complaints and prepare reports for the local resolution stage;
(e) introduction of a time limit for the local informal resolution stage to be resolved within 10 working days, although extensions are possible with agreement;
(f) formal local investigation should be considered and the response sent within 25 working days from when the complaint was received, which may be extended in complex cases. The investigation should however be completed within three calendar months from the date the complaint was made;
(g) the independent review stage in England will be taken over by the Commission for Social Care and Inspection (CSCI), which has been subject to recurrent postponements, pending further consideration of the results and recommendations of the various reports from the Shipman Inquiry and the realignment with the NHS complaints procedure. This is necessary due to the government plan to merge the CSCI with the Healthcare Commission by 2008.

In Wales the independent review stage will be conducted by an independent panel established by the Welsh Assembly, which will comprise lay people and people who have social services experience.

CHAPTER 19

The Ombudsmen

An Ombudsman's main role is to investigate complaints of injustice caused by maladministration, although there is no statutory definition of the term. Richard Crossman in the debates on the Parliamentary Commissioner Bill in 1967 referred to 'bias, neglect, inattention, delay, incompetence, ineptitude, perversity, turpitude, arbitrariness and so on', when describing the term. It was extended in the Health Service Ombudsman's annual report for 1993–4 to include:

- rudeness;
- unwillingness to treat the complainant as a person with rights;
- refusal to answer reasonable questions;
- neglecting to inform a complainant on request of his rights or entitlement;
- knowingly giving misleading or inadequate advice;
- ignoring valid advice or overruling consideration which would produce an uncomfortable result for the overruler;
- offering no redress or manifestly disproportionate redress;
- showing bias whether because of colour, sex or any other grounds;
- omission to notify those who thereby lose a right of appeal;
- refusal to inform adequately of the right of appeal;
- faulty procedures;
- failure by management to monitor compliance with adequate procedures;
- cavalier disregard of guidance which is intended to be followed in the interest of equitable treatment of those who use a service;
- partiality; and
- failure to mitigate the effects of rigid adherence to the letter of the law where that produces manifestly inequitable treatment.

19.1 LOCAL GOVERNMENT OMBUDSMEN

19.1.1 The statutory framework

The Local Government Ombudsmen (LGO) for England and Wales were established by the Local Government Act 1974 (LGA 1974) as amended by the Local Government and Housing Act 1989. In Wales, the Ombudsman is now governed by Part III of the Local Government Act 2000 and the Commission for Local Administration in Wales and Local Commissioner in Wales (Functions and Expenses) Regulations 2001, SI 2001/2275 (W.165)).

The LGO investigate complaints about district, borough, city or county councils and joint boards of local authorities, but not town or parish councils (LGA 1974, s.25). The LGO cannot investigate a complaint about action which affects all or most of the inhabitants of the authority's area (LGA 1974, s.26(7)).

19.1.2 Reform to the Ombudsman service

The Public Services Ombudsman (Wales) Act 2005, in force in April 2006, will abolish the LGO and bring various Ombudsmen under the umbrella of the Public Services Ombudsman. For the time being the Ombudsman for Wales is operating from one site with the Parliamentary and Health Service Ombudsmen: the posts are now held by one person.

The Cabinet Office has issued a consultation paper seeking views on possible reforms to the Public Sector Ombudsmen services in England. It wants to remove the restrictions on the Parliamentary Commission for Administration, the Health Service Ombudsman and Local Government Ombudsmen so that they can work more closely in cases where they cross issues. They hope to be able to delegate functions to other ombudsmen services, to issue advice and guidance on good administrative practices and other matters, to seek resolution of complaints, in addition to or instead of conducting a formal investigation and to allow investigation of some cases not first referred to local authorities.

19.1.3 The Local Government Ombudsman's offices

There are three Local Government Ombudsmen in England. See further the Local Government Ombudsman's website (**www.lgo.org.uk**) or Appendix 3 for details.

19.2 HEALTH SERVICE OMBUDSMAN

The Health Service Ombudsman (HSO) undertakes investigations into complaints made by or on behalf of people who have suffered a hardship or injustice because of the NHS' s failure to provide a service, a failure in a service, or maladministration (Health Service Commissioners Act 1993 (HSCA 1993), s.3). Since 1996, the HSO has been able to investigate clinical decisions and where this happens, a clinical adviser may assist with the investigation. The HSO also looks into complaints against private health providers, where the treatment or other service was funded by the NHS. The HSO does not have remit to investigate complaints against the National Institute for Health and Clinical Excellence or NHS Direct. In Wales the role of the Health Service Commission will be abolished once the Public Services Ombudsman (Wales) Act 2005 is in force (see **para.19.1.2** above). See Appendix 3 for contact details.

19.3 THE PROCEDURE

19.3.1 Local resolution

Prior to making a complaint to the Ombudsman, the aggrieved person should have tried to resolve the matter through the NHS or local authority complaints procedure, to give the authority a reasonable opportunity to investigate and reply to the complaint. A complaint made to the Ombudsman before the local process has been exhausted will usually be treated as premature. If the complainant is still dissatisfied with the outcome, a complaint can be made to the Ombudsman. The Ombudsman has been known to investigate when the local complaints process has not been exhausted, for example if the complaint includes allegation of delay in the local process (LGA 1974, s.26(5); HSCA 1993, s.9(5)).

19.3.2 Alternative remedies

The Ombudsman may not investigate a complaint where there is a right of appeal to a tribunal or a minister, or where the person aggrieved has a remedy by way of proceedings in a court of law, although there is discretion to investigate if the Ombudsman is satisfied in the particular circumstances that it is not reasonable to expect the aggrieved person to appeal or to go to court (LGA 1974, s.26(6); HSCA 1993, s.4).

Whether the Ombudsman should have investigated a complaint where judicial review of the authority's decision might have been possible was considered by the Court of Appeal in *R* v. *Local Commissioner for Administration in North and North East England ex p Liverpool City Council* [2001] 1 All ER 462. Henry LJ said in that case (para.23):

> What may not have been recognized back in 1974 was the emergence of judicial review to the point where most if not almost all matters which could form the basis for a complaint of maladministration are matters for which the elastic qualities of judicial review might provide a remedy.

He went on to say (para.28):

> In my judgement this was a clear case for the application of the proviso. Serious allegations of maladministration had been made. Such allegations could best be investigated by the resources and powers of the Commissioner, with her powers to compel both disclosure of documents, and the giving of assistance to the investigation. The Commissioner was in a position to get to the bottom of a prima facie case of maladministration, and the ratepayers would be unlikely to have reached that goal, having regard to the weakness of the coercive fact finding potential of judicial review. As she found, it would be very difficult, if not impossible, for the complainants to obtain the necessary evidence in judicial review proceedings. Additionally, the complainants were a group in modest housing, unlikely to have the means to pursue the remedy. The Commissioner was clearly right to use the proviso to continue her investigation. This case is a good example of a case where the Commissioner's investigation and report can provide the just remedy when judicial review might fail to; and can reach facts which might not emerge under the judicial review process.

As a result, complaints to the Ombudsman are often seen as an alternative to judicial review and may sometimes provide a better remedy. However, the Ombudsman will not investigate any complaint if the dispute concerns a point of law or statutory interpretation and a complaint is not a suitable remedy if there is a degree of urgency to the case. The Ombudsman considers the way the decision is reached and implemented rather than what those decisions or actions are. The complaint may result in changes being made to the way the authority works, even though its policy and practice may not be illegal.

19.3.3 The complainant

The Ombudsman will accept complaints made by the aggrieved person; or if that person is unable to act for himself or has died, a member of their family, partner or representative may act instead. It is also possible for an appropriate organisation to make a complaint, for example, where a number of individuals are affected by the same problem (LGA 1974, s.26; HSCA 1993, s.9(3)).

Cases in England can be referred to the HSO by the Healthcare Commission which undertakes the independent review stage of the NHS complaints procedure (NHS Complaints Regulations 2004, reg.16(2)(g)). The Commission for Social Care Inspection will eventually conduct the independent stage of local authority complaints, which has suffered a number of postponements but it is anticipated at the time of writing to commence in April 2006, with similar regulatory provision to refer complaints to the LGO. (See **Chapter 18** on Complaints.)

19.3.4 Time limits

The complaint must be submitted to the Ombudsman no later than 12 months from the date when the complainant became aware of the events which are the subject of the complaint. There is discretion to extend the time limit where the Ombudsman considers it is reasonable, such as the local investigation took longer than it should have done (LGA 1974, s.26(4); HSCA 1993, s.9).

19.3.5 The complaint form

The Ombudsman has standard complaint forms, which can be accessed from the website or by contacting the relevant office. The forms are easy to complete and self-explanatory but note that when completing the form:

1. Be clear about the complaint, provide specific dates, with details of all individuals involved.
2. Provide all documentation in chronological order, with a schedule of supporting documents to which you and the Ombudsman can easily refer.
3. The complainant should give written consent to seek health or social care records in the application.
4. Photocopy supporting documents, although if the originals are sent the Ombudsman will photocopy them (free of charge) and return the originals.

19.3.6 Discretion to investigate

The Ombudsman has wide discretion whether to initiate, continue or discontinue an investigation and must be satisfied that intervention would be helpful and likely to achieve something for the complainant. As such it is important to make sure that the Ombudsman has the complete facts and supporting documentation at the time of submission of the complaint. There is no cost to the complainant for the Ombudsman's work.

Once the complaint has been received, the Ombudsman will acknowledge receipt and a full response will be sent later. The Ombudsman has no set time limit in which to deal with the matter as this will depend on the complexity of the complaint. Initial enquiries are made and depending on the outcome there may be a decision to formally investigate the matter. If the Ombudsman decides not to investigate further, the complainant and the organisation are informed in writing with reasons.

19.3.7 The investigation

For the purposes of an investigation, the Ombudsman has the same powers as the High Court in respect of attendance and examination of the witnesses and the production of documents. Nobody is compelled to give evidence that they could not be compelled to give in civil proceedings before the High Court (LGA 1974, s.29; HSCA 1993, s.12). Anyone who, without lawful excuse, obstructs the Ombudsman in the performance of his function is guilty of an act or omission which, if the investigation were in the High Court, would constitute contempt of court.

When the Ombudsman decides to investigate the matter, the complainant and the authority concerned are sent a statement of complaint setting out the matters that will be investigated. This gives all parties an opportunity to make comments. The Ombudsman will then obtain all the relevant papers from the authority. The authority's responses are sent to the complainant for comment. Where necessary and appropriate the investigator may conduct interviews with relevant individuals.

Investigations must be conducted in private. The procedure for the conduct of an investigation is at the Ombudsman's discretion and will depend on the complexities of the case. The Ombudsman cannot mention the name of any person in a report on an investigation, unless it is considered necessary, but in the case of the LGO, a councillor must be named if that councillor has breached the National Code of Local Government Conduct unless the Ombudsman is satisfied that it would be unjust to do so.

It is common for the authority to offer to settle the matter during the investigation, so in many cases there will not be the need for a full report.

If during the investigation the Ombudsman forms the opinion that the complaint relates partly to a matter which could be the subject of a complaint to another public Ombudsman, then he must consult with that Ombudsman and if necessary inform the complainant of how to make a complaint to the other Ombudsman.

19.3.8 The report

At the end of the investigation a detailed report about the case is sent to the complainant, the authority concerned and the Secretary of State (LGA 1974, s.30; HSCA 1993, s.14). The Ombudsmen are not bound by precedent in reaching their conclusions and making recommendations but they should act consistently. If the complaint is justified the Ombudsman can make recommendations about the remedy, such as a change in practice and procedure, reimbursing the complainant in respect of any financial loss suffered, or awarding compensation as a consequence of the maladministration. The recommendations do not have to be followed but they must be considered. In the majority of cases the conclusions will be respected and recommendations followed.

Reports of completed investigations are available from the relevant Ombudsmen and are available on their websites.

19.3.9 Review of case

There is no appeal against the Ombudsman's findings, although the case may be reviewed if there is significant fresh evidence that was not available at the time the complaint was considered. The Ombudsman's decision is, however, open to judicial review.

CHAPTER 20

The Local Government Monitoring Officer

20.1 THE ROLE OF THE MONITORING OFFICER

Section 5 of the Local Government and Housing Act 1989 (LGHA 1989) creates a duty on local authorities to appoint a Monitoring Officer. The Act places responsibility on the Monitoring Officer to oversee *vires* issues, in particular, reporting to the local authority if the Monitoring Officer believes that any proposal, decision or omission would give rise to unlawfulness, or if any decision has given rise to maladministration (LGHA 1989, s.5(2)). The Monitoring Officer's role is to ensure lawfulness and fairness in the operation of the local authority's decision-making process, including investigation and reporting on issues that embrace all aspects of the local authority's functions.

The local authority has wide power to choose whom it designates as the Monitoring Officer except that it cannot be the Head of Paid Service and as such cannot be the Chief Executive (LGHA 1989, s.5(1)(b)). The position is frequently held by the Head of Legal Services.

The role has been extended by virtue of ss.59, 60 and 64 in England, and ss.70 and 71 in Wales, of the LGA 2000, to promote and maintain high standards of conduct within a local authority, in accordance with a published Code of Conduct, in particular through the provision of support to the local authority's Standards Committee. Regulations for the way in which such matters should be dealt with may be made under s.66 in England and s.73(1) in Wales.

20.2 REMEDIES

If there has been an alleged breach of policy, it can be useful to contact the Monitoring Officer particularly before legal proceedings are commenced.

If the Monitoring Officer considers that any proposal, decision or omission would give rise to unlawfulness or if any decision or omission has given rise to maladministration the Monitoring Officer must investigate the matter and report or make recommendations to the Full Council or where appropriate the Cabinet after first consulting with the Head of Paid Service and

Chief Finance Officer. In the case of ethical standards being investigated, the Monitoring Officer reports to the Standards Committee.

After the report has been sent to the committee, the members have 21 days to consider it (LGHA 1989, s.5(5)(a)). Any proposal or decision that is subject to such a report cannot be implemented until the report has been considered. The report can make recommendations and give legal advice as to the course of action to be taken.

Under LGHA 1989, s.92(1) where the local authority considers that maladministration has occurred and a person has been or may have been adversely affected by the action, the local authority can make a discretionary payment to that person.

CHAPTER 21

The Department of Health

21.1 DEFAULT POWERS

Section 7D of LASSA 1970 provides that if the Secretary of State is satisfied that a local authority has failed without reasonable excuse to comply with one of its social services functions (other than under the 1989 Act) then he may make an order declaring that the authority is in default in respect of that duty. Any order can contain a direction compelling the authority to comply with the duty within a certain time frame. If the authority fails to comply with this, the Secretary of State can apply to the High Court for a mandatory order compelling the authority to do this.

These powers are rarely used or exercised. The power can only be used in limited situations, such as where a duty, rather than a power has not been exercised. The Secretary of State needs to be satisfied that there has been no reasonable excuse for this failure. Experts in the community care area have indicated that this power has never been used by the Secretary of State (see Clements, *Community Care and the Law*, 3rd edn (LAG, 2004) at p.543).

The courts have found on some occasions that these powers should be used instead of judicial review (*R* v. *Devon CC ex p Baker*; *R* v. *Durham CC ex p Curtis* [1995] 1 All ER 73 with *R* v. *Westminster City Council* (1997–98) 1 CCLR 486 and *R* v. *Kirklees MBC ex p Good* (1997–98) 1 CCLR 506).

CHAPTER 22

The Children's Commissioner

22.1 THE BACKGROUND TO THE ROLE OF THE CHILDREN'S COMMISSIONER

The need for a Children's Commissioner arose out of the Waterhouse Inquiry into child abuse in North Wales (*Lost in Care*: Welsh Assembly, 2000) and the report by Lord Laming into the Victoria Climbie tragedy (**www.victoria-climbie-inquiry.org.uk**). It had long been felt by advocates for the rights of the child that children required an independent body that could investigate complaints made by them and that could look more generally at social and educational policy and make broader recommendations for changes to practice or policy.

22.2 THE COMMISSIONER IN ENGLAND

The Children Act 2004 created the role of a Children's Commissioner in England. The Children's Commissioner's function is to 'promote awareness of the views and interest of children in England'. This involves investigation of all services provided to children by central or local government or regulated by them (such as private fostering, day care and private hospitals).

The Commissioner may not investigate individual complaints made by children (Children Act 2004, s.2(7)) unless a complaint raises issues of public policy, but can consider and research the complaints procedure as far as it relates to children and consider or research any other matter relating to the interests of children (s.2(2)). He must consult children in these functions (s.2(4)). The Commissioner must publish reports on his research or advice, which can contain recommendations for action that must be carried out within a certain time frame. The Commissioner therefore has power to demand action and change.

The first Commissioner is Professor Al Aynsley Green. No regulations or policy guidance have yet been published on the role of the Commissioner and as yet no guidance given on making complaints. For further information, see the Commissioner's website (**www.childrenscommissioner.org**).

22.3 THE COMMISSIONER IN WALES

The Children's Commissioner in Wales was set up in October 2001 as a result of the CSA 2000 and the Children's Commissioner for Wales Act 2001 (see further **www.childcom.org.uk**). The post is currently held by Peter Clarke.

The Commissioner has power to investigate the position of children in respect of all aspects of functions provided to them by both central and local government and those aspects of private functions which are regulated by local or central government (see above for examples).

The Commissioner can, like his English counterpart, review and monitor the provision for dealing with complaints and ensure that proper action is taken. He also is to provide advocacy services for children, provide advice and information to them and most importantly can provide and examine cases involving particular children, if they are those to whom regulated children's services have been provided in Wales (pursuant to the Children's Commissioner for Wales Regulations 2001, SI 2001/2787 (W.237)). The services which he can investigate are those provided either by relevant public or private bodies or by individuals in respect of children, including education, health and social services sectors at a local or national level.

In order to make an individual examination of a case, a representation should be made by the child concerned or by a suitable representative on behalf of the child which raises a question of principle that has more general application or relevance to the rights or welfare of relevant children, which is wider than the particular case (SI 2001/2787, reg.6).

The Commissioner can also involve himself in proceedings concerning a particular child if he is of the view that the proceedings relate to a matter of general application or relevance to the rights and welfare of children in Wales, as well as assisting in making a complaint to the relevant provider of children's services.

The Commissioner must publish his reports and has the ability to demand action and report inadequate compliance with his recommendations (SI 2001/2787, reg.14).

22.4 USE OF THE COMMISIONER FOR REDRESS

The Children's Commissioner could provide a useful additional forum to ensure that the complaints procedures of local and national government are working properly and to provide assistance during the making of a complaint. The Children's Commissioner could also provide a route by which general investigation of policy problems or more general difficulties with service provision could be brought to the attention of health and social care providers.

CHAPTER 23

Judicial review

23.1 WHAT IS JUDICIAL REVIEW?

Judicial review is the procedure by which the courts can survey and enforce good administration by public bodies. In this procedure, the court decides whether or not a public body has breached its public law obligations and if so, what can or should be ordered by way of a remedy. The jurisdiction of the court (as set out in the Supreme Court Act 1981 and r.54 of the Civil Procedure Rules 1998, SI 1998/3132 (CPR)) is to permit individuals and/or organisations to challenge administrative decisions made by any public body which concern 'public law'. The role of the court is for the judiciary to provide a control mechanism as independent arbiters in order to protect individuals from abuse by public bodies or to ensure that public bodies are not 'above the law' and that their decisions are subject to independent scrutiny. Judicial review is brought in the Administrative Court, which is a branch of the Queen's Bench Division of the High Court.

Judicial review does not (usually) deal with the merits of the decision: it is called 'review' because it concerns whether or not the administrator or body has acted in a reasonable and fair manner: it is concerned with 'procedure' rather than 'merits'.

Public law is a wide concept, but involves decisions concerning either a statutory scheme or a set of laws, or administrative decisions which do not involve 'private rights', i.e. those rights which could be subject to enforcement via contract or tort. For example, a health authority would be acting as a public body when it made a policy decision about which new cancer drug it would provide to individuals who needed it. However, when it ordered that drug from the relevant pharmaceutical company, it would not be acting as a public body but instead it would be acting as a private body entering into a contractual relationship with another private body.

23.2 WHO CAN BE SUBJECT TO JUDICIAL REVIEW?

23.2.1 Public bodies subject to judicial review

Public bodies that are acting as public law bodies (and not as private bodies) can be subject to judicial review. In the context of this book, health authorities and social services authorities are public bodies, as are any bodies (generally) that exercise powers or duties deriving from statute. Central and local government bodies, organisations or quangos (e.g. NICE, CSCI, etc.) are all public bodies. Courts, Tribunals and Ombudsmen (e.g. Care Standards Tribunal, Local Government Ombudsmen) and bodies which act in a quasi-judicial capacity (for example, the Discipline Committee of the GMC) would also be subject to judicial review.

23.2.2 Private bodies subject to judicial review

Sometimes bodies whose activities may be considered to be 'private' may involve a sufficient public element to render the exercise of their powers in certain contexts subject to judicial review. Much depends upon whether or not that private body is undertaking a function which is underpinned by statute, or whether it is operating under the authority of government or is woven into the fabric of governmental regulation (*Aston Cantlow and Wilmcote with Billesley PCC* v. *Wallbank* [2003] UKHL 37; *Hampshire CC* v. *Beer* [2003] EWCA Civ 1506). For example, a social landlord was held to be acting as a public authority when evicting an individual from her home when she had previously been a local authority tenant in circumstances where the social landlord was bound up with her local council very heavily (*Poplar Housing & Regeneration Community Association Ltd* v. *Donoghue* [2002] QB 48). However, where a public body is under a statutory duty to make arrangements to provide a particular service, and contracts that service out to a company, then that company does not usually owe any public law duties; for example where a private company provided residential accommodation to a group of vulnerable adults, that company was not subject to judicial review (*R* v. *Servite Houses ex p Goldsmith* [2001] BLGR 55). In *R (on the application of Heather)* v. *Leonard Cheshire Foundation* [2002] EWCA Civ 366, the Court of Appeal found that an independent sector provider of residential care would not be subject to challenge as a public authority under the Human Rights Act 1998 (the same test as whether or not something is a public body), merely because a public authority is meeting the costs of the care it provides or because it is subject to a degree of statutory regulation.

In contrast, an independent sector provider running a psychiatric hospital has been found to be a public authority (*R (on the application of A)* v. *Partnerships in Care Ltd* [2002] EWHC 529) when deciding on the types of care that a particular ward would provide, because of the statutory underpinning of the hospital and the fact that detained patients have no choice about where they access a service. Given the extensive amount of 'contracting out' that occurs, particularly in a social services context, it is somewhat surprising that these companies have not, as yet, been held to be subject to public law jurisdiction. This area is subject to flux and much depends upon the actual facts of the relationship between the parties and the context of the decision taken by the body in question.

Judicial review does not lie against bodies which have no governmental or statutory flavour, even though their actions may impinge upon a great number of individuals. Judicial review does not lie against bodies whose powers are derived from agreement of the parties and when private law remedies are available against the bodies concerned. Who or what is a public body has been subject to considerable judicial debate, much of which still continues. Readers should refer to specialist textbooks, in particular, De Smith, Woolf and Jowell, *Administrative Law in Action* (Sweet and Maxwell, 2002) and Clive Lewis, *Judicial Remedies in Public Law* (Sweet and Maxwell, 2001).

23.3 WHAT DECISIONS OR ACTIONS CAN BE CHALLENGED BY WAY OF JUDICIAL REVIEW?

A claim for judicial review is defined in CPR r.54.1(2)(a) as a claim to review the lawfulness of an enactment or decision, action or failure to act. The courts have jurisdiction to uphold that English statute is in breach of either European Union law or the European Convention on Human Rights as enshrined into English law under the Human Rights Act 1998. Other than this, the courts cannot decide whether or not an Act of Parliament is lawful, as Parliament is sovereign (*Manuel* v. *Attorney General* [1983] Ch 77; *Jackson* v. *Attorney General* [2005] UKHL 56).

Subordinate legislation (i.e. regulations or Orders in Council) can be subject to judicial review unless it is economically sensitive or there is an element of bad faith or absurdity (*R* v. *Secretary of State for the Environment ex p Hammersmith and Fulham LBC* [1991] 1 AC 521). Other than this, the wide scope of CPR r.54 enables individuals or protest groups to ask for review of any unlawful exercise of public power or unlawful failure to perform a public duty. The courts have also been willing to intervene and review guidance, advice or recommendations made by public bodies, and the policies of both central and local government and other public bodies. Again, the specialist textbooks outline the wide and vast areas upon which the courts have intervened in this area. To give examples, the courts have intervened in the guidance issued to general practitioners (*Gillick* v. *West Norfolk and Wisbech Area Health Authority* [1986] AC 112), and about the policy of the GMC (*R (on the application of Burke)* v. *GMC* [2005] EWCA Civ 1003).

23.4 WHO CAN APPLY FOR JUDICIAL REVIEW?

A court cannot permit an individual or a group or a body to take judicial review proceedings unless they have sufficient interest in the matter to which the claim relates (Supreme Court Act 1981, s.31(3)). This is to stop 'busybodies' interfering in administrative decisions without good reason. Whether or not someone has sufficient interest in a case depends upon the relationship between the claimant and the claim. If someone has a direct personal interest in the outcome of the claim, then that person will obviously have an interest in it. If an individual has a general or public interest but no personal interest in the matter, then the court may still permit an application to be brought if there is a serious issue of public importance to be tried (*R* v. *Secretary of State for Foreign and Commonwealth Affairs ex p Lord Rees-Mogg* [1994] QB 552).

The court takes a relatively liberal approach as to whether or not public interest groups or pressure groups and charities have a sufficient interest to bring claims for judicial review. When deciding whether or not these groups have sufficient interest, the court will look at the nature of the challenge, the importance of the issue and the nature of the alleged breach and the role played by the group or body in question. Groups such as the Child Poverty Action Group and RADAR have brought judicial reviews against regional or national policies, which will affect their members (see *R* v. *Gloucestershire CC ex p RADAR* (1997–98) 1 CCLR 476). The court will recognise that the public interest group may be able to bring a challenge more easily than an individual and that this should be recognised when there is a policy which is of importance to groups of individuals.

23.5 WHAT ARE THE GROUNDS FOR JUDICIAL REVIEW?

23.5.1 Review of the procedure – not the decision

Judicial review is primarily concerned with reviewing the procedure used when making a decision, rather than the underlying decision itself. As stated above, public law is characterised by an overarching principle: the public body is the decision maker. Parliament has conferred on a public body a power to act under statute or regulations. Because Parliament has determined this, the High Court's role in judicial review is to review the legality of the decision. If the High Court were empowered to substitute its decision for that of the public body, then the court would be exercising a power that has been given to the public body. That would be the judiciary taking over the role of the executive, which under constitutional notions of separation of powers is impermissible.

Judicial review cannot be brought simply because the individual is unhappy with a decision: there must be some legal basis for a 'review'. In the main, in the area of health and social care in recent years the courts have stressed the need for practitioners in this area to focus upon breaches of the decision-making process, rather than try to use the process for the court to substitute its decision for that of the original decision maker.

In *R (on the application of P)* v. *Essex CC* [2004] EWHC 2027 (Admin), the court said:

> The present litigation exemplifies a certain type of judicial review case which experience suggests can too often end up following a less than desirable course: I have in mind community care, housing and other cases, involving either children or vulnerable adults, especially those where as here, the first task of the local or other public authority is the preparation of an assessment.
>
> This is not the first time that I have felt impelled to express my unease about this particular type of litigation . . . There is, I think, a problem here that needs to be addressed. Too often in my experience inadequate thought is given to what precisely the court is being asked or can properly be asked to do . . . it may be helpful to set out a few basic principles.
>
> What the claimants here seek to challenge are decisions taken by the public authority in pursuant of the statutory powers and duties conferred on it by [an] Act. So I am here concerned with an area of decision making Parliament has chosen to confer the relevant power on the [public authority] not on the court or anyone else. It follows that we are here within the realm of public law, not private law. It likewise follows that the primary decision maker is the [public authority] and not the court. The court's function in this type of dispute is essentially one of review – review of the [public authority's] decision, . . . rather than of primary decision making. It is not the function of the court itself to come to a decision on the merits.

The courts have been reluctant to interfere with decisions made by either social services departments or health authorities which often involve very difficult questions of competing considerations of resources (either physical or financial resources) or competing public policy considerations (see *R* v. *Secretary of State for Social Services ex p Hincks* (1980) 1 BMLR 93, CA; *R* v. *Central Birmingham Health Authority ex p Walker* (1987) 3 BMLR 32, CA; *R* v. *Cambridge District Health Authority ex p B (No.1)* [1995] 2 All ER 129, CA). Practitioners in this area need always to consider if they are straying into a challenge to the merits, which the courts will refuse.

More claims have been brought against social services, as the duties owed by them are often mandatory and individual in nature. Claims against health authorities are often difficult because the underlying legislation (the 1977 Act) creates 'target' duties, rather than providing a duty to each and every individual. It is very difficult for the individual concerned to enforce these duties (see *R (on the application of A)* v. *Lambeth LBC* [2003] UKHL 57 for an analysis of the law as it relates to the 1989 Act, s.17).

23.5.2 Error of law or illegality

Judicial review lies where an inferior court or tribunal or other public body makes an error of law in the way that is exercises its powers or performs its duties. If a body misunderstands or fails to act within the law then it has acted illegally (*Council of Civil Service Unions* v. *Minister for the Civil Service* [1985] AC 374, HL).

The courts have decided that matters are 'illegal' by looking at a number of different tests. These include:

1. A decision to act *ultra vires* – literally acting outside its powers, if the body or official in question has no power to take a decision or exceeds such powers that are given. An example of this is in *R* v. *North and East Devon Health Authority ex p Coughlan* [2001] QB 213, where the court found that criteria created by the local NHS Trust, which divested it of responsibility for the care of Ms Coughlan were unlawful and *ultra vires*.
2. If a public body makes an error of law in the course of a decision which affects the result, it is treated as having acted outside its powers, or having made a 'jurisdictional error' (*Anisminic Ltd* v. *Foreign Compensation Commission* [1969] 2 AC 147 at 198F–G). This would include deciding to do something when it has no power to do so (sometimes called acting *functus officio*), or declining to act when it has power.
3. If a public body acts for extraneous reasons and not for the purposes which Parliament intended (*Padfield* v. *Minister of Agriculture* [1968] AC 997 at 1030B–D) or if a body acts in bad faith or has an improper motive. However, this is difficult to prove (*British Oxygen Co Ltd* v. *Board of Trade* [1971] AC 610 at 624F–G). So, within a health care context it was held to be improper to use MHA 1983 to protect an unborn child when its mother, who had capacity, had refused to undergo a caesarean section (*St George's Health Care NHS Trust* v. *S* [1999] Fam 26).
4. Public bodies must take into account relevant considerations and disregard irrelevant ones. In *R* v. *Avon CC ex p M* [1994] 2 FLR 1006, a local authority was held to have ignored the claimant's psychological needs when deciding which residential placement should be allocated to him and it therefore failed to take into account a relevant consideration. The authority also decided not to permit the residential placement of the claimant's choice because it would 'set a precedent'. That was held to be an irrelevant consideration in this context.
5. If a public body has made a fundamental mistake of fact, material to a decision before it, it is a ground for review. This must be where the public body has made a decision where there are unsupported or unreasonable

factual conclusions or unfairness through ignorance or disregarding an established and material fact (*E* v. *Secretary of State for the Home Department* [2004] QB 1044 at paras.42 and 63).

6. Where a public body is given a wide discretion, it must not fetter that discretion, e.g. by applying a particular set of criteria in an inflexible manner, without permitting exceptions. An example of this in the health care context is *R* v. *North West Lancashire Health Authority ex p A* [2000] 1 WLR 977, where the authority's rigid and inflexible application of its mistaken policy on gender reassignment was held to be a fetter of its discretion, and *R (on the application of Rogers)* v. *Swindon NHS Primary Care Trust* [2006] EWCA Civ 392. Further, in *R* v. *Ealing LBC ex p Leaman* (1984) *The Times*, 10 February, the court found that a local authority could not fetter its discretion by not considering financial assistance for holidays under CSDPA 1970, s.2 simply because that holiday was not arranged by the authority. This particular ground of review can be useful in a health or social care context where resource rationing can often lead to the construction of blanket policies, which either admit no exceptions or where the exceptions are so rare as to be practically useless.
7. Where Parliament has indicated that a particular decision or power is to be given exclusively to a particular officer or body, it may be illegal to delegate it to another (*R* v. *Devon CC ex p George* [1989] AC 573, HL).

23.5.3 Perversity or irrationality

The Wednesbury *approach*

The courts have, until the implementation of the Human Rights Act 1998, set the bar fairly high for a finding that a public body has acted in a perverse fashion – something which is outrageous in its defiance of logic. The seminal judgment is *Associated Provincial Picture Houses Ltd* v. *Wednesbury* [1948] 1 KB 223, where the court held that perverse decision making occurred when it was still possible 'to say that although the local authority have kept within the four corners of the matters which they ought to consider, they have nevertheless come to a conclusion so unreasonable that no reasonable authority could have come to it'. For examples within the health and social care context, it has not been found to be irrational to cancel operations if staffing was restricted (*R* v. *Secretary of State for Social Services ex p Hincks* (1980) 1 BMLR 93, CA). However, in *R* v. *North Derbyshire Health Authority ex p Fisher* (1997–98) 1 CCLR 150, the court found that it would be irrational to have to survey every patient in the local NHS Trust area before prescribing a particular cancer drug.

The super Wednesbury *approach*

This test has been refined in recent years to indicate that a matter will be perverse if it is not 'within the range of reasonable responses open to a decision maker' (*Boddington* v. *British Transport Police* [1999] 2 AC 143 at 175H) or that in cases which involve fundamental rights, anxious scrutiny could be engaged (see *R* v. *Ministry of Defence ex p Smith* [1996] QB 517 at 554) – sometimes known as the 'super *Wednesbury* approach'.

In cases which involve fundamental rights (i.e. those rights enshrined in the European Convention on Human Rights or common law rights involving liberty or life) this approach has not been held to be enough, and a more rigorous review of decisions has been applied in these cases. In *R (on the application of Daly)* v. *Secretary of State for the Home Department* [2001] UKHL 26 at paras.27–28, the House of Lords recognised that in these cases the courts would use the concept of proportionality, which is more precise and sophisticated than the usual grounds of review, and which can involve the court having to look at the competing interests and the relative weight to be given to various considerations when deciding if a decision is lawful, rather than just looking at whether or not it is within the *Wednesbury* range. Furthermore, given the need within the context of the Human Rights Act 1998 to look at pressing social need and proportionality, this involves a review which necessarily looks at the merits of the underlying decision.

23.5.4 Procedural impropriety

Procedural fairness

Judicial review will be possible if there has been a breach of natural justice or procedural fairness (sometimes called in more recent case law 'procedural due process'). This will include a failure to comply with a particular statutory procedural obligation, such as the duty to consult. The rules of natural justice are broadly that a person should be given a fair hearing before a decision affecting him is taken and that the decision maker is not biased in the sense that there is no real danger that the decision maker will favour or not favour that individual (*Re Medicaments and Related Classes of Goods (No.2)* [2001] 1 WLR 700 and *Porter v. Magill* [2002] 2 WLR 37). What is fair depends very much on the circumstances of the case, and can vary widely, dependent upon the nature of the decision and the impact it will have on the individual. The rules of natural justice apply when an individual's liberty or life will be materially affected or where the individual's property or job will be affected (*Ridge* v. *Baldwin (No.1)* [1964] AC 40 being the seminal case on the issue of fair procedure, which involved the dismissal of a chief constable by his police authority). Health and social care bodies could act unfairly in the manner in which they operate their complaints procedures and also when social services make decisions about assessment under the National Health Service and Community Care Act 1990, s.47.

Legitimate expectation

Procedural impropriety also includes the areas where a party may have a 'legitimate expectation' of consultation before a decision is taken or a service is altered or withdrawn. Procedural legitimate expectation involves some reliance by the individual or group concerned on some open or communicated promise or practice, which clearly leads the claimant to expect some kind of procedural advantage. This can arise either from an express promise or from the existence of a regular practice by a particular public body (*Council of Civil Service Unions* v. *Minister for the Civil Service* [1985] AC 374 at 401b). For example, in *R (on the application of C)* v. *Brent, Kensington and Chelsea, and Westminster NHS Trust* [2002] Lloyd's Rep Med 231, the court found that as the accommodation provided for vulnerable adults with mental health problems was interim in nature, there was no basic duty or legitimate expectation for them to be consulted, and the assurance made of a home for life was not 'clear and unequivocal'. If the local authority was not to follow its eligibility criteria when determining an individual's social care needs, or if the NHS Trust was not to have followed a particular policy promulgated by NICE about the availability of certain treatments, then a claim for procedural or substantive legitimate expectations may lie.

Legitimate expectation can also extend to a substantive right for a service to continue, if representations have been made which the court will uphold. One of the leading cases in this area is the decision in *R* v. *North and East Devon Health Authority ex p Coughlan* [2001] QB 213, where Ms Coughlan alleged that she was given a promise by the local authority that she would have a home for life, and that, given these representations her care home should not be closed by the authority. The court stated at para.57(c) of the judgment that:

> Where the court considers that a lawful promise or practice has induced a legitimate expectation of a benefit which is substantive, not simply procedural, authority now establishes that here too the court will in a proper case decide whether to frustrate the expectation is so unfair that to take a new and different course will amount to an abuse of power. Here, once the legitimacy of the expectation is established, the court will have the task of weighing the requirements of fairness against any overriding interest relied upon for the change of policy.

The application of substantive legitimate expectation can have a great impact in community and health care decisions, as very often the complaint will involve the removal or alteration of a service that may have been provided for a long time and about which a 'promise' may have been made that it would not be withdrawn. There have certainly been several challenges to the closure of day centres and care homes for vulnerable adults, where substantive legitimate expectation has been successfully used to prevent their closure (see **para.13.3**).

Requirement to consult

Procedural impropriety also includes a duty to consult, which is of particular importance to patients or users of social and health care services. Local authorities are obliged, following LGA 2000, to have written constitutions, which will often require consultation on important decisions about social care – including the construction or alteration of eligibility criteria. Central government also has a duty to consult on many policy or practice decisions. The duty to consult has been used successfully to block the closure of care homes or hospitals (*R* v. *North and East Devon Health Authority ex p Pow* (1997–98) 1 CCLR 280; *R* v. *Bath Mental Healthcare Trust ex p Beck* (2000) 3 CCLR 5). In *R* v. *Devon CC ex p Baker* [1995] 1 All ER 73, QBD, the court held that the duty to consult

> . . . encompasses those cases in which it is held that a particular procedure not otherwise required by law in the protection of an interest must be followed consequent upon some specific promise or practice. Fairness requires that the public authority be held to it. There is often held to be a basic duty to consult, which must consist of the following (known as the Gunning principles: *R* v. *Brent LBC ex p Gunning* [1986] 84 LGR 168), 'First that the consultation must be at a time when the proposals are still at a formative stage. Second, the proposer must give sufficient reasons for any proposal to permit of intelligent consideration and response. Third . . . that adequate time must be given for consideration and response and finally, fourth, that the produce of consultation must be conscientiously taken into account in finalising any statutory proposals'.

There is central government guidance upon consultation, the Code of Practice on Consultation (Cabinet Office, October 2005, available from **www.cabinetoffice.gov.uk**).

Requirement to give reasons

Procedural due process also often includes the duty to give reasons. The courts have been increasingly willing in recent years to find that reasons should be given in all contexts where the administrative process is infused with the concept of fair treatment whenever those people are potentially affected by administrative action. The Social Services Complaints Panel, the Health Care Commission, the Ombudsmen and the Local and Central Government Ombudsmen are required to give reasons for their decisions under statute. On a non-statutory basis, the courts have held that reasons should be given in a number of health and social care contexts. For example, reasons were held to be required when an NHS body decided to depart from national guidance (*R* v. *North Derbyshire Health Authority ex p Fisher* (1997–98) 1 CCLR 150, QBD); when the local authority failed to give reasons for its failure to follow statutory guidance in a community care context (*R* v. *Islington LBC ex p Rixon* (1997–98) 1 CCLR 119); and when a local continuing care panel failed to produce reasons for its recommendations (*R (on the application of Goldsmith)* v. *Wandsworth LBC* [2004] EWCA Civ 1170). Reasons will always be required when the decision impacts upon the fundamental rights of an individual (*R* v. *Higher Education Funding Council ex p Institute of Dental Surgery* [1994] 1 All ER 651).

Where reasons are deemed to be necessary, they must communicate an adequate level of information, which is dependent upon all the circumstances. Reasons must be intelligible and informative and must enable the person affected by the decision to understand why they have won or lost (*R* v. *Brent LBC ex p Baruwa* (1997) 29 HLR 915 at 929). They must deal with the main points raised and must not be generalised incantations (*R (on the application of Gupta)* v. *BMC* (2001) *The Times*, 16 October).

Duty to act in accordance with directions

The last area of procedural fairness is the duty to act in accordance with directions issued by the Secretary of State or in accordance with governmental guidance. In *R* v. *North Yorkshire CC ex p Hargreaves* (unreported) 30 September 1994, the court quashed a decision by the local authority where it had failed to abide by the mandatory requirements set out in the 1990 policy guidance. So if the authority failed to comply with the Community Care Assessment Directions 2004 (LAC (2004) 24) in failing to consult the service users about their needs, then the court could quash that decision.

The courts have also held on a number of occasions that a failure to follow guidance issued under LASSA 1970, s.7 without good reason is unlawful and so the decision will be quashed (*R* v. *Islington LBC ex p Rixon* (1997–98) 1 CCLR 119).

23.6 REMEDIES IN JUDICIAL REVIEW

All remedies in judicial review are discretionary in nature. The remedies available as set out in CPR r.54.2 and CPR r.54.3 are as follows.

1. A mandatory order: this requires the court or public body to do something as is required under its public duties. It can require someone to do a particular act, or indicate to them that they can hear something or make a decision. A mandatory order cannot be made against the Crown, but can be made against a minister (*M* v. *Home Office* [1994] 1 AC 377 at 425).

2. A prohibitory order: this will restrain the public body from acting outside its jurisdiction or from otherwise abusing its powers.
3. A quashing order: this quashes or sets aside a decision or order of a public body or court. The court has power to remit the decision back to the court or decision maker to make a fresh decision.
4. An injunction: this can include an injunction restraining someone from doing something or compelling them to do something (a mandatory injunction –Supreme Court Act 1981, s.30) and follows general principles for the granting of injunctive relief (see CPR r.25 on the granting of interim remedies).
5. A declaratory order: this order has a special place with judicial review because it can be used in a wide-ranging and flexible manner, which can clearly identify what the claimant's position or the authority's position should be. In some cases the courts have been willing to give advisory declarations if it is in the public interest, even if there is no dispute or proposed action (*R (on the application of Quintavalle)* v. *Secretary of State for Health* [2001] EWHC 918 (Admin)); but see the caution to be applied in these situations (*R (on the application of Burke)* v. *GMC* [2005] EWCA Civ 1003).
6. A claim for damages, restitution or recovery of the amount due (but only in addition to another order). Damages can only be awarded if there is some statutory or private law cause of action which could enable the claimant to make a claim for damages in any event (i.e. under the Human Rights Act 1998: see *Anufrijeva* v. *Southwark LBC* [2004] QB 1124). The judicial review procedure does not create any new rights for individuals to seek damages but provides that if a claim for damages exists in private law, it may be claimed in judicial review procedure alongside a claim for a public law remedy.

The court has power to refuse the grant of judicial review or any relief under the Supreme Court Act 1981, if there has been undue delay in making an application and it would cause substantial hardship or prejudice to the rights of any person or would be detrimental to good administration. This could include where the claim was filed out of time. CPR r.54.5 provides that a claim for judicial review must be filed promptly or in any event within three months. 'Promptly' has often been found to be less than three months (*R* v. *Hammersmith and Fulham LBC ex p Burkett* [2002] 1 WLR 1593 indicates that this may not comply with EU laws on the need for legal certainty but has not yet quashed this rule). Even if filed in time, an application may be refused if it would cause prejudice to the wide public interest (*R* v. *Brent LBC ex p O'Malley* [1997] 10 Admin LR 265). If matters have become academic or if a remedy would serve no useful purpose, then it will not be granted. A remedy may be refused if the public body would reach the same decision irrespective of any error or the individual has suffered no prejudice. However, this will occur only exceptionally (*Berkeley* v. *Secretary of State for the Environment, Transport and the Regions (No.1)* [2001] 2 AC 603).

If a claim is brought prematurely, where the public body has not yet made a final decision, then relief could be refused (see *R* v. *East Lancashire Health Authority ex p B* [1997] COD 267, QBD).

23.7 ALTERNATIVE REMEDIES

23.7.1 Determining the alternative remedy

Most importantly in the health and social care context, the court may refuse permission to proceed with judicial review or refuse to grant a remedy, if there is an alternative remedy which could have been used by the claimant. Judicial review is meant to be a remedy of last resort, and the court will look at all the circumstances, including the nature of the issue and the suitability of the alternative remedy for resolving it, when deciding whether or not an alternative remedy should be used. Where there is a statutory right of appeal then it will only be in exceptional cases that a right of review will lie before such appeal rights have been exhausted (see *R* v. *Inland Revenue Commissioners ex p Preston* [1985] AC 835 at 852D–F). In the health and social care context, there are few rights of statutory appeal, save for the right to go before a Mental Health Review Tribunal and/or to seek disciplinary action against a health or social care professional.

However, there are statutory rights to use a complaints procedure or to go to the Secretary of State or Local Government Monitoring Officer or even the Ombudsman (see **Chapters 18, 19** and **20**). Whether or not a matter should go to the complaints procedure or should go to judicial review is going to depend, in the main, on the suitability of the alternative remedy to resolve the dispute, and the effectiveness and convenience of these alternative remedies (i.e. their speed and the technical knowledge of the participants) as well as the range of remedies that they can offer. In social care cases, the court has held that when deciding whether or not an alternative remedy should be used (in that case using the default procedures of the Secretary of State), the court should look at which is the more 'convenient, expeditious and effective' (*R* v. *Devon CC ex p Baker; R v. Durham CC ex p Curtis* [1995] 1 All ER 73 at 92F).

If the matter is primarily one of law, then judicial review may well be more suitable. In the *Baker* case, the court found that where the issue is entirely legal in a developing field, it is peculiarly appropriate for a decision to be made by the courts rather than by an alternative remedy (at 87B–C and 92F–H) and for a similar decision see *R* v. *Sutton LBC ex p Tucker* (1997–98) 1 CCLR 251 at 275B–G. Conversely, in a case without a question of law then the complaints procedure would be more suitable (*R* v. *Lambeth LBC ex p A*

(1998) 10 Admin LR 209, 228A; *R* v. *East Sussex CC ex p W* [1998] 2 FLR 1082; *R* v. *Barking and Dagenham LBC ex p L* [2001] 2 FLR 763). Likewise in *R* v. *Gloucestershire CC ex p RADAR* (1997–98) 1 CCLR 476, the statutory complaints procedure under LASSA 1970 was not held to be as suitable as judicial review when the matter concerned a point of principle about an authority's legal obligations. An issue concerning the flexibility of a policy was an appropriate question for judicial review (*R* v. *Nottingham City Council ex p Howitt* [1999] COD 530).

23.7.2 Alternative dispute resolution

The court has been robust in cases involving community care to indicate that alternative dispute resolution (ADR) should be explored prior to the commencement of proceedings. In *R (on the application of Cowl)* v. *Plymouth City Council* [2001] EWCA Civ 1935 the court stated clearly that parties should contemplate using ADR in cases involving the closure of care homes to save time, expense or stress (although the resultant procedure was purportedly more costly and longer than a review would have been). The court indicated that it was of paramount importance to avoid litigation in such disputes. See further *R (on the application of Dudley)* v. *East Sussex CC* [2003] EWHC 1093 (Admin). Pursuing such remedies does not affect the judicial review time limit, so parties may need to issue proceedings to cover their client's interests but then stay them pending the outcome of the ADR proceedings. Furthermore, the NHS complaints procedure and any Ombudsman procedure become abandoned when a complainant indicates he intends to litigate. ADR is therefore likely to be used either in parallel with judicial review proceedings or prior to their issue, rather than being used instead of such proceedings. Failure to take up ADR can lead to a party being penalised in costs (*Dunnett* v. *Railtrack Plc* [2002] 2 All ER 850).

23.7.3 Which division of the High Court?

In some cases involving the welfare of children or adults without capacity to make legal decisions, the court may decide that a matter should be determined by the Family Division rather than the Administrative Court (*A (A Patient)* v. *A Health Authority* [2002] Fam 213 at 72 and 97). Where a matter may involve issues around care plans and child placements it should be heard in the Family Division by judges who have Administrative Court experience (*C* v. *Bury MBC* [2002] EWHC 1438 (Fam)).

The 'best interests' jurisdiction involves review on the merits and has been used to determine which and how social care services should be provided to incapacitated adults (*R (on the application of A)* v. *East Sussex CC* [2003] EWHC 167 (Admin). It is always used in cases involving medical treatment for adults and children where there are disputes between the NHS and parents (*Wyatt* v. *Portsmouth Hospital NHS* [2005] EWCA Civ 1181, following *Airedale NHS Trust* v. *Bland* [1993] AC 789, HL, *Glass* v. *UK* [2004] 1 FLR 1019). For how to issue such a claim, see *Practice Note (Official Solicitor)* [2001] 2 FLR 158.

23.8 THE BASIC PROCEDURE

A detailed look at the procedure is beyond the scope of this book and reference should be made to specialist textbooks (*De Woolf, Smith and Jowell* (above), *Lewis* (above) and Michael Fordham *Judicial Review Handbook* (Hart Publishing, 2004)). However, practitioners should always pay particular attention to the following:

(a) the need to issue the claim promptly pursuant to CPR r.54.4;
(b) the need to follow the Pre-action Protocol for Judicial Review in Administrative Court actions (see **www.dca.gov.uk**). Failure to do so will lead to the court taking this into account when deciding case management and costs issues. Even if the matter is urgent, and so the usual time limits for reply to a pre-action protocol letter do not apply (14 days), it is still important to notify the defendant of the nature of the challenge and the interim relief sought. Practitioners should ensure that their letters are clear and focused upon precisely what the authority should do to remedy the unlawfulness;
(c) the ability to seek disclosure and further information under the Data Protection Act 1998, the Freedom of Information Act 2000 and the general procedural rules about disclosure;
(d) the need to review a claim once it has been issued to ensure that the claim is still relevant and necessary;
(e) in cases where the nature of the challenge may change but the underlying allegation is similar to the new challenge, then amending the claim, if necessary (*R (on the application of P)* v. *Essex CC* [2004] EWHC 2027 (Admin) at para.38 and pursuant to CPR r.54).

CHAPTER 24

Actions and claims under the Human Rights Act 1998

24.1 HUMAN RIGHTS ACT 1998

The Human Rights Act 1998 came into force on 1 October 2000. It was expected to make great changes to English law. Whilst there have been some amendments in this area, it cannot realistically be said that the Act has caused a fundamental shift in health and social care law. Nevertheless, a fundamental understanding of human rights law and its principles are central to the life of any practitioner, and in the area of health and social care they have become automatically considered. The European Convention on Human Rights is a wide-ranging document which deals with a spectrum of fundamental freedoms and to a lesser extent, social and economic rights. Some of the Articles are likely to be more relevant to health and social care practitioners than others and are considered in this Chapter. For an in-depth examination of the Act, see Lester and Pannick, *Human Rights Law and Practice*, 2nd edn (Butterworths, 2004) and Clayton and Tomlinson, *The Law of Human Rights* (OUP, 2003).

24.2 ARTICLE 2 – RIGHT TO LIFE

Article 2 is the most fundamental provision of the Convention and involves the right to life. The Article provides that a Member State may not take a life intentionally, but also places a positive obligation upon the State to put in place a statutory framework in order to safeguard the right to life to the greatest extent possible (*Kilic* v. *Turkey* (2001) 33 EHRR 58). This can include a positive obligation to protect an individual who is at risk of being murdered (*Osman* v. *UK* (2000) 29 EHRR 245).

The scope of this obligation has to be interpreted in such a way so as not to impose an impossible or disproportionate burden on society, bearing in mind the operational choices which have to be made (*Kilick*, above, at para.63).

24.2.1 Medical care and Article 2

In *X* v. *UK* (1978) 14 DR 31 the court found that a State was under an obligation to take adequate measures to protect life and suggested that in some circumstances the State may be under a duty to provide adequate health care. However, this must be considered within the wide operational discretion given to each Member State to determine its own health care systems, which can sometimes involve making resource decisions that may well curtail life (*R* v. *Cambridge District Health Authority ex p B (No.1)* [1995] 1 WLR 898 and *NHS Trust A* v. *M* [2001] Fam 348). The court has refused to compel an NHS Trust to provide an experimental drug regime, even though it would be in the best interests of the patients (*A* v. *A* [2003] Fam 83).

The unborn child

The court has been historically reluctant to determine whether or not an unborn child deserves protection under Art.2 (*Poku* v. *UK* (1996) 22 EHRR CD94) given the wide variety of views expressed by different Member States on this issue.

Euthanasia and assisted suicide

The court has also been reluctant to express a firm view as to the applicability of Art.2 to euthanasia and assisted suicide because of the large religious and cultural differences throughout European States. In *Pretty* v. *UK* (2002) 35 EHRR 1, the court indicated that the right under Art.2 is not a right to die, and does not create a right of self-determination to choose death rather than life (para.39 of the European Court decision). That does not mean that it will, however, be a breach of Art.2 to make assisted suicide lawful (see *R (on the application of Pretty)* v. *DPP* [2002] 1 AC 800 at para.68; and the law of the Netherlands and Switzerland); further see the Seventh Report of the Joint Committee on Human Rights (HL Paper 74, HC 547).

Withdrawal of nutrition and hydration

However, it is compatible with the right to life for an NHS Trust to withdraw nutrition and hydration (*NHS Trust B* v. *H* [2001] Fam 348). Furthermore, an individual's right to personal autonomy is such that, if he has adequate mental capacity, he may refuse medical treatment without this being a breach of Art.2 (*Re B (Adult: Refusal of Medical Treatment)* [2002] 2 All ER 449).

24.2.2 Investigations of death and Article 2

The right under Art.2 has also led to the courts finding that there must be effective, independent investigations into the deaths of individuals where the agents of the State may be engaged, for example in prisons (*R (on the application of Middleton)* v. *HM Coroner for Western Somerset* [2004] 2 AC 182; *Goodson* v. *Bedfordshire and Luton Coroner* [2004] EWHC 2931). Deaths in hospital would not automatically require an independent investigation (see *Goodson*). The right to an investigation can exist even if the individual dies outside the UK, providing the individual is under the jurisdiction of the UK (*R on the application of Al-Skeini)* v. Secretary of State for Defence [2005] EWCA Civ 1609).

24.2.3 Damages paid in Article 2 cases

The State, in its role as provider of health care, has had to settle a number of cases for breaches of Art.2 in claims involving deficiencies of care for patients detained under the Mental Health Act 1983 (see further *Clinical Risk*, Vol.11, No.2, March 2005). In addition, if something could be considered to be gross negligence, the State may well be liable for failings in its health care system as breaches of Art.2 (*R (on the application of Khan (Mohammed Farooq))* v. *Secretary of State for Health* [2003] EWCA Civ 1129).

24.2.4 Environment and Article 2

Significant environmental hazards may well be serious enough so that the State has a duty under Art.2 to protect the general public from life-threatening hazards. In *Oneryildiz* v. *Turkey* (2004) 39 EHRR 12 (judgment of 18 June 2002), a relative of individuals killed by a landslide from a rubbish tip successfully argued that it was a breach of Art.2 for the authorities to do nothing, when they knew that there was a real threat to people's lives.

24.3 ARTICLE 3 – RIGHT NOT TO BE SUBJECTED TO TORTURE, INHUMAN OR DEGRADING TREATMENT

Article 3 indicates that no one shall be subjected to torture, inhuman or degrading punishment. This is an absolute basic right, which applies regardless of the aims of the state, or the difficulties faced when investigating terrorism (*Chahal* v. *UK* (1997) 23 EHRR 413; *A* v. *Secretary of State for the Home Department* [2005] UKHL 71).

24.3.1 Threshold for breach of Article 3

The treatment alleged must attain a minimum level of severity to fall within the scope of Art.3. This assessment depends on the duration of the treatment, its physical and mental effects, and the age, sex, vulnerability and state of health of a particular individual (*Ireland* v. *UK* (1979–80) 2 EHRR 25 at para.162). In the UK, much discussion of this provision has centred around when destitute asylum seekers reach this threshold (*R (on the application of Limbuela)* v. *Secretary of State for the Home Department* [2005] UKHL 66; *R (on the application of Q)* v. *Secretary of State for the Home Department* [2003] EWHC 2507 (Admin)). Destitution can, therefore, in certain circumstances, reach the relevant threshold for breach of Art.3 if the individual is denied food, shelter and the most basic necessities of life.

The 'threshold' is lower for those in society who are more vulnerable (the elderly, the disabled, the mentally ill or children). In *Price* v. *UK* (2002) 34 EHRR 53, a disabled woman was detained in a police station and was unable to go to the toilet, so was at risk of developing sores. This amounted to a breach of Art.3 and entitled her to appropriate compensation. There would also need to be reasonable adjustments made to prevent degrading treatment occurring again.

24.3.2 Violation of Article 3 – medical treatment

In the spectrum of health care, forcible administration of medical treatment to a protesting patient (*R (on the application of Wilkinson)* v. *Broadmoor Hospital* [2001] EWCA Civ 1545) or the seclusion of mentally ill patients could amount to a violation of Art.3 in principle, although on its facts such a violation was not made out (*R (on the application of Munjaz)* v. *Mersey Care NHS Trust* [2005] UKHL 58). However, an individual's rights under Art.3 or Art.8 would not be breached if he lacked capacity to know whether or not he was ill and he required treatment as a matter of therapeutic necessity and had been detained under MHA 1983 (*R (on the application of B)* v. *S* [2006] EWCA Civ 28 and *R (on the application of B)* v. *Ashworth Hospital Authority* [2005] UKHL 20).

Treatment which causes mental suffering if there is a sufficient degree of intensity (*Ireland* v. *UK* (1979–80) 2 EHRR 25) and the threat of such inhuman and degrading treatment, even if not administered, can violate Art.3 (*Cosans* v. *UK* (1982) 4 EHRR 293, where although the court held that the threat of corporal punishment in schools was not enough to surmount the minimum threshold, the court upheld that principle as being right). Collective treatment of a group or community can also constitute breach of Art.3. An omission to provide effective medical care to a mentally ill person could also amount to a breach of Art.3 (*Keenan* v. *UK* (2001) 33 EHRR 38).

24.3.3 Abuse and Article 3

The State has a positive obligation to protect children and vulnerable adults from abuse. Where abuse has been suffered by an individual in the care of a public authority, there is a positive obligation for an independent and open investigation to be convened and a duty to take reasonable steps to prevent that ill-treatment. (See *Z* v. *UK* (2002) 34 EHRR 3; *Re F (Adult: Court's Jurisdiction)* [2000] 3 WLR 1740; *Assenov* v. *Bulgaria* (1999) 28 EHRR 652 and *A* v. *UK* (1999) 27 EHRR 611, where the court found a breach of Art.3 on the grounds that national law had failed to protect a child from abuse by his stepfather because of the law of 'reasonable chastisement' – see the Children Act 2004.) The State has personal responsibility, in particular in respect of vulnerable individuals, for the effective deterrence of breaches of personal integrity (*R (on the application of A)* v. *East Sussex CC (No.2)* [2003] EWHC 167). This could lead to the State being found to be negligent or having to pay damages under Art.3 for failing to prevent such abuse or breaches of personal integrity.

The introduction of Art.3 issues can mean that the traditional role of judicial review is not enough and the court has to determine and resolve disputes of fact, for example such as whether or not someone could consent to medical treatment (*R (on the application of Wilkinson)* v. *Broadmoor Hospital* [2001] EWCA Civ 1545), where, for example, the court hears live evidence.

24.3.4 Limitations of Article 3

There is a limit to the positive obligation of the State, and so obligations cannot be unlimited. Where there may be significant resource implications or macro social, economic or political considerations, the courts will be slower to find a breach of Art.3 (*Anufrijeva* v. *Southwark LBC* [2004] QB 1124; *R (on the application of A)* v. *East Sussex CC (No.2)* [2003] EWHC 167 and the destitute asylum seeker cases). As the example of corporal punishment shows, the 'threshold' for determining what is inhuman and degrading alters as society changes and evolves, and so, even over a relatively short period of time, systems of treatment and the provision of social welfare in the UK to certain individuals may well become subject to concerns that they breach Art.3, in particular, in respect of treatment in care homes or for those with disabilities or mental illness.

24.4 ARTICLE 5 – RIGHT TO LIBERTY

Article 5 prevents the State from detaining people except in certain defined instances. Article 5(1)(e) provides that individuals can be lawfully detained for the prevention of infectious diseases if they are of unsound mind, alcoholics, drug addicts or vagrants. Minors can also be detained for the purpose of educational supervision or to bring them before competent legal authority (Art.5(1)(d)). Article 5 is concerned solely with the deprivation of liberty, and does not deal with either treatment or conditions (*R (on the application of Cawser)* v. *Secretary of State for the Home Department* [2003] EWCA Civ 1522, CA).

24.4.1 Article 5 and detention under the Mental Health Act 1983

Article 5 obviously applies to those detained under MHA 1983 (and its successor in the Mental Health Bill 2004). An individual subject to compulsory detention, even though able to leave the hospital on occasions, could rely on Art.5 (*Ashingdane* v. *UK* (1985) 7 EHRR 528 at para.42).

In order for individuals to be lawfully detained, the requirement of lawfulness established in *Winterwerp* v. *Netherlands* (1979–80) 2 EHRR 387 must be met:

(a) the individual concerned must be reliably established to be of unsound mind by objective medical expertise;
(b) this is of a kind or degree which warrants compulsory detention; and
(c) the disorder persists throughout the detention so that it continues to be justified.

In an emergency an individual may be admitted to hospital under the doctrine of necessity (*R* v. *Bournewood Community and Mental Health NHS Trust ex p L* [1999] 1 AC 458, HL). The *Bournewood* case was considered by the European Court of Human Rights, which held that the absence of procedural safeguards failed to protect against arbitrary deprivations of liberty on grounds of necessity and so there had been a violation of Art.5(1) and there was no available procedure to review the decision, which was a breach of Art.5(4) (this is considered in more detail in at **para.12.6**).

The State does have discretion in making its own initial and subsequent assessment (*Aerts* v. *Belgium* (2000) 29 EHRR 50). Where an individual is found no longer to suffer from a mental disorder, there is no automatic right to immediate and unconditional release, and so the State is entitled to proceed with caution and, if necessary, impose supervisory conditions within a reasonable period of time on such an individual (*Johnson* v. *UK* (1999) 27 EHRR 296).

The introduction of Art.5 into domestic case law has found that MHA 1983, ss.72 and 73, which required a patient to prove that the criteria justifying his detention no longer existed, were wrong. Furthermore, where a patient has been ordered to be released under MHA 1983 following a decision of the Mental Health Review Tribunal, any deferral to enable conditions to be put in place must be done within a proportionate and reasonable time (*R (on the application of K)* v. *Camden and Islington Health Authority* [2001] EWCA Civ 240). However, in *R (on the application of H)* v. *Secretary of State for the Home Department* [2003] UKHL 59, the court found that in situations where individuals are still mentally ill and can only be safely released with conditions (and those conditions cannot be practically implemented), then there will be no breach of Art.5(1) by not releasing an individual, if the health authority has used its best endeavours to implement such conditions.

Under Art.5(4) every individual who is deprived of his liberty is entitled to take proceedings to have the lawfulness of his detention determined by a court and his release ordered. This includes proceedings before a Mental Health Review Tribunal. The proceedings must be determined speedily in the light of the particular case (*R (on the application of H)* v. *Secretary of State for the Home Department* [2002] EWCA Civ 646; *SSHD* v. *MHRT* [2002] EWCA Civ 1868; and *R (on the application of C)* v. *London and South West Region MHRT* [2001] EWCA Civ 1110).

24.5 ARTICLE 6 – RIGHT TO A FAIR HEARING

Article 6 provides that the parties have a right to a fair hearing when their civil or criminal rights are affected. This must be by a fair and public hearing within a reasonable time and by an independent and impartial tribunal established by law.

24.5.1 Application of Article 6 – the issue of 'civil' proceedings

The application of Art.6 to issues concerning health and social care (which will almost always fall into the remit of civil rather than criminal law) is complicated by the fact that the definition by the European Court of what should be considered to be a 'civil' right includes those obligations and rights which an individual has in private law. Rights which exist in public law are not always civil rights. What is a civil right depends and is dependent upon the meaning of the European Convention on Human Rights (*Alconbury* v. *SSETR* [2001] UKHL 23). As a general rule, it is the character of the right, rather than those who are parties to the proceedings, that is relevant. Rights which involve private persons in their relations between themselves are always civil rights, as are most rights which involve some form of pecuniary transaction (*Stran Greek Refineries* v. *Greece* (1995) 19 EHRR 293); for example, this would include the right to engage in a commercial activity, or the right to claim personal injury. The European Court has held that social security benefits, in the main, confer a benefit which is 'civil' in nature (*Salesi* v. *Italy* (1998) 26 EHRR 187; *McGinley* v. *UK* (1999) 27 EHRR 1).

Many of the social and health care rights explored in this book, however, do not involve private rights between individuals, and the court has been reluctant to characterise other forms of State intervention as creating 'civil' rights (see *R (on the application of B)* v. *Alperton Community School* [2001] EWHC 229 (Admin) on the issue of whether or not exclusion from school was a civil right justifying an independent tribunal hearing).

This is important because, in some cases, the tribunals which sit and hear appeals about health and social care matters are not independent and impartial. In *R (on the application of Beeson)* v. *Dorset CC* [2002] EWCA Civ 1812, the court found that a social services complaints panel was compliant with Art.6 (1) because of the presence of the availability of judicial review. Subsequent to the introduction of the Human Rights Act 1998, both the social care and health legislation have been altered to take account of the need for independence and impartiality (see **Chapter 18** for details).

24.6 ARTICLE 8 – RIGHT TO A FAMILY AND PRIVATE LIFE

Article 8 provides that all individuals have a right to respect for their family and private life, their home and correspondence. This right can only be interfered with if it is in accordance with the law, and necessary in a democratic society in order for society to protect others. This is a wide-ranging Article which encompasses the right to autonomous development, interaction and liberty, a right to a private sphere, where the State cannot intervene. It encompasses not just physical or bodily integrity but also personal identity, lifestyle, sexual identity and sexual orientation, reputation, family life, the home and all forms of communication (see *Pretty* v. *UK* (2002) 35 EHRR 1 at para.61). Decision makers have to weigh Art.8 rights when making decisions, for example as to how care is to be provided (*Gunter* v. *South Western Staffordshire Primary Care Trust* [2005] EWHC 1894 (Admin)).

24.6.1 Article 8 – a qualified right

Article 8 has the largest impact in health and social care law because it deals primarily with the State's provision of services to preserve bodily integrity, personal identity, lifestyle, and on occasions to provide a home. Article 8 is not unlimited in scope, and it must be remembered that there is only a right to 'respect' for those rights. Not all acts or omissions of a public authority which have an impact on an individual's autonomy will constitute an interference with Art.8. It is a qualified right, which the courts have found is subject to limitations, in particular in areas involving social rights (for example, the right to housing (*Harrow LBC* v. *Qazi* [2003] UKHL 43)). In every case involving Art.8, the court will be striking a balance between the general interest of the community and the interest of the individual (see *Cossey* v. *UK* (1991) 13 EHRR 622 at para.37).

Article 8 is primarily a negative right (i.e. the State does not have a right to interfere). It can impose positive obligations upon the State to take such steps as necessary to make Art.8 real and substantial, which could involve the requirement for some group of individuals to protect others, or may require the State to dedicate resources to enable vulnerable individuals to be protected. For example, in *X* v. *Netherlands* (1986) 8 EHRR 235, the State was under an obligation to protect individuals from sexual assault. In *R (on the application of Bernard)* v. *Enfield LBC* [2003] HRLR 4, the court was found to be under a duty to provide assistance under the National Assistance Act 1948 to a severely disabled woman in order to maintain her basic physical and psychological integrity. A failure to provide such services was held to be a breach of Art.8.

24.6.2 Treatment and Article 8

Article 8 provides that forced physical intervention and treatment is not permissible by the State (*Matter* v. *Slovakia* (2001) 31 EHRR 32; *R (on the application of Wooder)* v. *Feggetter* [2002] EWCA Civ 554) and is a breach of Art.8 if the individual has the requisite capacity. In *Glass* v. *UK* (2004) 39 EHRR 15, the court found that it was a breach of Art.8 for an NHS Trust to treat a child against the consent of the child's parents without seeking a declaration from the court. However, in *R (on the application of Burke)* v. *GMC* [2005] EWCA Civ 1003, the court stated that an individual did not have a right to have life-prolonging treatment to be provided for him in circumstances where it was not deemed clinically appropriate. In *Sentges* v. *Netherlands* (unreported, application 27677/02) 8 July 2003, the ECHR held that Art.8 was not applicable every time an individual's life was disrupted but only in exceptional circumstances. In *Pentiacova* v. *Moldova* (unreported, application 14462/03) 4 January 2005, the court held that there could be a breach of Art.8 if there was a lack of public funding for certain medical treatment.

24.6.3 Patients and Article 8

It would be a breach of Art.8 to label someone a patient under the rules of English civil procedure, which then takes away the right for him to manage his own affairs, as this is a breach of his mental integrity and personal freedom (*Masterman-Lister* v. *Brutton & Co and Jewell* [2003] 3 All ER 162 at para.17). The State can also be obliged to desist from steps which would have an adverse impact on the mental health of an individual (*Bensaid* v. *UK* [2001] INLR 325; *R (on the application of Razgar)* v. *Secretary of State for the Home Department (No.2)* [2002] EWHC 2554, QBD; *X (formerly known as Mary Bell)* v. *SO* [2003] EWHC 1101 at paras.20–24).

24.6.4 Abuse and Article 8

In *Stubbings* v. *UK* (1997) 23 EHRR 213, the court found that the State may well be required to adopt measures designed to secure respect for private life in the sphere of individuals between themselves. The *Stubbings* case involved the State having proper criminal and civil sanctions to ensure the prevention of child abuse. There can be a duty on the State to maintain the physical and psychological well being of an individual by giving appropriate financial assistance (*R (on the application of Bernard)* v. *Enfield LBC* [2003] HRLR 4). The State may also be required to provide individuals with information about their health (or rather, possible situations where their health could be compromised) (*McGinley* v. *UK* (1999) 27 EHRR 1).

24.6.5 Personal identity and Article 8

Article 8 also involves a right to develop one's personal identity. This has involved the State being under an obligation to provide a full picture for individuals of their background and origin, and so the need to provide appropriate details for those who have been adopted, or those who have been born as a result of donor insemination (*Gaskin* v. *UK* (1990) 12 EHRR 36). However, there is a limit to the right to know such information if it would involve impinging on the rights of others (*R (on the application of Addinell)* v. *Sheffield City Council* [2001] ACD 61; *Gunn-Russo* v. *Nugent Care Society* [2001] EWHC 566 (Admin)).

Right to self-determine

An extension of one's personal identity is the right to self-determination, which is the right to shape who you are through your personal choices and through wider social interactions (*Pretty* v. *UK* (2002) 35 EHRR 1). For example, the right to self-determination has been held to include the right not have medical treatment or the right to drink alcohol (*Whitefield* v. *GMC* [2003] HRLR 9). It can also include, in the case of individuals detained under the mental health legislation, the right to be consulted as to who is their next relative (*R (on the application of M)* v. *Secretary of State for Health* [2003] EWHC 1094).

In *Botta* v. *Italy* (1998) 26 EHRR 241, a disabled man relied upon Art.8 to argue that a private beach should be available to him. The European Court rejected the argument that the State had the right to regulate such actions, and argued that his access to the beach constituted interpersonal relations of such a broad and indeterminate scope that there could be no direct link between the measures the State was urged to take and an individual's private life. Had the right, however, been to access something vital to his everyday life (for example, his hospital or his house) then the decision may well have been decided otherwise. However, this case is useful to indicate that disabled persons should have access to the life of the community and essential economic and social activities. Visiting the beach, was not in this case, held to be essential economic or social activity.

24.6.6 Personal information and records and Article 8

Article 8 is also important in health and social care law because it assists in regulating and controlling the information that the State has on individuals. Records kept by health and social services departments will be subject to the right of the individual to privacy under Art.8(1), in particular where an individual cannot refute its contents (*Rotaru* v. *Rumania* (2000) 8 BHRC 449). The court has dealt with cases involving child protection registers (*R (on the application of Ellis)* v. *Chief Constable of Essex* [2003] EWHC 1321; *J v. West Sussex CC* [2002] EWHC 1143 (Admin) where disclosure was made of convictions). The maintenance of medical records may be a breach of the right to privacy (*Chare* v. *France* 71 Ddr 141 (1991)).

24.6.7 Right to family life and Article 8

Article 8 also involves the right to protect family life. What is a family is a question of fact and a family is the existence of close personal ties so that individuals can live together and develop normally. Family can mean an extended family, or those involved in same-sex relationships (*Mendoza* v. *Ghaidan* [2004] UKHL 30). The courts have dealt with the issue of whether reduction in benefit is a breach of the right of family life (*Hooper* v. *Secretary of State for Work and Pensions* [2005] UKHL 29).

24.6.8 Right to a home and Article 8

Article 8 can also be used to protect the right of an individual to have a home. This is a place where someone lives, irrespective of whether or not that person has any legal interest in the property (*Harrow LBC* v. *Qazi* [2003] UKHL 43). There is no right to a home under European law (*Chapman* v. *UK* (2001) 33 EHRR 18) and no right for every individual to have a home. However, individuals with severe disabilities may have a right to be provided with adequate housing (*Marzari* v. *Italy* (2000) 30 EHRR CD 218). Where an individual lawfully owns a home, then the individual's removal can only occur if it is done lawfully and proportionately (although what is proportionate is currently that which is permitted in law: see *Harrow LBC* v. *Qazi* (above)). In the case of *R* v. *North and East Devon Health Authority ex p Coughlan* [2001] QB 213, the court found that individuals who had lived for lengthy periods in residential care provision could call this their 'home' and where an individual had an expectation created by the authority that this would be a home for life, then it would be disproportionate to move him.

24.7 ARTICLE 14 – RIGHT NOT TO SUFFER DISCRIMINATION

Article 14 states that Convention rights should be secured without discrimination on any ground such as sex, race, colour, language, political or other opinion, national or social origin, association with a national minority property, birth or other status. This is a free-standing right which only comes into operation if it can be found that the discrimination comes within the ambit of one of the substantive convention provisions. There does not have to be a breach of any Convention right, however, and if the relevant authority has gone beyond the Convention in the providing of rights, it must still do so without discrimination. To come within the ambit of another Convention provision can be within even a 'tenuous' link and the English courts have been generous in their interpretation of the ambit of Art.14 (*Ghaidan* v. *Mendoza* [2004] UKHL 30; *Carson* v. *Secretary of State for Work and Pensions* [2005] UKHL 37). Discrimination has wide meaning under the Convention and has been interpreted in a multiplicity of situations.

24.7.1 The meaning of discrimination

Discrimination exists where there has been differential treatment (on less favourable grounds) and the State cannot provide reasonable and objective justification (*Carson* v. *Secretary of State for Work and Pensions* [2005] UKHL 37; *Hooper* v. *Secretary of State for Works and Pensions* [2005] UKHL 29; *Westminster City Council* v. *Morris* [2005] EWCA Civ 1184). In order to demonstrate justification, the state must demonstrate that the difference pursues a legitimate aim and that there is a reasonable relationship of proportionality between the means employed and the aim to be realised (*Petrovic* v. *Austria* (2001) 33 EHRR 14). The House of Lords and the European Court have held that each national authority has a wide margin of appreciation on the question of justification, which depends on the subject matter and background to the case. Whilst this means that it will be difficult for authorities to justify discrimination on the ground of race and sex (*Carson* (above) at para.7) and sexual orientation (*Ghaidan* v. *Mendoza* [2004] UKHL 30), it may well be easier for authorities to permit discrimination on other grounds, for example, economic or social differences.

24.8 CLAIMS UNDER THE HUMAN RIGHTS ACT 1998

Under the Human Rights Act 1998, s.6, a public authority cannot act in a way which is incompatible with the Convention rights unless there is an Act of Parliament which indicates that the authority could not have acted differently. There is no definition of public authority in the legislation, and it embraces 'hybrid' organisations which will only be acting publicly where their functions are of a public nature.

24.8.1 Meaning of public authority under the Human Rights Act 1998

Pure public authorities will include government departments, local authorities, the NHS, any governmental quango or regulatory body (such as the Healthcare Commission, NICE and CSCI). Hybrid bodies could include institutions which do not fulfil entirely governmental or public functions; for example, hospitals which have private and public law duties. Public bodies are those whose nature is governmental in a broad sense of that expression (*Aston Cantlow and Wilmcote with Billesley PCC* v. *Wallbank* [2003] UKHL 37).

24.8.2 Bodies of a public nature

Who is a public authority is particularly important in the health and social care area because of the large-scale privatisation (in effect) of the provision of much health and social care which was formerly provided directly by local or central government. Whilst the local authority may have residual responsibility under the legislation for the care provided, organisations acting on behalf of the local authority may well not be subject to the Human Rights Act 1998 as they are not public bodies. In *R (on the application of Heather)* v. *Leonard Cheshire Foundation* [2002] EWCA Civ 366 a charity providing care and support services for disabled children was not a public authority, even though the majority of residents in the homes were placed there by the social services of local authorities. In *Poplar Housing & Regeneration Community Association Ltd* v. *Donoghue* [2001] EWCA Civ 595, a housing association was held to be a public body but only in circumstances where it had adopted the functions of a local authority and where the relationship between the association and the local authority was particularly close. The court in that case found that a body which does not have responsibilities to the public does not necessarily become a public authority merely because it performs acts on behalf of a public authority which would constitute public functions if the acts were performed by the public body itself. These decisions have been subject to significant criticism as failing to provide effective remedies for those individuals placed within private residential care and day centre institutions (see Seventh Report of the Joint Committee on Human Rights – 2003/2004 (HL Hansard)).

24.8.3 The use by individuals of the Human Rights Act 1998

Individuals can use the Convention either to bring a claim against a public authority or as a shield or defence in proceedings brought against them by a public authority or against a court or tribunal (Human Rights Act 1998, s.7(6)).

Section 7 of the Human Rights Act 1998 allows a claim to be brought against a public authority for breach of the Act but only by those who are or would be a 'victim' under the European Convention on Human Rights (Art.34). A victim has to be someone whose rights have been violated by the Convention, or who runs the risk of such a violation (*Marckx* v. *Belgium* (1979–80) 2 EHRR 330), or be an indirect victim (such as a spouse or parent) of the affected person (*McCann* v. *UK* (1996) 21 EHRR 97). A company can be a victim under the Convention (*Observer and Guardian* v. *UK* (1992) 14 EHRR 153). Someone does not cease to be a victim just because the measure which is alleged to breach the Convention has not caused any prejudice (*Eckle* v. *Germany* (1983) 5 EHRR 1). Claims under the Human Rights Act 1998 involving pressure groups, for example, may not be enough for an individual to be a victim, unlike in judicial review proceedings when pressure groups (for example the Child Poverty Action Group) can bring claims. The Government and local authorities cannot be victims.

24.9 REMEDIES UNDER THE HUMAN RIGHTS ACT 1998

Under the Human Rights Act 1998, s.8, a court or tribunal can find any act unlawful and may grant any relief and remedy within its powers as it considers just and appropriate. This can include an award of damages (Human Rights Act 1998, s.8(6)) if the court or tribunal has power to award damages in civil proceedings (Human Rights Act 1998, s.8(2)). No award of damages can be made unless the court determines that this is necessary for 'just satisfaction' in the case, which should take into account the other relief or remedy granted. The courts have consistently found that an award of damages is a discretionary matter and not an entitlement (*Anufrijeva* v. *Southwark LBC* [2004] 1 QB 1124; *R (on the application of Greenfield)* v. *Secretary of State for the Home Department* [2005] 1 WLR 673). In deciding whether or not to award damages the court will take into account the principles applied by the European Court of Human Rights when it has awarded damages.

Unfortunately, there are few principles which do underlie such awards, save for the fundamental principle that an individual should be placed in the same position as if the Convention breach had not occurred. In cases involving financial loss, this is clear. However, cases involving non-pecuniary loss are less clear and involve the court looking at the nature of the breach and the Article involved. If the case involves Arts.2 or 3, the court has indicated that compensation should, in principle, be available, but in cases involving mere maladministration or delay the court has refused to award damages. The scale and manner of the violation, and the victims themselves are also taken into account. Compared to English awards for damages, the sums are modest and can include claims for stress and anxiety which do not amount to a recognisable psychiatric injury. The House of Lords in *Greenfield* (above) made it clear that the domestic courts should operate within the European Court of Human Rights framework.

In *R (on the application of Bernard)* v. *Enfield LBC* [2003] HRLR 4, a case where a disabled individual had lived in appalling housing conditions for an 18-month period, the court also decided that an award of damages should be made which was comparable to that which could be made by a Local Government Ombudsman and so awarded a sum of £10,000.

24.10 ISSUING PROCEEDINGS UNDER THE HUMAN RIGHTS ACT 1998

24.10.1 Which route to pursue?

Anufrijeva v. *Southwark LBC* [2004] 1 QB 1124 provides that cases involving the recovery of damages under the Human Rights Act 1998 for maladministration should usually be brought by ordinary claim in the Administrative Court. However, in *Andrews* v. *Reading BC* [2004] EWHC 970, the Administrative Court indicated that, unless the claim involved some kind of public law challenge which would require permission to proceed, then claims should not be brought ordinarily to the Administrative Court. In *Anufrijeva* (above) the court indicated clearly that if the issue is maladministration, before any claim for damages under the Human Rights Act 1998 could be permitted to continue by a judge, good reason would have to be given as to why the claim could not proceed to the Local Government Ombudsman or alternative source of compensation, or the claim should be stayed for ADR or be dealt with summarily by a master if it has merit.

24.10.2 The limitation period

Proceedings must, under the Human Rights Act 1998, s.7(5)(a), be brought within the period of one year beginning with the date on which the act complained of took place or such longer period as the court considers equitable having regard to all the circumstances. The court has not as yet, had to consider these claims in detail, but it is believed that the court is likely to approach the claim in a similar way as in a claim to disapply the limitation period under the Limitation Act 1980, s.33. Furthermore, s.7(5) provides that if a stricter time limit applies in relation to the judicial procedure to be engaged by claimants to ensure that the public authority respects their rights (for example in judicial review, a claim must be brought promptly or within three months) then a court could find that claims involving judicial review and claims under the Human Rights Act 1998 which involve a public law element which would usually require judicial review should be brought within the time limit for such actions (which pursuant to CPR r.54.5 is promptly or within three months).

24.10.3 Public funding and Human Rights Act 1998 proceedings

Public funding is available for cases against public authorities which raise 'significant' human rights issues. The Legal Services Commission's Funding criteria (Part 3C) make it clear that cases will be funded if they can make a difference to the outcome, and the allegations must be of at least borderline prospects of success.

CHAPTER 25

Other international law instruments

25.1 THE USE OF OTHER INTERNATIONAL LAW INSTRUMENTS

The United Kingdom is a party to a wide range of international human rights instruments. The European Convention on Human Rights was designed to enforce some of the rights referred to in the Universal Declaration of Human Rights proclaimed by the United Nations (UN) in 1948 (see Art.53 of the Convention). There will be times when practitioners may find it useful to refer to the jurisprudence or content of these International Conventions when trying to demonstrate to courts the contents of the European Convention on Human Rights or when developing or trying to enshrine such rights into the common law. Many of these treaties touch upon and deal with issues which will affect decision making in both health care and social care.

A detailed examination of these different treaties is beyond the scope of this book but for an in-depth discussion, see Lester and Pannick, *Human Rights Law and Practice*, 2nd edn (Butterworths, 2004) and Clayton and Tomlinson, *The Law of Human Rights* (OUP, 2003). Commonwealth members of the judiciary have, at the highest level, indicated that such instruments should be complementary to domestic law within the national courts (see Lester and Pannick at Chapter 9).

25.2 INTERNATIONAL COVENANT ON CIVIL AND POLITICAL RIGHTS

The International Covenant on Civil and Political Rights (ICCPR) enables the Human Rights Committee of the UN to report on the UK's compliance with this treaty once every five years and enables other countries to complain about its performance under the ICCPR. There is no right for a UK individual to complain about violation of the Covenant, although this option is open to citizens of other States. Its articles cover most of the issues raised by the European Convention on Human Rights, as well as the right not to be discriminated against on the grounds of race, colour, sex, language, religion, political or other opinion, national or social origin, birth or other status (Art.26) and the right to life (Art.6) which has been given a broader meaning than in the European Court of Human Rights, for example that the State has a positive obligation to attempt to reduce infant mortality and increase life expectancy.

25.3 UNITED NATIONS CONVENTION ON THE RIGHTS OF THE CHILD

This Convention was ratified by the UK Government in 1991 and has four main aims:

(a) the participation of children in decisions affecting their own destiny;
(b) the protection of children against discrimination and all forms of neglect and exploitation;
(c) the prevention of harm to children;
(d) the provision of assistance for their basic needs.

The House of Lords has found that the law should not be interpreted or power exercised in a manner inconsistent with these treaty obligations (*Venables* v. *News Group Newspapers Ltd* [2001] Fam 430 at 49F–H). In *Procurator Fiscal* v. *Watson* [2002] 4 All ER 1, the court found that the interpretation of the European Convention on Human Rights (in that case the right to a fair trial under Art.6 of the Convention) must be read, when dealing with children, in the light of the UN Convention on the Rights of the Child.

The latest report from the UN (in 2002) set out that in respect of children with disabilities there is unequal enjoyment of cultural, social and political rights. Obviously, these rights may well be used when arguing cases concerning the social and health care rights of children (see *R on the application of the Howard League for Penal Reform* v. *Secretary of State for the Home Department* [2002] EWHC 2497 (Admin), where the 1989 Act was held to apply to children in detention).

25.4 CONVENTIONS AGAINST TORTURE

The UK has also ratified the Convention against Torture and Other Cruel, Inhuman and Degrading Treatment or Punishment in December 1988 and also the European Convention for the Prevention of Torture and Inhuman and Degrading Treatment or Punishment in June 1988. Obviously, these have an interrelationship with Art.3 of the European Convention on Human Rights.

25.5 EUROPEAN SOCIAL CHARTER

The European Social Charter 1961 sets out a list of obligations which the UK is legally bound to accept. There is a monitoring body which reports on the compliance of States with this treaty, called the European Committee of Social Rights. It has found that the UK is in breach of Art.13 (the right to social and medical assistance) in its insistence that applicants for social assistance must meet a habitual residence test.

25.6 EUROPEAN CHARTER OF FUNDAMENTAL RIGHTS

This charter was 'proclaimed' in December 2000 and set out a range of civil, political, economic and social rights of European citizens and all persons resident in the European Union. It has not yet been incorporated into EU or UK law, but all EU legislative measures are checked for compatibility with the Charter. In *Council of the European Union* v. *Hautala* [2002] 1 CMLR 421, the court has found that the Charter is a 'source of guidance for the true nature of Community rules'. English judges have also cited the charter (see *R (on the application of the Howard League for Penal Reform)* v. *Secretary of State for the Home Department* [2002] EWHC 2497). In that case, Munby J indicated that these charters, whilst not legally binding, could be consulted in order to elucidate or reaffirm the content of human rights which are generally recognised in Europe through the European Convention on Human Rights.

CHAPTER 26

Actions for damages

26.1 WHEN CAN AN ACTION FOR DAMAGES BE BROUGHT?

The mere fact that a health or social care provider may not have acted in accordance with legislation is not enough for an individual to receive damages through the courts (the Ombudsman operates on different principles, which are set out in **Chapter 19**). An individual has to establish that the action of the health or social care provider is either a breach of contract or a tort to obtain damages.

26.1.1 The special status of local authorities

The same principles apply to health and social care providers in the public or private sector as apply to any other body, although the application of principles of tort have often been modified to take account of the special status of local authorities, often acting in extremely difficult areas involving public policy and competing resources (see *X* v. *Bedfordshire CC* [1995] AC 633 and *JD* v. *East Berkshire Community Health NHS Trust* [2005] UKHL 23). Conscious of the need for professionals to concentrate on investigating claims of abuse, or providing basic health and social care to often troubled individuals, the courts have been reluctant to find that health or social work professionals are liable to pay damages, for example, to children who may have been removed from their parents' care because of a negligent child abuse investigation. Detailed and complex questions of law and fact arise in these cases, which require specialist advice and assistance. For an overview of the law in the area reference should be made to specialist books, such as *Jackson & Powell on Professional Negligence*, 5th edn (Sweet & Maxwell, 2003) and *Clerk and Lindsell on Torts*, 18th edn (Sweet & Maxwell, 2003).

26.1.2 The increase in claims

The most obvious types of health care claim are claims against health care professionals for their negligent treatment, or negligent failure to treat individuals when they are under their care, or, in some cases, for abuse, whether physical, emotional or sexual, that they have meted out to vulnerable individuals. These claims are called 'clinical negligence' claims. Such claims have existed for a number of years, and there are a number of specialist solicitors who deal solely with them.

In the past 20 years, there has also been a growth of litigation against other professional bodies involved in social care (in particular social workers, teachers and educational psychologists) for their alleged failures, for example, to diagnose or spot various learning difficulties, or to prevent child abuse from occurring. Whilst the law in this area is dependent largely upon the practice in the particular field at the time in question, the law underlying all these types of claims is of common application.

26.2 CLAIMS OF TRESPASS

Trespass to the person is used in civil proceedings to cover acts which could amount to a criminal offence of harm to the body of an individual. It includes deliberate acts that cause an individual to apprehend unlawful violence. This will include sexual or physical abuse, unlawful imprisonment or medical treatment of that individual without his consent.

26.2.1 Vicarious liability for trespass

In *Lister* v. *Hesley Hall Ltd* [2001] UKHL 22, the House of Lords indicated that in cases where an employee commits acts of trespass which are closely connected with his employment, it would be fair and just to hold his employer vicariously liable for his action. In the *Lister* case, this meant that the local authority was held to be liable for the acts of a care warden in abusing children who were under his care and control. It is very likely that most individuals who carry out a caring role within care homes, or those who treat individuals in hospital or a day centre would be held to be carrying out acts of employment (albeit unlawful) if they abused individuals within their care, and so the care home or relevant local authority is likely to be liable for their actions.

26.2.2 Limitation period for trespass

Any claim for trespass must be brought within six years of the act complained of and cannot be extended (*Stubbings* v. *Webb* [1993] AC 498). In any claim for tortious damages, time does not begin to run when an individual is a child (under the age of 18) or a patient (within the meaning of MHA 1983) under the Limitation Act 1980.

26.3 CLAIM OF NEGLIGENCE

Health and social care providers may be liable in negligence, just as can any other individual or body. To prove a claim, an individual must show that the health or social care provider owed him a duty of care; that this duty was breached; and that the breach has caused him damage for which the English courts can compensate him.

The English courts are very conscious of the fact that litigation costs, in particular it costs the NHS a great deal of public money, and that most cases involving local authorities also involve the taxpayer being liable for the faults of the local council. They are also aware that many individuals working in particular in social care have difficult and demanding jobs which often involve balancing small budgets for large numbers of people, or which involve extremely serious decisions for example as to whether or not children can continue to live with their parents. They have been concerned in a number of cases with preventing 'defensive' practices arising which could stifle appropriate local authority and NHS activity.

26.3.1 Duty of care in health and social care cases

The courts have long recognised that a patient can sue for negligent treatment or failure to treat a medical condition. This area of law is relatively well defined and claims are brought regularly.

In cases involving other public bodies, and in particular social services, there are additional factors which the court will take into account when deciding whether or not there has been negligence. The first and most litigated over the past 20 years is whether or not these particular health or social care professionals or bodies owe a duty of care to the individual concerned. The law recognises that some types of harm which happen to individuals cannot be compensated by the courts and/or that in some circumstances there may well not have been an 'assumption of responsibility' by the relevant professional or body to the individual in question. The courts decide these questions by determining:

(a) whether or not there is any foreseeability of harm to the individual concerned;
(b) whether or not there is proximity between the individual harmed and the body concerned in the sense of a direct and close relationship in which, in all the circumstances of the case, liability can be imposed; and
(c) whether it is just and reasonable to impose a duty of care.

See *Caparo Industries Plc* v. *Dickman* [1990] 2 WLR 358.

26.3.2 The public policy element

Even where all these three factors can be shown to exist, the courts could still find that public policy means that a duty of care should not be imposed, although very often the courts will look at the public policy issues when deciding whether or not there is proximity or whether it would be just and reasonable to impose a duty of care. There is no single test for proximity or for justice and fairness (refer to *Caparo Industries Plc* v. *Dickman* [1990] 2 WLR 358; *X* v. *Bedfordshire CC* [1995] AC 633; *Phelps* v. *Hillingdon LBC* [2001] 2 AC 619; *Barrett* v. *Enfield LBC* [2001] 2 AC 550; *W* v. *Essex CC* [2001] 2 AC 592; and *JD* v. *East Berkshire Community Health NHS Trust* [2005] UKHL 23 for discussion of this issue in the context of claims involving child abuse investigations and education professionals). The courts have, historically, tended to extend the categories of negligence only incrementally (*Caparo* (above)). Over the past 10 years, however, the courts have tended to find that in many areas they cannot use policy reasons to justify refusing an individual compensation for tortious failures of local authorities.

26.3.3 The purpose of the statutory power

When looking at whether or not the courts will impose liability for acts of, in particular, health care bodies or local authorities when carrying out their statutory duties and powers, the court will look at the purpose for which a statutory power is conferred. The court will not impose a duty of care if it would discourage the performance of the duties and powers of the statutory body (*X* v. *Bedfordshire CC* [1995] AC 633). Furthermore, in cases involving health and social care bodies, the social services department may well be performing functions which require it to act in the public interest as a whole, which may involve the weighing of competing public interests or the allocation of resources. In those circumstances, it may be unfair to impose a duty of care. The greater role that 'policy' plays, the more likely it is that the issue is not 'justiciable', i.e. it is not possible to claim that a duty of care is owed. The courts have held on many occasions that they are not suited to deciding whether liability in negligence should arise in respect of the exercise of statutory discretion when matters involve social policy, or the balance of different public interests, or the allocation of resources within society. An example would be the allocation of resources between various budgets involving adult and child social care which could involve the cutting of services to a particular day centre. This could potentially cause psychological damage to individuals, but would not lead to the imposition of a duty of care.

The courts have also been reluctant to impose liability on individuals involved in regulating various systems, for example, Ofsted or the CSCI, which produces a critical report on a particular residential care home. In cases involving financial licensing and registration it has been found that no duty of care can be owed to individuals because of the broader requirements of these bodies to act in the public interest (*Davis* v. *Radcliffe* [1990] 1 WLR 821). Likewise, psychiatrists involved in investigating child abuse allegations did not owe a duty of care to the wrongly accused abuser (*JD* v. *East Berkshire Community Health NHS Trust* [2005] UKHL 23).

26.3.4 The unreasonable exercise of a statutory discretion

If a social care provider acts within the boundaries of his statutory discretion, then no liability for tort could arise as the action has been sanctioned and authorised by statute (*X* v. *Bedfordshire CC* [1995] AC 633 and *Barrett* v. *Enfield LBC* [2001] 2 AC 550). It is only if an individual can prove that the exercise of the discretion was so unreasonable that it was not really the exercise of a discretion at all, that liability for damages could be imposed. For example, a public body could think that a particular provision of the National Assistance (Assessment of Resources) Regulations 1992 did not apply and therefore wrongly charge an individual money. Whilst this may well be wrong in public law terms, this would not mean that the public body was at fault in negligence just because it made a mistake in a complex area of law, where all parties agree that the Regulations are complicated and problematic. It would only be in the most blatant case where it could be found that a body was negligent; for example, if a local authority decided that it would never provide accommodation to individuals under the National Assistance Act 1948, s.21 without any good reason for that decision. Even if that decision was held to be unreasonable, that does not mean that an individual could sue unless he could prove the three-stage test set out above.

26.3.5 Other routes for redress

Furthermore, the fact that judicial review is often available for complaints about the legality of acts of local authorities and the NHS, and that rights of appeal and/or use of the Ombudsman are available in many cases, could mean that it would be wrong to impose liability for negligence (*X* v. *Bedfordshire CC* [1995] AC 633 and *Jones* v. *Department of Employment* [1989] QB 1).

26.3.6 Failure to exercise statutory powers

Under the general principles of negligence a person is not liable for omitting to take an action unless he is under a duty to act because of the relationship he has with the individual who has been harmed. In *Stovin* v. *Wise* [1996] AC 923 and in *Gorringe* v. *Calderdale MBC* [2004] UKHL 15, the courts emphasised that it would only be in very limited situations that a public body would be liable for failing to exercise its statutory powers, in the sense that it was irrational or where there were exceptional grounds for holding that the policy of the statute required compensation to be paid to those who suffered loss because of the failure to exercise the power.

If there has been an 'assumption of responsibility', for example, if someone has an appointed social worker or has been taken into care, there may well be a duty owed if the social worker fails to act.

A public authority would not, in, general, be liable for the acts of third parties, unless there is such a special relationship so that the public body is responsible for the acts of that person. For example, prison officers have been held to be liable for the acts of young offenders who were allowed to escape (*Home Office* v. *Dorset Yacht Co* [1970] AC 1004).

26.3.7 The *Bolam* principle: the reasonably competent standard

Even assuming a duty of care can be established, in most cases involving public authorities a professional may be involved (for example a doctor, physiotherapist, social worker) and therefore a court will only find that there has been a breach of the duty of care if it can be demonstrated that the individual's performance fell below the standard of the reasonably competent individual performing that person's job (*Bolam* v. *Friern Hospital Management Committee* [1957] 1 WLR 582). The standard must be viewed as proper by a responsible body of professional opinion, which can include a view which is held by the 'minority' as long as it is held by a reasonable section of that profession. For example, there may be two alternative ways to perform an operation; a doctor will not be liable in negligence if he chooses one option over the other, providing that a reasonable body of opinion would support him in that decision.

26.3.8 Causation and loss

Even if a claimant can demonstrate a breach of the duty of care, he must also establish that the breach caused the loss, which often involves extremely difficult questions of fact or law. Reference to the standard textbooks (*McGregor on Damages*, 19th edn (Sweet & Maxwell, 2003)) should be made for further information on these issues.

26.3.9 Limitation

Claims for personal injury must be brought within three years of the date of the injury or three years of the date of knowledge of such injury (Limitation Act 1980, ss.11 and 14). The date of knowledge issue is complicated and involves issues around what an individual could or should have known at the time in question and the nature of the injury. Claims for other forms of damage (e.g. property damage) must be brought within six years. For further detail see *Butterworths Law of Limitation* (looseleaf).

26.4 CLAIM OF BREACH OF STATUTORY DUTY

There is only a very limited power for an individual to sue and claim a tortuous remedy for breach of statutory duty. The courts do not have a consistent attitude as to whether or not breaching a statute can in and of itself amount to a cause of action in which damages can be claimed. In circumstances where the statute indicates whether or not liability arises, then the matter is easy. Unfortunately, none of the health or social care statutes indicate this. The law in this area is beyond the scope of this book and reference should be made to the law of tort and the law relating to judicial review for further reference.

26.5 CLAIM OF FALSE IMPRISONMENT

A hospital or care home may be liable for false imprisonment if an individual suffers a complete deprivation of liberty for any period of time without lawful cause. The person imprisoned does not have to prove fault on behalf of the hospital as it is a tort of strict liability. It is not necessary that someone knows that they have been falsely imprisoned (*Murray* v. *Ministry of Defence* [1988] 1 WLR 692) and so adults with mental health problems and learning disabilities could still be falsely imprisoned. This tort is actionable per se, i.e. it is not necessary for an individual to prove that he has suffered any damage to start a claim.

26.6 CLAIMS OF RACE, SEX AND DISABILTY DISCRIMINATION

A health or social care body could be liable in damages for a claim for race, sex or disability discrimination under the Race Relations Act 1976, the Sex Discrimination Act 1975 and the Disability Discrimination Act 1995. The Race Relations (Amendment) Act 2000 provides that public authorities cannot discriminate in the provision of their functions. Furthermore, public authorities in their role as providers of services also owe duties not to discriminate on the grounds of race, sex or disability. For further discussion of this topic, see Palmer *et al.*, *Discrimination Law Handbook* (LAG, 2002).

26.7 CLAIMS OF MISFEASANCE IN PUBLIC OFFICE

Misfeasance in public office is the tort of dishonest or deliberate abuse of power by a public official. Such abuse may arise where the act is done maliciously, that is with the intention of injuring the claimant or knowing that the act will be outside the powers of the public body and knowing that the person will suffer loss (*Three Rivers DC* v. *Bank of England (No.3)* [2003] 2 AC 1). The individual has to act maliciously with the specific intention of injuring someone or act with reckless indifference knowing that he had no power to do the act complained of and that this act would injure an individual or class of individuals. This includes shutting his eyes to the obvious, if it can be proven that he may have known about a dishonesty.

This tort can be committed by an individual or by a corporate body, such as a local authority. A public authority will also be liable for acts of its employees if their unauthorised actions are a misguided and unauthorised method of performing their authorised duties. However, if employees act in a way which is so unconnected with their authorised duties as to be independent of and outside those duties, for example, if a social worker began to stalk and harass a client or an ex-client, the employer will not be liable. In *Jones* v. *Swansea City Council* [1990] 1 WLR 1453 a local authority was accused of misfeasance when an individual alleged that the refusal to grant a lease to her husband was caused by malice and a desire to cause harm to her husband's firm. This was due to an antipathy towards her husband because of his political involvement with the local authority. A corporate body can also be found to have caused malice if the majority of the council members can be seen to have acted with malice.

This is a tort which, until recently, had been rarely litigated and there are few cases which set out the principles for recovery of damages. However it seems that individuals now are more willing to use this tort, in particular when dealing with the behaviour of regulatory authorities in cases of large-scale financial loss (*Three Rivers* (above) and *Weir* v. *Secretary of State for Transport (No.2)* [2005] EWHC 2192).

26.8 CLAIMS FOR RESTITUTION

Individuals may well be charged for social and health care services, or be asked to pay towards the cost of their residential care. It could turn out that the body has, in fact, no right and no statutory power to levy such money. Money paid by way of taxes or other public levies, if the demand is outside the statutory tax-raising powers of the local authority, should then be repaid by the authority irrespective of whether or not the local council had made a mistake (*Woolwich Building Society* v. *Inland Revenue Commissioners* [1993] AC 70).

In cases where money has been paid to the local authority as a result of a mistake arising from an agreement which the local authority could not within its jurisdictional powers enter into, the money is recoverable from the local authority (*Kleinwort Benson Ltd* v. *Lincoln City Council* [1998] 3 WLR 1095). A person who pays money under a mistake of law, even if at the time of the payment the parties were of the view that the agreement was lawful, is entitled to have his money repaid.

An authority can argue that it would be inequitable to order restitution, or that the judicial principle of certainty requires that the money is not repaid because of the consequences for the council of repaying large sums of money.

In order to bring a claim for restitution, an individual will need to prove that the payment made has been made wrongly and under a mistake as to the rules and regulations governing such payments. He will then need to assert his right to recovery of the money.

26.9 EU LAW

The UK Government can be liable in damages for losses caused to an individual by breaches of EU law (*Francovich* v. *Italy* [1991] ECR I–5357) and this is becoming increasingly important in health care related topics (*R (on the application of Watts)* v. *Bedford Primary Care Trust* [2004] EWCA Civ 166). Liability in damages can arise where the rule of law infringed has been intended to confer rights on an individual: there must be a sufficiently serious breach and a direct causal link between the breach and the damage suffered (see *R* v. *Secretary of State for Transport ex p Factortrame Ltd (No.5)* [2000] 1 AC 524). Loss of profit or restitutionary claims may well be made available, and the state may be required to alter the law. For further discussion of this area of the law, which is particularly complex and requires specialist advice, refer to Lewis *Remedies and the Enforcement of European Community Law* (Sweet and Maxwell, 1996) and Lewis *Judicial Remedies in Public Law* 3rd Edn (Sweet and Maxwell, 2004).

APPENDIX 1

Statutory legislation

A National Assistance Act 1948 (ss.21–24, 26, 29–30, 30A, 32–33)
B Health Services and Public Health Act 1968 (s.45)
C Chronically Sick and Disabled Persons Act 1970 (ss.1–2)
D Local Authority Social Services Act 1970 (ss.6, 7, 7A, 7C, 7D, 7E)
E Local Government Act 1972 (s.113)
F National Health Service Act 1977 (ss.1–3, 8, 21–22, 28, Sched.8)
G Health and Social Services and Social Security Adjudications Act 1983 (s.17, 21, 22, 24, Sched.9)
H Mental Health Act 1983 (s.117)
I Disabled Persons (Services, Consultation and Representation) Act 1986 (ss.4, 8)
J Children Act 1989 (ss.3, 17–18, 20–23, 23A–23E, 24, 24A–24D, 25–26, 26A, 27–30, Sched.2)
K National Health Service and Community Care Act 1990 (ss.46–47)
L Carers (Recognition and Services) Act 1995 (s.1)
M Local Government Act 2000 (ss.1–3, 92)
N Carers and Disabled Children Act 2000 (ss.1–6, 6A)
O Health and Social Care Act 2001 (ss.49, 53–58)

A. NATIONAL ASSISTANCE ACT 1948

PART III LOCAL AUTHORITY SERVICES

Provision of Accommodation

21. Duty of local authorities to provide accommodation

(1) Subject to and in accordance with the provisions of this Part of this Act, a local authority may with the approval of the Secretary of State, and to such extent as he may direct shall, make arrangements for providing –

(a) residential accommodation for persons aged 18 or over who by reason of age, illness, disability or any other circumstances are in need of care and attention which is not otherwise available to them; and
(aa) residential accommodation for expectant and nursing mothers who are in need of care and attention which is not otherwise available to them.
(b) [*repealed*]

(1A) A person to whom section 115 of the Immigration and Asylum Act 1999 (exclusion from benefits) applies may not be provided with residential accommodation under subsection (1)(a) if his need for care and attention has arisen solely –

(a) because he is destitute; or
(b) because of the physical effects, or anticipated physical effects, of his being destitute.

(1B) Subsections (3) and (5) to (8) of section 95 of the Immigration and Asylum Act 1999, and paragraph 2 of Schedule 8 to that Act, apply for the purposes of subsection (1A) as they apply for the purposes of that section, but for the references in subsections (5) and (7) of that section and in that paragraph to the Secretary of State substitute references to a local authority.
(2) In making any such arrangements a local authority shall have regard to the welfare of all persons for whom accommodation is provided, and in particular to the need for providing accommodation of different descriptions suited to different descriptions of such persons as are mentioned in the last foregoing subsection.
(2A) In determining for the purposes of paragraph (a) or (aa) of subsection (1) of this section whether care and attention are otherwise available to a person, a local authority shall disregard so much of the person's resources as may be specified in, or determined in accordance with, regulations made by the Secretary of State for the purposes of this subsection.
(2B) In subsection (2A) of this section the reference to a person's resources is a reference to his resources within the meaning of regulations made for the purposes of that subsection.
(3) [*repealed*]
(4) Subject to the provisions of section 26 of this Act accommodation provided by a local authority in the exercise of their functions under this section shall be provided in premises managed by the authority or, to such extent as may be determined in accordance with the arrangements under this section, in such premises managed by another local authority as may be agreed between the two authorities and on such terms, including terms as to the reimbursement of expenditure incurred by the said other authority, as may be so agreed.
(5) References in this Act to accommodation provided under this Part thereof shall be construed as references to accommodation provided in accordance with this and the five next following sections, and as including references to board and other services, amenities and requisites provided in connection with the accommodation except where in the opinion of the authority managing the premises their provision is unnecessary.
(6) References in this Act to a local authority providing accommodation shall be construed, in any case where a local authority agree with another local authority for the provision of accommodation in premises managed by the said other authority, as references to the first-mentioned authority.
(7) Without prejudice to the generality of the foregoing provisions of this section, a local authority may –

(a) provide, in such cases as they may consider appropriate, for the conveyance of persons to and from premises in which accommodation is provided for them under this Part of the Act;
(b) make arrangements for the provision on the premises in which accommodation is being provided of such other services as appear to the authority to be required.

. . .

(8) . . . nothing in this section shall authorise or require a local authority to make any provision authorised or required to be made (whether by that or by any other authority) by or under any enactment not contained in this Part of this Act or authorised or required to be provided under the National Health Service Act 1977.

22. Charges to be made for accommodation

(1) Subject to section 26 of this Act, where a person is provided with accommodation under this Part of this Act the local authority providing the accommodation shall recover from him the amount of the payment which he is liable to make in accordance with the following provisions of this section.
(2) Subject to the following provisions of this section, the payment which a person is liable to make for any such accommodation shall be in accordance with a standard rate fixed for that accommodation by the authority managing the premises in which it is provided and that standard rate shall represent the full cost to the authority of providing that accommodation.
(3) Where a person for whom accommodation in premises managed by any local authority is provided, or proposed to be provided, under this Part of this Act satisfies the local authority that he is unable to pay therefor at the standard rate, the authority shall assess his ability to pay . . ., and accordingly determine at what lower rate he shall be liable to pay for the accommodation.

. . .

(4) In assessing for the purposes of the last foregoing subsection a person's ability to pay, a local authority shall assume that he will need for his personal requirements such sum per week as may be prescribed by the Minister, or such other sum as in special circumstances the authority may consider appropriate.
(4A) Regulations made for the purposes of subsection (4) of this section may prescribe different sums for different circumstances.
(5) In assessing as aforesaid a person's ability to pay, a local authority shall give effect to regulations made by the Secretary of State for the purposes of this subsection except that, until the first such regulations come into force, a local authority shall give effect to Part III of Schedule 1 to the Supplementary Benefits Act 1976, as it had effect immediately before the amendments made by Schedule 2 to the Social Security Act 1980.
(5A) If they think fit, an authority managing premises in which accommodation is provided for a person shall have power on each occasion when they provide accommodation for him, irrespective of his means, to limit to such amount as appears to them reasonable for him to pay the payments required from him for his accommodation during a period commencing when they begin to provide the accommodation for him and ending not more the eight weeks after that.
(6) [*repealed*]
(7) [*repealed*]
(8) Where accommodation is provided by a local authority in premises managed by another local authority, the payment therefor under this section shall be made to

the authority managing the premises and not to the authority providing accommodation, but the authority managing the premises shall account for the payment to the authority providing the accommodation.

(8A) This section shall have effect subject to any regulations under section 15 of the Community Care (Delayed Discharges etc.) Act 2003 (power to require certain community care services and services for carers to be provided free of charge).

(9) [*repealed*]

23. Management of premises in which accommodation provided

(1) Subject to the provisions of this Part of this Act, a local authority may make rules as to the conduct of premises under their management in which accommodation is provided under this Part of this Act and as to the preservation of order in the premises.

(2) Rules under this section may provide that where by reason of any change in a person's circumstances he is no longer qualified to receive accommodation under this Part of the Act or where a person has otherwise become unsuitable therefor, he may be required by the local authority managing the premises to leave the premises in which the accommodation is provided.

(3) Rules under this section may provide for the waiving of part of the payments due under the last foregoing section where in compliance with the rules persons for whom accommodation is provided assist in the running of the premises.

24. Authority liable for provision of accommodation

(1) The local authority empowered under this Part of this Act to provide residential accommodation for any person shall subject to the following provisions of this Part of this Act be the authority in whose area the person is ordinarily resident.

(2) [*repealed*]

(3) Where a person in the area of a local authority –

(a) is a person with no settled residence

(b) not being ordinarily resident in the area of the local authority, is in urgent need of residential accommodation under this Part of this Act,

the authority shall have the like power to provide residential accommodation for him as if he were ordinarily resident in their area.

(4) Subject to and in accordance with the arrangements under section twenty-one of this Act, a local authority shall have power, as respects a person ordinarily resident in the area of another local authority, with the consent of that other authority to provide residential accommodation for him in any case where the authority would have a duty to provide such accommodation if he were ordinarily resident in their area.

(5) Where a person is provided with residential accommodation under this Part of this Act, he shall be deemed for the purposes of this Act to continue to be ordinarily resident in the area in which he was ordinarily resident immediately before the residential accommodation was provided for him.

(6) For the purposes of the provision of residential accommodation under this Part of this Act, a patient in a hospital vested in the Secretary of State, a Primary Care Trust, an NHS Trust or an NHS foundation trust shall be deemed to be ordinarily resident in the area, if any, in which he was ordinarily resident immediately before he was admitted as a patient to the hospital, whether or not he in fact continues to be ordinarily resident in that area.

(7) In subsection (6) above 'NHS trust' means a National Health Service trust established under Part I of the National Health Service and Community Care Act 1990 or under the National Health Service (Scotland) Act 1978, and 'Primary Care Trust' means a Primary Care Trust established under 16A of the National Health Service Act 1977.

25. [*repealed*]

26. Provision of accommodation in premises maintained by voluntary organisations

(1) Subject to subsections (1A) and (1C) below, arrangements under section 21 of this Act may include arrangements made with a voluntary organisation or with any other person who is not a local authority where –

(a) that organisation or person manages premises which provide for reward accommodation falling within subsection (1)(a) or (aa) of that section, and
(b) the arrangements are for the provision of such accommodation in those premises.

(1A) Arrangements must not be made by virtue of this section for the provision of accommodation together with nursing or personal care for persons such as are mentioned in section 3(2) of the Care Standards Act 2000 (care homes) unless –

(a) the accommodation is to be provided, under the arrangements, in a care home (within the meaning of that Act) which is managed by the organisation or person in question; and
(b) that organisation or person is registered under Part II of that Act in respect of the home.

(1B) [*repealed*]
(1C) Subject to subsection (1D) below, no arrangements may be made by virtue of this section for the provision of accommodation together with nursing without the consent of such Primary Care Trust or Health Authority as may be determined in accordance with regulations.
(1D) Subsection (1C) above does not apply to the making by an authority of temporary arrangements for the accommodation of any person as a matter of urgency; but, as soon as practicable after any such temporary arrangements have been made, the authority shall seek the consent required by subsection (1C) above to the making of appropriate arrangements for the accommodation of the person concerned.
(1E) [*repealed*]
(2) Any arrangements made by virtue of . . . this section shall provide for the making by the local authority to the other party thereto of payments in respect of the accommodation provided at such rates as may be determined by or under the arrangements and subject to subsection (3A) below the local authority shall recover from each person for whom accommodation is provided under the arrangements the amount of the refund which he is liable to make in accordance with the following provisions of this section.
(3) Subject to subsection (3A) below a person for whom accommodation is provided under any such arrangements shall, in lieu of being liable to make payment therefore in accordance with section twenty-two of this Act, refund to the local authority any payments made in respect of him under the last foregoing subsection. Provided that where a person for whom accommodation is provided, or proposed to be provided, under any such arrangements satisfies the local

authority that he is unable to make a refund at the full rate determined under that subsection, subsections (3) and (5) of section twenty-two of this Act shall, with the necessary modifications, apply as they apply where a person satisfies the local authority of his inability to pay at the standard rate as mentioned in the said subsection (3).

(3A) Where accommodation in any premises is provided for any person under arrangements made by virtue of this section and the local authority, the person concerned and the voluntary organisation or other person managing the premises (in this subsection referred to as 'the provider') agree that this subsection shall apply –

(a) so long as the person concerned makes the payments for which he is liable under paragraph (b) below, he shall not be liable to make any refund under subsection (3) above and the local authority shall not be liable to make any payment under subsection (2) above in respect of the accommodation provided for him;
(b) the person concerned shall be liable to pay to the provider such sums as he would otherwise (under subsection (3) above) be liable to pay by way of refund to the local authority; and
(c) the local authority shall be liable to pay to the provider the difference between the sums paid by virtue of paragraph (b) above and the payments which, but for paragraph (a) above, the authority would be liable to pay under subsection (2) above.

(4) Subsections (5A) . . . (7) and (9) of the said section twenty-two shall, with the necessary modifications, apply for the purposes of the last foregoing subsection as they apply for the purposes of the said section twenty-two.

(4AA) Subsections (2) to (4) shall have effect subject to any regulations under section 15 of the Community Care (Delayed Discharges etc.) Act 2003 (power to require certain community care services and services for carers to be free of charge).

(4A) Section 21(5) of this Act shall have effect as respects accommodation provided under arrangements made by virtue of this section with the substitution for the reference to the authority managing the premises of a reference to the authority making the arrangements.

(5) Where in any premises accommodation is being provided under . . . this section in accordance with arrangements made by any local authority, any person authorised in that behalf by the authority may at all reasonable times enter and inspect the premises.

(6) [*repealed*]

(7) In this section the expression 'voluntary organisation' includes any association which is a housing association for the purposes of the Housing Act 1936 . . . and 'exempt body' means an authority or body constituted by an Act of Parliament or incorporated by Royal Charter.

26A. [*repealed*]

27. [*repealed*]

28. [*repealed*]

29. Welfare arrangements for blind, deaf, dumb and crippled persons, etc

(1) A local authority may, with the approval of the Secretary of State, and to such extent as he may direct in relation to persons ordinarily resident in the area of the local authority shall make arrangements for promoting the welfare of persons to whom this section applies, that is to say persons aged eighteen or over who are blind, deaf or dumb or who suffer from mental disorder of any description, and other persons aged eighteen or over who are substantially and permanently handicapped by illness, injury, or congenital deformity or such other disabilities as may be prescribed by the Minister.
(2) [*repealed*]
(3) [*repealed*]
(4) Without prejudice to the generality of the provisions of subsection (1) of this section, arrangements may be made thereunder –

(a) for informing persons to whom arrangements under that subsection relate of the services available for them thereunder;
(b) for giving such persons instruction in their own homes or elsewhere in methods of overcoming the effects of their disabilities;
(c) for providing workshops where such persons may be engaged (whether under a contract of service or otherwise) in suitable work, and hostels where persons engaged in the workshops, and other persons to whom arrangements under subsection (1) of this section relate and for whom work or training is being provided in pursuance of the Disabled Persons (Employment) Act 1944 or the Employment and Training Act 1973 may live;
(d) for providing persons to whom arrangements under subsection (1) of this section relate with suitable work (whether under a contract of service or otherwise) in their own homes or elsewhere;
(e) for helping such persons in disposing of the produce of their work;
(f) for providing such persons with recreational facilities in their own homes or elsewhere;
(g) for compiling and maintaining classified registers of the persons to whom arrangements under subsection (1) of this section relate.

(4A) Where accommodation in a hostel is provided under paragraph (c) of subsection (4) of this section –

(a) if the hostel is managed by a local authority, section 22 of this Act shall apply as it applies where accommodation is provided under section 21;
(b) if the accommodation is provided in a hostel managed by a person other than a local authority under arrangements made with that person, subsections (2) to (4A) of section 26 of this Act shall apply as they apply where accommodation is provided under arrangements made by virtue of that section; and
(c) sections 32 and 43 of this Act shall apply as they apply where accommodation is provided under sections 21 to 26;

and in this subsection references to 'accommodation' include references to board and other services, amenities and requisites provided in connection with the accommodation, except where in the opinion of the authority managing the premises or, in the case mentioned in paragraph (b) above, the authority making the arrangements their provision is unnecessary.

(5) [*repealed*]
(6) Nothing in the foregoing provisions of this section shall authorise or require –

(a) the payment of money to persons to whom this section applies, other than persons for whom work is provided under arrangements made by virtue of paragraph (c) or paragraph (d) of subsection (4) of this section or who are engaged in work which they are enabled to perform in consequence of anything done in pursuance of arrangements made under this section; or
(b) the provision of any accommodation or services required to be provided under the National Health Service Act 1977 . . .

(7) A person engaged in work in a workshop provided under paragraph (c) of subsection (4) of this section, or a person in receipt of a superannuation allowance granted on his retirement from engagement in any such workshop, shall be deemed for the purposes of this Act to continue to be ordinarily resident in the area in which he was ordinarily resident immediately before he was accepted for work in that workshop; and for the purposes of this subsection a course of training in such a workshop shall be deemed to be work in that workshop.

30. Voluntary organisations for disabled persons' welfare

(1) A local authority may, in accordance with arrangements made under section 29 of this Act, employ as their agent for the purposes of that section any voluntary organisation or any person carrying on, professionally or by way of trade or business, activities which consist of or include the provision of services for any of the persons to whom section 29 above applies, being an organisation or person appearing to the authority to be capable of providing the service to which the arrangements apply.
(2) [*repealed*]
(3) [*repealed*]

30A. Research

Without prejudice to any powers conferred on them by any other Act, –
(a) the Secretary of State may promote research into any matter relating to the functions of local authorities under this Part of this Act, and, in particular, may participate with or assist other persons in conducting such research; and
(b) a local authority may conduct or assist other persons in conducting research into any matter relating to the functions of local authorities under this Part of this Act.

31. [*repealed*]

Financial adjustments between local authorities

32. Adjustments between authority providing accommodation, etc, and authority area of residence

(1) Any expenditure which apart from this section would fall to be borne by a local authority –

(a) in the provision under this Part of this Act of accommodation for a person ordinarily resident in the area of another local authority, or
(b) in the provision under section twenty-nine of this Act of services for a person ordinarily so resident, or
(c) in providing under paragraph (a) of subsection (7) of section twenty-one of this Act for the conveyance of a person ordinarily resident as aforesaid,

shall be recoverable from the said other local authority, and in this subsection any reference to another local authority includes a reference to a local authority in Scotland.

(2) For the purposes of paragraph (a) of the last foregoing subsection it shall be assumed that the expenditure incurred by a local authority in providing accommodation for any person is, as respects accommodation provided in premises managed by a local authority, at the rate for the time being fixed for that accommodation under subsection (2) of section twenty-two of this Act, and, as respects accommodation provided pursuant to an arrangement made under section twenty-six of this Act, at the rate referred to in subsection (2) of that section.

(3) Any question arising under this Part of this Act as to the ordinary residence of a person shall be determined by the Minister.

33. Local authorities for purposes of Part III

(1) In this Part of this Act the expression 'local authority' means a council which is a local authority for the purposes of the Local Authority Social Services Act 1970 in England or Wales, and a council constituted under section 2 of the Local Government etc (Scotland) Act 1994 in Scotland.

. . .

(2) [*repealed*]

B. HEALTH SERVICES AND PUBLIC HEALTH ACT 1968

45. Promotion by local authorities of the welfare of old people

(1) A local authority may with the approval of the Secretary of State, and to such extent as he may direct shall, make arrangements for promoting the welfare of old people.

(2) [*repealed*]

(3) A local authority may employ as their agent for the purposes of this section any voluntary organisation or any person carrying on, professionally or by way of trade or business, activities which consist of or include the provision of services for old people, being an organisation or person appearing to the authority to be capable of promoting the welfare of old people.

(4) No arrangements under this section shall provide –

(a) for the payment of money to old people except in so far as the arrangements may provide for the remuneration of old people engaged in suitable work in accordance with the arrangements;

(b) for making available any accommodation or services required to be provided under the National Health Service Act 1977.

(4A) No arrangements under this section may be given effect to in relation to a person to whom section 115 of the Immigration and Asylum Act 1999 (exclusion from benefits) applies solely –

(a) because he is destitute; or

(b) because of the physical effects, or anticipated physical effects, of his being destitute.

(4B) Subsections (3) and (5) to (8) of section 95 of the Immigration and Asylum Act 1999, and paragraph 2 of Schedule 8 to that Act, apply for the purposes of subsection (4A) as they apply for the purposes of that section, but for the references in subsections (5) and (7) of that section and in that paragraph to the Secretary of State substitute references to a local authority.

(5) The National Assistance Act 1948 shall have effect as if the following references included a reference to this section, that is to say, –

(a) the reference, in section 32, to section 29 of that Act;
(b) the references, in sections 35, . . . 45, 52 . . ., to Part III of that Act;
(c) the references, in sections . . . 56 and 59, to that Act.

(6) [*repealed*]
(7) [*repealed*]
(8) [*repealed*]
(9) The Health Visiting and Social Work (Training) Act 1962 shall have effect in relation to functions of local authorities under this section as it does in relation to functions of local authorities under Part III of the National Assistance Act 1948.
(10) [*repealed*]
(11) In this section 'local authority' (except where used in the expression 'public or local authority') means the council of a county, other than a metropolitan county, or of a county borough, metropolitan district or London Borough or the Common Council of the City of London, and 'voluntary organisation' means a body the activities of which are carried on otherwise than for profit but does not include any public or local authority.
(12) [*repealed*]

C. CHRONICALLY SICK AND DISABLED PERSONS ACT 1970

Welfare and housing

1. Information as to the need for and existence of welfare services

(1) It shall be the duty of every local authority having functions under section 29 of the National Assistance Act 1948 to inform themselves of the number of persons to whom that section applies within their area and of the need for the making by the authority of arrangements under that section for such persons.
(2) Every such local authority –

(a) shall cause to be published from time to time at such times and in such manner as they consider appropriate general information as to the services provided under arrangements made by the authority under the said section 29 which are for the time being available in the area; and
(b) shall ensure that any such person as aforesaid who uses any of those services is informed of any other service provided by the authority (whether under any such arrangements or not) which in the opinion of the authority is relevant to his needs and of any service provided by any other authority or organisation which in the opinion of the authority is so relevant and of which particulars are in the authorities' possession.

2. Provision of welfare services

(1) Where a local authority having functions under section 29 of the National Assistance Act 1948 are satisfied in the case of any person to whom that section applies who is ordinarily resident in their area that it is necessary in order to meet the needs of that person for that authority to make arrangements for all or any of the following matters, namely –

(a) the provision of practical assistance for that person in his home;
(b) the provision for that person of, or assistance to that person in obtaining, wireless, television, library or similar recreational facilities;
(c) the provision for that person of lectures, games, outings or other recreational facilities outside his home or assistance to that person in taking advantage of educational facilities available to him;
(d) the provision for that person of facilities for, or assistance in, travelling to and from his home for the purpose of participating in any services provided under arrangements made by the authority under the said section 29 or, with the approval of the authority, in any services provided otherwise than as aforesaid which are similar to services which could be provided under such arrangements;
(e) the provision of assistance for that person in arranging for the carrying out of any works of adaptation in his home or the provision of any additional facilities designed to secure his greater safety, comfort or convenience;
(f) facilitating the taking of holidays by that person, whether at holiday homes or otherwise and whether provided under arrangements made by the authority or otherwise
(g) the provision of meals for that person in his home or otherwise;
(h) the provision for that person of, or assistance to that person, in obtaining, a telephone and any special equipment necessary to enable him to use the telephone;

then subject to the provisions of section 7(1) of the Local Authority Social Services Act 1970 (which requires local authorities in the exercise of certain functions, including functions under the said section 29, to act under the general guidance of the Secretary of State) it shall be the duty of that authority to make those arrangements in exercise of their functions under the said section 29.

(2) [*repealed*]

D. LOCAL AUTHORITY SOCIAL SERVICES ACT 1970

6. The director of social services

(A1) A local authority in England shall appoint an officer, to be known as the director of adult social services, for the purposes of their social services functions, other than those for which the authority's director of children's services is responsible under section 18 of the Children Act 2004.
(1) A local authority in Wales shall appoint an officer, to be known as the director of social services, for the purposes of their social services functions.
(2) Two of more local authorities may, if they consider that the same person can efficiently discharge, for both or all of them, the functions of director of adult social services or (as the case may be) social services, concur in the appointment of a person as director of adult services or (as the case may be) social services for both or all of those authorities.
(3) [*repealed*]
(4) [*repealed*]
(5) [*repealed*]
(6) A local authority which have appointed, or concurred in the appointment of, a person under this section, shall secure the provision of adequate staff for assisting him in the exercise of his functions.
(7) [*repealed*]
(8) [*repealed*]

7. Local authorities to exercise social services functions under guidance of Secretary of State

(1) Local authorities shall, in the exercise of their social services functions, including the exercise of any discretion conferred by any relevant enactment, act under the general guidance of the Secretary of State.
(2) [*repealed*]
(3) [*repealed*]

7A. Directions by the Secretary of State as to exercise of social services functions

(1) Without prejudice to section 7 of this Act, every local authority shall exercise their social services functions in accordance with such directions as may be given to them under this section by the Secretary of State.
(2) Directions under this section –

  (a) shall be given in writing; and
  (b) may be given to a particular authority, or to authorities of a particular class, or to authorities generally.

7B. Complaints procedure

[*(1), (2), (3), (4) are not yet in force.*]

7C. Inquiries

(1) The Secretary of State may cause an inquiry to be held in any case where, whether on representations made to him or otherwise, he considers it advisable to do so in connection with the exercise by any local authority of any of their social services functions (except in so far as those functions relate to persons under the age of eighteen).
(2) Subsections (2) to (5) of section 250 of the Local Government Act 1972 (powers in relation to local inquiries) shall apply in relation to an inquiry under this section as they apply in relation to an inquiry under that section.

7D. Default powers of Secretary of State as respects social services functions of local authorities

(1) If the Secretary of State is satisfied that any local authority have failed, without reasonable excuse, to comply with any of their duties which are social services functions (other than a duty imposed by or under the Children Act 1989, section 1 or 2(4) of the Adoption (Intercountry Aspects) Act 1999 or the Adoption and Children Act 2002), he may make an order declaring that authority to be in default with respect to the duty in question.
(2) An order under subsection (1) may contain such directions for the purpose of ensuring that the duty is complied with within such period as may be specified in the order as appear to the Secretary of State to be necessary.
(3) Any such direction shall, on the application of the Secretary of State, be enforceable by mandamus.

7E. Grants to local authorities in respect of social services for the mentally ill

The Secretary of State may, with the approval of the Treasury, make grants out of money provided by Parliament towards any expenses of local authorities incurred in connection with the exercise of their social services functions in relation to persons suffering from mental illness.

E. LOCAL GOVERNMENT ACT 1972

113. Placing of staff of local authorities at disposal of other local authorities

(1) Without prejudice to any powers exercisable apart from this section, a local authority may enter into an agreement with another local authority for the placing at the disposal of the latter for the purposes of their functions, on such terms as may be provided by the agreement, of the services of officers employed by the former, but shall not enter into any such agreement with respect to any officer without consulting him.

(1A) Without any prejudice to any power exercisable apart from this section, a local authority may enter into an agreement with the Health Protection Agency, a Health Authority, Special Health Authority, Primary Care trust, NHS trust or NHS foundation trust –

(a) for the placing at the disposal of the Health Protection Agency, the Health Authority, Special Health Authority, Primary Care Trust, NHS trust or NHS foundation trust for the purposes of their functions, on such terms as may be provided by the agreement, of the services of officers employed by the local authority;

(b) for the placing at the disposal of the local authority for the purposes of their functions, on such terms as may be provided by the agreement, of the services of officers employed by the Health Protection Agency, the Health Authority, Special Health Authority, Primary Care Trust, NHS trust or NHS foundation trust

but a local authority shall not enter into an agreement in pursuance of paragraph (a) of this subsection in respect of any officer without consulting him.

(2) For superannuation purposes service rendered by an officer of a local authority whose services are placed at the disposal of another local authority in pursuance of this section is service rendered to the authority by whom he is employed, but any such officer shall be treated for the purposes of any enactment relating to the discharge of local authorities' functions as an officer of that other local authority.

(3) An officer whose services are placed at the disposal of a local authority in pursuance of subsection (1A) of this section shall be treated as an officer of the authority for the purposes of any enactment relating to the discharge of local authorities' functions.

(4) In subsection (1A) above 'NHS trust' means a National Health Service trust established under Part I of the National Health Service and Community Care Act 1990 and 'Primary Care Trust' means a Primary Care Trust established under section 16A of the National Health Service Act 1977.

F. NATIONAL HEALTH SERVICE ACT 1977

1. Secretary of State's duty as to health service

(1) It is the Secretary of State's duty to continue the promotion in England and Wales of a comprehensive health service designed to secure improvement –

(a) in the physical and mental health of the people of those countries, and
(b) in the prevention, diagnosis and treatment of illness,

and for that purpose to provide or secure the effective provision of services in accordance with this Act.

(2) The services so provided shall be free of charge except in so far as the making and recovery of charges is expressly provided for by or under any enactment, whenever passed.

2. Secretary of State's general power as to services

Without prejudice to the Secretary of State's powers apart from this section, he has power –

(a) to provide such services as he considers appropriate for the purpose of discharging any duty imposed on him by this Act; and
(b) to do any other thing whatsoever which is calculated to facilitate, or is conducive or incidental to, the discharge of such a duty.

This section is subject to section 3(3) below.

3. Services generally

(1) It is the Secretary of State's duty to provide throughout England and Wales, to such extent as he considers necessary to meet all reasonable requirements –

(a) hospital accommodation;
(b) other accommodation for the purpose of any service provided under this Act;
(c) medical, dental, nursing and ambulance services;
(d) such other facilities for the care of expectant and nursing mothers and young children as he considers are appropriate as part of the health service;
(e) such facilities for the prevention of illness, the care of persons suffering from illness and the after-care of persons who have suffered from illness as he considers are appropriate as part of the health service;
(f) such other services as are required for the diagnosis and treatment of illness.

(1A) The Secretary of State may provide or secure the provision of anything mentioned in subsection (1) above outside England and Wales.

(2) Where any hospital provided by the Secretary of State in accordance with this Act was a voluntary hospital transferred by virtue of the National Health Service Act 1946, and –

(a) the character and associations of that hospital before its transfer were such as to link it with a particular religious denomination, then
(b) regard shall be had in the general administration of the hospital to the preservation of that character and those associations.

(3) Nothing in section 2 above or in this section affects the provisions of Part II of this Act (which relates to arrangements with practitioners for the provision of . . . ophthalmic and pharmaceutical services).
(4) For the purposes of the duty in subsection (1), services provided under –

(a) section 16CA(2) or 16CC(2) below, or
(b) a general medical services contract or a general dental services contract,

are to be regarded as provided by the Secretary of State.

8. Health authorities and Strategic Health Authorities

(1) It is the duty of the Secretary of State to establish, in accordance with Part 1 of Schedule 5 to this Act, authorities to be called –

(a) Strategic Health Authorities, in the case of authorities established for areas in England;
(b) Health Authorities, in the case of authorities established for areas in Wales.

(2) Subject to subsection (4) below –

(a) a Strategic Health Authority shall be established for such area of England as is specified in the order establishing the authority; and
(b) a Health Authority shall be established for such area of Wales as is so specified, or, if the order so provides, for the whole of Wales.

(3) A Strategic Health Authority or a Health Authority shall be known by such name, in addition to the title 'Strategic Health Authority' or 'Health Authority', as –

(a) appears to the Secretary of State appropriately to signify the connection of the authority with the area for which they are established; and
(b) is specified in the order establishing the authority.

(4) The Secretary of State may by order –

(a) vary the area of a Strategic Health Authority or Health Authority;
(b) abolish a Strategic Health Authority or Health Authority;
(c) establish a new Strategic Health Authority or Health Authority;
(d) change the name by which a Strategic Health Authority or Health Authority are known.

(5) No order shall be made under this section relating to a Strategic Health Authority until after the completion of such consultation as may be prescribed.
(6) Consultation requirements contained in regulations under subsection (5) are in addition to, and not in substitution for, any other consultation requirements which may apply.
(7) The Secretary of State shall act under this section so as to ensure –

(a) that the areas for which Strategic Health Authorities are at any time established together comprise the whole of England;
(b) that the areas for which Health Authorities are at any time established together comprise the whole of Wales; and
(c) that no area for which a Strategic Health Authority or a Health Authority are established extends both into England and into Wales.

(8) The power to make incidental or supplemental provision conferred by section 126(4) below includes, in particular, in its application to orders made under this

section, power to make provision for the transfer of staff, property, rights and liabilities.

21. Local social services authorities

(1) Subject to paragraphs (d) and (e) of section 3(1) above, the services described in Schedule 8 to this Act in relation to –

(a) care of mothers . . .,
(b) prevention, care and after-care,
(c) home help and laundry facilities,

are functions exercisable by local social services authorities, and that Schedule has effect accordingly.

(2) A local social services authority who provide premises, furniture or equipment for any of the purposes of this Act may permit the use of the premises, furniture or equipment –

(a) by any local social services authority, or
(b) by any of the bodies constituted under this Act, or
(c) by a local education authority.

This permission may be on such terms (including terms with respect to the services of any staff employed by the authority giving permission) as may be agreed.

(3) A local social services authority may provide (or improve or furnish) residential accommodation –

(a) for officers employed by them for the purposes of any of their functions as a local social services authority, or
(b) for officers employed by a voluntary organisation for the purposes of any services provided under this section and Schedule 8.

22. Co-operation between health authorities and local authorities

(1) In exercising their respective functions NHS bodies (on one hand) and local authorities (on the other) shall co-operate with one another in order to secure and advance the health and welfare of the people of England and Wales.

(1A) In this section 'NHS body' means-

(za) a Strategic Health Authority;
(a) a Health Authority;
(b) a Special Health Authority;
(c) a Primary Care Trust; or
(cc) a Local Health Board;
(d) an NHS trust;
(e) an NHS foundation trust.

(2) [*repealed*]
(3) [*repealed*]
(4) [*repealed*]
(5) [*repealed*]
(6) [*repealed*]

28. Supply of goods and services by local authorities

(1) In the Local Authorities (Goods and Services) Act 1970 the expression 'public body' includes any Strategic Health Authority, Health Authority, Special Health Authority, Primary Care Trust, or Local Health Board and so far as relates to his functions under this Act includes the Secretary of State.

(2) The provisions of subsection (1) above have effect as if made by an order under section 1(5) of that Act of 1970, and accordingly may be varied or revoked by such an order.

(3) Every local authority shall make available to Strategic Health Authorities, Health Authorities, Special Health Authorities, Primary Care Trusts, Local Health Boards, NHS trusts, and NHS foundation trusts acting in the area of the local authority the services of persons employed by the local authority for the purposes of the local authority's functions under the Local Authorities Social Services Act 1970 so far as is reasonably necessary and practicable to enable Strategic Health Authorities, Health Authorities, Special Health Authorities, Primary Care Trusts, Local Health Boards, NHS trusts, and NHS foundation trusts to discharge their functions under this Act, the National Health Service and Community Care Act 1990 and Part 1 of the Health and Social Care (Community Health and Standards) Act 2003.

(4) [*repealed*]

SCHEDULE 8 LOCAL SOCIAL SERVICES AUTHORITIES

Care of mothers and young children

1. (1) A local social services authority may, with the Secretary of State's approval, and to such extent as he may direct shall, make arrangements for the care of expectant and nursing mothers (other than for the provision of residential accommodation for them) . . .

(2) [*repealed*]

Prevention, care and after-care

2. (1) A local social services authority may, with the Secretary of State's approval, and to such extent as he may direct shall, make arrangements for the purpose of the prevention of illness and for the care of persons suffering from illness and for the after-care of persons who have been suffering and in particular for –

(a) [*repealed*]
(b) the provision, for persons whose care is undertaken with a view to preventing them from becoming ill, persons suffering from illness and persons who have been so suffering, of centres or other facilities for training them or keeping them suitably occupied and the equipment and maintenance of such centres;
(c) the provision, for the benefit of such persons as are mentioned in paragraph (b) above, of ancillary or supplemental services; and
(d) for the exercise of the functions of the authority in respect of persons suffering from mental disorder who are received into guardianship under Part II or III of the Mental Health Act 1983 (whether the guardianship of the local social services authority or of other persons).

Such authority shall neither have the power nor be subject to a duty to make under this paragraph arrangements to provide facilities for any of the purposes mentioned in section 15(1) of the Disabled Persons (Employment) Act 1944.

(2) No arrangements under this paragraph shall provide for the payment of money to persons for whose benefit they are made except –

(a) in so far as they may provide for the remuneration of such persons engaged in suitable work in accordance with the arrangements; . . .

(b) [*repealed*]

of such amounts as the local social services authority think fit in respect of their occasional personal expenses where it appears to that authority that no such payment would otherwise be made.

(2A) No arrangements under this paragraph may be given effect to in relation to a person to whom section 115 of the Immigration and Asylum Act 1999 (exclusion from benefits) applies solely –

(a) because he is destitute; or

(b) because of the physical effects, or anticipated physical effects, of his being destitute.

(2B) Subsections (3) and (5) to (8) of section 95 of the Immigration and Asylum Act 1999, and paragraph 2 of Schedule 8 to that Act, apply for the purposes of subsection (2A) as they apply for the purposes of that section, but for the references in subsections (5) and (7) of that section and in that paragraph to the Secretary of State substitute references to a local social services authority.

(3) The Secretary of State may make regulations as to the conduct of premises in which, in pursuance of arrangements made under this paragraph, are provided for persons whose care is undertaken with a view to preventing them from becoming sufferers from mental disorder within the meaning of that Act of 1983 or who are, or have been, so suffering, . . . facilities for training them or keeping them suitably occupied.

(4) [*repealed*]

(4A) This paragraph does not apply in relation to persons under the age of 18.

(4AA) No authority is authorised or may be required under this paragraph to provide residential accommodation for any person.

(5) [*repealed*]

3. (1) It is the duty of every local social services authority to provide on such a scale as is adequate for the needs of their area, or to arrange for the provision on such a scale as is so adequate, of home help for households where such help is required owing to the presence of . . . a person who is suffering from illness, lying-in, an expectant mother, aged, handicapped as a result of having suffered from illness or by congenital deformity, . . . and every such authority has power to provide or arrange for the provision of laundry facilities for households for which home help is being, or can be, provided under this sub-paragraph.

(2) [*repealed*]

Research

4. Without prejudice to any powers conferred on them by any other Act, a local social services authority may conduct or assist other persons in conducting research into matters relating to the functions of local services authorities under this Schedule.

G. HEALTH AND SOCIAL SERVICES AND SOCIAL SECURITY ADJUDICATIONS ACT 1983

17. (1) Subject to subsection (3) below, an authority providing a service to which this section applies may recover such charge (if any) for it as they consider reasonable.

(2) This section applies to services provided under the following enactments –

(a) section 29 of the National Assistance Act 1948 (welfare arrangements for blind, deaf, dumb and crippled persons etc.);
(b) section 45(1) of the Health Services and Public Health Act 1968 (welfare of old people);
(c) Schedule 8 to the National Health Service Act 1977 (care of mothers and young children, prevention of illness and care and after- care and home help and laundry facilities);
(d) Section 8 of the Residential Homes Act 1980 (meals and recreation for old people); and
(e) Paragraph 1 of part II of Schedule 9 to this Act other than the provision of services for which payment may be required under section 22 or 26 of the National Assistance Act 1948.
(f) section 2 of the Carers and Disabled Children Act 2000.

(3) If a person –

(a) avails himself of a service to which this section applies, and
(b) satisfies the authority providing the service that his means are insufficient for it to be reasonably practicable for him to pay for the service the amount which he would otherwise be obliged to pay for it,

the authority shall not require him to pay more for it than it appears to them that it is reasonably practicable for him to pay.

(4) Any charge under this section may, without prejudice to any other method of recovery, be recovered summarily as a civil debt.

(5) This section has effect subject to any regulations under section 15 of the Community Care (Delayed Discharges, etc) Act 2003 (Power to require certain community care services and services for carers to be free of charge).

21. (1) Subject to the following provisions of this section, where –

(a) a person avails himself of Part III accommodation; and
(b) that person knowingly and with the intention of avoiding charges for the accommodation –
   (i) has transferred any asset to which this section applies to some other person or persons not more than six months before the date on which he begins to reside in such accommodation; or
   (ii) transfers any such asset to some other person or persons while residing in the accommodation; and

(c) either –
(i) the consideration for the transfer is less than the value of the asset; or
(ii) there is no consideration for the transfer,

The person or persons to whom the asset is transferred by the person availing himself of the accommodation shall be liable to pay the local authority providing the accommodation or arranging for its provision the difference between the amount assessed as due to be paid for the accommodation by the person availing himself of it and the amount which the local authority receive from him for it.

(2) This section applies to cash and any other asset which falls to be taken into account for the purpose of assessing under section 22 of the National Assistance Act 1948 the ability to pay for the accommodation of the person availing himself of it.

(3) Subsection 1(1) above shall have effect in relation to a transfer by a person who leaves Part III accommodation and subsequently resumes residence in such accommodation as if the period of six months mentioned in paragraph (b)(i) were a period of six months before the date on which he resumed residence in such accommodation.

(3A) If the Secretary of State so directs, subsection (1) above shall not apply in such cases as may be specified in the direction.

(4) Where a person has transferred an asset to which this section applies to more than one person, the liability of each of the persons to whom it was transferred shall be in proportion to the benefit accruing to him from the transfer.

(5) A person's liability under this section shall not exceed the benefit accruing to him from the transfer.

(6) Subject to subsection (7) below, the value of any asset to which this section applies, other than cash, which has been transferred shall be taken to be the amount of the consideration which would have been realised for it if it had been sold on the open market by a willing seller at the time of the transfer.

(7) For the purpose of calculating the value of an asset under subsection (6) above there shall be deducted from the amount of the consideration –

(b) the amount of any incumbrance on the asset; and
(c) a reasonable amount in respect of the expenses of the sale.

(8) In this Part of this Act 'Part III accommodation' means accommodation provided under sections 21 to 26 of the National Assistance Act 1948, and, in the application of this Part of this Act to Scotland, means accommodation provided under the Social Work (Scotland) Act 1968 or section 7 (functions of local authorities) of the Mental Health (Scotland) Act 1984.

22. (1) Subject to subsection (2) below, where a person who avails himself of Part III accommodation provided by a local authority in England, Wales or Scotland –

(a) fails to pay any sum assessed as due to be paid by him for the accommodation; and
(b) has a beneficial interest in land in England and Wales,

the local authority may create a charge in their favour on his interest in the land.

(2) In the case of a person who has interests in more than one parcel of land the charge under this section shall be upon his interest in such one of the parcels as the local authority may determine.

(2A) In determining whether to exercise their power under subsection (1) above and in making any determination under subsection (2) above, the local authority shall comply with any directions given to them by the Secretary of State as to the exercise of those functions.

(3) [*repealed*]

(4) Subject to subsection (5) below, a charge under this section shall be in respect of any amount assessed as due to be paid which is outstanding from time to time.

(5) The charge on the interest of the equitable joint tenant in land shall be in respect of the amount not exceeding the value of the interest that he would enjoy in the land if the joint tenancy were severed but the creation of such a charge shall not sever the joint tenancy.

(6) On the death of an equitable joint tenant in land whose interest in the land is subject to a charge under this section –

(a) if there are surviving joint tenants, their interests in the land; and

(b) if the land vests in one person, or one person is entitled to have it vested in him, his interest in it,

shall become subject to a charge for an amount not exceeding the amount of the charge to which the interest of the deceased joint tenant was subject by virtue of subsection (5) above.

(7) A charge under this section shall be created by a declaration in writing made by the local authority.

(8) Any such charge, other than a charge on the interest of an equitable joint tenant in land, shall in the case of unregistered land be a land charge of Class B within the meaning of section 2 of the Land Charges Act 1972 and in the case of registered land be a registerable charge taking effect as a charge by way of a legal mortgage.

24. (1) Any sum charged on or secured over an interest in land under this Part of this Act shall bear interest from the day after that on which the person for whom the local authority provided the accommodation dies.

(2) The rate of interest shall be such reasonable rate as the Secretary of State may direct or, if no such direction is given, as the local authority may determine.

SCHEDULE 9

Part II Meals and Recreation for Old People

1. A district council or Welsh county council or county borough council shall have power to make such arrangements as they may from time to time determine for providing meals and recreation for old people in their homes or elsewhere and may employ as their agent for the purpose of this paragraph any voluntary organisation whose activities consist in or include the provision of meals or recreation for old people.
2. A district council or Welsh county council or county borough council may assist any such organisation as is referred to in paragraph 1 above to provide meals or recreation for old people –

(a) by contributing to the funds of the organisation;

(b) by permitting them to use premises belonging to the council on such terms as may be agreed; and

(c) by making available furniture, vehicles or equipment (whether by way of gift or loan or otherwise) and the services of any staff who are employed by the council in connection with the premises or other things which they permit the organisation to use.

3. (1) District councils or Welsh county councils or county borough councils shall exercise their functions under this Part of this Schedule (including any discretion conferred on them under it) in accordance with the provisions of any regulations of the Secretary of State made for the purposes of this paragraph; and without prejudice to the generality of this paragraph, regulations under this paragraph –

(a) may provide for conferring on officers of the Secretary of State authorised under the regulations such powers of inspection as may be prescribed in relation to the exercise of functions under this Part of this Schedule by or by arrangement with or on behalf of district councils; and

(b) may make provision with respect to the qualifications of officers employed by district councils for the purposes of this Part of this Schedule or by voluntary organisations acting under arrangements with or on behalf of district councils for those purposes.

(2) The power to make regulations under this paragraph shall be exercisable by statutory instrument which shall be subject to annulment in pursuance of a resolution of either House of Parliament.

4. In this Part of this Schedule –
'functions' includes powers and duties; and
'voluntary organisation' means a body the activities of which are carried on otherwise than for profit, but does not include any public or local authority.

H. MENTAL HEALTH ACT 1983

117. (1) This section applies to persons who are detained under section 3 above, or admitted to a hospital in pursuance of a hospital order made under section 37 above, or transferred to a hospital in pursuance of a hospital direction made under section 45A above or a transfer direction made under section 47 or 48 above, and then cease to be detained and (whether or not immediately after so ceasing) leave hospital.

(2) It shall be the duty of the Primary Care Trust or Health Authority and of the local social services authority to provide, in co-operation with relevant voluntary agencies, after-care services for any person to whom this section applies until such time as the Primary Care Trust or Health Authority and the local social services authority are satisfied that the person concerned is no longer in need of such services; but they shall not be so satisfied in the case of a patient who is subject to after-care under supervision at any time while he remains so subject.

(2A) It shall be the duty of the Primary Care Trust or Health Authority to secure that at all times while a patient is subject to after-care under supervision –

(a) a person who is a registered medical practitioner approved for the purposes of section 12 above by the Secretary of State as having special experience in the diagnosis or treatment of mental disorder is in charge of the medical treatment provided for the patient as part of the after-care services provided for him under this section; and

(b) a person professionally concerned with any of the after-care services so provided is supervising him with a view to securing that he receives the after-care services so provided.

(2B) Section 32 above shall apply for the purposes of this section as it applies for the purposes of Part II of this Act.

(3) In this section 'the Primary Care Trust or Health Authority' means the Primary Care Trust or Health Authority, and 'the local social services authority' means the local social services authority, for the area in which the person concerned is resident or to which he is sent on discharge by the hospital in which he was detained.

I. DISABLED PERSONS (SERVICES, CONSULTATION AND REPRESENTATION) ACT 1986

4. When requested to do so by –

(a) a disabled person,
(b) his authorised representative, or
(c) any person who provides care for him in the circumstances mentioned in section 8,

a local authority shall decide whether the needs of the disabled person call for the provision by the authority of any services in accordance with section 2(1) of the 1970 Act (provision of welfare services).

8. (1) Where –

(a) a disabled person is living at home and receiving a substantial amount of care on a regular basis from another person (who is not a person employed to provide such care by any body in the exercise of its functions under any enactment), and
(b) it falls to a local authority to decide whether the disabled person's needs call for the provision by them of any services for him under any of the welfare enactments, the local authority shall, in deciding that question, have regard to the ability of that other person to continue to provide such care on a regular basis.

(2) Where that other person is unable to communicate, or (as the case may be) be communicated with, orally or in writing (or in each of those ways) by reason of any mental or physical incapacity, the local authority shall provide such services as, in their opinion, are necessary to ensure that any such incapacity does not prevent the authority from being properly informed as to the ability of that person to continue to provide care as mentioned in subsection (1).

J. CHILDREN ACT 1989

3. Meaning of 'parental responsibility'

(1) In this Act 'parental responsibility' means all the rights, duties, powers, responsibilities and authority which by law a parent of a child has in relation to the child and his property.

(2) It also includes the rights, powers and duties which a guardian of the child's estate (appointed, before the commencement of section 5, to act generally) would have had in relation to the child and his property.
(3) The rights referred to in subsection (2) include, in particular, the right of the guardian to receive or recover in his own name, for the benefit of the child, property of whatever description and wherever situated which the child is entitled to receive or recover.
(4) The fact that a person has, or does not have, parental responsibility for a child shall not affect –

(a) any obligation which he may have in relation to the child (such as a statutory duty to maintain the child); or
(b) any rights which, in the event of the child's death, he (or any other person) may have in relation to the child's property.

(5) A person who –

(a) does not have parental responsibility for a particular child; but
(b) has care of the child,

may (subject to the provisions of this Act) do what is reasonable in all the circumstances of the case for the purpose of safeguarding or promoting the child's welfare.

PART III LOCAL AUTHORITY SUPPORT FOR CHILDREN AND FAMILIES

Provision of services for children and their families

17. Provision of services for children in need, their families and others

(1) It shall be the general duty of every local authority (in addition to the other duties imposed on them by this Part) –
(a) to safeguard and promote the welfare of children within their area who are in need; and
(b) so far as is consistent with that duty, to promote the upbringing of such children by their families,

by providing a range and level of services appropriate to those children's needs.
(2) For the purpose principally of facilitating the discharge of their general duty under this section, every local authority shall have the specific duties and powers set out in Part 1 of Schedule 2.
(3) Any service provided by an authority in the exercise of functions conferred on them by this section may be provided for the family of a particular child in need or for any member of his family, if it is provided with a view to safeguarding or promoting the child's welfare.
(4) The Secretary of State may by order amend any provision of Part I of Schedule 2 or add any further duty or power to those for the time being mentioned there.
(5) Every local authority –

(a) shall facilitate the provision by others (including in particular voluntary organisations) of services which the authority have power to provide by virtue of this section, or section 18, 20, 23 or 24; and
(b) may make such arrangements as they see fit for any person to act on their behalf in the provision of any such service.

(6) The services provided by a local authority in the exercise of functions conferred on them by this section may include giving assistance in kind or, in exceptional circumstances, in cash.
(7) Assistance may be unconditional or subject to conditions as to the repayment of the assistance or of its value (in whole or in part).
(8) Before giving any assistance or imposing any conditions, a local authority shall have regard to the means of the child concerned and of each of his parents.
(9) No person shall be liable to make any repayment of assistance or of its value at any time when he is in receipt of income support or family credit under the Social Security Act 1986.
(10) For the purposes of this Part a child shall be taken to be in need if –

(a) he is unlikely to achieve or maintain, or to have the opportunity of achieving or maintaining, a reasonable standard of health or development without the provision for him of services by a local authority under this Part;
(b) his health or development is likely to be significantly impaired, or further impaired, without the provision for him of such services; or
(c) he is disabled,

and 'family', in relation to such a child, includes any person who has parental responsibility for the child and any other person with whom he has been living.
(11) For the purposes of this Part, a child is disabled if he is blind, deaf or dumb or suffers from mental disorder of any kind or is substantially and permanently handicapped by illness, injury or congenital deformity or such other disability as may be prescribed; and in this Part –
'development' means physical, intellectual, emotional, social or behavioural development; and
'health' means physical or mental health.

18. Day care for pre-school and other children

(1) Every local authority shall provide such day care for children in need within their area who are –

(a) aged five or under; and
(b) not yet attending schools,

as is appropriate.
(2) A local authority may provide day care for children within their area who satisfy the conditions mentioned in subsection (1)(a) and (b) even though they are not in need.
(3) A local authority may provide facilities (including training, advice, guidance and counselling) for those –

(a) caring for children in day care; or
(b) who at any time accompany such children while they are in day care.

(4) In this section 'day care' means any form of care or supervised activity provided for children during the day (whether or not it is provided on a regular basis).
(5) Every local authority shall provide for children in need within their area who are attending any school such care or supervised activities as is appropriate –

(a) outside school hours; or
(b) during school holidays.

(6) A local authority may provide such care or supervised activities for children within their area who are attending any school even though those children are not in need.
(7) In this section 'supervised activity' means an activity supervised by a responsible person.

Provision of accommodation for children

20. Provision of accommodation for children: general

(1) Every local authority shall provide accommodation for any child in need within their area who appears to them to require accommodation as a result of –

(a) there being no person who has parental responsibility for him;
(b) his being lost or having been abandoned; or
(c) the person who has been caring for him being prevented (whether or not permanently, and for whatever reason) from providing him with suitable accommodation or care.

(2) Where a local authority provide accommodation under subsection (1) for a child who is ordinarily resident in the area of another local authority, that other local authority may take over the provision of accommodation for the child within –

(a) three months of being notified in writing that the child is being provided with accommodation; or
(b) such other longer period as may be prescribed.

(3) Every local authority shall provide accommodation for any child in need within their area who has reached the age of sixteen and whose welfare the authority consider is likely to be seriously prejudiced if they do not provide him with accommodation.
(4) A local authority may provide accommodation for any child within their area (even though a person who has parental responsibility for him is able to provide him with accommodation) if they consider that to do so would safeguard or promote the child's welfare.
(5) A local authority may provide accommodation for any person who has reached the age of sixteen but is under twenty-one in any community home which takes children who have reached the age of sixteen if they consider that to do so would safeguard or promote his welfare.
(6) Before providing accommodation under this section, a local authority shall, so far as is reasonably practicable and consistent with the child's welfare –

(a) ascertain the child's wishes regarding the provision of accommodation; and
(b) give due consideration (having regard to his age and understanding) to such wishes of the child as they have been able to ascertain.

(7) A local authority may not provide accommodation under this section for any child if any person who –

(a) has parental responsibility for him; and
(b) is willing and able to –
 (i) provide accommodation for him; or
 (ii) arrange for accommodation to be provided for him,

objects.

(8) Any person who has parental responsibility for a child may at any time remove the child from accommodation provided by or on behalf of the local authority under this section.

(9) Subsections (7) and (8) do not apply while any person –

(a) in whose favour a residence order is in force with respect to the child; or

(b) who has care of the child by virtue of an order made in the exercise of the High Court's inherent jurisdiction with respect to children,

agrees to the child being looked after in accommodation provided by or on behalf of the local authority.

(10) Where there is more than one such person as is mentioned in subsection (9), all of them must agree.

(11) Subsections (7) and (8) do not apply where a child who has reached the age of sixteen agrees to being provided with accommodation under this section.

21. Provision of accommodation for children in police protection or detention or on remand, etc

(1) Every local authority shall make provision for the reception and accommodation of children who are removed or kept away from home under Part V.

(2) Every local authority shall receive, and provide accommodation for, children –

(a) in police protection whom they are requested to receive under section 46(3)(f);

(b) whom they are requested to receive under section 38(6) of the Police and Criminal Evidence Act 1984;

(c) who are –

(i) on remand under paragraph 7(5) of Schedule 7 to the Powers of Criminal Courts (Sentencing) Act 2000 or section 23(1) of the Children and Young Persons Act 1969; or

(ii) the subject of a supervision order imposing a local authority residence requirement under paragraph 5 of Schedule 6 to that Act of 2000 or a foster parent residence requirement under paragraph 5A of that Schedule,

and with respect to whom they are the designated authority.

(3) Where a child has been –

(a) removed under Part V; or

(b) detained under section 38 of the Police and Criminal Evidence Act 1984,

and he is not being provided with accommodation by a local authority or in a hospital vested in the Secretary of State or a Primary Care Trust, or otherwise made available pursuant to arrangements made by a Health Authority or a Primary Care Trust, any reasonable expenses of accommodating him shall be recoverable from the local authority in whose area he is ordinarily resident.

Duties of local authorities in relation to children looked after by them

22. General duty of local authority in relation to children looked after by them

(1) In this Act, any reference to a child who is looked after by a local authority is a reference to a child who is –

(a) in their care; or
(b) provided with accommodation by the authority in the exercise of any functions (in particular those under this Act) which are social services functions within the meaning of the Local Authority Social Services Act 1970, apart from functions under sections 17, 23B and 24B.

(2) In subsection (1) 'accommodation' means accommodation which is provided for a continuous period of more than 24 hours.
(3) It shall be the duty of a local authority looking after any child –

(a) to safeguard and promote his welfare; and
(b) to make such use of services available for children cared for by their own parents as appears to the authority reasonable in his case.

(3A) The duty of a local authority under subsection (3)(a) to safeguard and promote the welfare of a child looked after by them includes in particular a duty to promote the child's educational achievement.
(4) Before making any decision with respect to a child whom they are looking after, or proposing to look after, a local authority shall, so far as is reasonably practicable, ascertain the wishes and feelings of –

(a) the child;
(b) his parents;
(c) any person who is not a parent of his but who has parental responsibility for him; and
(d) any other person whose wishes and feelings the authority consider to be relevant,

regarding the matter to be decided.
(5) In making any such decision a local authority shall give due consideration –

(a) having regard to his age and understanding, to such wishes and feelings of the child as they have been able to ascertain;
(b) to such wishes and feelings of any person mentioned in subsection (4)(b) to (d) as they have been able to ascertain; and
(c) to the child's religious persuasion, racial origin and cultural and linguistic background.

(6) If it appears to a local authority that it is necessary, for the purpose of protecting members of the public from serious injury, to exercise their powers with respect to a child whom they are looking after in a manner which may not be consistent with their duties under this section, they may do so.
(7) If the Secretary of State considers it necessary, for the purpose of protecting members of the public from serious injury, to give directions to a local authority with respect to the exercise of their powers with respect to a child whom they are looking after, he may give such directions to the authority.
(8) Where any such directions are given to an authority they shall comply with them even though doing so is inconsistent with their duties under this section.

23. Provision of accommodation and maintenance by local authority for children whom they are looking after

(1) It shall be the duty of any local authority looking after a child –

(a) when he is in their care, to provide accommodation for him; and
(b) to maintain him in other respects apart from providing accommodation for him.

(2) A local authority shall provide accommodation and maintenance for any child whom they are looking after by –

(a) placing him (subject to subsection (5) and any regulations made by the Secretary of State) with –
(i) a family;
(ii) a relative of his; or
(iii) any other suitable person,

on such terms as to payment by the authority and otherwise as the authority may determine subject to section 49 of the Children Act 2004;

(aa) maintaining him in an appropriate children's home; or
(b) [*repealed*]
(c) [*repealed*]
(d) [*repealed*]
(e) [*repealed*]
(f) making such other arrangements as –
(i) seem appropriate to them; and
(ii) comply with any regulations made by the Secretary of State.

(2A) Where under subsection (2)(aa) a local authority maintains a child in a home provided, equipped and maintained by the Secretary of State under section 82(5), it shall do so on such terms as the Secretary of State may from time to time determine.

(3) Any person with whom a child has been placed under subsection (2)(a) is referred to in this Act as a local authority foster parent unless he falls within subsection (4).

(4) A person falls within this subsection if he is –

(a) a parent of the child;
(b) a person who is not a parent of the child but who has parental responsibility for him; or
(c) where the child is in care and there was a residence order in force with respect to him immediately before the care order was made, a person in whose favour the residence order was made.

(5) Where a child is in the care of a local authority, the authority may only allow him to live with a person who falls within subsection (4) in accordance with regulations made by the Secretary of State.

(5A) For the purposes of subsection (5) a child shall be regarded as living with a person if he stays with that person for a continuous period of more than 24 hours.

(6) Subject to any regulations made by the Secretary of State for the purposes of this subsection, any local authority looking after a child shall make arrangements to enable him to live with –

(a) a person falling within subsection (4); or
(b) a relative, friend or other person connected with him,

unless that would not be reasonably practicable or consistent with his welfare.

(7) Where a local authority provide accommodation for a child whom they are looking after, they shall, subject to the provisions of this Part and so far as is reasonably practicable and consistent with his welfare, secure that –

(a) the accommodation is near his home; and
(b) where the authority are also providing accommodation for a sibling of his, they are accommodated together.

(8) Where a local authority provide accommodation for a child whom they are looking after and who is disabled, they shall, so far as is reasonably practicable, secure that the accommodation is not unsuitable to his particular needs.
(9) Part II of Schedule 2 shall have effect for the purposes of making further provision as to children looked after by local authorities and in particular as to the regulations that may be made under subsections (2)(a) and (f) and (5).
(10) In this Act –
'appropriate children's home' means a children's home in respect of which a person is registered under Part II of the Care Standards Act 2000; and
'children's home' has the same meaning as in that Act.

23A. The responsible authority and relevant children

(1) The responsible local authority shall have the functions set out in section 23B in respect of a relevant child.
(2) In subsection (1) 'relevant child' means (subject to subsection (3)) a child who –

(a) is not being looked after by any local authority;
(b) was, before last ceasing to be looked after, an eligible child for the purposes of paragraph 19B of Schedule 2; and
(c) is aged sixteen or seventeen.

(3) The Secretary of State may prescribe –

(a) additional categories of relevant children; and
(b) categories of children who are not to be relevant children despite falling within subsection (2).

(4) In subsection (1) the 'responsible local authority' is the one which last looked after the child.
(5) If under subsection (3)(a) the Secretary of State prescribes a category of relevant children which includes children who do not fall within subsection (2)(b) (for example, because they were being looked after by a local authority in Scotland), he may in the regulations also provide for which local authority is to be the responsible local authority for those children.

23B. Additional functions of the responsible authority in respect of relevant children

(1) It is the duty of each local authority to take reasonable steps to keep in touch with a relevant child for whom they are the responsible authority, whether he is within their area or not.
(2) It is the duty of each local authority to appoint a personal adviser for each relevant child (if they have not already done so under paragraph 19C of Schedule 2).
(3) It is the duty of each local authority, in relation to any relevant child who does not already have a pathway plan prepared for the purposes of paragraph 19B of Schedule 2 –

(a) to carry out an assessment of his needs with a view to determining what advice, assistance and support it would be appropriate for them to provide him under this Part; and
(b) to prepare a pathway plan for him.

(4) The local authority may carry out such an assessment at the same time as any assessment of his needs is made under any enactment referred to in sub-paragraphs (a) to (c) of paragraph 3 of Schedule 2, or under any other enactment.
(5) The Secretary of State may by regulations make provision as to assessments for the purposes of subsection (3).
(6) The regulations may in particular make provision about –

(a) who is to be consulted in relation to an assessment;
(b) the way in which an assessment is to be carried out, by whom and when;
(c) the recording of the results of an assessment;
(d) the considerations to which the local authority are to have regard in carrying out an assessment.

(7) The authority shall keep the pathway plan under regular review.
(8) The responsible local authority shall safeguard and promote the child's welfare and, unless they are satisfied that his welfare does not require it, support him by –

(a) maintaining him;
(b) providing him with or maintaining him in suitable accommodation; and
(c) providing support of such other descriptions as may be prescribed.

(9) Support under subsection (8) may be in cash.
(10) The Secretary of State may by regulations make provision about the meaning of 'suitable accommodation' and in particular about the suitability of landlords or other providers of accommodation.
(11) If the local authority have lost touch with a relevant child, despite taking reasonable steps to keep in touch, they must without delay –

(a) consider how to re-establish contact; and
(b) take reasonable steps to do so,

and while the child is still a relevant child must continue to take such steps until they succeed.
(12) Subsections (7) to (9) of section 17 apply in relation to support given under this section as they apply in relation to assistance given under that section.
(13) Subsections (4) and (5) of section 22 apply in relation to any decision by a local authority for the purposes of this section as they apply in relation to the decisions referred to in that section.

23C. Continuing functions in respect of former relevant children

(1) Each local authority shall have the duties provided for in this section towards –

(a) a person who has been a relevant child for the purposes of section 23A (and would be one if he were under eighteen), and in relation to whom they were the last responsible authority; and
(b) a person who was being looked after by them when he attained the age of eighteen, and immediately before ceasing to be looked after was an eligible child,

and in this section such a person is referred to as a 'former relevant child'.

(2) It is the duty of the local authority to take reasonable steps –

(a) to keep in touch with a former relevant child whether he is within their area or not; and
(b) if they lose touch with him, to re-establish contact.

(3) It is the duty of the local authority –

(a) to continue the appointment of a personal adviser for a former relevant child; and
(b) to continue to keep his pathway plan under regular review.

(4) It is the duty of the local authority to give a former relevant child –

(a) assistance of the kind referred to in section 24B(1), to the extent that his welfare requires it;
(b) assistance of the kind referred to in section 24B(2), to the extent that his welfare and his educational or training needs require it;
(c) other assistance, to the extent that his welfare requires it.

(5) The assistance given under subsection (4)(c) may be in kind or, in exceptional circumstances, in cash.

(6) Subject to subsection (7), the duties set out in subsections (2), (3) and (4) subsist until the former relevant child reaches the age of twenty-one.

(7) If the former relevant child's pathway plan sets out a programme of education or training which extends beyond his twenty-first birthday –

(a) the duty set out in subsection (4)(b) continues to subsist for so long as the former relevant child continues to pursue that programme; and
(b) the duties set out in subsections (2) and (3) continue to subsist concurrently with that duty.

(8) For the purposes of subsection (7)(a) there shall be disregarded any interruption in a former relevant child's pursuance of a programme of education or training if the local authority are satisfied that he will resume it as soon as is reasonably practicable.

(9) Section 24B(5) applies in relation to a person being given assistance under subsection (4)(b) as it applies in relation to a person to whom section 24B(3) applies.

(10) Subsections (7) to (9) of section 17 apply in relation to assistance given under this section as they apply in relation to assistance given under that section.

Personal advisers and pathway plans

23D. Personal advisers

(1) The Secretary of State may by regulations require local authorities to appoint a personal adviser for children or young persons of a prescribed description who have reached the age of sixteen but not the age of twenty-one who are not –

(a) children who are relevant children for the purposes of section 23A;
(b) the young persons referred to in section 23C; or
(c) the children referred to in paragraph 19C of Schedule 2.

(2) Personal advisers appointed under or by virtue of this Part shall (in addition to any other functions) have such functions as the Secretary of State prescribes.

23E. Pathway plans

(1) In this Part, a reference to a 'pathway plan' is to a plan setting out –

(a) in the case of a plan prepared under paragraph 19B of Schedule 2 –
(i) the advice, assistance and support which the local authority intend to provide a child under this Part, both while they are looking after him and later; and
(ii) when they might cease to look after him; and
(b) in the case of a plan prepared under section 23B, the advice, assistance and support which the local authority intend to provide under this Part,

and dealing with such other matters (if any) as may be prescribed.

(2) The Secretary of State may by regulations make provision about pathway plans and their review.

24. Persons qualifying for advice and assistance

(1) In this Part 'a person qualifying for advice and assistance' means a person to whom subsection (1A) or (1B) applies.

(1A) This subsection applies to a person –

(a) who has reached the age of sixteen but not the age of twenty-one;
(b) with respect to whom a special guardianship order is in force (or, if he has reached the age of eighteen, was in force when he reached that age); and
(c) who was, immediately before the making of that order, looked after by a local authority.

(1B) This subsection applies to a person to whom subsection (1A) does not apply, and who –

(a) is under twenty-one; and
(b) at any time after reaching the age of sixteen but while still a child was, but is no longer, looked after, accommodated or fostered.

(2) In subsection (1B)(b), 'looked after, accommodated or fostered' means –

(a) looked after by a local authority;
(b) accommodated by or on behalf of a voluntary organisation;
(c) accommodated in a private children's home;
(d) accommodated for a consecutive period of at least three months –
(i) by any Health Authority, Special Health Authority, Primary Care Trust or local education authority, or
(ii) in any care home or independent hospital or in any accommodation provided by a National Health Service trust; or an NHS Foundation Trust
(e) privately fostered.

(3) Subsection (2)(d) applies even if the period of three months mentioned there began before the child reached the age of sixteen.

(4) In the case of a person qualifying for advice and assistance by virtue of subsection (2)(a), it is the duty of the local authority which last looked after him to take such steps as they think appropriate to contact him at such times as they think appropriate with a view to discharging their functions under sections 24A and 24B.

(5) In each of sections 24A and 24B, the local authority under the duty or having the power mentioned there ('the relevant authority') is –

(za) in the case of a person to whom subsection (1A) applies, a local authority determined in accordance with regulations made by the Secretary of State;
(a) in the case of a person qualifying for advice and assistance by virtue of subsection (2)(a), the local authority which last looked after him; or
(b) in the case of any other person qualifying for advice and assistance, the local authority within whose area the person is (if he has asked for help of a kind which can be given under section 24A or 24B).

24A. Advice and assistance

(1) The relevant authority shall consider whether the conditions in subsection (2) are satisfied in relation to a person qualifying for advice and assistance.
(2) The conditions are that –

(a) he needs help of a kind which they can give under this section or section 24B; and
(b) in the case of a person to whom section 24(1A) applies, or to whom section 24(1B) applies, and who was not being looked after by any local authority, they are satisfied that the person by whom he was being looked after does not have the necessary facilities for advising or befriending him.

(3) If the conditions are satisfied –

(a) they shall advise and befriend him if he is a person to whom section 24(1A) applies, or he is a person to whom section 24(1B) applies and he was being looked after by a local authority or was accommodated by or on behalf of a voluntary organisation; and
(b) in any other case they may do so.

(4) Where as a result of this section a local authority are under a duty, or are empowered, to advise and befriend a person, they may also give him assistance.
(5) The assistance may be in kind and, in exceptional circumstances, assistance may be given –

(a) by providing accommodation, if in the circumstances assistance may not be given in respect of the accommodation under section 24B, or
(b) in cash.

(6) Subsections (7) to (9) of section 17 apply in relation to assistance given under this section or section 24B as they apply in relation to assistance given under that section.

24B. Employment, education and training

(1) The relevant local authority may give assistance to any person who qualifies for advice and assistance by virtue of section 24(1A) or section 24(2)(a) by contributing to expenses incurred by him in living near the place where he is, or will be, employed or seeking employment.
(2) The relevant local authority may give assistance to a person to whom subsection (3) applies by –

(a) contributing to expenses incurred by the person in question in living near the place where he is, or will be, receiving education or training; or
(b) making a grant to enable him to meet expenses connected with his education or training.

(3) This subsection applies to any person who –

(a) is under twenty-four; and
(b) qualifies for advice and assistance by virtue of section 24(1A) or section 24(2)(a), or would have done so if he were under twenty-one.

(4) Where a local authority are assisting a person under subsection (2) they may disregard any interruption in his attendance on the course if he resumes it as soon as is reasonably practicable.

(5) Where the local authority are satisfied that a person to whom subsection (3) applies who is in full-time further or higher education needs accommodation during a vacation because his term-time accommodation is not available to him then, they shall give him assistance by –

(a) providing him with suitable accommodation during the vacation; or
(b) paying him enough to enable him to secure such accommodation himself.

(6) The Secretary of State may prescribe the meaning of 'full-time', 'further education', 'higher education' and 'vacation' for the purposes of subsection (5).

24C. Information

(1) Where it appears to a local authority that a person –

(a) with whom they are under a duty to keep in touch under section 23B, 23C or 24; or
(b) whom they have been advising and befriending under section 24A; or
(c) to whom they have been giving assistance under section 24B,

proposes to live, or is living, in the area of another local authority, they must inform that other authority.

(2) Where a child who is accommodated –

(a) by a voluntary organisation or in a private children's home;
(b) by any Health Authority, Special Health Authority, Primary Care Trust or local education authority; or
(c) in any care home or independent hospital or any accommodation provided by a National Health Service trust or NHS Foundation Trust,

ceases to be so accommodated, after reaching the age of sixteen, the organisation, authority or (as the case may be) person carrying on the home shall inform the local authority within whose area the child proposes to live.

(3) Subsection (2) only applies, by virtue of paragraph (b) or (c), if the accommodation has been provided for a consecutive period of at least three months.

24D. Representations: sections 23A to 24B

(1) Every local authority shall establish a procedure for considering representations (including complaints) made to them by –

(a) a relevant child for the purposes of section 23A or a young person falling within section 23C;
(b) a person qualifying for advice and assistance; or
(c) a person falling within section 24B(2),

about the discharge of their functions under this Part in relation to him.

(1A) Regulations may be made by the Secretary of State imposing time limits on the making of representations under subsection (1).

(2) In considering representations under subsection (1), a local authority shall comply with regulations (if any) made by the Secretary of State for the purposes of this subsection.

Secure accommodation

25. Use of accommodation for restricting liberty

(1) Subject to the following provisions of this section, a child who is being looked after by a local authority may not be placed, and, if placed, may not be kept, in accommodation provided for the purpose of restricting liberty ('secure accommodation') unless it appears –

(a) that –
  (i) he has a history of absconding and is likely to abscond from any other description of accommodation; and
  (ii) if he absconds, he is likely to suffer significant harm; or

(b) that if he is kept in any other description of accommodation he is likely to injure himself or other persons.

(2) The Secretary of State may by regulations –

(a) specify a maximum period –
  (i) beyond which a child may not be kept in secure accommodation without the authority of the court; and
  (ii) for which the court may authorise a child to be kept in secure accommodation;

(b) empower the court from time to time to authorise a child to be kept in secure accommodation for such further period as the regulations may specify; and

(c) provide that applications to the court under this section shall be made only by local authorities.

(3) It shall be the duty of a court hearing an application under this section to determine whether any relevant criteria for keeping a child in secure accommodation are satisfied in his case.

(4) If a court determines that any such criteria are satisfied, it shall make an order authorising the child to be kept in secure accommodation and specifying the maximum period for which he may be so kept.

(5) On any adjournment of the hearing of an application under this section, a court may make an interim order permitting the child to be kept during the period of the adjournment in secure accommodation.

(6) No court shall exercise the powers conferred by this section in respect of a child who is not legally represented in that court unless, having been informed of his right to apply for representation funded by the Legal Services Commission as part of the Community Legal Service or Criminal Defence Service and having had the opportunity to do so, he refused or failed to apply.

(7) The Secretary of State may by regulations provide that –

(a) this section shall or shall not apply to any description of children specified in the regulations;

(b) this section shall have effect in relation to children of a description specified in the regulations subject to such modifications as may be so specified;

(c) such other provisions as may be so specified shall have effect for the purpose of determining whether a child of a description specified in the regulations may be placed or kept in secure accommodation.

(8) The giving of an authorisation under this section shall not prejudice any power of any court in England and Wales or Scotland to give directions relating to the child to whom the authorisation relates.
(9) This section is subject to section 20(8).

Supplemental

26. Review of cases and enquiries into representations

(1) The Secretary of State may make regulations requiring the case of each child who is being looked after by a local authority to be reviewed in accordance with the provisions of the regulations.
(2) The regulations may, in particular, make provision –

(a) as to the manner in which each case is to be reviewed;
(b) as to the considerations to which the local authority are to have regard in reviewing each case;
(c) as to the time when each case is first to be reviewed and the frequency of subsequent reviews;
(d) requiring the authority, before conducting any review, to seek the views of –
(i) the child;
(ii) his parents;
(iii) any person who is not a parent of his but who has parental responsibility for him; and
(iv) any other person whose views the authority consider to be relevant,
including, in particular, the views of those persons in relation to any particular matter which is to be considered in the course of the review;
(e) requiring the authority . . . in the case of a child who is in their care –
(i) to keep the section 31A plan for the child under review and, if they are of the opinion that some change is required, to revise the plan, or make a new plan, accordingly,
(ii) to consider whether an application should be made to discharge their care order;
(f) requiring the authority . . ., in the case of a child in accommodation provided by the authority –
(i) if there is no plan for the future care of the child, to prepare one,
(ii) if there is such a plan for the child, to keep it under review and, if they are of the opinion that some change is required, to revise the plan or make a new plan, accordingly,
(iii) to consider whether the accommodation accords with the requirements of this Part;
(g) requiring the authority to inform the child, so far as is reasonably practicable, of any steps he may take under this Act;
(h) requiring the authority to make arrangements, including arrangements with such other bodies providing services as it considers appropriate, to implement any decision which they propose to make in the course, or as a result, of the review;
(i) requiring the authority to notify details of the result of the review and of any decision taken by them in consequence of the review to –

(i) the child;
(ii) his parents;
(iii) any person who is not a parent of his but who has parental responsibility for him; and
(iv) any other person whom they consider ought to be notified;

(j) requiring the authority to monitor the arrangements which they have made with a view to ensuring that they comply with the regulations.
(k) for the authority to appoint a person in respect of each case to carry out in the prescribed manner the functions mentioned in subsection (2A) and any prescribed function.

(2A) The functions referred to in subsection (2)(k) are –

(a) participating in the review of the case in question,
(b) monitoring the performance of the authority's functions in respect of the review,
(c) referring the case to an officer of the Children and Family Court Advisory and Support Service, if the person appointed under subsection (2)(k) considers it appropriate to do so.

(2B) A person appointed under subsection (2)(k) must be a person of a prescribed description.

(2C) In relation to children whose cases are referred to officers under subsection (2A)(c), the Lord Chancellor may by regulations –

(a) extend any functions of the officers in respect of family proceedings (within the meaning of section 12 of the Criminal Justice and Court Services Act 2000) to other proceedings,
(b) require any functions of the officers to be performed in the manner prescribed by the regulations.

(2D) The power to make regulations in subsection (2C) is exercisable in relation to functions of Welsh family proceedings officers only with the consent of the National Assembly for Wales.

(3) Every local authority shall establish a procedure for considering any representations (including any complaint) made to them by –

(a) any child who is being looked after by them or who is not being looked after by them but is in need;
(b) a parent of his;
(c) any person who is not a parent of his but who has parental responsibility for him;
(d) any local authority foster parent;
(e) such other person as the authority consider has a sufficient interest in the child's welfare to warrant his representations being considered by them,

about the discharge by the authority of any of their qualifying functions in relation to the child.

(3A) The following are qualifying functions for the purposes of subsection (3) –

(a) functions under this Part,
(b) such functions under Part 4 or 5 as are specified by the Secretary of State in regulations.

(3B) The duty under subsection (3) extends to representations (including complaints) made to the authority by –

(a) any person mentioned in section 3(1) of the Adoption and Children Act 2002 (persons for whose needs provision is made by the Adoption Service) and any other person to whom arrangements for the provision of adoption support services (within the meaning of that Act) extend,
(b) such other person as the authority consider has sufficient interest in a child who is or may be adopted to warrant his representations being considered by them,

about the discharge by the authority of such functions under the Adoption and Children Act 2002 as are specified by the Secretary of State in regulations.

(3C) The duty under subsection (3) extends to any representations (including complaints) which are made to the authority by –

(a) a child with respect to whom a special guardianship order is in force,
(b) a special guardian or a parent of such a child,
(c) any other person the authority consider has a sufficient interest in the welfare of such a child to warrant his representations being considered by them, or
(d) any person who has applied for an assessment under section 14F(3) or (4),

about the discharge by the authority of such functions under section 14F as may be specified by the Secretary of State in regulations.

(4) The procedure shall ensure that at least one person who is not a member or officer of the authority takes part in –

(a) the consideration; and
(b) any discussions which are held by the authority about the action (if any) to be taken in relation to the child in the light of the consideration.

but this subsection is subject to subsection (5A).

(4A) Regulations may be made by the Secretary of State imposing time limits on the making of representations under this section.

(5) In carrying out any consideration of representations under this section a local authority shall comply with any regulations made by the Secretary of State for the purpose of regulating the procedure to be followed.

(5A) Regulations under subsection (5) may provide that subsection (4) does not apply in relation to any consideration or discussion which takes place as part of a procedure for which provision is made by the regulations for the purpose of resolving informally the matters raised in the representations.

(6) The Secretary of State may make regulations requiring local authorities to monitor the arrangements that they have made with a view to ensuring that they comply with any regulations made for the purposes of subsection (5).

(7) Where any representation has been considered under the procedure established by a local authority under this section, the authority shall –

(a) have due regard to the findings of those considering the representation; and
(b) take such steps as are reasonably practicable to notify (in writing) –
   (i) the person making the representation;
   (ii) the child (if the authority consider that he has sufficient understanding); and
   (iii) such other persons (if any) as appear to the authority to be likely to be affected,

of the authority's decision in the matter and their reasons for taking that decision and of any action which they have taken, or propose to take.

(8) Every local authority shall give such publicity to their procedure for considering representations under this section as they consider appropriate.

26A. Advocacy services

(1) Every local authority shall make arrangements for the provision of assistance to –

(a) persons who make or intend to make representations under section 24D; and
(b) children who make or intend to make representations under section 26.

(2) The assistance provided under the arrangements shall include assistance by way of representation.
(3) The arrangements –

(a) shall secure that a person may not provide assistance if he is a person who is prevented from doing so by regulations made by the Secretary of State; and
(b) shall comply with any other provision made by the regulations in relation to the arrangements.

(4) The Secretary of State may make regulations requiring local authorities to monitor the steps that they have taken with a view to ensuring that they comply with regulations made for the purposes of subsection (3).
(5) Every local authority shall give such publicity to their arrangements for the provision of assistance under this section as they consider appropriate.

27. Co-operation between authorities

(1) Where it appears to a local authority that any authority . . . mentioned in subsection (3) could, by taking any specified action, help in the exercise of any of their functions under this Part, they may request the help of that other authority . . ., specifying the action in question.
(2) An authority whose help is so requested shall comply with the request if it is compatible with their own statutory or other duties and obligations and does not unduly prejudice the discharge of any of their functions.
(3) The authorities are –

(a) any local authority,
(b) any local education authority;
(c) any local housing authority;
(d) any Health Authority, Special Health Authority, Primary Care Trust, or National Health Service Trust or NHS foundation trust; and
(e) any person authorised by the Secretary of State for the purposes of this section.

(4) [*repealed*]

28. Consultation with local education authorities

(1) Where –

(a) a child is being looked after by a local authority; and

(b) the authority propose to provide accommodation for him in an establishment at which education is provided for children who are accommodated there,

they shall, so far as is reasonably practicable, consult the appropriate local education authority before doing so.

(2) Where any such proposal is carried out, the local authority shall, as soon as is reasonably practicable, inform the appropriate local education authority of the arrangements that have been made for the child's accommodation.

(3) Where the child ceases to be accommodated as mentioned in subsection (1)(b), the local authority shall inform the appropriate local education authority.

(4) In this section 'the appropriate local education authority' means –

(a) the local education authority within whose area the local authority's area falls; or,

(b) where the child has special educational needs and a statement of his needs is maintained under Part IV of the Education Act 1996, the local education authority who maintain the statement.

29. Recoupment of cost of providing services etc

(1) Where a local authority provide any service under section 17 or 18, other than advice, guidance or counselling, they may recover from a person specified in subsection (4) such charge for the service as they consider reasonable.

(2) Where the authority are satisfied that that person's means are insufficient for it to be reasonably practicable for him to pay the charge, they shall not require him to pay more than he can reasonably be expected to pay.

(3) No person shall be liable to pay any charge under section (1) for a service provided under section 17 or section 18(1) or (5) at any time when he is in receipt of income support under Part VII of the Social Security Contributions and Benefits Act 1992 of any element of child tax credit other than the family element, of working tax credit or of an income-based jobseeker's allowance.

(3A) No person shall be liable to pay any charge under subsection (1) for a service provided under section 18(2) or (6) at any time when he is in receipt of income support under Part VII of the Social Security Contributions and Benefits Act 1992 or of an income-based jobseeker's allowance.

(3B) No person shall be liable to pay any charge under subsection (1) for a service provided under section 18(2) or (6) at any time when –

(a) he is in receipt of guarantee state pension credit under section 1(3)(a) of the State Pension Credit Act 2002, or

(b) he is a member of a married or unmarried couple (within the meaning of that Act) the other member of which is in receipt of guarantee state pension credit.

(4) The persons are –

(a) where the service is provided for a child under sixteen, each of his parents;

(b) where it is provided for a child who has reached the age of sixteen, the child himself; and

(c) where it is provided for a member of the child's family, that member.

(5) Any charge under subsection (1) may, without prejudice to any other method of recovery, be recovered summarily as a civil debt.

(6) Part III of Schedule 2 makes provision in connection with contributions towards the maintenance of children who are being looked after by local authorities and

consists of the re-enactment with modifications of provisions in Part V of the Child Care Act 1980.

(7) Where a local authority provide any accommodation under section 20(1) for a child who was (immediately before they began to look after him) ordinarily resident within the area of another local authority, they may recover from that other authority any reasonable expenses incurred by them in providing the accommodation and maintaining him.

(8) Where a local authority provide accommodation under section 21(1) or (2)(a) or (b) for a child who is ordinarily resident within the area of another local authority and they are not maintaining him in –

(a) a community home provided by them;
(b) a controlled community home; or
(c) a hospital vested in the Secretary of State or a Primary Care Trust, or any other hospital made available pursuant to arrangements made by a Strategic Health Authority, Health Authority or a Primary Care Trust,

they may recover from that other authority any reasonable expenses incurred by them in providing the accommodation and maintaining him.

(9) Except where subsection (10) applies, where a local authority comply with any request under section 27(2) in relation to a child or other person who is not ordinarily resident within their area, they may recover from the local authority in whose area the child or person is ordinarily resident any reasonable expenses incurred by them in respect of that person.

(10) Where a local authority ('authority A') comply with any request under section 27(2) from another local authority ('authority B') in relation to a child or other person –

(a) whose responsible authority is authority B for the purposes of section 23B or 23C; or
(b) whom authority B are advising or befriending or to whom they are giving assistance by virtue of section 24(5)(a),

authority A may recover from authority B any reasonable expenses incurred by them in respect of that person.

30. Miscellaneous

(1) Nothing in this Part shall affect any duty imposed on a local authority by or under any other enactment.

(2) Any question arising under section 20(2), 21(3) or 29(7) to (9) as to the ordinary residence of a child shall be determined by agreement between the local authorities concerned or, in default of agreement, by the Secretary of State.

(3) Where the functions conferred on a local authority by this Part and the functions of a local education authority are concurrent, the Secretary of State may by regulations provide by which authority the functions are to be exercised.

(4) The Secretary of State may make regulations for determining, as respects any local education authority functions specified in the regulations, whether a child who is being looked after by a local authority is to be treated, for purposes so specified, as a child of parents of sufficient resources or as a child of parents without resources.

SCHEDULE 2 LOCAL AUTHORITY SUPPORT FOR CHILDREN AND FAMILIES

PART I PROVISION OF SERVICES FOR FAMILIES

Identification of children in need and provision of information

1. (1) Every local authority shall take reasonable steps to identify the extent to which there are children in need within their area.

(2) Every local authority shall –

(a) publish information –

(i) about services provided by them under sections 17, 18, 20, 23B to 23D, 24A and 24B; and

(ii) where they consider it appropriate, about the provision by others (including, in particular, voluntary organisations) of services which the authority have power to provide under those sections; and

(b) take such steps as are reasonably practicable to ensure that those who might benefit from the services receive the information relevant to them.

Children's services plans

1A. (1) Every local authority shall, on or before 31st March 1997 –

(a) review their provision of services under sections 17, 20, 21, 23 and 24; and

(b) having regard to that review and to their most recent review under section 19, prepare and publish a plan for the provision of services under Part III.

(2) Every local authority –

(a) shall, from time to time review the plan prepared by them under sub-paragraph (1)(b) (as modified or last substituted under this sub-paragraph), and

(b) may, having regard to that review and to their most recent review under section 19, prepare and publish –

(i) modifications (or, as the case may be, further modifications) to the plan reviewed; or

(ii) a plan in substitution for that plan.

(3) In carrying out any review under this paragraph and in preparing any plan or modifications to a plan, a local authority shall consult –

(a) every Local Health Board, Health Authority or Primary Care Trust the whole or any part of whose area lies within the area of the local authority;

(b) every National Health Service trust which manages a hospital, establishment or facility (within the meaning of the National Health Service and Community Care Act 1990) in the authority's area;

(ba) every NHS foundation trust which manages a hospital (within the meaning of the Health and Social Care (Community Health and Standards) Act 2003) in the authority's area;

(c) if the local authority is not itself a local education authority, every local education authority the whole or any part of whose area lies within the area of the local authority;

(d) any organisation which represents schools in the authority's area which are grant-maintained schools or grant-maintained special schools (within the meaning of the Education Act 1993);
(e) the governing body of every such school in the authority's area which is not so represented;
(f) such voluntary organisations as appear to the local authority –
 (i) to represent the interests of persons who use or are likely to use services provided by the local authority under Part III; or
 (ii) to provide services in the area of the local authority which, were they to be provided by the local authority, might be categorised as services provided under that Part;
(g) the chief constable of the police force for the area;
(h) the probation committee for the area;
(i) such other persons as appear to the local authority to be appropriate; and
(j) such other persons as the Secretary of State may direct.

(4) Every local authority shall, within 28 days of receiving a written request from the Secretary of State, submit to him a copy of –

(a) the plan prepared by them under sub-paragraph (1); or
(b) where that plan has been modified or substituted, the plan as modified or last substituted.

Maintenance of a register of disabled children

2. (1) Every local authority shall open and maintain a register of disabled children within their area.
(2) The register may be kept by means of a computer.

Assessment of children's needs

3. Where it appears to a local authority that a child within their area is in need, the authority may assess his needs for the purposes of this Act at the same time as any assessment of his needs is made under –

(a) the Chronically Sick and Disabled Persons Act 1970;
(b) Part IV of the Education Act 1996;
(c) the Disabled Persons (Services, Consultation and Representation) Act 1986; or
(d) any other enactment.

Prevention of neglect and abuse

4. (1) Every local authority shall take reasonable steps, through the provision of services under Part III of this Act, to prevent children within their area suffering ill-treatment or neglect.
(2) Where a local authority believe that a child who is at any time within their area –

(a) is likely to suffer harm; but
(b) lives or proposes to live in the area of another local authority

they shall inform that other local authority.
(3) When informing that other local authority they shall specify –

(a) the harm that they believe he is likely to suffer; and
(b) (if they can) where the child lives or proposes to live.

Provision of accommodation in order to protect child

5. (1) Where –

(a) it appears to a local authority that a child who is living on particular premises is suffering, or is likely to suffer, ill treatment at the hands of another person who is living on those premises; and
(b) that other person proposes to move from the premises,

the authority may assist that other person to obtain alternative accommodation.

(2) Assistance given under this paragraph may be in cash.
(3) Subsections (7) to (9) of section 17 shall apply in relation to assistance given under this paragraph as they apply in relation to assistance given under that section.

Provision for disabled children

6. Every local authority shall provide services designed –

(a) to minimise the effect on disabled children within their area of their disabilities; and
(b) to give such children the opportunity to lead lives which are as normal as possible.

Provision to reduce need for care proceedings etc.

7. Every local authority shall take reasonable steps designed –

(a) to reduce the need to bring –
   (i) proceedings for care or supervision orders with respect to children within their area;
   (ii) criminal proceedings against such children;
   (iii) any family or other proceedings with respect to such children which might lead to them being placed in the authority's care; or
   (iv) proceedings under the inherent jurisdiction of the High Court with respect to children;
(b) to encourage children within their area not to commit criminal offences; and
(c) to avoid the need for children within their area to be placed in secure accommodation.

Provision for children living with their families

8. Every local authority shall make such provision as they consider appropriate for the following services to be available with respect to children in need within their area while they are living with their families –

(a) advice, guidance and counselling;
(b) occupational, social, cultural or recreational activities;
(c) home help (which may include laundry facilities);

(d) facilities for, or assistance with, travelling to and from home for the purpose of taking advantage of any other service provided under this Act or of any similar service;
(e) assistance to enable the child concerned and his family to have a holiday.

Family centres

9. (1) Every local authority shall provide such family centres as they consider appropriate in relation to children within their area.
(2) 'Family centre' means a centre at which any of the persons mentioned in sub-paragraph (3) may –

(a) attend for occupational, social, cultural or recreational activities;
(b) attend for advice, guidance or counselling; or
(c) be provided with accommodation while he is receiving advice, guidance or counselling.

(3) The persons are –

(a) a child;
(b) his parents;
(c) any person who is not a parent of his but who has parental responsibility for him;
(d) any other person who is looking after him.

Maintenance of the family home

10. Every local authority shall take such steps as are reasonably practicable, where any child within their area who is in need and whom they are not looking after is living apart from his family –

(a) to enable him to live with his family; or
(b) to promote contact between him and his family,

if, in their opinion, it is necessary to do so in order to safeguard or promote his welfare.

Duty to consider racial groups to which children in need belong

11. Every local authority shall, in making any arrangements –

(a) for the provision of day care within their area; or
(b) designed to encourage persons to act as local authority foster parents,

have regard to the different racial groups to which children within their area who are in need belong.

PART II CHILDREN LOOKED AFTER BY LOCAL AUTHORITIES

Regulations as to placing of children with local authority foster parents

12. Regulations under section 23(2)(a) may, in particular, make provision –

(a) with regard to the welfare of children placed with local authority foster parents;

(b) as to the arrangements to be made by local authorities in connection with the health and education of such children;
(c) as to the records to be kept by local authorities;
(d) for securing that a child is not placed with a local authority foster parent unless that person is for the time being approved as a local authority foster parent by such local authority as may be prescribed;
(e) for securing that where possible the local authority foster parent with whom a child is to be placed is –
  (i) of the same religious persuasion as the child; or
  (ii) gives an undertaking that the child will be brought up in that religious persuasion;
(f) for securing that children placed with local authority foster parents, and the premises in which they are accommodated, will be supervised and inspected by a local authority and that the children will be removed from those premises if their welfare appears to require it;
(g) as to the circumstances in which local authorities may make arrangements for duties imposed on them by the regulations to be discharged, on their behalf.

Regulations as to arrangements under section 23(2)(f)

13. Regulations under section 23(2)(f) may, in particular, make provisions as to –

(a) the persons to be notified of any proposed arrangements;
(b) the opportunities such persons are to have to make representations in relation to the arrangements proposed;
(c) the persons to be notified of any proposed changes in arrangements;
(d) the records to be kept by local authorities;
(e) the supervision by local authorities of any arrangements made.

Regulations as to conditions under which child in care is allowed to live with parent, etc

14. Regulations under section 23(5) may, in particular, impose requirements on a local authority as to –

(a) the making of any decision by a local authority to allow a child to live with any person falling within section 23(4) (including requirements as to those who must be consulted before the decision is made, and those who must be notified when it has been made);
(b) the supervision or medical examination of the child concerned;
(c) the removal of the child, in such circumstances as may be prescribed, from the care of the person with whom he has been allowed to live;
(d) the records to be kept by local authorities.

Promotion and maintenance of contact between child and family

15. (1) Where a child is being looked after by a local authority, the authority shall, unless it is not reasonably practicable or consistent with his welfare, endeavour to promote contact between the child and –

(a) his parents;
(b) any person who is not a parent of his but who has parental responsibility for him; and
(c) any relative, friend or other person connected with him.

(2) Where a child is being looked after by a local authority –

(a) the authority shall take such steps as are reasonably practicable to secure that –
(i) his parents; and
(ii) any person who is not a parent of his but who has parental responsibility for him,
are kept informed of where he is being accommodated; and
(b) every such person shall secure that the authority are kept informed of his or her address.

(3) Where a local authority ('the receiving authority') take over the provision of accommodation for a child from another local authority ('the transferring authority') under section 20(2) –

(a) the receiving authority shall (where reasonably practicable) inform –
(i) the child's parents; and
(ii) any person who is not a parent of his but who has parental responsibility for him;
(b) sub-paragraph (2)(a) shall apply to the transferring authority, as well as the receiving authority, until at least one such person has been informed of the change; and
(c) sub-paragraph (2)(b) shall not require any person to inform the receiving authority of his address until he has been so informed.

(4) Nothing in this paragraph requires a local authority to inform any person of the whereabouts of a child if –

(a) the child is in the care of the authority; and
(b) the authority has reasonable cause to believe that informing the person would prejudice the child's welfare.

(5) Any person who fails (without reasonable excuse) to comply with sub-paragraph (2)(b) shall be guilty of an offence and liable on summary conviction to a fine not exceeding level 2 on the standard scale.

(6) It shall be a defence in any proceedings under sub-paragraph (5) to prove that the defendant was residing at the same address as another person who was the child's parent or had parental responsibility for the child and had reasonable cause to believe that the other person had informed the appropriate authority that both of them were residing at that address.

Visits to or by children: expenses

16. (1) This paragraph applies where –

(a) a child is being looked after by a local authority; and
(b) the conditions mentioned in sub-paragraph (3) are satisfied.

(2) The authority may –

(a) make payments to –

(i) a parent of the child;
(ii) any person who is not a parent of his but who has parental responsibility for him; or
(iii) any relative, friend or other person connected with him,

in respect of travelling, subsistence or other expenses incurred by that person in visiting the child; or

(b) make payments to the child, or to any person on his behalf, in respect of travelling, subsistence or other expenses incurred by or on behalf of the child in his visiting –
(i) a parent of his;
(ii) any person who is not a parent of his but who has parental responsibility for him; or
(iii) any relative, friend or other person connected with him.

(3) The conditions are that –

(a) it appears to the authority that the visit in question could not otherwise be made without undue financial hardship; and
(b) the circumstances warrant the making of the payments.

Appointment of visitor for child who is not being visited

17. (1) Where it appears to a local authority in relation to any child that they are looking after that –

(a) communication between the child and –
(i) a parent of his, or
(ii) any person who is not a parent of his but who has parental responsibility for him,

has been infrequent; or

(b) he has not visited or been visited by (or lived with) any such person during the preceding twelve months,

and that it would be in the child's best interests for an independent person to be appointed to be his visitor for the purposes of this paragraph, they shall appoint such a visitor.

(2) A person so appointed shall –

(a) have the duty of visiting, advising and befriending the child; and
(b) be entitled to recover from the authority who appointed him any reasonable expenses incurred by him for the purposes of his functions under this paragraph.

(3) A person's appointment as a visitor in pursuance of this paragraph shall be determined if –

(a) he gives notice in writing to the authority who appointed him that he resigns the appointment; or
(b) the authority give him notice in writing that they have terminated it.

(4) The determination of such an appointment shall not prejudice any duty under this paragraph to make a further appointment.

(5) Where a local authority propose to appoint a visitor for a child under this paragraph, the appointment shall not be made if –

(a) the child objects to it; and
(b) the authority are satisfied that he has sufficient understanding to make an informed decision.

(6) Where a visitor has been appointed for a child under this paragraph, the local authority shall determine the appointment if –

(a) the child objects to its continuing; and
(b) the authority are satisfied that he has sufficient understanding to make an informed decision.

(7) The Secretary of State may make regulations as to the circumstances in which a person appointed as a visitor under this paragraph is to be regarded as independent of the local authority appointing him.

Power to guarantee apprenticeship deeds etc

18. (1) While a child is being looked after by a local authority, or is a person qualifying for advice and assistance, the authority may undertake any obligation by way of guarantee under any deed of apprenticeship or articles of clerkship which he enters into.

(2) Where a local authority have undertaken any such obligation under any deed or articles they may at any time (whether or not they are still looking after the person concerned) undertake the like obligation under any supplemental deed or articles.

Arrangements to assist children to live abroad

19. (1) A local authority may only arrange for, or assist in arranging for, any child in their care to live outside England and Wales with the approval of the court.

(2) A local authority may, with the approval of every person who has parental responsibility for the child arrange for, or assist in arranging for, any other child looked after by them to live outside England and Wales.

(3) The court shall not give its approval under sub-paragraph (1) unless it is satisfied that –

(a) living outside England and Wales would be in the child's best interests;
(b) suitable arrangements have been, or will be, made for his reception and welfare in the country in which he will live;
(c) the child has consented to living in that country; and
(d) every person who has parental responsibility for the child has consented to his living in that country.

(4) Where the court is satisfied that the child does not have sufficient understanding to give or withhold his consent, it may disregard sub-paragraph (3)(c) and give its approval if the child is to live in the country concerned with a parent, guardian, special guardian, or other suitable person.

(5) Where a person whose consent is required by sub-paragraph (3)(d) fails to give his consent, the court may disregard that provision and give its approval if it is satisfied that that person –

(a) cannot be found;
(b) is incapable of consenting; or
(c) is withholding his consent unreasonably.

(6) Section 85 of the Adoption and Children Act 2002 (which imposes restrictions on taking children out of the United Kingdom) shall not apply in the case of any child who is to live outside England and Wales with the approval of the court given under this paragraph.

(7) Where a court decides to give its approval under this paragraph it may order that its decision is not to have effect during the appeal period.

(8) In sub-paragraph (7) 'the appeal period' means –

(a) where an appeal is made against the decision, the period between the making of the decision and the determination of the appeal; and

(b) otherwise, the period during which an appeal may be made against the decision.

(9) This paragraph does not apply to a local authority placing a child for adoption with prospective adopters.

Preparation for ceasing to be looked after

19A. It is the duty of the local authority looking after a child to advise, assist and befriend him with a view to promoting his welfare when they have ceased to look after him.

19B. (1) A local authority shall have the following additional functions in relation to an eligible child whom they are looking after.

(2) In sub-paragraph (1) 'eligible child' means, subject to sub-paragraph (3), a child who –

(a) is aged sixteen or seventeen; and

(b) has been looked after by a local authority for a prescribed period, or periods amounting in all to a prescribed period, which began after he reached a prescribed age and ended after he reached the age of sixteen.

(3) The Secretary of State may prescribe –

(a) additional categories of eligible children; and

(b) categories of children who are not to be eligible children despite falling within sub-paragraph (2).

(4) For each eligible child, the local authority shall carry out an assessment of his needs with a view to determining what advice, assistance and support it would be appropriate for them to provide him under this Act –

(a) while they are still looking after him; and

(b) after they cease to look after him,

and shall then prepare a pathway plan for him.

(5) The local authority shall keep the pathway plan under regular review.

(6) Any such review may be carried out at the same time as a review of the child's case carried out by virtue of section 26.

(7) The Secretary of State may by regulations make provision as to assessments for the purposes of sub-paragraph (4).

(8) The regulations may in particular provide for the matters set out in section 23B(6).

Personal advisers

19C. A local authority shall arrange for each child whom they are looking after who is an eligible child for the purposes of paragraph 19B to have a personal adviser.

Death of children being looked after by local authorities

20. (1) If a child who is being looked after by a local authority dies, the authority –

(a) shall notify the Secretary of State and the Commission for Social Care Inspection;
(b) shall, so far as is reasonably practicable, notify the child's parents and every person who is not a parent of his but who has parental responsibility for him;
(c) may, with the consent (so far as it is reasonably practicable to obtain it) of every person who has parental responsibility for the child, arrange for the child's body to be buried or cremated; and
(d) may, if the conditions mentioned in sub-paragraph (2) are satisfied, make payments to any person who has parental responsibility for the child, or any relative, friend or other person connected with the child, in respect of travelling, subsistence or other expenses incurred by that person in attending the child's funeral.

(2) The conditions are that –

(a) it appears to the authority that the person concerned could not otherwise attend the child's funeral without undue financial hardship; and
(b) that the circumstances warrant the making of the payments.

(3) Sub-paragraph (1) does not authorise cremation where it does not accord with the practice of the child's religious persuasion.
(4) Where a local authority have exercised their power under sub-paragraph (1)(c) with respect to a child who was under sixteen when he died, they may recover from any parent of the child any expenses incurred by them.
(5) Any sums so recoverable shall, without prejudice to any other method of recovery, be recoverable summarily as a civil debt.
(6) Nothing in this paragraph affects any enactment regulating or authorising the burial, cremation or anatomical examination of the body of a deceased person.

PART III CONTRIBUTIONS TOWARDS MAINTENANCE OF CHILDREN LOOKED AFTER BY LOCAL AUTHORITIES

Liability to contribute

21. (1) Where a local authority are looking after a child (other than in the cases mentioned in sub-paragraph (7)) they shall consider whether they should recover contributions towards the child's maintenance from any person liable to contribute ('a contributor').
(2) An authority may only recover contributions from a contributor if they consider it reasonable to do so.
(3) The persons liable to contribute are –

(a) where the child is under sixteen, each of his parents;
(b) where he has reached the age of sixteen, the child himself.

(4) A parent is not liable to contribute during any period when he is in receipt of income support under Part VII of the Social Security Contributions and Benefits Act 1992, of any element of child tax credit other than the family element, of working tax credit or of an income-based jobseeker's allowance.
(5) A person is not liable to contribute towards the maintenance of a child in the care of a local authority in respect of any period during which the child is allowed by the authority (under section 23(5)) to live with a parent of his.
(6) A contributor is not obliged to make any contribution towards a child's maintenance except as agreed or determined in accordance with this Part of this Schedule.
(7) The cases are where the child is looked after by a local authority under –

(a) section 21;
(b) an interim care order;
(c) section 92 of the Powers of Criminal Courts (Sentencing) Act 2000.

Agreed contributions

22. (1) Contributions towards a child's maintenance may only be recovered if the local authority have served a notice ('a contribution notice') on the contributor specifying –

(a) the weekly sum which they consider that he should contribute; and
(b) arrangements for payment.

(2) The contribution notice must be in writing and dated.
(3) Arrangements for payment shall, in particular, include –

(a) the date on which liability to contribute begins (which must not be earlier than the date of the notice);
(b) the date on which liability under the notice will end (if the child has not before that date ceased to be looked after by the authority); and
(c) the date on which the first payment is to be made.

(4) The authority may specify in a contribution notice a weekly sum which is a standard contribution determined by them for all children looked after by them.
(5) The authority may not specify in a contribution notice a weekly sum greater than that which they consider –

(a) they would normally be prepared to pay if they had placed a similar child with local authority foster parents; and
(b) it is reasonably practicable for the contributor to pay (having regard to his means).

(6) An authority may at any time withdraw a contribution notice (without prejudice to their power to serve another).
(7) Where the authority and the contributor agree –

(a) the sum which the contributor is to contribute; and
(b) arrangements for payment,

(whether as specified in the contribution notice or otherwise) and the contributor notifies the authority in writing that he so agrees, the authority may recover summarily as a civil debt any contribution which is overdue and unpaid.

(8) A contributor may, by serving a notice in writing on the authority, withdraw his agreement in relation to any period of liability falling after the date of service of the notice.

(9) Sub-paragraph (7) is without prejudice to any other method of recovery.

Contribution orders

23. (1) Where a contributor has been served with a contribution notice and has –

(a) failed to reach any agreement with the local authority as mentioned in paragraph 22(7) within the period of one month beginning with the day on which the contribution notice was served; or

(b) served a notice under paragraph 22(8) withdrawing his agreement,

the authority may apply to the court for an order under this paragraph.

(2) On such an application the court may make an order ('a contribution order') requiring the contributor to contribute a weekly sum towards the child's maintenance in accordance with arrangements for payment specified by the court.

(3) A contribution order –

(a) shall not specify a weekly sum greater than that specified in the contribution notice; and

(b) shall be made with due regard to the contributor's means.

(4) A contribution order shall not—

(a) take effect before the date specified in the contribution notice; or

(b) have effect while the contributor is not liable to contribute (by virtue of paragraph 21); or

(c) remain in force after the child has ceased to be looked after by the authority who obtained the order.

(5) An authority may not apply to the court under sub-paragraph (1) in relation to a contribution notice which they have withdrawn.

(6) Where –

(a) a contribution order is in force;

(b) the authority serve another contribution notice; and

(c) the contributor and the authority reach an agreement under paragraph 22(7) in respect of that other contribution notice,

the effect of the agreement shall be to discharge the order from the date on which it is agreed that the agreement shall take effect.

(7) Where an agreement is reached under sub-paragraph (6) the authority shall notify the court –

(a) of the agreement; and

(b) of the date on which it took effect.

(8) A contribution order may be varied or revoked on the application of the contributor or the authority.

(9) In proceedings for the variation of a contribution order, the authority shall specify –

(a) the weekly sum which, having regard to paragraph 22, they propose that the contributor should contribute under the order as varied; and

(b) the proposed arrangements for payment.

(10) Where a contribution order is varied, the order –

(a) shall not specify a weekly sum greater than that specified by the authority in the proceedings for variation; and
(b) shall be made with due regard to the contributor's means.

(11) An appeal shall lie in accordance with rules of court from any order made under this paragraph.

Enforcement of contribution orders etc

24. (1) A contribution order made by a magistrates' court shall be enforceable as a magistrates' court maintenance order (within the meaning of section 150(1) of the Magistrates' Courts Act 1980).

(2) Where a contributor has agreed, or has been ordered, to make contributions to a local authority, any other local authority within whose area the contributor is for the time being living may –

(a) at the request of the local authority who served the contributions notice; and
(b) subject to agreement as to any sum to be deducted in respect of services rendered,

collect from the contributor any contributions due on behalf of the authority who served the notice.

(3) In sub-paragraph (2) the reference to any other local authority includes a reference to –

(a) a local authority within the meaning of section 1(2) of the Social Work (Scotland) Act 1968; and
(b) a Health and Social Services Board established under Article 16 of the Health and Personal Social Services (Northern Ireland) Order 1972.

(4) The power to collect sums under sub-paragraph (2) includes the power to –

(a) receive and give a discharge for any contributions due; and
(b) (if necessary) enforce payment of any contributions,

even though those contributions may have fallen due at a time when the contributor was living elsewhere.

(5) Any contribution collected under sub-paragraph (2) shall be paid (subject to any agreed deduction) to the local authority who served the contribution notice.

(6) In any proceedings under this paragraph, a document which purports to be –

(a) a copy of an order made by a court under or by virtue of paragraph 23; and
(b) certified as a true copy by the designated officer for the court,

shall be evidence of the order.

(7) In any proceedings under this paragraph, a certificate which –

(a) purports to be signed by the clerk or some other duly authorised officer of the local authority who obtained the contribution order; and
(b) states that any sum due to the authority under the order is overdue and unpaid,

shall be evidence that the sum is overdue and unpaid.

Regulations

25. The Secretary of State may make regulations –

(a) as to the considerations which a local authority must take into account in deciding –
   (i) whether it is reasonable to recover contributions; and
   (ii) what the arrangements for payment should be;

(b) as to the procedures they must follow in reaching agreements with –
   (i) contributors (under paragraphs 22 and 23); and
   (ii) any other local authority (under paragraph 23).

K. NATIONAL HEALTH SERVICE AND COMMUNITY CARE ACT 1990

General provisions concerning community care services

46. Local authority plans for community care services

(1) Each local authority –

(a) shall, within such period after the day appointed for the coming into force of this section as the Secretary of State may direct, prepare and publish a plan for the provision of community care services in their area;

(b) shall keep the plan prepared by them under paragraph (a) above and any further plans prepared by them under this section under review; and

(c) shall, at such intervals as the Secretary of State may direct, prepare and publish modifications to the current plan, or if the case requires, a new plan.

(2) In carrying out any of their functions under paragraphs (a) to (c) of subsection (1) above, a local authority shall consult –

(a) any Health Authority and any Local Health Board the whole or any part of whose area lies within the area of the local authority;

(b) [*repealed*];

(c) in so far as any proposed plan, review or modifications of a plan may affect or be affected by the provision or availability of housing and the local authority is not itself a local housing authority, within the meaning of the Housing Act 1985, every such local housing authority whose area is within the area of the local authority;

(d) such voluntary organisations as appear to the authority to represent the interests of persons who use or are likely to use any community care services within the area of the authority or the interests of private carers who, within that area, provide care to persons for whom, in the exercise of their social services functions, the local authority have a power or a duty to provide a service.

(e) such voluntary housing agencies and other bodies as appear to the local authority to provide housing or community care services in their area; and

(f) such other persons as the Secretary of State may direct.

(3) In this section –
'local authority' means the council of a county, a county borough, a metropolitan district or a London borough or the Common Council of the City of London;
'community care services' means services which a local authority may provide or arrange to be provided under any of the following provisions –

(a) Part III of the National Assistance Act 1948;
(b) section 45 of the Health Services and Public Health Act 1968;
(c) section 21 of and Schedule 8 to the National Health Service Act 1977; and
(d) section 117 of the Mental Health Act 1983; and

'private carer' means a person who is not employed to provide the care in question by any body in the exercise of its functions under any enactment.

47. Assessment of needs for community care services

(1) Subject to subsections (5) and (6) below, where it appears to a local authority that any person for whom they may provide or arrange for the provision of community care services may be in need of any such services, the authority –

(a) shall carry out an assessment of his needs for those services; and
(b) having regard to the results of that assessment, shall then decide whether his needs call for the provision by them of any such services.

(2) If at any time during the assessment of the needs of any person under subsection (1)(a) above it appears to a local authority that he is a disabled person, the authority –

(a) shall proceed to make such a decision as to the services he requires as is mentioned in section 4 of the Disabled Persons (Services, Consultation and Representation) Act 1986 without his requesting them to do so under that section; and
(b) shall inform him that they will be doing so and of his rights under that Act.

(3) If at any time during the assessment of the needs of any person under subsection (1)(a) above, it appears to a local authority –

(a) that there may be a need for the provision to that person by such Primary Care Trust or Health Authority as may be determined in accordance with regulations of any services under the National Health Service Act 1977, or
(b) that there may be a need for the provision to him of any services which fall within the functions of a local housing authority (within the meaning of the Housing Act 1985) which is not the local authority carrying out the assessment,

the local authority shall notify that Primary Care Trust, Health Authority or local housing authority and invite them to assist, to such extent as is reasonable in the circumstances, in the making of the assessment; and, in making their decision as to the provision of the services needed for the person in question, the local authority shall take into account any services which are likely to be made available for him by that Primary Care Trust, Health Authority or local housing authority.

(4) The Secretary of State may give directions as to the manner in which an assessment under this section is to be carried out or the form it is to take but, subject to any such directions and to subsection (7) below, it shall be carried out in such manner and take such form as the local authority consider appropriate.

(5) Nothing in this section shall prevent a local authority from temporarily providing or arranging for the provision of community care services for any person without carrying out a prior assessment of his needs in accordance with the preceding provisions of this section if, in the opinion of the authority, the condition of that person is such that he requires those services as a matter of urgency.

(6) If, by virtue of subsection (5) above, community care services have been provided temporarily for any person as a matter of urgency, then, as soon as practicable thereafter, an assessment of his needs shall be made in accordance with the preceding provisions of this section.

(7) This section is without prejudice to section 3 of the Disabled Persons (Services, Consultation and Representation) Act 1986.

(8) In this section –
'disabled person' has the same meaning as in that Act; and
'local authority' and 'community care services' have the same meanings as in section 46 above.

L. CARERS (RECOGNITION AND SERVICES) ACT 1995

1. Assessment of ability of carers to provide care: England and Wales

(1) Subject to subsection (3) below, in any case where –

(a) a local authority carry out an assessment under section 47(1)(a) of the National Health Service and Community Care Act 1990 of the needs of a person ('the relevant person') for community care services, and
(b) an individual ('the carer') provides or intends to provide a substantial amount of care on a regular basis for the relevant person,

the carer may request the local authority, before they make their decision as to whether the needs of the relevant person call for the provision of any services, to carry out an assessment of his ability to provide and to continue to provide care for the relevant person; and if he makes such a request, the local authority shall carry out such an assessment and shall take into account the results of that assessment in making that decision.

(2) Subject to subsection (3) below, in any case where –

(a) a local authority assess the needs of a disabled child for the purposes of Part III of the Children Act 1989 or section 2 of the Chronically Sick and Disabled Persons Act 1970, and
(b) an individual ('the carer') provides or intends to provide a substantial amount of care on a regular basis for the disabled child,

the carer may request the local authority, before they make their decision as to whether the needs of the disabled child call for the provision of any services, to carry out an assessment of his ability to provide and to continue to provide care for the disabled child; and if he makes such a request, the local authority shall carry out such an assessment and shall take into account the results of that assessment in making that decision.

(2A) For the purposes of an assessment under subsection (1) or (2), the local authority may take into account, so far as it considers it to be material, an assessment under section 1 or 6 of the Carers and Disabled Children Act 2000.

(2B) In any case where –

(a) a local authority are carrying out an assessment mentioned in paragraph (a) of either subsection (1) or subsection (2) above in relation to the relevant person or (as the case may be) a disabled child, and
(b) it appears to the local authority that an individual may be entitled to request (but has not requested) an assessment under the subsection in question of his ability to provide and to continue to provide care for the relevant person or the disabled child,

the local authority must inform the individual that he may be so entitled before they make their decision as to the needs of the relevant person or the disabled child.

(2C) An assessment under subsection (1) or (2) above must include consideration of whether the carer –

(a) works or wishes to work,
(b) is undertaking, or wishes to undertake, education, training or any leisure activity.

(3) No request may be made under subsection (1) or (2) above by an individual who provides or will provide the care in question –

(a) by virtue of a contract of employment or other contract with any person; or
(b) as a volunteer for a voluntary organisation.

(4) The Secretary of State may give directions as to the manner in which an assessment under subsection (1) or (2) above is to be carried out or the form it is to take but, subject to any such directions, it shall be carried out in such manner and take such form as the local authority consider appropriate.

(5) Section 8 of the Disabled Persons (Services, Consultation and Representation) Act 1986 (duty of local authority to take into account ability of carers) shall not apply in any case where –

(a) an assessment is made under subsection (1) above in respect of an individual who provides the care in question for a disabled person; or
(b) an assessment is made under subsection (2) above.

(6) In this section –
'community care services' has the meaning given by section 46(3) of the National Health Service and Community Care Act 1990;
'child' means a person under the age of eighteen;
'disabled child' means a child who is disabled within the meaning of Part III of the Children Act 1989;
'disabled person' means a person to whom section 29 of the National Assistance Act 1948 applies;
'local authority' has the meaning given by section 46(3) of the National Health Service and Community Care Act 1990; and
'voluntary organisation' has the same meaning as in the National Assistance Act 1948.

(7) In Schedule 1 to the Local Authority Social Services Act 1970 (enactments conferring functions assigned to social services committees) at the end there shall be inserted –
'Carers (Recognition and Services) Act 1995
Section 1 Assessment of ability of carers to provide care.'

M. LOCAL GOVERNMENT ACT 2000

PART I PROMOTION OF ECONOMIC, SOCIAL OR ENVIRONMENTAL WELL-BEING ETC

Interpretation

1. Meaning of 'local authority' in Part I

In this Part 'local authority' means –
(a) in relation to England –
  (i) a county council,
  (ii) a district council,
  (iii) a London borough council,
  (iv) the Common Council of the City of London in its capacity as a local authority,
  (v) the Council of the Isles of Scilly,
(b) in relation to Wales, a county council or a county borough council.

Promotion of well-being

2. Promotion of well-being

(1) Every local authority are to have power to do anything which they consider is likely to achieve any one or more of the following objects –

  (a) the promotion or improvement of the economic well-being of their area,
  (b) the promotion or improvement of the social well-being of their area, and
  (c) the promotion or improvement of the environmental well-being of their area.

(2) The power under subsection (1) may be exercised in relation to or for the benefit of –

  (a) the whole or any part of a local authority's area, or
  (b) all or any persons resident or present in a local authority's area.

(3) In determining whether or how to exercise the power under subsection (1), a local authority must have regard to their strategy under section 4.
(4) The power under subsection (1) includes power for a local authority to –

  (a) incur expenditure,
  (b) give financial assistance to any person,
  (c) enter into arrangements or agreements with any person,
  (d) co-operate with, or facilitate or co-ordinate the activities of, any person,
  (e) exercise on behalf of any person any functions of that person, and
  (f) provide staff, goods, services or accommodation to any person.

(5) The power under subsection (1) includes power for a local authority to do anything in relation to, or for the benefit of, any person or area situated outside their area if they consider that it is likely to achieve any one or more of the objects in that subsection.
(6) Nothing in subsection (4) or (5) affects the generality of the power under subsection (1).

3. Limits on power to promote well-being

(1) The power under section 2(1) does not enable a local authority to do anything which they are unable to do by virtue of any prohibition, restriction or limitation on their powers which is contained in any enactment (whenever passed or made).

(2) The power under section 2(1) does not enable a local authority to raise money (whether by precepts, borrowing or otherwise).

(3) The Secretary of State may by order make provision preventing local authorities from doing, by virtue of section 2(1), anything which is specified, or is of a description specified, in the order.

(3A) The power under subsection (3) may be exercised in relation to –

(a) all local authorities,
(b) particular local authorities, or
(c) particular descriptions of local authority.

(4) Subject to subsection (4A) before making an order under subsection (3), the Secretary of State must consult such representatives of local government and such other persons (if any) as he considers appropriate.

(4A) Subsection (4) does not apply to an order under this section which is made only for the purpose of amending an earlier order under this section –

(a) so as to extend the earlier order, or any provision of the earlier order, to a particular authority or to authorities of a particular description, or
(b) so that the earlier order, or any provision of the earlier order, ceases to apply to a particular authority or to authorities of a particular description.

(5) Before exercising the power under section 2(1), a local authority must have regard to any guidance for the time being issued by the Secretary of State about the exercise of that power.

(6) Before issuing any guidance under subsection (5), the Secretary of State must consult such representatives of local government and such other persons (if any) as he considers appropriate.

(7) In its application to Wales, this section has effect as if for any reference to the Secretary of State there were substituted a reference to the National Assembly for Wales.

(8) In this section 'enactment' includes an enactment comprised in subordinate legislation (within the meaning of the Interpretation Act 1978).

Maladministration etc.

92. Payments in cases of maladministration etc.

(1) Where a relevant authority consider –

(a) that action taken by or on behalf of the authority in the exercise of their functions amounts to, or may amount to, maladministration, and
(b) that a person has been, or may have been, adversely affected by that action,

the authority may, if they think appropriate, make a payment to, or provide some other benefit for, that person.

(2) Any function which is conferred on the Greater London Authority under this section is to be exercisable by the Mayor of London and the London Assembly acting jointly on behalf of the Authority.

(3) In this section –

'action' includes failure to act,
'relevant authority' has the same meaning as in Part III of this Act.

N. CARERS AND DISABLED CHILDREN ACT 2000

1. Right of carers to assessment

(1) If an individual aged 16 or over ('the carer') –

(a) provides or intends to provide a substantial amount of care on a regular basis for another individual aged 18 or over ('the person cared for'); and
(b) asks a local authority to carry out an assessment of his ability to provide and to continue to provide care for the person cared for,

the local authority must carry out such an assessment if it is satisfied that the person cared for is someone for whom it may provide or arrange for the provision of community care services.

(2) For the purposes of such an assessment, the local authority may take into account, so far as it considers it to be material, an assessment under section 1(1) of the Carers (Recognition and Services) Act 1995.

(3) Subsection (1) does not apply if the individual provides or will provide the care in question –

(a) by virtue of a contract of employment or other contract with any person; or
(b) as a volunteer for a voluntary organisation.

(3A) An assessment under subsection (1) must include consideration of whether the carer –

(a) works or wishes to work,
(b) is undertaking, or wishes to undertake, education, training or any leisure activity.

(4) The Secretary of State (or, in relation to Wales, the National Assembly for Wales) may give directions as to the manner in which an assessment under subsection (1) is to be carried out or the form it is to take.

(5) Subject to any such directions, it is to be carried out in such manner, and is to take such form, as the local authority considers appropriate.

(6) In this section, 'voluntary organisation' has the same meaning as in the National Assistance Act 1948.

2. Services for carers

(1) The local authority must consider the assessment and decide –

(a) whether the carer has needs in relation to the care which he provides or intends to provide;
(b) if so, whether they could be satisfied (wholly or partly) by services which the local authority may provide; and
(c) if they could be so satisfied, whether or not to provide services to the carer.

(2) The services referred to are any services which –

(a) the local authority sees fit to provide; and
(b) will in the local authority's view help the carer care for the person cared for,

and may take the form of physical help or other forms of support.

(3) A service, although provided to the carer –

(a) may take the form of a service delivered to the person cared for if it is one which, if provided to him instead of to the carer, could fall within community care services and they both agree it is to be so delivered; but
(b) if a service is delivered to the person cared for it may not, except in prescribed circumstances, include anything of an intimate nature.

(4) Regulations may make provision about what is, or is not, of an intimate nature for the purposes of subsection (3).

3. Vouchers

(1) Regulations may make provision for the issue of vouchers by local authorities.
(2) 'Voucher' means a document whereby, if the local authority agrees with the carer that it would help him care for the person cared for if the carer had a break from caring, the person cared for may secure that services in lieu of the care which would otherwise have been provided to him by the carer are delivered temporarily to him by another person by way of community care services.
(3) The regulations may, in particular, provide –

(a) for the value of a voucher to be expressed in terms of money, or of the delivery of a service for a period of time, or both;
(b) for the person who supplies a service against a voucher, or for the arrangement under which it is supplied, to be approved by the local authority;
(c) for vouchers to be issued to the carer or to the person cared for;
(d) for a maximum period during which a service (or a service of a prescribed description) can be provided against a voucher.

4. Assessments and services for both carer and person cared for

(1) In section 1 of the Carers (Recognition and Services) Act 1995 (which provides for carers to be assessed as to their ability to care in connection with an assessment of the needs of the individual cared for), after subsection (2) insert –

'(2A) For the purposes of an assessment under subsection (1) or (2), the local authority may take into account, so far as it considers it to be material, an assessment under section 1 or 6 of the Carers and Disabled Children Act 2000.'

(2) Subsection (4) applies if the local authority –

(a) is either providing services under this Act to the carer, or is providing community care services to or in respect of the person cared for (but not both); and
(b) proposes to provide another service to (or in respect of) the one who is not receiving any such service,

and the new service, or any service already being provided, is one which could be provided either under this Act, or by way of community care services.

(3) Subsection (4) also applies if –

(a) the local authority is not providing services to the carer (under this Act) or to the person cared for (by way of community care services), but proposes to provide services to each of them following an assessment under section 1 and under section 47 of the National Health Service and Community Care Act 1990; or

(b) the local authority is providing services both to the carer (under this Act) and to the person cared for (by way of community care services), and proposes to provide to either of them a new service,

and (in a paragraph (a) case) any of the services, or (in a paragraph (b) case) the new service, is one which could be provided either under this Act, or by way of community care services.

(4) In the case of each such service, the local authority must decide whether the service is, or is in future, to be provided under this Act, or by way of community care services (and hence whether it is, or is in future, to be provided to the carer, or to the person cared for).

(5) The local authority's decision under subsection (4) is to be made without regard to the means of the carer or of the person cared for.

5. Direct payments

In section 1(1) of the Community Care (Direct Payments) Act 1996 (which provides for the making of payments for securing the provision of services which a person is assessed as needing) –

(a) in paragraph (a), at the end insert 'or under section 2(1) of the Carers and Disabled Children Act 2000 (services for carers) to provide a person with services under that Act,';

(b) for paragraph (b), substitute –

'(b) in the case of a person –

(i) whose needs the local authority have decided call for the provision of community care services, he is of a description which is specified for the purposes of this subsection by regulations made by the Secretary of State, or

(ii) whom the local authority have decided to provide with services under the Carers and Disabled Children Act 2000, he is not of a description so specified by regulations made by the Secretary of State,'; and

(c) after 'his needs call' insert 'or, as the case may be, they have decided to provide (or arrange to provide)'.

6. Assessments: persons with parental responsibility for disabled children

(1) If a person with parental responsibility for a disabled child –

(a) provides or intends to provide a substantial amount of care on a regular basis for the child; and

(b) asks a local authority to carry out an assessment of his ability to provide and to continue to provide care for the child,

the local authority must carry out such an assessment if it is satisfied that the child and his family are persons for whom it may provide or arrange for the provision of services under section 17 of the Children Act 1989 ('the 1989 Act').

(2) For the purposes of such an assessment, the local authority may take into account, so far as it considers it to be material, an assessment under section 1(2) of the Carers (Recognition and Services) Act 1995.

(2A) An assessment under subsection (1) must include consideration of whether the person with parental responsibility for the child –

(a) works or wishes to work,
(b) is undertaking, or wishes to undertake, education, training or any leisure activity.

(3) The Secretary of State (or, in relation to Wales, the National Assembly for Wales) may give directions as to the manner in which an assessment under subsection (1) is to be carried out or the form it is to take.

(4) Subject to any such directions, it is to be carried out in such manner, and is to take such form, as the local authority considers appropriate.

(5) The local authority must take the assessment into account when deciding what, if any, services to provide under section 17 of the 1989 Act.

(6) Terms used in this section have the same meaning as in Part III of the 1989 Act.

6A. Duty to inform carers of right to assessment

(1) Subsection (2) applies if it appears to a local authority that it would be required to carry out a carer's assessment on being asked to do so by –

(a) the carer, or
(b) a person with parental responsibility for a disabled child ('the responsible person').

(2) The local authority must inform the carer or, as appropriate, the responsible person that he may be entitled to a carer's assessment (but this is subject to subsections (3) and (4)).

(3) Subsection (2) does not apply in relation to the carer if the local authority has previously –

(a) carried out a carer's assessment for him in relation to the person cared for,
(b) informed him that he may be entitled to a carer's assessment in relation to the person cared for, or
(c) carried out an assessment of him under section 4(3) of the Community Care (Delayed Discharges etc.) Act 2003 in relation to the person cared for.

(4) Subsection (2) does not apply in relation to the responsible person if the local authority has previously carried out a carer's assessment for him in relation to the disabled child or informed him that he may be entitled to a carer's assessment in relation to the disabled child.

(5) In this section 'carer's assessment' means –

(a) in the case of the carer, an assessment under section 1 of his ability to provide and to continue to provide care for the person cared for,
(b) in the case of the responsible person, an assessment under section 6 of his ability to provide and to continue to provide care for the disabled child.

O. HEALTH AND SOCIAL CARE ACT 2001

PART 4 SOCIAL CARE

Nursing care

49. Exclusion of nursing care from community care services

(1) Nothing in the enactments relating to the provision of community care services shall authorise or require a local authority, in or in connection with the provision of any such services, to –

(a) provide for any person, or
(b) arrange for any person to be provided with,

nursing care by a registered nurse.

(2) In this section 'nursing care by a registered nurse' means any services provided by a registered nurse and involving –

(a) the provision of care, or
(b) the planning, supervision or delegation of the provision of care,

other than any services which, having regard to their nature and the circumstances in which they are provided, do not need to be provided by a registered nurse.

Measures to increase availability of Part 3 accommodation

53. Disregarding of resources when determining need for residential accommodation

In section 21 of the 1948 Act (duties of local authorities to provide accommodation), for subsections (2A) and (2B) there shall be substituted –

'(2A) In determining for the purposes of paragraph (a) or (aa) of subsection (1) of this section whether care and attention are otherwise available to a person, a local authority shall disregard so much of the person's resources as may be specified in, or determined in accordance with, regulations made by the Secretary of State for the purposes of this subsection.

(2B) In subsection (2A) of this section the reference to a person's resources is a reference to his resources within the meaning of regulations made for the purposes of that subsection.'

54. Funding by resident etc. of more expensive accommodation

(1) Regulations may make provision for and in connection with the making, in respect of the provision of Part 3 accommodation, of additional payments –

(a) by persons for whom such accommodation is provided ('residents'); or
(b) by other persons (including persons liable to maintain residents by virtue of section 42 of the 1948 Act).

(2) In this section 'additional payments', in relation to a resident, means payments which –

(a) are made for the purpose of meeting all or part of the difference between the actual cost of his Part 3 accommodation and the amount that the local authority providing it would usually expect to pay in order to provide Part 3 accommodation suitable for a person with the assessed needs of the resident; and
(b) (in the case of additional payments by the resident) are made out of such of his resources as may be specified in, or determined in accordance with, regulations under subsection (1);

and for this purpose 'resources' has the meaning given by such regulations.

(3) In this Part 'Part 3 accommodation' means accommodation provided under sections 21 to 26 of the 1948 Act.

55. Power for local authorities to take charges on land instead of contributions

(1) Where a person ('the resident') –

(a) is availing himself of Part 3 accommodation provided by a local authority, or is proposing to do so, and
(b) is liable, or would be liable, to pay for the accommodation (whether at the full standard rate determined in accordance with section 22(2) or 26(2) of the 1948 Act or at any lower rate),

the local authority may enter into a deferred payment agreement with the resident.

(2) The relevant authority may by directions require local authorities, where –

(a) they provide or are to provide Part 3 accommodation for a person falling within subsection (1) ('the resident'), and
(b) any conditions specified in the directions are satisfied,

to enter into a deferred payment agreement with the resident.

(3) A 'deferred payment agreement' is an agreement whereby –

(a) during the exempt period the resident will not be required to make payment to the authority of any relevant contributions in respect of periods (or parts of periods) falling within the exempt period, but
(b) the total amount of the relevant contributions shall become payable to the authority on the day after the date on which the exempt period ends, and
(c) the resident will grant the authority a charge in their favour in respect of any land specified in the agreement in which he has a beneficial interest (whether legal or equitable) for the purpose of securing the payment to the authority of the total amount payable to them as mentioned in paragraph (b).

(4) 'The exempt period', in relation to a deferred payment agreement, is the period beginning with the time when the agreement takes effect and ending –

(a) 56 days after the date of the resident's death, or
(b) with any earlier date which, in accordance with the agreement, the resident has specified in a notice given by him to the authority for the purposes of subsection (5)(b).

(5) The provisions of any deferred payment agreement and any such charge as is mentioned in subsection (3)(c) –

(a) shall be determined by the authority in accordance with any directions given by the relevant authority; but

(b) shall secure that the agreement and any such charge may be terminated by notice given to the authority by the resident on payment of the full amount which he is liable to pay as mentioned in subsection (3)(a) down to the date of the payment.

(6) Where a deferred payment agreement is in force in respect of the resident –

(a) no interest shall accrue at any time on or before the date on which the exempt period ends in respect of any sum which he is liable to pay as mentioned in subsection (3)(a); but

(b) as from the day after that date, any such sum shall bear interest at such reasonable rate as the relevant authority may direct or, if no such directions are given, as the authority may determine;

and accordingly any charge granted in pursuance of subsection (3)(c) shall secure payment to the authority of any interest falling due by virtue of paragraph (b) above.

(7) Any reference in this section to relevant contributions is a reference to so much of the payments which the resident is liable to pay to an authority for Part 3 accommodation (including any payments which are additional payments for the purpose of section 54) as may be specified, or determined in accordance with, regulations made for the purposes of this subsection.

(8) Any directions given by the relevant authority under this section shall be given to local authorities generally.

56. Cross-border placements

(1) Regulations may make provision for and in connection with authorising a local authority to make arrangements under section 21 of the 1948 Act for a person to be provided with residential accommodation in Scotland, Northern Ireland, any of the Channel Islands or the Isle of Man.

(2) Regulations under this section may, in particular, make provision –

(a) specifying conditions which must be satisfied before a local authority make any arrangements in pursuance of the regulations in respect of a person;

(b) for the application of provisions of the 1948 Act in relation to –

(i) any such arrangements, or

(ii) the person in respect of whom any such arrangements are made,

with or without modifications.

Direct payments

57. Direct payments

(1) Regulations may make provision for and in connection with requiring or authorising the responsible authority in the case of a person of a prescribed description who falls within subsection (2) to make, with that person's consent, such payments to him as they may determine in accordance with the regulations in respect of his securing the provision of the service mentioned in paragraph (a) or (b) of that subsection.

(2) A person falls within this subsection if a local authority ('the responsible authority') have decided –

(a) under section 47 of the 1990 Act (assessment by local authorities of needs for community care services) that his needs call for the provision by them of a particular community care service (within the meaning of section 46 of that Act), or
(b) under section 2(1) of the Carers and Disabled Children Act 2000 (c. 16) (services for carers) to provide him with a particular service under that Act.

(3) Regulations under this section may, in particular, make provision –

(a) specifying circumstances in which the responsible authority are not required or authorised to make any payments under the regulations to a person, whether those circumstances relate to the person in question or to the particular service mentioned in paragraph (a) or (b) of subsection (2);
(b) for any payments required or authorised by the regulations to be made to a person by the responsible authority ('direct payments') to be made to that person ('the payee') as gross payments or alternatively as net payments;
(c) for the responsible authority to make for the purposes of subsection (4) or (5) such determination as to –
(i) the payee's means, and
(ii) the amount (if any) which it would be reasonably practicable for him to pay to the authority by way of reimbursement or contribution,
as may be prescribed;
(d) as to the conditions falling to be complied with by the payee which must or may be imposed by the responsible authority in relation to the direct payments (and any conditions which may not be so imposed);
(e) specifying circumstances in which the responsible authority –
(i) may or must terminate the making of direct payments,
(ii) may require repayment (whether by the payee or otherwise) of the whole or part of the direct payments;
(f) for any sum falling to be paid or repaid to the responsible authority by virtue of any condition or other requirement imposed in pursuance of the regulations to be recoverable as a debt due to the authority;
(g) displacing functions or obligations of the responsible authority with respect to the provision of the service mentioned in subsection (2)(a) or (b) only to such extent, and subject to such conditions, as may be prescribed;
(h) authorising direct payments to be made to any prescribed person on behalf of the payee.

(4) For the purposes of subsection (3)(b) 'gross payments' means payments –

(a) which are made at such a rate as the authority estimate to be equivalent to the reasonable cost of securing the provision of the service concerned; but
(b) which may be made subject to the condition that the payee pays to the responsible authority, by way of reimbursement, an amount or amounts determined under the regulations.

(5) For the purposes of subsection (3)(b) 'net payments' means payments –

(a) which are made on the basis that the payee will himself pay an amount or amounts determined under the regulations by way of contribution towards the cost of securing the provision of the service concerned; and
(b) which are accordingly made at such a rate below that mentioned in subsection (4)(a) as reflects any such contribution by the payee.

(6) Regulations under this section shall provide that, where direct payments are made in respect of a service which, apart from the regulations, would be provided under section 117 of the Mental Health Act 1983 (after-care) –

(a) the payments shall be made at the rate mentioned in subsection (4)(a); and
(b) subsection (4)(b) shall not apply.

(7) Regulations made for the purposes of subsection (3)(a) may provide that direct payments shall not be made in respect of the provision of residential accommodation for any person for a period in excess of a prescribed period.
(8) In this section 'prescribed' means specified in or determined in accordance with regulations under this section.

58. Direct payments in respect of children

For section 17A of the Children Act 1989 (c. 41) there shall be substituted –

'17A Direct payments

(1) The Secretary of State may by regulations make provision for and in connection with requiring or authorising the responsible authority in the case of a person of a prescribed description who falls within subsection (2) to make, with that person's consent, such payments to him as they may determine in accordance with the regulations in respect of his securing the provision of the service mentioned in that subsection.
(2) A person falls within this subsection if he is –

(a) a person with parental responsibility for a disabled child,
(b) a disabled person with parental responsibility for a child, or
(c) a disabled child aged 16 or 17,

and a local authority ("the responsible authority") have decided for the purposes of section 17 that the child's needs (or, if he is such a disabled child, his needs) call for the provision by them of a service in exercise of functions conferred on them under that section.
(3) Subsections (3) to (5) and (7) of section 57 of the 2001 Act shall apply, with any necessary modifications, in relation to regulations under this section as they apply in relation to regulations under that section.
(4) Regulations under this section shall provide that, where payments are made under the regulations to a person falling within subsection (5) –

(a) the payments shall be made at the rate mentioned in subsection (4)(a) of section 57 of the 2001 Act (as applied by subsection (3)); and
(b) subsection (4)(b) of that section shall not apply.

(5) A person falls within this subsection if he is –

(a) a person falling within subsection (2)(a) or (b) and the child in question is aged 16 or 17, or
(b) a person who is in receipt of income support, working families' tax credit or disabled person's tax credit under Part 7 of the Social Security Contributions and Benefits Act 1992 (c. 4) or of an income-based jobseeker's allowance.

(6) In this section –
"the 2001 Act" means the Health and Social Care Act 2001;
"disabled" in relation to an adult has the same meaning as that given by section 17(11) in relation to a child;
"prescribed" means specified in or determined in accordance with regulations under this section (and has the same meaning in the provisions of the 2001 Act mentioned in subsection (3) as they apply by virtue of that subsection).'

APPENDIX 2

Government directions and guidance

A National Assistance Act 1948 (Choice of Accommodation) Directions 1992 (as amended)
B Local Authority Circular LAC (93) 10
C Local Authority Circular LAC (2004) 20
D Delayed Discharges (Continuing Care) Directions 2004
E Community Care Assessment Directions 2004

A. NATIONAL ASSISTANCE ACT 1948 (CHOICE OF ACCOMMODATION) DIRECTIONS 1992 (AS AMENDED)

The Secretary of State in exercise of the powers conferred by section 7A of the Local Authority Social Services Act 1970 and of all other powers enabling her in that behalf hereby makes the following Directions –

1. Citation, commencement and extent

(1) These Directions may be cited as the National Assistance Act 1948 (Choice of Accommodation) Directions 1992 and shall come into force on 1st April 1993.
(2) These Directions extend only to England.

2. Local authorities to provide preferred accommodation

Where a local authority have assessed a person under section 47 of the National Health Service and Community Care Act 1990 (assessment) and have decided that accommodation should be provided pursuant to section 21 of the National Assistance Act 1948 (provision of residential accommodation), the local authority shall, subject to paragraph 3 of these Directions, make arrangements for accommodation pursuant to section 21 for that person at the place of his choice within England and Wales (in these Directions called 'preferred accommodation') if he has indicated that he wishes to be accommodated in preferred accommodation.

3. Conditions for provision of preferred accommodation

Subject to paragraph 4 of these Directions the local authority shall only be required to make or continue to make arrangements for a person to be accommodated in his preferred accommodation if –

(a) the preferred accommodation appears to the authority to be suitable in relation to his needs as assessed by them;
(b) the cost of making arrangements for him at his preferred accommodation would not require the authority to pay more than they would usually expect to pay having regard to his assessed needs;
(c) the preferred accommodation is available;
(d) the persons in charge of the preferred accommodation provide it subject to the authority's usual terms and conditions, having regard to the nature of the accommodation, for providing accommodation for such a person under Part III of the National Assistance Act 1948.

B. LOCAL AUTHORITY CIRCULAR LAC (93) 10

DEPARTMENT OF HEALTH

To: The Chief Executive: Metropolitan District Councils, County Councils – In England; London Borough Councils; Common Council of the City of London

Council of the Isles of Scilly

Directors of Social Services – for information

March 1993

Approvals and Directions for arrangements from 1 April 1993 made under Schedule 8 to the National Health Service Act 1977 and sections 21 and 29 of the National Assistance Act 1948

SUMMARY

This circular contains guidance on the consolidated approvals and directions made by the Secretary of State for Health on local authorities continuing responsibilities, from 1 April 1993, to provide residential accommodation and welfare services, insofar as they are provided under sections 21 and 29 of the National Assistance Act, 1948 and paragraphs 1 and 2 of Schedule 9 of the NHS Act, 1977.

ACTION

1. This circular contains approvals and directions made by the Secretary of State in exercise of the powers conferred by sections 21(1) and 29(1) of the National Assistance Act 1948 and paragraphs 1 and 2 of Schedule 8 to the National Health Service Act 1977.
2. It consolidates the existing approvals and directions contained in LAC 13/74, LAC 19/74, LAC (74) 28 and Annexes 1 and 2 of LAC (91) 12. This circular does not of itself create any additional responsibilities which have not previously been expected of local social services authorities. This circular also updates existing guidance on registration practice and related statistics.

BACKGROUND

3. Social services authorities' powers under sections 21 and 29 of the 1948 Act and under Schedule 8 to the 1977 Act are subject to the requirement to act with the approval and under the direction of the Secretary of State. The relevant information is at:

Appendix 1 – Approvals and Directions under section 21(1) of the 1948 Act.
Appendix 2 – Approvals and Directions under section 29(1) of the 1948 Act.
Appendix 3 – Approvals and Directions under paras 1 and 2 of Schedule 8 of the 1977 Act.

4. The approvals and directions contained in this circular take account of the amendments made to Part III of the 1948 Act and Schedule 8 of the 1977 Act by the Mental Health Act 1983, the Children Act 1989, the National Health Service and Community Care Act 1990 and the Community Care (Residential Accommodation) Act 1992.

   It is the view of the Department that the amendments introduced into the 1948 Act by section 1 of the Community Care (Residential Accommodation) Act 1992 will require authorities to make some direct provision for residential care under Part III of the 1948 Act.

5. From 1 April 1993, when section 43 of the 1990 Act comes into force, authorities will not be able to provide accommodation to people ordinarily resident in independent homes immediately before that date with preserved rights to the higher levels of Income Support. The new section 26A(3) of the 1948 Act, inserted by section 43 of the 1990 Act, gives the Secretary of State power to make exceptions. These are set out in LAC (93) 6 together with SI 1993 No 477.
6. Paragraphs 1 and 2 of the Schedule 8 to the National Health Service Act 1977 will remain in force after 1 April 1993, but they will be amended so that local authorities will no longer be able to provide residential accommodation under them. For convenience, the approvals and directions previously contained in Circulars 19/74 and 74/28, which related to services other than the provision of accommodation have been included in this Circular.
7. The opportunity has been taken to consolidate and update circulars 25/61, 17/74, (74) 37 and (78) 20 concerning registration practice and statistics. Appendix 4 refers.

WHITE PAPER AND POLICY GUIDANCE

8. It will be the responsibility of Social Services Departments to make maximum possible use of private and voluntary providers and so increase the available range of options and widen consumer choice (paragraph 1.11 of the White Paper 'Caring for People' (Cm 849)). The Government welcomes the action being taken by authorities to review the range of services they are currently providing, as part of a comprehensive review of the needs and services available in their area. Social services authorities will continue to play a valuable role in the provision of services, but in those cases where they are currently the main or sole providers of services, they will be expected to take all reasonable steps to secure diversity of provision (paragraph 3.4.1). Regarding the circumstances in which direct provision may be needed the White Paper said (paragraph 3.4.11) that the Government will expect local authorities to retain the ability to act as direct service providers, if other forms of service provision are unforthcoming or unsuitable. This is likely to be particularly important in services for people with high levels of dependency, or particularly challenging patterns of behaviour, whose care it is essential to safeguard.
9. The role of housing and social services authorities in relation to housing and community care is set out in the joint circular from the Departments of Health (LAC (92) 12) and the Environment (10/92). This circular has also been issued to housing associations by the Housing Corporation.

10. By virtue of section 2 of the Chronically Sick and Disabled Persons Act 1970 the matters dealt with in sub section (1) of that section do not need to be included in the arrangements contained in Appendix 2.
11. It is not necessary for the arrangements contained in this circular to cover the provision by local authorities of sheltered employment as this is provided under powers deriving from the Disabled Persons (Employment) Acts 1944 and 1958.
12. The Secretary of State hopes that authorities will keep in mind the needs of individuals, families and groups to ensure that the services provided are administered flexibly and in accordance with changing needs. For the purpose of any of these arrangements, where no express statutory power exists for authorities to use outside service providers, the Secretary of State has also approved the use by authorities of suitable accommodation, services or facilities made available by another authority, voluntary body or person on such conditions as may be agreed. Thus, for example, authorities may continue to make use on a repayment basis of suitable residential or training places made available by other authorities, though they are asked nevertheless to bear in mind the importance of such services being provided as near to the person's home place as is practicable.
13. Social services authorities' powers to prevent mental disorder or provide care for those who are or have been suffering from mental disorder are embraced in their wider powers under paragraph 2 of Schedule 8 to the 1977 Act to prevent illness and provide care for those who are or have been suffering from it. In addition, if authorities wish to provide services other than accommodation specifically for persons who are alcoholic or drug-dependent, the Secretary of State has approved them so doing. Because authorities' powers to provide accommodation under paragraph 2 of Schedule 8 are being repealed, the Approvals and Directions in relation to the provision of accommodation for the prevention of mental disorder or for persons who are or who have been suffering from mental disorder, or specifically for persons who are alcoholic or drug-dependent, have all been transferred to section 21(1) of the 1948 Act. Further guidance on the provision of alcohol and drug services within community care is contained in LAC (93) 2.

EFFECTIVE DATE

14. The Approvals and Directions are effective from 1 April 1993.

CANCELLATION OF CIRCULARS

15. This circular cancels LAC 13/74, LAC 19/74, LAC (74) 28, LAC 17/74, LAC (74) 37 and LAC (78) 20. It also cancels Annexes 1 and 2 of LAC (91) 12. Authorities should note however the saving provision contained in paragraph 6(3) of Appendix 1 to this circular in relation to the directions contained in Annexes 1 and 2 of circular LAC (91) 12.

ENQUIRIES

16. Enquiries about this circular should be made to CS1 Division, Department of Health on 071 972 4237.

CS1 Division
Wellington House
133–155 Waterloo Road
LONDON SE1 8UG
Tel: 071 972 4237
EAR 100

(c) Crown Copyright

Appendix 1 to LAC (93) 10

SECRETARY OF STATE'S APPROVALS AND DIRECTIONS UNDER SECTION 21(1) OF THE NATIONAL ASSISTANCE ACT 1948

The Secretary of State for Health, in exercise of the powers conferred on her by section 21(1) of the National Assistance Act 1948, hereby makes the following Approvals and Directions:

1. Commencement, interpretation and extent

(1) These Approvals and Directions shall come into force on 1st April 1993.
(2) In these Approvals and Directions, unless the context otherwise requires, 'the Act' means the National Assistance Act 1948.
(3) The Interpretation Act 1978 applies to these Approvals and Directions as it applies to an Act of Parliament.
(4) These Approvals and Directions shall apply only to England and Wales.

2. Residential accommodation for persons in need of care and attention

(1) The Secretary of State hereby –

(a) approves the making by local authorities of arrangements under section 21(1)(a) of the Act in relation to persons with no settled residence and, to such extent as the authority may consider desirable, in relation to persons who are ordinarily resident in the area of another local authority, with the consent of that other authority; and
(b) directs local authorities to make arrangements under section 21(1)(a) of the Act in relation to persons who are ordinarily resident in their area and other persons who are in urgent need thereof,

to provide residential accommodation for persons aged 18 or over who by reason of age, illness, disability or any other circumstance are in need of care and attention not otherwise available to them.
(2) Without prejudice to the generality of sub-paragraph (1), the Secretary of State hereby directs local authorities to make arrangements under section 21(1)(a) of the Act to provide temporary accommodation for persons who are in urgent need thereof in circumstances where the need for that accommodation could not reasonably have been foreseen.
(3) Without prejudice to the generality of sub-paragraph (1), the Secretary of State hereby directs local authorities to make arrangements under section 21(1)(a) of the Act to provide accommodation –

(a) in relation to persons who are or have been suffering from mental disorder, or
(b) for the purposes of the prevention of mental disorder,

for persons who are ordinarily resident in their area and for persons with no settled residence who are in the authority's area.

(4) Without prejudice to the generality of sub-paragraph (1) and subject to section 24(4) of the Act, the Secretary of State hereby approves the making by local authorities of arrangements under section 21(1)(a) of the Act to provide residential accommodation –

(a) in relation to persons who are or have been suffering from mental disorder; or
(b) for the purposes of the prevention of mental disorder,

for persons who are ordinarily resident in the area of another local authority but who following discharge from hospital have become resident in the authority's area.

(5) Without prejudice to the generality of sub-paragraph (l), the Secretary of State hereby approves the making by local authorities of arrangements under section 21(1)(a) of the Act to provide accommodation to meet the needs of persons for –

(a) the prevention of illness;
(b) the care of those suffering from illness; and
(c) the aftercare of those so suffering.

(6) Without prejudice to the generality of sub-paragraph (l), the Secretary of State hereby approves the making by local authorities of arrangements under section 21(1)(a) of the Act specifically for persons who are alcoholic or drug-dependent.

3. Residential accommodation for expectant and nursing mothers

The Secretary of State hereby approves the making by local authorities of arrangements under section 21(1)(aa) of the Act to provide residential accommodation (in particular mother and baby homes) for expectant and nursing mothers (of any age) who are in need of care and attention which is not otherwise available to them.

4. Arrangements to provide services for residents

The Secretary of State hereby directs local authorities to make arrangements in relation to persons provided with accommodation under section 21(1) of the Act for all or any of the following purposes –

(a) for the welfare of all persons for whom accommodation is provided;
(b) for the supervision of the hygiene of the accommodation so provided;
(c) to enable persons for whom accommodation is provided to obtain –
    (i) medical attention,
    (ii) nursing attention during illnesses of a kind which are ordinarily nursed at home, and
    (iii) the benefit of any services provided by the National Health Service of which they may from time to time be in need,

but nothing in this paragraph shall require a local authority to make any provision authorised or required to be provided under the National Health Service Act 1977;

(d) for the provision of board and such other services, amenities and requisites provided in connection with the accommodation, except where in the opinion of the authority managing the premises their provision is unnecessary;

(e) to review regularly the provision made under the arrangements and to make such improvements as the authority considers necessary.

5. Arrangements for the conveyance of residents

The Secretary of State hereby approves the making by local authorities of arrangements under section 21(1) of the Act to provide, in such cases as the authority considers appropriate, for the conveyance of persons to and from premises in which accommodation is provided for them under Part III of the Act.

6. Duties in respect of residents in transferred accommodation

(1) Where a person is provided with accommodation pursuant to section 21(1) of the Act, and –

(a) the residential accommodation is local authority accommodation provided pursuant to section 21(4) of the 1948 Act;

(b) the local authority transfer the management of the residential accommodation to a voluntary organisation who –

(i) manages it as a residential care home within the meaning of Part I of the Registered Homes Act 1984, and

(ii) is registered under that Part or is not required to be so registered by virtue of being an exempt body; and

(c) the person is accommodated in the residential accommodation immediately before and after the transfer,

while that person remains accommodated in that residential accommodation, the local authority shall remain under a duty to make arrangements to provide accommodation for him after any transfer to which paragraph (b) of this sub-paragraph refers.

(2) For the purposes of paragraph (c) of sub-paragraph (l), a person shall be regarded as accommodated in residential accommodation if –

(a) he is temporarily absent from such accommodation (including circumstances in which he is in hospital or on holiday);

(b) before 1st April 1993, that accommodation was provided under paragraph 2(1) of Schedule 8 to the National Health Service Act 1977.

(3) Where immediately before these Approvals and Directions come into force a local authority was under a duty to provide a person with accommodation by virtue of –

(a) the Secretary of State's former Directions under Section 21(1) of the National Assistance Act 1948 contained in Annex 1 of Department of Health Circular LAC (91) 12; or

(b) the Secretary of State's former Directions under paragraph 2 of Schedule 8 to the National Health Service Act 1977 contained in Annex 2 of Department of Health Circular LAC (91) 12, while that person remains accommodated in that residential accommodation, the local authority shall remain under a duty to make arrangements to provide that person with accommodation from the date on which these Directions come into force.

7. Powers to make arrangements with other local authorities and voluntary organisations etc.

For the avoidance of doubt, these Approvals and Directions are without prejudice to any of the powers conferred on local authorities by section 21(4) and section 26(1) of the Act (arrangements with voluntary organisations etc.).

ANN DE PEYER

Dated 17/3/1993 Signed on behalf of the Secretary of State for Health

Appendix 2 to LAC (93) 10

SECRETARY OF STATE'S APPROVALS AND DIRECTIONS UNDER SECTION 29(1) OF THE NATIONAL ASSISTANCE ACT 1948

The Secretary of State for Health, in exercise of the powers conferred on her by section 29(1) of the National Assistance Act 1948, hereby makes the following Approvals and Directions:

1. Commencement, interpretation and extent

(1) These Approvals and Directions shall come into force on 1st April 1993.
(2) In these Approvals and Directions, unless the context otherwise requires, 'the Act' means the National Assistance Act 1948.
(3) The Interpretation Act 1978 applies to these Approvals and Directions as it applies to an Act of Parliament.
(4) These Approvals and Directions shall apply only to England and Wales.

2. Powers and duties to make welfare arrangements

(1) The Secretary of State hereby approves the making by local authorities of arrangements under section 29(1) of the Act for all persons to whom that subsection applies and directs local authorities to make arrangements under section 29(1) of the Act in relation to persons who are ordinarily resident in their area for all or any of the following purposes –

(a) to provide a social work service and such advice and support as may be needed for people in their own homes or elsewhere;
(b) to provide, whether at centres or elsewhere, facilities for social rehabilitation and adjustment to disability including assistance in overcoming limitations of mobility or communication;
(c) to provide, whether at centres or elsewhere, facilities for occupational, social, cultural and recreational activities and, where appropriate, the making of payments to persons for work undertaken by them;

(2) The Secretary of State hereby directs local authorities to make the arrangements referred to in section 29(4)(g) of the Act (compiling and maintaining registers) in relation to persons who are ordinarily resident in their area.

(3) The Secretary of State hereby approves the making by local authorities of arrangements under section 29(1) of the Act for all persons to whom that subsection applies for the following purposes –

(a) to provide holiday homes;
(b) to provide free or subsidised travel for all or any persons who do not otherwise qualify for travel concessions but only in respect of travel arrangements for which concessions are available;
(c) to assist a person in finding accommodation which will enable him to take advantage of any arrangements made under section 29(1) of the Act;
(d) to contribute to the cost of employing a warden on welfare functions in warden assisted housing schemes;
(e) to provide warden services for occupiers of private housing.

(4) Save as is otherwise provided for under this paragraph, the Secretary of State hereby approves the making by local authorities of all or any of the arrangements referred to in section 29(4) of the Act (welfare arrangements etc.) for all persons to whom section 29(1) applies.

3. Welfare arrangements with another local authority

The Secretary of State hereby approves the making by local authorities of arrangements under section 29(1) of the Act, where appropriate, with another local authority for the provision of any of the services referred to in these Approvals and Directions.

4. Welfare arrangements with voluntary organisations and otherwise

For the avoidance of doubt, these Approvals and Directions are without prejudice to the powers conferred on local authorities by section 30(1) of the Act (voluntary organisations for disabled persons welfare).

ANN DE PEYER

Dated 17/3/1993 Signed on behalf of the Secretary of State for Health

Appendix 3 to LAC (93) 10

SECRETARY OF STATE'S APPROVALS AND DIRECTIONS UNDER PARAGRAPHS 1 AND 2 OF SCHEDULE 8 TO THE NATIONAL HEALTH SERVICE ACT 1977

The Secretary of State for Health, in exercise of the powers conferred on her by paragraphs l(l) and 2(1) of Schedule 8 to the National Health Service Act 1977, hereby makes the following Approvals and Directions:

l. Commencement, interpretation and extent

(1) These Approvals and Directions shall come into force on 1st April 1993.
(2) In these Approvals and Directions, unless the context otherwise requires, 'the Act' means the National Health Service Act 1977.
(3) The Interpretation Act 1978 applies to these Approvals and Directions as it applies to an Act of Parliament.
(4) For the avoidance of doubt, these Approvals and Directions apply only to England and Wales.

2. Services for expectant and nursing mothers

The Secretary of State hereby approves the making of arrangements under paragraph 1(1) of Schedule 8 to the Act for the care of expectant and nursing mothers (of any age) other than the provision of residential accommodation for them.

3. Services for the purpose of the prevention of illness etc.

(1) The Secretary of State hereby approves the making by local authorities of arrangements under paragraph 2(1) of Schedule 8 to the Act for the purpose of the prevention of illness, and the care of persons suffering from illness and for the aftercare of persons who have been so suffering and in particular for –

(a) the provision, for persons whose care is undertaken with a view to preventing them becoming ill, persons suffering from illness and persons who have been so suffering, of centres or other facilities for training them or keeping them suitably occupied and the equipment and maintenance of such centres;

(b) the provision, for the benefit of such persons as are mentioned in paragraph (a) above, of ancillary or supplemental services.

(2) The Secretary of State hereby directs local authorities to make arrangements under paragraph 2(1) of Schedule 8 to the Act for the purposes of the prevention of mental disorder, or in relation to persons who are or who have been suffering from mental disorder –

(a) for the provision of centres (including training centres and day centres) or other facilities (including domiciliary facilities), whether in premises managed by the local authority or otherwise, for training or occupation of such persons;

(b) for the appointment of sufficient social workers in their area to act as approved social workers for the purposes of the Mental Health Act 1983;

(c) for the exercise of the functions of the authority in respect of persons suffering from mental disorder who are received into guardianship under Part II or III of the Mental Health Act 1983 (whether the guardianship of the local social services authority or of other persons);

(d) for the provision of social work and related services to help in the identification, diagnosis, assessment and social treatment of mental disorder and to provide social work support and other domiciliary and care services to people living in their homes and elsewhere.

(3) Without prejudice to the generality of sub-paragraph (1), the Secretary of State hereby approves the making by local authorities of arrangements under paragraph 2(1) of Schedule 8 to the Act for the provision of –

(a) meals to be served at the centres or other facilities referred to in sub-paragraphs (1)(a) and (2)(a) above and meals-on-wheels for house-bound people not provided for –

(i) under section 45(1) of the Health Services and Public Health Act 1968, or

(ii) by a district council under paragraph 1 of Part II of Schedule 9 to the Health and Social Services and Social Security Adjudications Act 1983;

(b) remuneration for persons engaged in suitable work at the centres or other facilities referred to in sub-paragraphs (1)(a) and (2)(a) above, subject to paragraph 2(2)(a) of Schedule 8 to the Act;
(c) social services (including advice and support) for the purposes of preventing the impairment of physical or mental health of adults in families where such impairment is likely, and for the purposes of preventing the break-up of such families, or for assisting in their rehabilitation;
(d) night-sitter services;
(e) recuperative holidays;
(f) facilities for social and recreational activities;
(g) services specifically for persons who are alcoholic or drug-dependent.

4. Services made available by another local authority etc.

For the purposes of any arrangements made under these Approvals and Directions, the Secretary of State hereby approves the use by local authorities of services or facilities made available by another authority, voluntary body or person on such conditions as may be agreed, but in making such arrangements, a local authority shall have regard to the importance of services being provided as near to a person's home as is practicable.

ANN DE PEYER

Dated 17/3/1993 Signed on behalf of the Secretary of State for Health

Appendix 4 to LAC (93) 10

SECTION 29 0F THE NATIONAL ASSISTANCE ACT 1948 – REGISTRATION PRACTICE AND RELATED STATISTICS

1. The guidance contained in this Appendix was previously contained in Local Authority Circulars 25/61 (dated 14 September 1961) 17/74 (dated 18 March 1974), (74) 37 (dated 30 December 1974) and (78) 20 (dated 9 October 1978). This Circular updates, but does not significantly change, the guidance contained in the earlier documents.

General

2. For certain statutory purposes unconnected with section 29 of the National Assistance Act, 1948* provision needs to be made for the registration of persons to whom that section applies. The keeping of registers is therefore included in those arrangements which are the subject of the direction given in Appendix 2 of this Circular. For the purposes of planning and providing services authorities will also wish to keep a record of persons to whom the section applies – both those who are receiving services and those who at some future date may be in need of help – and in the view of the Department it will be convenient for these records to be designated registers. In this way a single set of records can assist authorities in planning their services and also provide the means for establishing

* Various benefits for blind persons are dependent on registration – notably an allowance set against income tax. More generally registration under section 29 may have a significance for the purposes of the Housing Finance Act 1972 and the Furnished Lettings (Rent Allowances) Act 1973.

the eligibility of individuals for certain benefits not deriving from section 29. The form of registers is not prescribed and the Department hopes that this will enable authorities to keep registers in whatever form and by whatever method will most readily meet their operational requirements. As indicated in paragraph 10 below the Department's annual statistical returns relating to persons to whom section 29 applies will continue to be based on information included in registers.

3. Authorities should note, however, that once it is established that a person comes within the scope of section 29, the giving of assistance under that section as extended by section 2 of the Chronically Sick and Disabled Persons Act 1970, is not dependent on formal registration – i.e. registration is not a prerequisite to giving assistance. If, therefore, a person has indicated a specific wish not to have their name included in the formal register this wish must be respected and such assistance should not on that account be withheld. The Department hopes, however, that the person concerned will be made aware that registration is no more than a routine process of record keeping. Furthermore, it will only be fair to explain that normal administrative practice requires that a written record is kept of anyone to whom help is given, or in respect of whom information is kept by the authority in case they should at some future date require help. If the nature of registration is explained in this way the Department hopes that the number of people specifically expressing a wish not to have their names included on the register will be small.

4. Authorities are reminded that registration under section 29 is entirely distinct from registration as a disabled person by the Department of Employment under the Disabled Persons (Employment) Acts 1944 and 1958. It would be helpful if authorities would avoid the use of the term 'disabled person' in relation to registration under section 29 and use instead the phrase 'registered as a handicapped person' or a similar phrase. In addition, where any document is separately issued confirming registration under section 29, and where that document is not confined to a particular and specified purpose (e.g. in relation to blind persons, for a reduced television licence fee) it would be helpful if that document could bear a note indicating that it is issued pursuant to section 29 of the 1948 Act and has no significance in relation to the Disabled Persons (Employment) Acts.

Criteria for determining whether or not a person comes within the scope of section 29

5. As indicated above, once it has been established that a person comes within the scope of section 29, the matter of registration on no way affects eligibility to receive help – in other words the material question in determining that eligibility is whether, for the purposes of section 29, the person is to be regarded as having a hearing, vision or speech impairment or is substantially and permanently handicapped by illness, injury or congenital deformity. The following paragraphs concern the interpretation of these terms. From 1 April 1974, a local authority requiring medical advice over registration has consulted the District Health Authority which has been, and remains, responsible for arranging for such advice to be given and for meeting any charges that may arise.

Visually impaired people

6. There are well established procedures for determining whether a visually impaired person is blind or partially sighted and thus whether the terms of section 29(1) – and registration – apply. Authorities are asked to note that the effective date of registration should be the same as that of certification. This is

to obviate the risk that delay in registration will adversely affect the blind person's eligibility for certain benefits not related to section 29.

Hearing impaired people

7. There are no formal examination procedures for determining whether a person is deaf or hard of hearing for the purposes of section 29, and there is no intention of introducing any new procedure in this respect.

Handicapped people in the General Classes

8. It is convenient to continue to use the term 'General Classes' to apply to those persons within the scope of section 29 whose primary handicap is neither visual nor auditory. It has not proved possible to give precise guidance on the interpretation of the phrase 'substantially and permanently handicapped'. However, as hitherto, authorities are asked to give a wide interpretation to the term 'substantial', which the Department fully recognises must always take full account of individual circumstances. With regard to the term 'permanent', authorities will also wish to interpret this sufficiently flexibly to ensure that they do not feel inhibited from giving help under section 29 in cases where they are uncertain of the likely duration of the condition.

Guidance on registration practice and the collection of statistics

9. As indicated in paragraph 2, authorities are free to choose the method or form of registration which will most readily meet their operational requirements. Depending on the form of register adopted, authorities may find it convenient to have separate sections for each of the groups of persons to whom section 29 applies as follows:

   Blind
   Partially sighted
   Deaf with speech
   Deaf without speech
   Hard of hearing
   General classes (i.e. those persons coming within the scope of section 29 whose primary handicap is neither visual nor auditory).

   Subject to what is said in paragraph 10 below national statistics will continue to relate separately to these groups.

10. Authorities will wish to consider what information to include in registers for their own purposes. For the purpose of compiling national statistics the Department will seek information about the age of all persons registered, subject to what is said in paras 13–14 below about mentally disordered persons. In respect of particular classes, additional information will be sought as follows:

    (a) *Blind and partially sighted*: The Local Authority Social Services letter, LASSL (90) 1, dated January 1990, announced changes to form BD8 concerning the certification of blind and partially sighted persons. The provisions of LASSL (90) 1 remain in force, and forms BD8 should continue to be sent to SSDs and to OPCS as appropriate.

Information on those aged over 65 and *registered* with authorities as blind will continue to be collected for every three years on form SSDA 902.

(b) *Hearing impaired people*: It is proposed that the register should continue to be maintained in accordance with the guidance contained at Annex 2 to this Appendix.

(c) *General class*: since 1 April 1974 the Department discontinued the collection of data into the formerly defined ten categories of impairment, although authorities could continue to record this information if they so wished. From the year ending 31 March 1976, authorities have been asked to provide data as follows:

   (i) very severe handicap (i.e. broadly people in categories 1–3* as used in the Report 'Handicapped and Impaired in Great Britain')

   (ii) severe or appreciable handicap (i.e. broadly people in categories 4–6* as used in the Report 'Handicapped and Impaired in Great Britain')

   (iii) other persons (e.g. including those suffering from a less severe heart or chest condition or from epilepsy)

11. At present the Department is not collecting information on the kind of 'help' provided to those registered with the authority. ('Help' is meant to cover the giving of any specific help or the involvement of social work time) but authorities may wish to retain the collection of this information.

12. Authorities are reminded that the value, both locally and nationally, of registers and related statistics will be lessened if registers are not kept up to date. It is desirable to regularly review the information held and to remove the names of those who, for any reason, should no longer be included. The continued co-operation of authorities in providing information to the Department is appreciated.

Persons suffering from a mental disorder within the meaning of the Mental Health Act 1983

13. Under the Mental Health Act 1983 persons suffering from a mental disorder came within the ambit of section 29 of the National Assistance Act 1948. The Chronically Sick and Disabled Persons Act 1970 (particularly sections 1 and 2) applies to the mentally disordered as well as to the physically handicapped. Local authority social services for the mentally disordered are generally provided under section 12 of the Health Services and Public Health Act and not under section 29 of the National Assistance Act.

14. Mentally disordered persons should be regarded as coming within the general class of handicapped persons but where they are registered they should be separately identified. (This applies only to persons whose sole disability is a mental disorder; those suffering also from a significant physical handicap should be registered on that account). As the number of mentally disordered persons who may be expected to register for purposes of the Housing Finance Act is likely to be only a small proportion of all mentally disordered persons known to local authorities, there would be little value in compiling detailed national statistics of those who register. Form SSDA 911, the triennial return on the General Classes of the Register of Handicapped Persons, specifically excludes all those who are registered solely on the grounds of mental disorder. Authorities will be expected to avoid making any overt difference in their handling of questions of registration between people who are mentally disordered and those who are not.

* for convenience the six categories are shown in Annex 1 to this Appendix.

Annex 1 to Appendix 4 of LAC (93) 10

Extract from the Report 'Handicapped and Impaired in Great Britain'

Category 1 includes those who need help going to or using the WC practically every night. In addition, most of those in this group need to be fed and dressed or, if they can feed and/or dress themselves, they need a lot of help during the day with washing and WC, or are incontinent.

Category 2 includes those who need help with the WC during the night but not quite so much help with feeding, washing, dressing, while not needing night-time help with the WC need a great deal of day-time help with feeding and/or washing and the WC.

Category 3 includes those who are permanently bedfast or confined to a chair and need help to get in and out, or are senile or mentally impaired, or are not able to care for themselves as far as normal everyday functions are concerned, but who do not need as much help as categories 1 and 2.

Category 4 includes those who either have difficulty doing everything, or find most things difficult and some impossible.

Category 5 includes those who find most things difficult, or three or four items difficult and some impossible.

Category 6 includes those who can do a fair amount for themselves but have difficulty with some items, or have to have help with one or two minor items.

Annex 2 to Appendix 4 of LAC (93) 10

Ministry of Health Circular 25/61

NATIONAL ASSISTANCE ACT 1948 WELFARE SERVICES FOR THE DEAF

1. I am directed by the Minister of Health to say that his Advisory Committee on the Health and Welfare of Handicapped Persons have considered the recommendations concerning welfare services for the deaf in the Report of the Working Party on Social Workers in the Local Authority Health and Welfare Services (The 'Younghusband Report').

Revision of definitions of deaf and hard-of-hearing

2. Paragraph 277 of the Report noted the desirability of revising the present definitions of the deaf and the hard-of-hearing, as contained in the notes on Clause 1(3) of the outline scheme for deaf or dumb persons (Part II of Appendix 1 of Circular 32/51). The Advisory Committee agree that the great advances made in the last four or five years, both in design of electronic hearing aids and in the ascertainment and auditory training of very young deaf children, have rendered out of date much of the descriptive matter applied to the deaf in Circular 32/51. They recommend that in future all persons who suffer from a disabling loss of hearing should be regarded as forming a single class which for registration for welfare services should be sub-divided on the following lines, according to the person's present condition and needs rather than according to the origin of his disability:

   Deaf without speech: Those who have no useful hearing and whose normal method of communication is by signs, finger spelling or writing.

Deaf with speech: Those who (even with a hearing aid) have little or no useful hearing but whose normal method of communication is by speech and lip-reading.

Hard-of-hearing: Those who (with or without a hearing aid) have some useful hearing and whose normal method of communication is by speech, listening and lip-reading.

3. The Minister hopes that local authorities will in future adopt those definitions. They will involve no alterations to approved schemes for the deaf or dumb. (The notes on the outline scheme contained in Appendix I of Circular 32/51 should, however, be read in conjunction with this circular.)

The Register

4. From 1 January 1962, registers should be maintained in the three revised categories set out in paragraph 2 above, and each category sub-divided into sexes and into the three age groups (children under age 16, persons aged 16 to 64 and persons aged 65 and over) in which the numbers on the register are already supplied to the Department at 31 December each year. Authorities should continue to record such general information as will help them to determine the type and degree of welfare assistance necessary in the best interests of the handicapped person.

Future development of services

5. The future development of all local health and welfare services must be considered in the light of what is said in Circular 21/61 on the economic situation. That circular contemplates the continued expansion of community care. It is an important part of this to develop the capacities of the handicapped to the fullest possible extent, and enable them to live as nearly as possible an independent life in the community.
6. Paragraph 10 of Circular 10/61, which dealt with the Younghusband Report, referred in particular to services for the deaf. The attention of authorities is particularly drawn to the recommendations in paragraph 693 of the Report, which, if acted on, will help to bring the welfare services for the deaf and hard-of-hearing into closer touch with other welfare services:
   (i) Some welfare officers in each area should learn to make adequate contact with the deaf people for whose welfare they are responsible.
   (ii) A casework service should be provided for the deaf people who need it, even if this must be attempted through an interpreter at first. This should be developed as trained staff become available.
   (iii) Clubs or social activities can be an important part in the life of the deaf. Voluntary organisations are often willing to provide them or assist in running them and local authorities may themselves be able to fill any gaps.
7. It is hoped that authorities will arrange for welfare officers concerned with the care of the deaf to visit hospitals and local health authority deaf diagnostic and training clinics, and also special schools and classes for the deaf and partially deaf, in order to widen their knowledge of deafness and of how deaf people can be helped. When dealing with the deaf without speech, it is of great importance that the welfare officer should be skilled in interpretation and have a thorough understanding of their special needs.

8. Authorities should ensure that in the services which local government provides or can influence, due attention is given to the availability of appropriate facilities for the deaf.
9. The Minister suggests that authorities should devote particular attention to the needs of the increasing group of the deaf with speech. The needs of this group differ in a number of ways from those met by the services traditionally provided for the deaf. For a long time to come, the group will consist largely of younger people who need facilities for continued auditory training and speech practice and whose other welfare needs are similar to those of the hard of hearing. In planning to meet them, welfare officers should seek the co-operation of youth employment officers, education officers and others concerned with the welfare of young people, as suggested in paragraph 998 of the Report. At least one large authority has found that adults who are deaf with speech or hard-of-hearing have benefited substantially from auditory training and speech practice at classes provided at an establishment of further education.
10. The deaf and hard-of hearing of all ages (excluding adults medically diagnosed as suffering from permanent total deafness) should be encouraged to seek periodic reassessment of hearing and helped to appreciate the importance of persevering with medical treatment. Perseverance, too, is necessary before a person supplied with a hearing aid becomes fully adjusted to its use; and where there is any doubt whether they are making proper use of it, they should be urged to seek advice. Those dependent on lip-reading as their main means of communication should also be encouraged to seek periodic reassessment of vision.
11. Local authorities providing their own services for the deaf will realise that some can better be provided by voluntary organisations. Spiritual ministration to the deaf is an outstanding example. The Minister is sure that local authorities work in close collaboration with bodies able to supplement the local authorities' own services in these and other ways.

C. LOCAL AUTHORITY CIRCULAR LAC (2004) 20

DEPARTMENT OF HEALTH

To: The Chief Executive: County Councils, Metropolitan District Councils, Shire Unitary Councils – England; London Borough Councils; Common Council of the City of London; Council of the Isles of Scilly

Chief Executive – Care Trusts

Chief Executive – Strategic Health Authorities

The Director of Social Services

14 October 2004

Guidance on:

National Assistance Act 1948 (Choice of Accommodation) Directions 1992

National Assistance (Residential Accommodation) (Additional Payments and Assessment of Resources) (Amendment) (England) Regulations 2001

1. SUMMARY

This guidance replaces the guidance that accompanied the Choice of Accommodation Directions 1992 ('the Directions'), and the further guidance included in LAC (2001) 29 to take account of the National Assistance Act 1948 (Choice of Accommodation) (Amendment) (England) Directions 2001 and the National Assistance (Additional Payments and Assessment of Resources) (Amendment) (England) Regulations 2001 ('the Regulations').

The Directions are intended to ensure that when councils with social services responsibilities ('councils') make placements in care homes or care homes providing nursing care, that, within reason, individuals are able to exercise genuine choice over where they live.

The Regulations give individuals the right to enter into more expensive accommodation than they would otherwise have been offered in certain circumstances, these are outlined in paragraph 3 of this guidance.

This guidance sets out what individuals should be able to expect from the council that is responsible for funding their care, subject to the individual's means, when arranging a care home place for them. This guidance is intended to describe the minimum of choice that councils should offer individuals. Even when not required to act in a certain way by the Directions or the Regulations, councils should make all reasonable efforts to maximise choice as far as possible within available resources.

This guidance is issued under Section 7(1) of the Local Authority Social Services Act 1970.

2. ACTION

Authorities are asked to take the following action: from October 14 2004 councils should use this guidance where the decision to provide residential accommodation under section 21 of the National Assistance Act 1948 either permanently or temporarily (intermediate care or short-term break or any interim care arrangement) has been made.

3. CANCELLATION OF CIRCULARS

The following Circulars should now be cancelled:

LAC (92) 27.

LAC (2001) 29.

4. ENQUIRIES

Enquiries about this Circular [and its enclosures] should be made to:

Department of Health
Older People and Disability Division
Care Services Directorate
Area 233
Wellington House
133–155 Waterloo Road
London SE1 8UG
Tel: 020 7972 4715
Email: OPDEnquiries@doh.gsi.gov.uk

From: Older People and Disability Division, Care Services Directorate, Area 233, Wellington House, 133–155 Waterloo Road, London SE1 8UG.

© Crown copyright 2004

Guidance on:

National Assistance Act 1948 (Choice of Accommodation) Directions 1992

National Assistance (Residential Accommodation) (Additional Payments and Assessment of Resources) (Amendment) (England) Regulations 2001

1. SUMMARY

1.1 If, after an assessment of need, made in accordance with the General Principles of Assessment in LAC (2002) 13 *Fair Access to Care Services* and, where applicable, in accordance with a specific assessment framework and discussion with the individual and their carers, a council decides to provide residential accommodation under section 21 of the National Assistance Act 1948 either permanently or temporarily (intermediate care or short term break or any interim care arrangement), it will make a placement on behalf of the individual in suitable accommodation. Nearly all placements under section 21 of the National Assistance Act 1948 are made in registered care homes. However, some adults are placed under section 21 of the National Assistance Act 1948 in unregistered settings where they need neither nursing care or personal care. While the detail of this guidance applies to registered care homes, the principles apply to adults placed in unregistered settings.

1.2 When the term 'residential care' is used in this guidance, it covers placements made on both a long-term and a temporary (which includes short-term care) basis to care homes, whether they provide nursing care or not.

1.3 If the individual concerned expresses a preference for particular accommodation ('preferred accommodation') within England and Wales, the council must arrange for care in that accommodation, provided:

- The accommodation is suitable in relation to the individual's assessed needs (see paragraphs 2.5.1 to 2.5.3)
- To do so would not cost the council more than what it would usually expect to pay for accommodation for someone with the individual's assessed needs see paragraphs 2.5.4 to 2.5.8). This is referred to throughout this guidance as the usual cost.
- The accommodation is available (see paragraphs 2.5.9 and 2.5.15)

- The provider of the accommodation is willing to provide accommodation subject to the council's usual terms and conditions for such accommodation (see paragraphs 2.5.16 to 2.5.17)

1.4 If an individual requests it, the council must also arrange for care in accommodation more expensive than it would usually fund provided a third party or, in certain circumstances, the resident, is willing and able to pay the difference between the cost the council would usually expect to pay and the actual cost of the accommodation (to 'top up'). These are the only circumstances where either a third party or the resident may be asked to top up (see paragraph 3).

2. PREFERRED ACCOMMODATION

2.1 As with all aspects of service provision, there should be a general presumption in favour of individuals being able to exercise reasonable choice over the service they receive. The limitations on councils' obligation to provide preferred accommodation set out in the Directions and the Regulations are not intended to deny individuals reasonable freedom of choice but to ensure that councils are able to fulfil their obligations for the quality of service provided and for value for money. The terms of the Directions and the Regulations are explained more fully below. Where, for any reason, a council decides not to arrange a place for someone in their preferred accommodation it must have a clear and reasonable justification for that decision which relates to the criteria of the Directions and is not in breach of the Regulations.

2.2 Arrangements under section 26(3A) of the National Assistance Act 1948 require the agreement of all parties. Individuals should not be refused their preferred accommodation without a full explanation from councils, in writing, of their reasons for doing so.

2.3 The location of the preferred accommodation need not be limited by the boundaries of the funding council. Councils are obliged to cater for placements falling within the Directions or the Regulations in any permitted care home within England or Wales. Any extension to this beyond England and Wales is subject to any future regulations governing cross-border placements (but see LAC (93) 18 in respect of placements involving Scotland and the Department of Health/Welsh Assembly protocol on NHS funded nursing care for cross border placements).

2.4 Funding councils may refer to their own usual costs when making placements in another council's area. However, because costs vary from area to area, if in order to meet a resident's assessed need it is necessary to place an individual in another area at a higher rate than the funding council's usual costs, the placing council should meet the additional cost itself.

2.5 The Directions state that a council must arrange for care in an individual's preferred accommodation subject to four considerations:

(a) Suitability of accommodation

2.5.1 Suitability will depend on the council's assessment of individual need. Each case must be considered on its merits.

2.5.2 Accommodation provided in a care home will not necessarily be suitable for the individual's needs simply because it satisfies registration standards. On the other hand, accommodation will not necessarily be unsuitable simply because it fails to conform to the council's preferred model of provision, or to meet to the letter a standard service specification laid down by the council.

2.5.3 The Directions and Regulations do not affect Section 26(1A) of the National Assistance Act 1948 as amended by the Care Standards Act 2000. Arrangements should not be made for the provision of accommodation together with nursing or personal care in a care home unless the accommodation to be provided is managed by an organisation or person who is registered under Part II of the Care Standards Act 2000. Similarly, the Directions and the Regulations do not require a council to contract with any accommodation where for any other reason it is prevented by law from doing so.

(b) Cost

2.5.4 One of the conditions associated with the provision of preferred accommodation is that such accommodation should not require the council to pay more than they would usually expect to pay, having regard to assessed needs (the 'usual cost'). This cost should be set by councils at the start of a financial or other planning period, or in response to significant changes in the cost of providing care, to be sufficient to meet the assessed care needs of supported residents in residential accommodation. A council should set more than one usual cost where the cost of providing residential accommodation to specific groups is different. In setting and reviewing their usual costs, councils should have due regard to the actual costs of providing care and other local factors. Councils should also have due regard to Best Value requirements under the Local Government Act 1999.

2.5.5 Individual residents should not be asked to pay more towards their accommodation because of market inadequacies or commissioning failures. Where an individual has not expressed a preference for more expensive accommodation, but there are not, for whatever reason, sufficient places available at a given time at the council's usual costs to meet the assessed care needs of supported residents, the council should make a placement in more expensive accommodation. In these circumstances, neither the resident nor a third party should be asked to contribute more than the resident would normally be expected to contribute and councils should make up the cost difference between the resident's assessed contribution and the accommodation's fees. Only when an individual has expressed a preference for more expensive accommodation than a council would usually expect to pay, can a third party or the resident be asked for a top up (see paragraph 3.1). Costs of accommodation should be compared on the basis of gross costs before income from charging. Given the different amounts that councils will recover from individuals by ways of charges, it would not be appropriate for a council to determine a usual net cost that it would expect to pay.

2.5.6 For the cost of placements in other councils' areas see paragraph 2.3.

2.5.7 Councils should not set arbitrary ceilings on the amount they expect to pay for an individual's residential care. Residents and third parties should not routinely be required to make up the difference between what the council will pay and the actual fees of a home. Councils have a statutory duty to provide residents with the level of service they could expect if the possibility of resident and third party contributions did not exist.

2.5.8 Costs can vary according to the type of care provided. For example, the cost a council might usually expect to pay for short-term care might be different from its usual cost for long-term care. There are also a number of situations where there may be higher costs incurred in providing residential care, be it long or short-term. Examples include specialist care for specific user groups with high levels of need or where necessary to prepare special diets and provide additional facilities for medical or cultural reasons. Councils should be prepared to meet these higher costs in order to ensure an individual's needs are appropriately met.

(c) Availability

2.5.9 Generally, good commissioning by councils should ensure there is sufficient capacity so individuals should not have to wait for their assessed (that is, eligible) needs to be met. However, waiting is occasionally inevitable, particularly when individuals have expressed a preference towards a particular care home where there are no current vacancies. Where individuals may need to wait at home or elsewhere, their access to the most appropriate (and possibly, preferred) service should be based solely on their assessed need, and councils should ensure that in the interim adequate alternative services are provided. Waiting for the preferred care home should not mean that the person's care needs are not met in the interim or that they wait in a setting unsuitable for their assessed needs, and this includes an acute hospital bed, until the most suitable or preferred accommodation becomes available. In view of the Community Care (Delayed Discharges etc.) Act 2003, councils should have contingency arrangements in place, that address the likelihood that an individual's preferred accommodation will not always be readily available. These arrangements should meet the needs of the individual and sustain or improve their level of independence. For some, the appropriate interim arrangement could be an enhanced care package at home.

2.5.10 Councils should give individuals an indication of the likely duration of the interim arrangement. Councils should place the individual on the waiting list of the preferred accommodation and aim to move them into that accommodation as soon as possible. Information about how the waiting list is handled should be clear and the individual should be kept informed of progress. If the duration of the interim arrangement exceeds a reasonable time period, e.g. 12 weeks, the individual should be reassessed to ensure that the interim and preferred accommodation are still able to meet the individual's assessed needs and to prevent any unnecessary moves between care homes that are unable to meet the individual's assessed needs. As part of this reassessment, individuals should also be asked if their preference is now to remain in the interim accommodation or whether they wish to continue waiting for their original preferred accommodation (see paragraph 2.5.14 for guidance on individuals who choose to remain in the interim accommodation).

2.5.11 Councils should ensure that while waiting in temporary residential accommodation, if an individual has to contribute towards their care costs it is in accordance with the National Assistance (Assessment of Resources) Regulations 1992. Individuals who are waiting in these circumstances should not be asked to pay more than their assessed financial contribution to meet the costs of these residential care services which have been arranged by the council to temporarily meet their assessed needs and councils should make up the cost difference between the resident's assessed contribution and the accommodation's fees. Only when an individual has expressed a preference for more expensive accommodation than a council would usually expect to pay, can a third party or the resident be asked for a top up (see paragraph 3.1).

2.5.12 Councils should take all reasonable steps to gain an individual's agreement to an interim care home or care package. Councils should make reasonable efforts to take account of the individual's desires and preferences. In doing this, councils should ascertain all relevant facts and take into account all the circumstances relevant to the person, and ensure that the individual (and their family or carers) understands the consequences of failing to come to an agreement. Where patients have been assessed as no longer requiring NHS continuing inpatient care, they do not have the right to occupy indefinitely an NHS bed. If an individual continues to unreasonably refuse the interim care home or care package, the council is entitled to consider that it has fulfilled its statutory duty to assess and offer services, and may then inform the individual, in writing, they will need to make their own arrangements. This position also applies to the unreasonable refusal of a permanent care home, not just the interim care home or care package. If at a later date further contact is made with social services regarding the individual, the council should re-open the care planning process, if it is satisfied that the individual's needs remain such to justify the provision of services and there is no longer reason to think that the individual will persist in refusing such services unreasonably. Councils should refer to Annex A of LAC (2003) 21 – *The Community Care (Delayed Discharges etc) Act 2003 Guidance for Implementation*. Councils may wish to take their own legal advice in such circumstances.

2.5.13 In all but a very small number of cases where an individual is being placed under Part II of the Mental Health Act 1983, individuals have the right to refuse to enter a care home. This includes patients who are awaiting discharge from hospital. In such cases the social services department should work with the person, his or her family and carers, and NHS partners, (and potentially housing partners), to explore alternative options, including a package of health and social care in the person's own home or suitable alternative accommodation.

2.5.14 In some cases, individuals who move into a care home for an interim period may choose to remain there, even if a place in their original preferred accommodation becomes available. If the care home is able to accept the individual on a long-term basis, they should be taken off the waiting list of their original preferred accommodation. If the cost of the interim care home is higher than the usual cost the council would expect to pay for their assessed need, upon making the choice to remain in that home, a third party or the resident could be approached for the total difference between the two rates. This should be clearly explained to individuals before they enter the home. See paragraph 3.2 for fuller details.

2.5.15 The Directions only apply to individuals whose care is being arranged by a council under Part 3 of the National Assistance Act 1948. For example, where hospital patients need to move to a different type of care, and social services are not involved, this is a matter for the NHS and the individual patient and the Directions do not apply. For good practice on handling these situations, see the Hospital Discharge Workbook.

(d) Terms and conditions

2.5.16 In order to ensure that they are able to exercise proper control over the use of their funds, councils need to be able to impose certain contractual conditions, for example, in relation to payment regimes, review, access, monitoring, audit, record keeping, information sharing, insurance, sub-contracting, etc.

2.5.17 The contractual conditions required of preferred accommodation should be broadly the same as those councils would impose on any other similar operation. Stricter conditions should never be used as a way of avoiding or deterring a placement. As with suitability, account should be taken of the nature and location of the accommodation. There may be occasions where it would be unreasonable for a council not to adapt its standard conditions and others where it would be unreasonable to expect it to do so. For example, councils should take into account the fact that care homes in other areas, or those that take residents from many areas, may have geared themselves to the normal requirements of other councils. Councils should be flexible in such circumstances and avoid adding to the administrative burden of care homes.

3. MORE EXPENSIVE ACCOMMODATION

3.1 The guidance set out in paragraphs 3.2 to 3.5.11, applies only where a resident explicitly chooses to enter accommodation other than that which the council offers them, and where that preferred accommodation is more expensive than the council would usually expect to pay.

3.2 In certain circumstances, councils can make placements in more expensive accommodation than they would usually expect to pay for, provided a resident or a third party is able and willing to make up the difference (to 'top up'). Residents that are subject to the 12 week property disregard or have agreed a deferred payments agreement with the council may make top-ups from specified resources on their own behalf. These are the only situations where the resident may top up. The most common arrangement is that a third party is providing the top-up. A third party in this case might be a relative, a friend, or any other source. For liable relatives see paragraph 3.5.10.

3.3 When setting its usual cost(s) a council should be able to demonstrate that this cost is sufficient to allow it to meet assessed care needs and to provide residents with the level of care services that they could reasonably expect to receive if the possibility of resident and third party contributions did not exist.

3.4 Councils should not seek resident or third party contributions in cases where the council itself decides to offer someone a place in more expensive accommodation in order to meet assessed needs, or for other reasons. Where there are no placements at the council's usual rate, councils should not leave individuals to make their own arrangements having determined that they need to enter residential accommodation and do not have care and attention otherwise available to them. In these instances, councils should make suitable alternative arrangements and seek no contribution from the individual other than their contribution as assessed under the National Assistance (Assessment of Resources) Regulations 1992. Councils must never encourage or otherwise imply that care home providers can or should seek further contributions from individuals in order to meet assessed needs.

3.5 This paragraph deals with considerations that apply where either residents or third parties are making further contributions to costs over and above the resident's assessed contribution under the National Assistance (Assessment of Resources) Regulations 1992.

(a) Responsibility for costs of accommodation

3.5.1 When making arrangements for residential care for an individual under the National Assistance Act 1948, a council is responsible for the full cost of that accommodation. Therefore, where a council places someone in more expensive accommodation, it must contract to pay the accommodation's fees in full. The resident's or the third party's contribution will be treated as part of the resident's income for charging purposes and the council will be able to recover it in that way. However, under a deferred payments agreement, where the resident is topping up against the value of their home, their top-up contribution is added to their deferred contribution.

3.5.2 Councils will be aware that under section 26(3A) of the National Assistance Act 1948 (as inserted by the NHS and Community Care Act 1990), it is open to them to agree with both the resident and the person in charge of their accommodation that, instead of paying a contribution to the council, the resident may pay the same amount direct to the accommodation, with the council paying the difference. In such a case, the third party would also pay the accommodation direct on behalf of the resident. However, it should be noted that even where there is such an agreement for the resident to make payments direct to the accommodation, the council continues to be liable to pay the full costs of the accommodation should either the resident or relative fail to pay the required amount.

3.5.3 Where top-ups are required from a resident or third party, the resident will therefore need to demonstrate that either they or the third party is able and willing to pay the difference between the council's usual rate and the accommodation's actual fees.

3.5.4 In order to safeguard both residents and councils from entering into top-up arrangements that are likely to fail, the resident or the third party must reasonably be expected to be able to continue to make top-up payments for the duration of the arrangements. Councils should, therefore, assure themselves that residents or third parties will have the resources to continue to make the required top-up payments. Councils should seek similar assurances when residents top-up against the value of their home when the home is subject to a deferred payments agreement. When the home is eventually sold, it should be possible for the resident or their estate to pay back the deferred contribution including the resident top-ups.

(b) The amount of the resident or third party top-up

3.5.5 The amount of resident or third party top-up payments should be the difference between the actual fee for the accommodation and the amount that otherwise the council would usually have expected to pay for someone with the individual's assessed needs. In determining the precise amounts in individual cases, the council will take account of the guidance give in paragraphs 2.5.4 to 2.5.8 above.

3.5.6 The amount of the resident or third party top-up should be calculated on gross costs; that is, the difference between the preferred accommodation's fees and the fees that a council would usually expect to pay. The fact that a resident might not have been able to meet the full cost of the accommodation that the council would otherwise have arranged does not affect their ability to benefit from the additional top-up payments.

(c) Price increases

3.5.7 Arrangements between the council, resident and third party will need to be reviewed from time to time to take account of changes to accommodation fees. There will also be changes to the council's usual cost, which should be reasonable and set in accordance with paragraphs 2.5.4 to 2.5.8. However, fees and usual costs may not change at the same rate, and residents and third parties should be told that there cannot be a guarantee that any increases in the accommodation's fees will automatically be shared evenly between the council and/or the resident or third party, should the particular accommodation's fees rise more quickly than the costs the council would usually expect to pay for similar individuals. A council may find it useful to agree with the resident (or third party) that the resident's (or third party's) contribution will be reviewed on a regular basis on the understanding that clear explanations for proposed increases are given. It is also important that individuals know when, and in what circumstances, the fees for their accommodation will be reviewed.

(d) Responsibilities of residents and third parties

3.5.8 Councils should make clear to residents and third parties, in writing, the basis on which arrangements are to be made when they seek to exercise their right to more expensive preferred accommodation. It should be clear from the outset to the resident, third party and person providing the accommodation that:

- failure to keep up top-up payments may result in the resident having to move to other accommodation unless, after an assessment of need, it is shown that assessed needs can only be met in the current accommodation. In these circumstances, councils should make up the cost difference between the resident's assessed contribution and the accommodation's fees. Where a resident's top-ups are being made against the value of property subject to a deferred payments agreement, a council will have assured itself from the outset that top-up payments are viable and recoverable when the home is sold;
- an increase in the resident's income will not necessarily lessen the need for a top-up contribution, since the resident's own income will be subject to means testing by the council in the normal way;
- a rise in the accommodation's fees will not automatically be shared equally between council, resident (if making a top-up), and third party.

(e) Suitability and conditions

3.5.9 With reference to paragraphs 2.5.1 to 2.5.3 and 2.5.16 to 2.5.17 above, the criteria of suitability and willingness to provide on the basis of normal conditions should be applied in the same way as for other preferred accommodation. An exception to this is that it would be reasonable to expect providers entering this kind of arrangement to agree to do so on the basis that the council has the right, subject to notice, to terminate the contract should the resident's or third party's top-up payments cease to be adequate.

(f) Liable relatives

3.5.10 Liable relatives who are making maintenance contributions cannot act as third parties for the care of the relative to whose care they are already contributing under section 42 of the National Assistance Act 1948. This limitation does not apply to top-up arrangements agreed prior to 1 October 2001 with liable relatives. Neither does the limitation apply to liable relatives who are not making contributions under section 42 of the 1948 Act.

4. INDIVIDUALS ALREADY RESIDENT IN RESIDENTIAL CARE

4.1 Individuals already placed by a council in residential accommodation, and those already in residential accommodation as self-funders but who, because of diminishing resources, are on the verge of needing council support, have the same rights under these Directions as those who have yet to be placed by the council. Any such individual who wishes to move to different or more expensive accommodation may seek to do so on the same basis as anyone about to enter residential care for the first time. Should a self-funder who is resident in a care home that is more expensive than a council would usually expect to pay later become the responsibility of the council due to diminishing funds, this may result in the resident having to move to other accommodation, unless, after an assessment of need, it is shown that assessed needs can only be met in the current accommodation. In these circumstances, neither the resident nor a third party should be asked for a top-up payment and councils should make up the cost difference between the resident's assessed contribution and the accommodation's fees.

5. INDIVIDUALS WHO ARE UNABLE TO MAKE THEIR OWN CHOICES

5.1 There will be cases in which prospective residents lack capacity to express a preference for themselves. It would be reasonable to expect councils to act on the preferences expressed by their advocate, carer or legal guardian in the same way that they would on the resident's own wishes, unless that would in the council's opinion be against the best interests of the resident.

6. EFFECT ON CONTRACTING

6.1 Any block contract or other form of contract that a council may have with a provider should not serve to limit choice. An individual should not be limited to care homes that hold such contracts with the funding council, or cares homes that are run by councils. It would not be reasonable for a council to use as a test for the suitability of accommodation, its presence or absence from a previously compiled list of preferred suppliers. The Directions and Regulations do not, however, prevent an authority having a list of preferred providers with which it will contract where a potential resident expresses no preference for particular accommodation, nor from recommending such providers to prospective residents.

7. INFORMATION

7.1 Individuals, and/or those who represent them, need information on the options open to them if they are to be able to exercise genuine choice. They should be given fair and balanced information with which to make the best choice of accommodation for them. Councils should explain to individuals their rights under the Directions and the Regulations. Councils should also consider providing material in a range of forms including written leaflets in local community languages, Braille, on audio tape and in accessible language e.g. easy words, short sentences, large print and pictures (for those with learning disabilities). Councils should supply copies of the Directions and this guidance if requested in appropriate forms. They should work with local Primary Care Trusts (PCTs) and local hospitals to provide clear information to hospital patients as early as possible in their stay about what the council will be able to provide should they require short or long-term residential care at the end of their hospital stay. Individuals should be told explicitly that:

- they are free to choose any accommodation that is likely to meet their needs subject to the constraints set out in the Directions and the Regulations.
- they may allow the council to make a placement decision on their behalf; and
- they may choose from a preferred list (if the authority operates such a system).

7.2 Councils should ensure that individuals are informed that they have a choice of accommodation irrespective of whether they express a preference for particular accommodation. Individuals should also be told what will happen if the preferred accommodation is not available. Councils may also wish to cover the matters described in paragraph 2.5.12. Wherever possible, the individual should be encouraged to have a relative, carer or advocate present during the conversation. A written record of the conversation should be kept, in particular, recording any decisions taken or preferences expressed by the individual. This record should be shared with the individual.

8. COMPLAINTS

8.1 Complaints about the application of the Directions and the Regulations and decisions taken in individual cases will fall within the scope of councils' statutory complaints procedure. As in all aspects of their activity, councils should ensure that prospective residents are aware of and understand the existence of the complaints procedure and their rights under it.

D. DELAYED DISCHARGES (CONTINUING CARE) DIRECTIONS 2004

The Secretary of State for Health, in exercise of the powers conferred on him by section 17 of the National Health Service Act 1977 and all other powers enabling him in that behalf, hereby makes the following Directions:

Commencement, application and interpretation

1. (1) These Directions come into force on 27th February 2004 and apply to every NHS body.

(2) In these Directions –
'the Act' means the Community Care (Delayed Discharges etc.) Act 2003;
'continuing care' means care provided over an extended period of time to a person aged 18 or over to meet physical or mental health needs which have arisen as the result of disability, accident or illness;
'eligibility criteria' means those criteria established by each Strategic Health Authority pursuant to paragraph 2(2) of the NHS Responsibilities Directions;
'NHS body' means a National Health Service trust or a Primary Care Trust in England;
'the NHS Responsibilities Directions' means the Continuing Care (National Health Service Responsibilities) Directions 2004;
'patient' means someone who is or is expected to become a 'qualifying hospital patient' as defined in section 1(1) of the Act;
'relevant social services authority' means the social services authority appearing to the NHS body to be the authority in whose area the patient is ordinarily resident;
'social services authority' means a local authority for the purposes of the Local Authority Social Services Act 1970.

Duties of NHS bodies

2. (1) Before an NHS body gives notice of a patient's case to a social services authority incompliance with its duty under section 2(2) of the Act, it must comply with paragraphs (2) to (5).
(2) The NHS body must carry out such an assessment as it considers appropriate of the patient's need for continuing care, in consultation, where it considers it appropriate, with the relevant social services authority.
(3) The NHS body must consult with the patient and, where it considers it appropriate, the patient's carer when carrying out the assessment.
(4) Having regard to the outcome of that assessment and applying any relevant eligibility criteria, the NHS body must decide whether the patient's needs call for the provision by an NHS body of continuing care.
(5) The NHS body must –

(a) notify the patient of the decision and make a record of it in the patient's notes; and
(b) inform the patient that if he is dissatisfied about –
(i) the procedure followed by the NHS body in reaching the decision about his need for continuing care; or
(ii) the application by the NHS body of any relevant eligibility criteria in relation to the decision,

he may apply for a review of the decision pursuant to paragraph 4(3) of the NHS Responsibilities Directions.

E. THE COMMUNITY CARE ASSESSMENT DIRECTIONS 2004

The Secretary of State for Health, in exercise of the powers conferred on him by section 47(4) of the National Health Service and Community Care Act 1990 hereby makes the following Directions:

Commencement, application and interpretation

1. (1) These Directions come into force on 1 September 2004 and apply to every local authority in England.
(2) In these Directions –
'the Act' means the National Health Service and Community Care Act 1990;
'community care services' has the same meaning as in section 46(3) of the Act;
'local authority' has the same meaning as in section 46(3) of the Act.

Manner and form of assessment of needs for community care services

2. (1) In assessing the needs of a person under section 47(1) of the Act a local authority must comply with paragraphs (2) to (4).
(2) The local authority must consult the person, consider whether the person has any carers and, where they think it appropriate, consult those carers.
(3) The local authority must take all reasonable steps to reach agreement with the person and, where they think it appropriate, any carers of that person, on the community care services which they are considering providing to him to meet his needs.
(4) The local authority must provide information to the person and, where they think it appropriate, any carers of that person, about the amount of the payment (if any) which the person will be liable to make in respect of the community care services which they are considering providing to him.

APPENDIX 3

Useful contacts

GOVERNMENT DEPARTMENTS

Department of Health

Publications Orderline

PO Box 777
London SE1 6XH

Tel: 0870 155 5455
www.dh.gov.uk

Customer Service Centre

Richmond House
79 Whitehall
London SW1A 2NS

Tel: 020 7210 4850

Information Commissioner
Wycliffe House
Water Lane
Wilmslow
Cheshire SK9 5AF

Tel: 01625 545745 (helpline)
www.dataprotection.gov.uk

Official Solicitor of the Supreme Court
81 Chancery Lane
London
WC2A 1DD

Tel: 020 7911 7127
Fax: 020 7911 7105
DX: 0012 London/Chancery Lane
www.officialsolicitor.gov.uk

Public Guardianship Office
Archway Tower
2 Junction Road
London
N19 5SZ

Tel: 020 7664 7000
Fax: 020 7664 7168
DX: 1141150 Archway 2 London
www.guardianship.gov.uk/

Welsh Assembly

For publications enquiries

Crown Buildings
Cathays Park
Cardiff CF10 3NQ
www.wales.gov.uk

NON-GOVERNMENT ORGANISATIONS

Citizens Advice (National Association of Citizens Advice Bureaux)
Myddelton House
115–123 Pentonville Road
London
N1 9LZ

Tel: 020 7833 2181 (admin only)
Fax: 020 7833 4371 (admin only)
www.citizensadvice.org.uk

The Law Centres Federation
Duchess House
18–19 Warren Street
London
W1P 5DB

Tel: 020 7387 8570
Fax: 020 7387 8368
Email: info@lawcentres.org.uk
www.lawcentres.org.uk

Independent Complaints Advocacy Services (ICAS)

An ICAS has been set up in every Primary Care Trust to provide an advocacy service for those making a formal complaint about NHS services. These are in the main run through Citizens Advice Bureaux, Carers Federation, POhWER and the South East Advocacy Projects. For more details see the Department of Health website:

www.dh.gov.uk/PolicyAndGuidance/OrganisationPolicy/ComplaintsPolicy/NHSComplaintsProcedure/fs/en

Community Health Councils

In Wales the advocacy service is provided through the Community Health Council. Details can be obtained from:

The Board of Community Health Councils
Ground Floor
Park House
Greyfriars Road
Cardiff
CF10 3AF

Tel: 029 2023 5558
Fax : 029 2023 5574
www.patienthelp.wales.nhs.uk

The Disability Rights Commission

The Disability Rights Commission is an independent body established in April 2000 by Disability Rights Commission 1999 Act to stop discrimination and promote equality of opportunity for disabled people. The DRC's role is to:

- give advice and information to disabled people, employers and service providers;
- help solve problems;
- take on test cases;
- provide an Independent Disability Conciliation Service for disabled people and service providers through Mediation UK (provided through the DRC where considered appropriate);
- campaign to strengthen the law;
- organise campaigns to change policy, practice and awareness;
- produce policy statements and research on disability issues; and publications on rights and good practice for disabled people, employers and service providers.

DRC Helpline
FREEPOST MID02164
Stratford upon Avon
CV37 9BR

Tel: 08457 622633
Tel: 08457 622644 (text phone)
Fax: 08457 778 878
www.drc-gb.org

Health Care Commission
Finsbury Tower
103–105 Bunhill Row
London
EC1Y 8TG

Tel: 020 7448 9200
www.healthcarecommission.org.uk

Commission for Social Care Inspection
33 Greycoat Street
London
SW1P 2QF

Tel: 020 7979 2000
Fax: 020 7979 2111
www.csci.org.uk

Independent Review Secretariat (Wales)

Mid and West Wales

PO Box 2
Brecon
Powys
LD3 0XR

Tel: 01874 712748
Fax: 01874 712756

South Wales

PO Box 21
Cardiff
CF10 2ZR

Tel: 029 2040 2262
Fax: 029 2040 2398

North Wales

PO Box 125
Mold
CH7 1WH

Tel: 01352 700227
Fax: 01352 754649

Local Government Ombudsman

For complaints about London boroughs north of the river Thames (including Richmond but not Harrow or Tower Hamlets), Essex, Kent, East Sussex, West Sussex, Surrey, Berkshire, Buckinghamshire, Hertfordshire, Suffolk and Coventry City:

Local Government Ombudsman
10th Floor, Millbank Tower
Millbank
London
SW1P 4QP

Tel: 020 7217 4620
Fax: 020 7217 4621
Email: enquiries.london@lgo.org.uk

For complaints about the London Borough of Tower Hamlets, Birmingham City, Solihull MBC, Cheshire, Derbyshire, Nottinghamshire, Lincolnshire and the north of England (except the cities of Manchester, York and Lancaster):

Local Government Ombudsman
Beverley House
17 Shipton Road
York
YO30 5FZ

Tel: 01904 380200
Fax: 01904 380269
Email: enquiries.york@lgo.org.uk

For complaints about London boroughs south of the river Thames (except Richmond) and Harrow; the cities of Manchester, York and Lancaster; and the rest of England not included in the areas above:

Local Government Ombudsman
The Oaks No 2
Westwood Way
Westwood Business Park
Coventry
CV4 8JB

Tel: 024 7682 0000
Fax: 024 7682 0001
Email: enquiries.coventry@lgo.org.uk

Health Service Ombudsman
Millbank Tower
Millbank
London
SW1P 4QP

Tel: 020 7217 4051
Tel: 0845 015 4033 (calls charged at local rates)
Email: enquiries@ombudsman.gsi.gov.uk
www.ombudsman.org.uk

Public Services Ombudsman for Wales
1 Ffordd yr Hen Gae
Pencoed
CF35 5LJ

Tel: 01656 641150
Fax: 01656 641199
Email: enquiries@ombudsman-wales.org.uk
www.ombudsman-wales.org.uk

The current Ombudsman services in Wales provided by the Commission for Local Administration in Wales, the Health Service Commissioner for Wales and the Welsh Administration Ombudsman are to be combined into a single Ombudsman service known as the Public Services Ombudsman for Wales.

SOLICITORS

The Law Society keeps all records of practising solicitors in England and Wales. You can locate a solicitor through their website and using the search facility:
http://www.lawsociety.org.uk/choosingandusing/findasolicitor.law

The relevant search areas are: mental health and incapacity; administrative and public law; and human rights. The Law Society has a panel of specialist Mental Health Lawyers. It does not have a search facility for health and social care or community care law.

You may also find a solicitor through organisations such as:

Solicitors for the Elderly
PO Box 257
Broxbourne
EN10 7YY

Tel: 01992 471568
www.solicitorsfortheelderly.com

The Housing Law Practitioners Association
88 Old Street
London
EC1V 9HU

Tel: 020 7505 4693
Fax: 020 7505 2168
Email: admin@hlpa.org.uk
www.hlpa.org.uk

The Human Rights Lawyers Association
Administration office
2nd Floor
289–293 High Holborn
London
WC1V 7HZ

Tel: 020 7242 1289
Email: SMontgomery@barcouncil.org.uk
www.hrla.co.uk

Immigration Law Practitioners Association
Lindsey House
40–42 Charterhouse Street
London
EC1M 6JN

Tel: 020 7251 8383
Fax: 020 7251 8384
Email: info@ilpa.org.uk
www.ilpa.org.uk

Solicitors who undertake legal aid work

Legal aid may be available to those on low income for health or social care problems via solicitors' firms, Citizens Advice Bureaux, legal advice centres, local authorities services and other similar organisations that have a contract with the Legal Services Commission (LSC).

The LSC has a useful website that calculates whether a person will qualify for legal aid and gives names of those that hold a LSC contract: www.clsdirect.org.uk/index.jsp

To find a legal aid lawyer contact the Community Legal Service Direct National Helpline 0845 345 4345 or the Legal Aid Practitioners' Group.

Legal Aid Practitioners Group
10 Greycoat Place
London
SW1P 1SB

Tel: 020 7960 6068
Fax: 020 7960 6168
www.lapg.co.uk

The Public Law Project
150 Caledonian Road
London
N1 9RD
Tel: 020 7697 2190
Fax: 020 7837 7048
Email: admin@publiclawproject.org.uk
www.publiclawproject.org.uk

The advice line 020 7697 2194 is open on Tuesday mornings between 10.00am and 1.00pm for those that provide advice, but without a contract to do so with the Legal Services Commission. The Human Rights and Public Law Line 0808 808 4546, is open on Tuesday and Thursday mornings as above and also on Monday and Wednesday afternoons between 2.00pm and 5.00pm for those that provide advice with a contract with the Legal Services Commission. They will accept complex case referrals via the advice lines.

The Public Law Project provides an advice and consultancy service for advice agencies and solicitors' practices.

ADVOCACY GROUPS

An advocacy group can find or provide an advocate who can give support to enable people to express themselves or to pass on the person's wishes and views. Some may be involved with complaints and disputes. Some organisations act as direct providers of advocates and others act as referrers. They may be paid or act as volunteers. Advocacy should be independent of the organisations from which people may be seeking justice or redress, although this is not always the case for example, where funding for the service has come from the local authority that is subject to the complaint.

Advocacy services are geographically patchy and may be available for certain types of client groups but not others. Advocacy services are often in place for people who are mentally ill or have learning disabilities. To locate an advocate see:

www.oneforus.com
www.advocacyresource.net

Charities and carers groups

A number of charities operate advocacy services, but most do not have full national coverage. Contact will need to be made in the first instance with the relevant charity's head office. Many charities also provide advice in the form of information sheets and telephone lines. Some will also take on test cases. There are many other charities and carers groups that provide local support and practical help. The following list is confined to national charities that give legal advice and/or provide advocacy services.

MENTAL HEALTH SUPPORT

Mind (Head Office)
15–19 Broadway
London
E15 4BQ

Tel: 020 8519 2122
Fax: 020 8522 1725
Email: contact@mind.org.uk
www.mind.org.uk

Mind (for help and information)
Mind
PO Box 277
Manchester
M60 3XN

Tel: 0845 766 0163
Email: info@mind.org.uk
www.mind.org.uk/About+Mind/
Mindinfoline.htm

Mind Cymru
3rd Floor
Quebec House
Castlebridge
5–19 Cowbridge Road East
Cardiff
CF11 9AB

Tel: 029 2039 5123
Fax: 029 2034 6585

Rural Minds
c/o South Staffs CVS
1 Stafford Street
Brewood
Staffs
ST19 9DX

Tel: 024 7641 4366
Fax: 024 7641 4369
Email: ruralminds@ruralnet.org.uk

Together: Working for Wellbeing
National Office
1st Floor
Lincoln House
296–302 High Holborn
London
WC1V 7JH

Tel: 020 7061 3400
Fax: 020 7061 3401
Email: contactus@together-uk.org
www.together-uk.org

London and East of England

1st Floor
89 Turners Hill
Cheshunt
Hertfordshire
EN8 9BD

Tel: 01992 622000
Fax: 01992 622621
Email: londonandeast@together-uk.org

South of England

94b High Street
Epsom
Surrey
KT19 8BJ

Tel: 01372 722970
Fax: 01372 722980
Email: south@together-uk.org

Midlands and North of England

Maca House
Yorkshire Street
Rochdale
Lancashire
OL12 0DS

Tel: 01706 640027
Fax: 01706 752480
Email: midlandsandnorth@
together-uk.org

LEARNING DISABILITIES SUPPORT

British Institute of Learning Disabilities (BILD)
Campion House
Green Street
Kidderminster
Worcestershire
DY10 1JL

Tel: 01562 723010
Fax: 01562 723029
Email: enquiries@bild.org.uk
www.bild.org.uk

Mencap
123 Golden Lane
London
EC1Y 0RT

Tel: 020 7454 0454
Fax: 020 7696 5540
Email: information@mencap.org.uk
www.mencap.org.uk

Mencap Cymru
31 Lambourne Crescent
Cardiff Business Park
Llanishen
Cardiff
CF14 5GF

Tel: 029 2074 7588
Fax: 029 2074 7550
Email:
information.wales@mencap.org.uk

PHYSICAL DISABILITIES SUPPORT

Disability Alliance
Universal House
88–94 Wentworth Street
London
E1 7SA

Tel: 020 7247 8776 (voice and minicom)
Fax: 020 7247 8765
www.disabilityalliance.org

Disabled Living Centres Council (now Assist UK)
Redbank House
4 St Chad's Street
Manchester
M8 8QA

Tel: 0870 770 2866 (national call rate)
Text phone: 0870 770 5813
www.assist-uk.org

Disabled Living Foundation
380–384 Harrow Road
London
W9 2HU

Tel: 0845 130 9177 (helpline, local call rate)
Text phone: 020 7432 8009
www.dlf.org.uk

Disablement Information and Advice Lines (Dial UK)
St Catherine's
Tickhill Road
Doncaster
South Yorkshire
DN4 8QN

Tel: 01302 310123
Fax: 01302 310404
www.dialuk.info

Royal Association for Disability and Rehabilitation (RADAR)
12 City Forum
250 City Road
London
EC1V 8AF

Tel: 020 7250 3222
Fax: 020 7250 0212
Email: radar@radar.org.uk
www.radar.org.uk

Royal National Institute for the Blind (RNIB)
105 Judd Street
London
WC1H 9NE

Tel: 020 7388 1266
Tel: 0845 766 9999 (helpline)
Fax: 020 7388 2034
Email: helpline@rnib.org.uk
www.rnib.org.uk

Royal National Institute for Deaf People (RNID)
19–23 Featherstone Street
London
EC1Y 8SL

Tel: 020 7296 8000
Tel: 0808 808 0123 (information line)
Fax: 020 7296 8199
Email: information@rnid.org.uk

AGE SUPPORT

Age Concern England
Astral House
1268 London Road
London
SW16 4ER

Tel: 0800 00 99 66 (free helpline)
www.ace.org.uk

Age Concern Cymru
Ty John Pathy
13/14 Neptune Court
Vanguard Way
Cardiff
CF24 5PJ

Tel: 029 2043 1555
Email: enquiries@accymru.org.uk
www.accymru.org.uk

Help the Aged England
207–221 Pentonville Road
London
N1 9UZ

Tel: 020 7278 1114
Fax: 020 7278 1116
www.helptheaged.org.uk

Help the Aged Wales
12 Cathedral Road
Cardiff
CF11 9LJ

Tel: 029 2034 6550
Fax: 029 2039 0898

(NB: Help the Aged takes on test cases.)

Alzheimer's Society
Gordon House
10 Greencoat Place
London
SW1P 1PH

Tel: 020 7306 0606
Tel: 0845 300 0336 (helpline)
Fax: 020 7306 0808
Email: enquiries@alzheimers.org.uk
www.alzheimers.org.uk

CHILDREN'S SUPPORT

Child Poverty Action Group (CPAG)
94 White Lion Street
London
N1 9PF

Tel: 020 7837 7979
Tel: 020 7833 4627 (advice line for advice agencies 2pm–4pm)
Fax: 020 7837 6414
www.cpag.org.uk

(NB: CPAG advice lines are 'second tier' services for advice agencies only. They do not have the resources to provide direct advice to people who are claiming benefits or to their friends and families.)

Children's Legal Centre
University of Essex
Wivenhoe Park
Colchester
Essex
CO4 3SQ

Tel: 01206 872466
Tel: 0845 456 6811 (education law advice line)
Email: clc@essex.ac.uk
Fax: 01206 874026
www.childrenslegalcentre.com

The Children's Society
Edward Rudolf House
Margery Street
London
WC1X 0JL

Tel: 0845 300 1128 (local rate)
www.the-childrens-society.org.uk

CARERS' SUPPORT

The Princess Royal Trust for Carers
142 Minories
London
EC3N 1LB

Tel: 020 7480 7788
Fax: 020 7481 4729
Email: help@carers.org
www.carers.org

Carers UK
20–25 Glasshouse Yard
London
EC1A 4JT

Tel: 020 7490 8818
Fax: 020 7490 8824
www.carersuk.org/Home

The Relatives and Residents Association
The Ivories
6–18 Northampton Street
London
N1 2HY

Tel: 020 7359 8148
Tel: 020 7359 8136 (helpline)
Fax: 020 7226 6603
Email: info@relres.org
www.relres.org

REFUGEES AND ASYLUM SEEKERS SUPPORT

JCWI (Joint Council for the Welfare of Immigrants)
115 Old Street
London
EC1V 9RT

Tel: 020 7251 8708
Fax: 020 7251 8707
Email: info@jcwi.org.uk
www.jcwi.org.uk

Refugee Legal Centre
153–157 Commercial Road
London
E1 2DA

Tel: 020 7780 3200
Fax: 020 7780 3201
www.refugee-legal-centre.org.uk

Immigration Advisory Service
County House
190 Great Dover Street
London
SE1 4YB

Tel: 020 7967 1200
Fax: 020 7378 0665
www.iasuk.org

The Refugee Council
240–250 Ferndale Road
London
SW9 8BB

Tel: 020 7346 6700
Tel: 020 7346 6777 (advice line)
Fax: 020 7346 6701
www.refugeecouncil.org.uk

APPENDIX 4

Websites

The following links are to documents and websites that are referred to in this Handbook, sorted alphabetically by author and title. There is also a quick links section to useful websites organised alphabetically at the end of this appendix.

CABINET OFFICE

Code of Practice on Consultation (October 2005)
www.cabinetoffice.gov.uk/regulation/consultation/code/index.asp

DCA

Making Decisions: Helping People who have Difficulty Deciding for Themselves: a Guide for Family and Friends (May 2003)
www.dca.gov.uk/family/mi/mibooklets/guide4.htm#top

Pre-action Protocol for Judicial Review
www.dca.gov.uk/civil/procrules_fin/contents/protocols/prot_jrv.htm

DEPARTMENT FOR EDUCATION AND SKILLS

Getting the Best from Complaints: Consultation on the Changes to the Social Services Complaints Procedures for Children, Young People and Other People Making a Complaint (Consultation, 29 October 2004)
www.dfes.gov.uk/consultations/conResults.cfm?consultationId=1274

DEPARTMENT OF HEALTH

Advice on the decision of the European Court of Human Rights in the case of *HL* v. *UK* (the 'Bournewood' Case) (10 December 2004)
www.dh.gov.uk/assetRoot/04/09/79/92/04097992.pdf

Alcohol and Drugs Services within Community Care (LAC (93) 2) (January 2003)
www.dh.gov.uk/assetRoot/04/01/25/02/04012502.pdf

A–Z of substance misuse guidance and publications
www.dh.gov.uk/PolicyAndGuidance/HealthAndSocialCareTopics/SubstanceMisuse/HealthySchoolsProjectAZ

Better Care Higher Standards (LAC (2001) 6, HSC 2001/006)
www.dh.gov.uk/assetRoot/04/01/27/31/04012731.pdf

Care Homes for Adults (18–65) and *Supplementary Standards for Care Homes Accommodating Young People aged 16 and 17* (February 2003)
www.dh.gov.uk/assetRoot/04/03/28/52/04032852.pdf

Charging for Residential Accommodation Guide (CRAG) (updated March 2004)
www.dh.gov.uk/assetRoot/04/07/00/48/04070048.pdf

Community and equipment services (guidance)
www.dh.gov.uk/PolicyAndGuidance/HealthAndSocialCareTopics/CommunityEquipment/fs/en?CONTENT_ID=4015916&chk=CODJRI

Direct payments information
www.dh.gov.uk/PolicyAndGuidance/OrganisationPolicy/FinanceAndPlanning/DirectPayments

Establishing the Responsible Commissioner – Guidance for PCT Commissioners on the Application of the Legal Framework on PCTs' Secondary Care Commissioning Responsibilities (October 2003)
www.dh.gov.uk/assetRoot/04/06/97/97/04069797.pdf

Fair Access to Care Services – Guidance on Eligibility Criteria for Adult Social Care (LAC (2002)13)
www.dh.gov.uk/assetRoot/04/01/27/16/04012716.pdf

Guidance on the Single Assessment Process for Older People (HSC 2002/001, LAC (2002) 1) (28 January 2002)
www.dh.gov.uk/assetRoot/04/01/22/89/04012289.pdf

Guidance to Support Implementation of the National Health Service (Complaints) Regulations 2004
www.dh.gov.uk/assetRoot/04/08/81/57/04088157.pdf

HIV key documents
www.dh.gov.uk/PolicyAndGuidance/HealthAndSocialCareTopics/HIV/HIVGeneralInformation

Hospital Travel Costs Scheme (updated guidance) (May 2005)
www.dh.gov.uk/assetRoot/04/11/86/92/04118692.pdf

Independent Complaints Advocacy Services (ICAS)
www.dh.gov.uk/PolicyAndGuidance/OrganisationPolicy/ComplaintsPolicy/NHSComplaintsProcedure

Joint Investment Plan guidance
www.dh.gov.uk/PolicyAndGuidance/OrganisationPolicy/IntegratedCare/JointInvestmentPlans

Learning from Complaints: Consultation on Changes to the Social Services Complaints Procedure for Adults (October 2004)
www.dh.gov.uk/assetRoot/04/09/80/31/04098031.pdf

Mental Health Policy Implementation Guide: Dual Diagnosis Good Practice Guide
www.dh.gov.uk/assetRoot/04/06/04/35/04060435.pdf

National Service Frameworks (NSFs), England (launched in April 1998)
www.dh.gov.uk/PolicyAndGuidance/HealthAndSocialCareTopics/HealthAndSocialCareArticle/fs/en?CONTENT_ID=4070951&chk=W3ar/W

National Minimum Standards for Voluntary Adoption Agencies and Local Authority Adoption Services in England and Wales (2003)
www.dh.gov.uk/assetRoot/04/06/21/27/04062127.pdf

National Minimum Standards for Accommodation of Students under Eighteen by Further Education Colleges
www.dh.gov.uk/assetRoot/04/03/43/32/04034332.pdf

National Minimum Standards for Adult Placement Schemes (August 2004)
www.dh.gov.uk/assetRoot/04/08/73/90/04087390.pdf

National Minimum Standards for Adult Placements, 2nd edition (July 2003)
www.dh.gov.uk/assetRoot/04/01/96/60/04019660.pdf

National Minimum Standards for Boarding Schools (2002)
www.dh.gov.uk/assetRoot/04/03/43/14/04034314.pdf

National Minimum Standards for Care Homes for Older People (2002)
www.dh.gov.uk/assetRoot/04/05/40/07/04054007.pdf

National Minimum Standards for Children's Homes (2002)
www.dh.gov.uk/assetRoot/04/03/43/19/04034319.pdf

National Minimum Standards for Domiciliary Care (February 2003)
www.dh.gov.uk/assetRoot/04/01/86/71/04018671.pdf

National Minimum Standards for Fostering Services (2002)
www.dh.gov.uk/assetRoot/04/03/43/84/04034384.pdf

National Minimum Standards for Nurse Agencies (January 2003)
www.dh.gov.uk/assetRoot/04/07/24/64/04072464.pdf

National Minimum Standards for Residential Family Centres Regulations (December 2002)
www.dh.gov.uk/assetRoot/04/03/44/12/04034412.pdf

National Minimum Standards for Residential Special Schools (2002)
www.dh.gov.uk/assetRoot/04/08/02/35/04080235.pdf

Ordinary Residence (LAC (93) 7)
www.dh.gov.uk/assetRoot/04/01/25/04/04012504.pdf

Overseas treatment for NHS patients
www.dh.gov.uk/PolicyAndGuidance/International/OverseasTreatmentGuidanceForNHS

Protection of Vulnerable Adults Scheme in England and Wales for Care Homes and Domiciliary Care Agencies (26 July 2004)
www.dh.gov.uk/assetRoot/04/09/03/19/04090319.pdf

Single Assessment Process (for determining older people's social care requirements)
www.dh.gov.uk/PolicyAndGuidance/HealthAndSocialCareTopics/SocialCare/SingleAssessmentProcess

Single Assessment Process for Older People – Assessment tools and accreditation (updated 2 January 2004)
www.dh.gov.uk/assetRoot/04/07/32/76/04073276.pdf

The Transfer of Frail Older NHS Patients to Other Long Stay Settings (Circular HSC 1998/048) (2 April 1998)
www.dh.gov.uk/assetRoot/04/01/17/25/04011725.pdf

Fairer Charging Policies for Home Care and other Non-residential Social Services: Practice Guidance (August 2002)
www.dh.gov.uk/assetRoot/04/06/74/50/04067450.pdf

No Secrets: Guidance on Developing and Implementing Multi-agency Policies and Procedures to Protect Vulnerable Adults from Abuse (Department of Health and Home Office)
www.dh.gov.uk/assetRoot/04/07/45/44/04074544.pdf

Framework for the Assessment of Children in Need and Their Families (2000) (Department of Health, Department for Education and Employment, Home Office)
www.dh.gov.uk/assetRoot/04/01/44/30/04014430.pdf

GENERAL MEDICAL COUNCIL

Withholding and Withdrawing Life-prolonging Treatments: Good Practice in Decision-making
www.gmcuk.org/guidance/library/standards/witholding_lifeprolonging_guidance.asp

GLOUCESTERSHIRE COUNCIL

Scrutiny Inquiry into Care Homes (report following the death of Violet Townsend)
www.gloucestershire.gov.uk/index.cfm?articleid=4397

HEALTH AND SAFETY EXECUTIVE

Scalding Risks from Hot Water in Health and Social Care (LAC 79/5, revised January 2003)
www.hse.gov.uk/lau/lacs/79–5.htm

Social Services: Social Inclusion and Elective Risk (SIM, 07/2000/08) (7 April 2000)
www.hse.gov.uk/foi/internalops/sectors/public/7_00_08.pdf

WALES

Charging for Residential Accommodation Guide (CRAG Amendment no. 20) (2005)
www.wales.gov.uk/subisocialpolicy/content/circulars/crag/crag-2005–e.pdf

Charging for Residential Accommodation Guide (CRAG Amendment no.16) (3 April 2003)
www.wales.gov.uk/subisocialpolicy/content/circulars/crag/crag16–e.pdf

Complaints in the NHS: A Guide to Handling Complaints in Wales (April 2003)
www.wales.nhs.uk/documents/complaints-leaflet-e.pdf

Creating a Unified and Fair System for Assessing and Managing Care
www.wales.gov.uk/subisocialpolicysocialservices/content/managingcare.pdf

Direct payments guidance
www.wales.gov.uk/subisocialpolicy/content/directpayment/policy-e.pdf

General Power for Best Value Authorities to Charge for Discretionary Services: Guidance on the Power in the Local Government Act 2003 (November 2004)
www.wales.gov.uk/subilocalgov/content/guidance/charge-discretionary-services-e.pdf

Guidance on Planning for Social Services
www.wales.gov.uk/subisocialpolicy/content/pdf/guid_plan_e.pdf

In Safe Hands: Implementing Adult Protection Procedures in Wales (July 2004)
www.wales.gov.uk/subisocialpolicy/content/pdf/safehands_e.pdf

National Minimum Standards and Regulations made under the Care Standards Act 2000
www.wales.gov.uk/subisocialpolicycarestandards/content/regulationsfinal-e.htm

Ordinary Residence – Personal Social Services (Circular WOC 41/93)
www.wales.gov.uk/subisocialpolicy/content/circulars/per-soc-serv-e.htm

National Service Frameworks (NSFs), Wales (March 2005)
www.wales.nhs.uk/sites/home.cfm?OrgID=334

NHS Funded Nursing Care in Care Homes Guidance 2004 (Circular WHC 2004/24: NAFWC 25/04O)
www.wales.nhs.uk/documents/ACF3BFA.pdf

General Power for Best Value Authorities to charge for Discretionary Services (November 2003)
www.odpm.gov.uk/stellent/groups/odpm_localgov/documents/page/odpm_locgov_038898.pdf

Consultation on the Representations Procedure (Children) (Wales) Regulations 2005 (October 2005)
www.welshconfed.org/reso/1776/image/P7%205–10–05.pdf

Consultation on the Social Services Complaints Procedures (Wales) Regulations 2005 (October 2005)
www.welshconfed.org/reso/1776/image/P6%205–10–05.pdf

QUICK LINKS

Care Standards Tribunal	**www.carestandardstribunal.gov.uk**
Children's Commissioner	**www.childrencommissioner.org**
Children's Commissioner for Wales	**www.childcom.org.uk**
Commission for Social Care Inspection	**www.csci.org.uk**
Community Health Councils	**www.wales.nhs.uk/chc/index.cfm**
Criminal Records Bureau	**www.crb.gov.uk**
Department for Constitutional Affairs	**www.dca.gov.uk**
Department for Education and Skills	**www.dfes.gov.uk**
Department for Work and Pensions	**www.dwp.gov.uk**
Department of Health	**www.dh.gov.uk**
Every Child Matters	**www.everychildmatters.gov.uk**
General Medical Council	**www.gmc-uk.org**
Health and Safety Executive	**www.hse.gov.uk**
Information Commissioner	**www.informationcommissioner.gov.uk**
Local Government Ombudsman	**www.lgo.org.uk**
Monitor (independent regulator of Foundation Hospital Trusts)	**www.monitor-nhsft.gov.uk**
National Assembly for Wales	**www.wales.gov.uk**
National Asylum Support Service	**www.asylumsupport.info/nass.htm**
National Health Service, Wales	**www.wales.nhs.uk**
National Treatment Agency for Substance Misuse	**www.nta.nhs.uk**
National Wheelchair Managers' Forum	**www.wheelchairmanagers.nhs.uk**
Office of the Deputy Prime Minister	**www.odpm.gov.uk**
Official Solicitor and Public Trustee	**www.offsol.demon.co.uk**
Parliamentary and Health Service Ombudsman	**www.ombudsman.org.uk**
Prescription Pricing Authority	**www.ppa.org.uk**
Public Services Ombudsman for Wales	**www.ombudsman-wales.org.uk/**
Solicitors for the Elderly	**www.solicitorsfortheelderly.com**
Valuing People (Department of Health plan for making the lives of people with learning disabilities and their families better) (2004)	**www.valuingpeople.gov.uk**
Victoria Climbie Inquiry	**www.victoria-climbie-inquiry.org.uk**
Welsh NHS Confederation	**www.welshconfed.org**

Index